HENRY WADSWORTH LONGFELLOW COLLECTION

EVANGELINE, THE SONG OF HIAWATHA, THE COURTSHIP OF MILES STANDISH, PAUL REVERE'S RIDE & OTHER TALES OF A WAYSIDE INN, THE CHILDREN'S HOUR, BIRDS OF FLIGHT, POEMS ON SLAVERY & MORE

HENRY WADSWORTH LONGFELLOW

CONTENTS

POEMS ON SLAVERY

EVANGELINE

THE SONG OF HIAWATHA

THE COURTSHIP OF MILES STANDISH

BIRDS OF PASSAGE

TALES OF A WAYSIDE INN

POEMS ON SLAVERY

POEMS ON SLAVERY

TO WILLIAM E. CHANNING

The pages of thy book I read,
  And as I closed each one,
My heart, responding, ever said,
  "Servant of God! well done!"

Well done! Thy words are great and bold;
  At times they seem to me,
Like Luther's, in the days of old,
  Half-battles for the free.

Go on, until this land revokes
  The old and chartered Lie,
The feudal curse, whose whips and yokes
  Insult humanity.

A voice is ever at thy side
  Speaking in tones of might,
Like the prophetic voice, that cried
  To John in Patmos, "Write!"

Write! and tell out this bloody tale;
  Record this dire eclipse,

This Day of Wrath, this Endless Wail,
  This dread Apocalypse!

THE SLAVE'S DREAM

Beside the ungathered rice he lay,
  His sickle in his hand;
His breast was bare, his matted hair
  Was buried in the sand.
Again, in the mist and shadow of sleep,
  He saw his Native Land.

Wide through the landscape of his dreams
  The lordly Niger flowed;
Beneath the palm-trees on the plain
  Once more a king he strode;
And heard the tinkling caravans
  Descend the mountain-road.

He saw once more his dark-eyed queen
  Among her children stand;
They clasped his neck, they kissed his cheeks,
  They held him by the hand!—
A tear burst from the sleeper's lids
  And fell into the sand.

And then at furious speed he rode
  Along the Niger's bank;
His bridle-reins were golden chains,
  And, with a martial clank,
At each leap he could feel his scabbard of steel
  Smiting his stallion's flank.

Before him, like a blood-red flag,
  The bright flamingoes flew;
From morn till night he followed their flight,
  O'er plains where the tamarind grew,
Till he saw the roofs of Caffre huts,
  And the ocean rose to view.

At night he heard the lion roar,
  And the hyena scream,

And the river-horse, as he crushed the reeds
  Beside some hidden stream;
And it passed, like a glorious roll of drums,
  Through the triumph of his dream.

The forests, with their myriad tongues,
  Shouted of liberty;
And the Blast of the Desert cried aloud,
  With a voice so wild and free,
That he started in his sleep and smiled
  At their tempestuous glee.

He did not feel the driver's whip,
  Nor the burning heat of day;
For Death had illumined the Land of Sleep,
  And his lifeless body lay
A worn-out fetter, that the soul
  Had broken and thrown away!

THE GOOD PART THAT SHALL NOT BE TAKEN AWAY

She dwells by Great Kenhawa's side,
  In valleys green and cool;
And all her hope and all her pride
  Are in the village school.

Her soul, like the transparent air
  That robes the hills above,
Though not of earth, encircles there
  All things with arms of love.

And thus she walks among her girls
  With praise and mild rebukes;
Subduing e'en rude village churls
  By her angelic looks.

She reads to them at eventide
  Of One who came to save;
To cast the captive's chains aside
  And liberate the slave.

And oft the blessed time foretells

When all men shall be free;
And musical, as silver bells,
   Their falling chains shall be.

And following her beloved Lord,
   In decent poverty,
She makes her life one sweet record
   And deed of charity.

For she was rich, and gave up all
   To break the iron bands
Of those who waited in her hall,
   And labored in her lands.

Long since beyond the Southern Sea
   Their outbound sails have sped,
While she, in meek humility,
   Now earns her daily bread.

It is their prayers, which never cease,
   That clothe her with such grace;
Their blessing is the light of peace
   That shines upon her face.

THE SLAVE IN THE DISMAL SWAMP

In dark fens of the Dismal Swamp
   The hunted Negro lay;
He saw the fire of the midnight camp,
And heard at times a horse's tramp
   And a bloodhound's distant bay.

Where will-o'-the-wisps and glow-worms shine,
   In bulrush and in brake;
Where waving mosses shroud the pine,
And the cedar grows, and the poisonous vine
   Is spotted like the snake;

Where hardly a human foot could pass,
   Or a human heart would dare,
On the quaking turf of the green morass
He crouched in the rank and tangled grass,
   Like a wild beast in his lair.

A poor old slave, infirm and lame;
  Great scars deformed his face;
On his forehead he bore the brand of shame,
And the rags, that hid his mangled frame,
  Were the livery of disgrace.

All things above were bright and fair,
  All things were glad and free;
Lithe squirrels darted here and there,
And wild birds filled the echoing air
  With songs of Liberty!

On him alone was the doom of pain,
  From the morning of his birth;
On him alone the curse of Cain
Fell, like a flail on the garnered grain,
  And struck him to the earth!

THE SLAVE SINGING AT MIDNIGHT

Loud he sang the psalm of David!
He, a Negro and enslaved,
Sang of Israel's victory,
Sang of Zion, bright and free.

In that hour, when night is calmest,
Sang he from the Hebrew Psalmist,
In a voice so sweet and clear
That I could not choose but hear,

Songs of triumph, and ascriptions,
Such as reached the swart Egyptians,
When upon the Red Sea coast
Perished Pharaoh and his host.

And the voice of his devotion
Filled my soul with strange emotion;
For its tones by turns were glad,
Sweetly solemn, wildly sad.

Paul and Silas, in their prison,
Sang of Christ, the Lord arisen,
And an earthquake's arm of might

Broke their dungeon-gates at night.

But, alas! what holy angel
Brings the Slave this glad evangel?
And what earthquake's arm of might
Breaks his dungeon-gates at night?

THE WITNESSES

In Ocean's wide domains,
  Half buried in the sands,
Lie skeletons in chains,
  With shackled feet and hands.

Beyond the fall of dews,
  Deeper than plummet lies,
Float ships, with all their crews,
  No more to sink nor rise.

There the black Slave-ship swims,
  Freighted with human forms,
Whose fettered, fleshless limbs
  Are not the sport of storms.

These are the bones of Slaves;
  They gleam from the abyss;
They cry, from yawning waves,
  "We are the Witnesses!"

Within Earth's wide domains
  Are markets for men's lives;
Their necks are galled with chains,
  Their wrists are cramped with gyves.

Dead bodies, that the kite
  In deserts makes its prey;
Murders, that with affright
  Scare school-boys from their play!

All evil thoughts and deeds;
  Anger, and lust, and pride;
The foulest, rankest weeds,
  That choke Life's groaning tide!

These are the woes of Slaves;
  They glare from the abyss;
They cry, from unknown graves,
  "We are the Witnesses!

THE QUADROON GIRL

The Slaver in the broad lagoon
  Lay moored with idle sail;
He waited for the rising moon,
  And for the evening gale.

Under the shore his boat was tied,
  And all her listless crew
Watched the gray alligator slide
  Into the still bayou.

Odors of orange-flowers, and spice,
  Reached them from time to time,
Like airs that breathe from Paradise
  Upon a world of crime.

The Planter, under his roof of thatch,
  Smoked thoughtfully and slow;
The Slaver's thumb was on the latch,
  He seemed in haste to go.

He said, "My ship at anchor rides
  In yonder broad lagoon;
I only wait the evening tides,
  And the rising of the moon.

Before them, with her face upraised,
  In timid attitude,
Like one half curious, half amazed,
  A Quadroon maiden stood.

Her eyes were large, and full of light,
  Her arms and neck were bare;
No garment she wore save a kirtle bright,
  And her own long, raven hair.

And on her lips there played a smile

As holy, meek, and faint,
As lights in some cathedral aisle
   The features of a saint.

"The soil is barren,—the farm is old";
   The thoughtful planter said;
Then looked upon the Slaver's gold,
   And then upon the maid.

His heart within him was at strife
   With such accursed gains:
For he knew whose passions gave her life,
   Whose blood ran in her veins.

But the voice of nature was too weak;
   He took the glittering gold!
Then pale as death grew the maiden's cheek,
   Her hands as icy cold.

The Slaver led her from the door,
   He led her by the hand,
To be his slave and paramour
   In a strange and distant land!

THE WARNING

Beware! The Israelite of old, who tore
   The lion in his path,—when, poor and blind,
He saw the blessed light of heaven no more,
   Shorn of his noble strength and forced to grind
In prison, and at last led forth to be
A pander to Philistine revelry,—

Upon the pillars of the temple laid
   His desperate hands, and in its overthrow
Destroyed himself, and with him those who made
   A cruel mockery of his sightless woe;
The poor, blind Slave, the scoff and jest of all,
Expired, and thousands perished in the fall!

There is a poor, blind Samson in this land,
   Shorn of his strength and bound in bonds of steel,

Who may, in some grim revel, raise his hand,
  And shake the pillars of this Commonweal,
Till the vast Temple of our liberties.
A shapeless mass of wreck and rubbish lies.

EVANGELINE

A TALE OF ACADIE

EVANGELINE

A TALE OF ACADIE

THIS is the forest primeval. The murmuring pines and the hemlocks,
  Bearded with moss, and in garments green, indistinct in the twilight,
  Stand like Druids of eld, with voices sad and prophetic,
  Stand like harpers hoar, with beards that rest on their bosoms.
  Loud from its rocky caverns, the deep-voiced neighboring ocean
  Speaks, and in accents disconsolate answers the wail of the forest.

  This is the forest primeval; but where are the hearts that beneath it
  Leaped like the roe, when he hears in the woodland the voice of the
      huntsman?
  Where is the thatch-roofed village, the home of Acadian farmers,—
  Men whose lives glided on like rivers that water the woodlands,
  Darkened by shadows of earth, but reflecting an image of heaven?
  Waste are those pleasant farms, and the farmers forever departed!
  Scattered like dust and leaves, when the mighty blasts of October
  Seize them, and whirl them aloft, and sprinkle them far o'er the ocean.
  Naught but tradition remains of the beautiful village of Grand-Pré.

  Ye who believe in affection that hopes, and endures, and is patient,
  Ye who believe in the beauty and strength of woman's devotion,
  List to the mournful tradition still sung by the pines of the forest;
  List to a Tale of Love in Acadie, home of the happy.

PART THE FIRST

I.

IN the Acadian land, on the shores of the Basin of Minas,
  Distant, secluded, still, the little village of Grand-Pré
  Lay in the fruitful valley. Vast meadows stretched to the eastward,
  Giving the village its name, and pasture to flocks without number.
  Dikes, that the hands of the farmers had raised with labor incessant,
  Shut out the turbulent tides; but at stated seasons the flood-gates
  Opened, and welcomed the sea to wander at will o'er the meadows.
  West and south there were fields of flax, and orchards and cornfields
  Spreading afar and unfenced o'er the plain; and away to the northward
  Blomidon rose, and the forests old, and aloft on the mountains
  Sea-fogs pitched their tents, and mists from the mighty Atlantic
  Looked on the happy valley, but ne'er from their station descended.
  There, in the midst of its farms, reposed the Acadian village.
  Strongly built were the houses, with frames of oak and of chestnut,
  Such as the peasants of Normandy built in the reign of the Henries.
  Thatched were the roofs, with dormer-windows; and gables projecting
  Over the basement below protected and shaded the door-way.
  There in the tranquil evenings of summer, when brightly the sunset
  Lighted the village street, and gilded the vanes on the chimneys,
  Matrons and maidens sat in snow-white caps and in kirtles
  Scarlet and blue and green, with distaffs spinning the golden
  Flax for the gossiping looms, whose noisy shuttles within doors
  Mingled their sound with the whir of the wheels and the songs of the
    maidens.
  Solemnly down the street came the parish priest, and the children
  Paused in their play to kiss the hand he extended to bless them.
  Reverend walked he among them; and up rose matrons and maidens,
  Hailing his slow approach with words of affectionate welcome.
  Then came the laborers home from the field, and serenely the sun sank
  Down to his rest, and twilight prevailed. Anon from the belfry
  Softly the Angelus sounded, and over the roofs of the village
  Columns of pale blue smoke, like clouds of incense ascending,
  Rose from a hundred hearths, the homes of peace and contentment.
  Thus dwelt together in love these simple Acadian farmers,—
  Dwelt in the love of God and of man. Alike were they free from
  Fear, that reigns with the tyrant, and envy, the vice of republics.
  Neither locks had they to their doors, nor bars to their windows;
  But their dwellings were open as day and the hearts of the owners;
  There the richest was poor, and the poorest lived in abundance.

Somewhat apart from the village, and nearer the Basin of Minas,
Benedict Bellefontaine, the wealthiest farmer of Grand-Pré,
Dwelt on his goodly acres; and with him, directing his household,
Gentle Evangeline lived, his child, and the pride of the village.
Stalworth and stately in form was the man of seventy winters;
Hearty and hale was he, an oak that is covered with snow-flakes;
White as the snow were his locks, and his cheeks as brown as the oak-leaves.
Fair was she to behold, that maiden of seventeen summers.
Black were her eyes as the berry that grows on the thorn by the wayside,
Black, yet how softly they gleamed beneath the brown shade of her tresses!
Sweet was her breath as the breath of kine that feed in the meadows.
When in the harvest heat she bore to the reapers at noontide
Flagons of home-brewed ale, ah! fair in sooth was the maiden.
Fairer was she when, on Sunday morn, while the bell from its turret
Sprinkled with holy sounds the air, as the priest with his hyssop
Sprinkles the congregation, and scatters blessings upon them,
Down the long street she passed, with her chaplet of beads and her missal,
Wearing her Norman cap, and her kirtle of blue, and the ear-rings,
Brought in the olden time from France, and since, as an heirloom,
Handed down from mother to child, through long generations.
But a celestial brightness—a more ethereal beauty—
Shone on her face and encircled her form, when, after confession,
Homeward serenely she walked with God's benediction upon her.
When she had passed, it seemed like the ceasing of exquisite music.

Firmly builded with rafters of oak, the house of the farmer
Stood on the side of a hill commanding the sea; and a shady
Sycamore grew by the door, with a woodbine wreathing around it.
Rudely carved was the porch, with seats beneath; and a footpath
Led through an orchard wide, and disappeared in the meadow.
Under the sycamore-tree were hives overhung by a penthouse,
Such as the traveller sees in regions remote by the roadside,
Built o'er a box for the poor, or the blessed image of Mary.
Farther down, on the slope of the hill, was the well with its moss-grown
Bucket, fastened with iron, and near it a trough for the horses.
Shielding the house from storms, on the north, were the barns and the farm-
    yard,
There stood the broad-wheeled wains and the antique ploughs and the
    harrows;
There were the folds for the sheep; and there, in his feathered seraglio,
Strutted the lordly turkey, and crowed the cock, with the selfsame
Voice that in ages of old had startled the penitent Peter.
Bursting with hay were the barns, themselves a village. In each one
Far o'er the gable projected a roof of thatch; and a staircase,

Under the sheltering eaves, led up to the odorous corn-loft.
There too the dove-cot stood, with its meek and innocent inmates
Murmuring ever of love; while above in the variant breezes
Numberless noisy weathercocks rattled and sang of mutation.

 Thus, at peace with God and the world, the farmer of Grand-Pré
Lived on his sunny farm, and Evangeline governed his household.
Many a youth, as he knelt in the church and opened his missal,
Fixed his eyes upon her, as the saint of his deepest devotion;
Happy was he who might touch her hand or the hem of her garment!
Many a suitor came to her door, by the darkness befriended,
And, as he knocked and waited to hear the sound of her footsteps,
Knew not which beat the louder, his heart or the knocker of iron;
Or at the joyous feast of the Patron Saint of the village,
Bolder grew, and pressed her hand in the dance as he whispered
Hurried words of love, that seemed a part of the music.
But, among all who came, young Gabriel only was welcome;
Gabriel Lajeunesse, the son of Basil the blacksmith,
Who was a mighty man in the village, and honored of all men;
For, since the birth of time, throughout all ages and nations,
Has the craft of the smith been held in repute by the people.
Basil was Benedict's friend. Their children from earliest childhood
Grew up together as brother and sister; and Father Felician,
Priest and pedagogue both in the village, had taught them their letters
Out of the selfsame book, with the hymns of the church and the plain-song.
But when the hymn was sung, and the daily lesson completed,
Swiftly they hurried away to the forge of Basil the blacksmith.
There at the door they stood, with wondering eyes to behold him
Take in his leathern lap the hoof of the horse as a plaything,
Nailing the shoe in its place; while near him the tire of the cart-wheel
Lay like a fiery snake, coiled round in a circle of cinders.
Oft on autumnal eves, when without in the gathering darkness
Bursting with light seemed the smithy, through every cranny and crevice,
Warm by the forge within they watched the laboring bellows,
And as its panting ceased, and the sparks expired in the ashes,
Merrily laughed, and said they were nuns going into the chapel.
Oft on sledges in winter, as swift as the swoop of the eagle,
Down the hillside bounding, they glided away o'er the meadow.
Oft in the barns they climbed to the populous nests on the rafters,
Seeking with eager eyes that wondrous stone, which the swallow
Brings from the shore of the sea to restore the sight of its fledglings;
Lucky was he who found that stone in the nest of the swallow!
Thus passed a few swift years, and they no longer were children.
He was a valiant youth, and his face, like the face of the morning,

Gladdened the earth with its light, and ripened through into action.
She was a woman now, with the heart and hopes of a woman.
"Sunshine of Saint Eulalie" was she called; for that was the sunshine
Which, as the farmers believed, would load their orchards with apples;
She, too, would bring to her husband's house delight and abundance,
Filling it full of love and the ruddy faces of children.

II.

NOW had the season returned, when the nights grow colder and longer,
And the retreating sun the sign of the Scorpion enters.
Birds of passage sailed through the leaden air, from the ice-bound,
Desolate northern bays to the shores of tropical islands.
Harvests were gathered in; and wild with the winds of September
Wrestled the trees of the forest, as Jacob of old with the angel.
All the signs foretold a winter long and inclement.
Bees, with prophetic instinct of want, had hoarded their honey
Till the hives overflowed; and the Indian hunters asserted
Cold would the winter be, for thick was the fur of the foxes.
Such was the advent of autumn. Then followed that beautiful season,
Called by the pious Acadian peasants the Summer of All-Saints!
Filled was the air with a dreamy and magical light; and the landscape
Lay as if new-created in all the freshness of childhood.
Peace seemed to reign upon earth, and the restless heart of the ocean
Was for a moment consoled. All sounds were in harmony blended.
Voices of children at play, the crowing of cocks in the farm-yards,
Whir of wings in the drowsy air, and the cooing of pigeons,
All were subdued and low as the murmurs of love, and the great sun
Looked with the eye of love through the golden vapors around him;
While arrayed in its robes of russet and scarlet and yellow,
Bright with the sheen of the dew, each glittering tree of the forest
Flashed like the plane-tree the Persian adorned with mantles and jewels.

Now recommenced the reign of rest and affection and stillness.
Day with its burden and heat had departed, and twilight descending
Brought back the evening star to the sky, and the herds to the homestead.
Pawing the ground they came, and resting their necks on each other,
And with their nostrils distended inhaling the freshness of evening.
Foremost, bearing the bell, Evangeline's beautiful heifer,
Proud of her snow-white hide, and the ribbon that waved from her collar,
Quietly paced and slow, as if conscious of human affection.
Then came the shepherd back with his bleating flocks from the seaside,
Where was their favorite pasture. Behind them followed the watch-dog,

Patient, full of importance, and grand in the pride of his instinct,
Walking from side to side with a lordly air, and superbly
Waving his bushy tail, and urging forward the stragglers;
Regent of flocks was he when the shepherd slept; their protector,
When from the forest at night, through the starry silence, the wolves howled.
Late, with the rising moon, returned the wains from the marshes,
Laden with briny hay, that filled the air with its odor.
Cheerily neighed the steeds,. with dew on their manes and their fetlocks,
While aloft on their shoulders the wooden and ponderous saddles,
Painted with brilliant dyes, and adorned with tassels of crimson,
Nodded in bright array, like hollyhocks heavy with blossoms.
Patiently stood the cows meanwhile, and yielded their udders
Unto the milkmaid's hand; whilst loud and in regular cadence
Into the sounding pails the foaming streamlets descended.
Lowing of cattle and peals of laughter were heard in the farm-yard,
Echoed back by the barns. Anon they sank into stillness;
Heavily closed, with a jarring sound, the valves of the barn-doors,
Rattled the wooden bars, and all for a season was silent.

In-doors, warm by the wide-mouthed fireplace, idly the farmer
Sat in his elbow-chair; and watched how the flames and the smoke-wreaths
Struggled together like foe in a burning city. Behind him,
Nodding and mocking along the wall, with gestures fantastic,
Darted his own huge shadow, and vanished away into darkness.
Faces, clumsily carved in oak, on the back of his arm-chair
Laughed in the flickering light, and the pewter plates on the dresser
Caught and reflected the flame, as shields of armies the sunshine.
Fragments of song the old man sang, and carols of Christmas,
Such as at home, in the olden time, his fathers before him
Sang in their Norman orchards and bright Burgundian vineyards.
Close at her father's side was the gentle Evangeline seated,
Spinning flax for the loom, that stood in the corner behind her.
Silent awhile were its treadles, at rest was its diligent shuttle,
While the monotonous drone of the wheel, like the drone of a bagpipe,
Followed the old man's song, and united the fragments together.
As in a church, when the chant of the choir at intervals ceases,
Footfalls are heard in the aisles, or words of the priest at the altar,
So, in each pause of the song, with measured motion the clock clicked.

Thus as they sat, there were footsteps heard, and, suddenly lifted,
Sounded the wooden latch, and the door swung back on its hinges.
Benedict knew by the hob-nailed shoes it was Basil the blacksmith,
And by her beating heart Evangeline knew who was with him.
"Welcome!" the farmer exclaimed, as their footsteps paused on the threshold,

"Welcome, Basil, my friend! Come, take thy place on the settle
Close by the chimney-side, which is always empty without thee;
Take from the shelf overhead thy pipe and the box of tobacco;
Never so much thyself art thou as when through the curling
Smoke of the pipe or the forge thy friendly and jovial face gleams
Round and red as the harvest moon through the mist of the marshes."
Then, with a smile of content, thus answered Basil the blacksmith,
Taking with easy air the accustomed seat by the fireside:—
"Benedict Bellefontaine, thou hast ever thy jest and thy ballad!
Ever in cheerfullest mood art thou, when others are filled with
Gloomy forebodings of ill, and see only ruin before them.
Happy art thou, as if every day thou hadst picked up a horseshoe."
Pausing a moment, to take the pipe that Evangeline brought him,
And with a coal from the embers had lighted, he slowly continued:—
"Four days now are passed since the English ships at their anchors
Ride in the Gaspereau's mouth, with their cannon pointed against us,
What their design may be is unknown; but all are commanded
On the morrow to meet in the church, where his Majesty's mandate
Will be proclaimed as law in the land. Alas! in the mean time
Many surmises of evil alarm the hearts of the people."
Then made answer the farmer:—"Perhaps some friendlier purpose
Brings these ships to our shores. Perhaps the harvests in England
By untimely rains or untimelier heat have been blighted,
And from our bursting barns they would feed their cattle and children."
"Not so thinketh the folk in the village," said, warmly, the blacksmith,
Shaking his head, as in doubt; then, heaving a sigh, he continued:—
"Louisburg is not forgotten, nor Beau Séjour, nor Port Royal.
Many already have fled to the forest, and lurk on its outskirts,
Waiting with anxious hearts the dubious fate of to-morrow.
Arms have been taken from us, and warlike weapons of all kinds;
Nothing is left but the blacksmith's sledge and the scythe of the mower."
Then with a pleasant smile made answer the jovial farmer:—
"Safer are we unarmed, in the midst of our flocks and our cornfields,
Safer within these peaceful dikes, besieged by the ocean,
Than our fathers in forts, besieged by the enemy's cannon.
Fear no evil, my friend, and to-night may no shadow of sorrow
Fall on this house and hearth; for this is the night of the contract.
Built are the house and the barn. The merry lads of the village
Strongly have built them and well; and, breaking the glebe round about
     them,
Filled the barn with hay, and the house with food for a twelvemonth.
René Leblanc will be here anon, with his papers and inkhorn.
Shall we not then be glad, and rejoice in the joy of our children?"
As apart by the window she stood, with her hand in her lover's,

Blushing Evangeline heard the words that her father had spoken,
And, as they died on his lips, the worthy notary entered.

III.

BENT like a laboring oar, that toils in the surf of the ocean,
  Bent, but not broken, by age was the form of the notary public;
  Shocks of yellow hair, like the silken floss of the maize, hung
  Over his shoulders; his forehead was high; and glasses with horn bows
  Sat astride on his nose, with a look of wisdom supernal.
  Father of twenty children was he, and more than a hundred
  Children's children rode on his knee, and heard his great watch tick.
  Four long years in the times of the war had he languished a captive,
  Suffering much in an old French fort as the friend of the English.
  Now, though warier grown, without all guile or suspicion,
  Ripe in wisdom was he, but patient, and simple, and childlike.
  He was beloved by all, and most of all by the children;
  For he told them tales of the Loup-garou in the forest,
  And of the goblin that came in the night to water the horses,
  And of the white Létiche, the ghost of a child who unchristened
  Died, and was doomed to haunt unseen the chambers of children;
  And how on Christmas eve the oxen talked in the stable,
  And how the fever was cured by a spider shut up in a nutshell,
  And of the marvellous powers of four-leaved clover and horseshoes,
  With whatsoever else was writ in the lore of the village.
  Then up rose from his seat by the fireside Basil the blacksmith,
  Knocked from his pipe the ashes, and slowly extending his right hand,
  "Father Leblanc," he exclaimed, "thou hast heard the talk in the village,
  And, perchance, canst tell us some news of these ships and their errand."
  Then with modest demeanor made answer the notary public:—
  "Gossip enough have I heard, in sooth, yet am never the wiser;
  And what their errand may be I know not better than others.
  Yet am I not of those who imagine some evil intention
  Brings them here, for we are at peace; and why then molest us?"
  "God's name!" shouted the hasty and somewhat irascible blacksmith;
  "Must we in all things look for the how, and the why, and the wherefore?
  Daily injustice is done, and might is the right of the strongest!"
  But, without heeding his warmth, continued the notary public:—
  "Man is unjust, but God is just; and finally justice
  Triumphs; and well I remember a story, that often consoled me,
  When as a captive I lay in the old French fort at Port Royal."
  This was the old man's favorite tale, and he loved to repeat it
  When his neighbors complained that any injustice was done them.

"Once in an ancient city, whose name I no longer remember,
Raised aloft on a column, a brazen statue of Justice
Stood in the public square, upholding the scales in its left hand,
And in its right a sword, as an emblem that justice presided
Over the laws of the land, and the hearts and homes of the people.
Even the birds had built their nests in the scales of the balance,
Having no fear of the sword that flashed in the sunshine above them.
But in the course of time the laws of the land were corrupted;
Might took the place of right, and the weak were oppressed, and the mighty
Ruled with an iron rod. Then it chanced in a nobleman's palace
That a necklace of pearls was lost, and erelong a suspicion
Fell on an orphan girl who lived as maid in the household.
She, after form of trial condemned to die on the scaffold,
Patiently met her doom at the foot of the statue of Justice.
As to her Father in heaven her innocent spirit ascended,
Lo! o'er the city a tempest rose; and the bolts of the thunder
Smote the statue of bronze, and hurled in wrath from its left hand
Down on the pavement below the clattering scales of the balance,
And in the hollow thereof was found the nest of a magpie,
Into whose clay-built walls the necklace of pearls was inwoven."
Silenced, but not convinced, when the story was ended, the blacksmith
Stood like a man who fain would speak, but findeth no language;
All his thoughts were congealed into lines on his face, as the vapors
Freeze in fantastic shapes on the window-panes in the winter.

    Then Evangeline lighted the brazen lamp on the table,
Filled, till it overflowed, the pewter tankard with home-brewed
Nut-brown ale, that was famed for its strength in the village of Grand-Pré;
While from his pocket the notary drew his papers and inkhorn,
Wrote with a steady hand the date and the age of the parties,
Naming the dower of the bride in flocks of sheep and in cattle.
Orderly all things proceeded, and duly and well were completed,
And the great seal of the law was set like a sun on the margin.
Then from his leathern pouch the farmer threw on the table
Three times the old man's fee in solid pieces of silver;
And the notary rising, and blessing the bride and the bridegroom,
Lifted aloft the tankard of ale and drank to their welfare.
Wiping the foam from his lip, he solemnly bowed and departed,
While in silence the others sat and mused by the fireside,
Till Evangeline brought the draught-board out of its corner.
Soon was the game begun. In friendly contention the old men
Laughed at each lucky hit, or unsuccessful manoeuver,
Laughed when a man was crowned, or a breach was made in the king-row.
Meanwhile apart, in the twilight gloom of a window's embrasure,

Sat the lovers, and whispered together, beholding the moon rise
Over the pallid sea and the silvery mist of the meadows.
Silently one by one, in the infinite meadows of heaven,
Blossomed the lovely stars, the forget-me-nots of the angels.

   Thus passed the evening away. Anon the bell from the belfry
Rang out the hour of nine, the village curfew, and straightway
Rose the guests and departed; and silence reigned in the household.
Many a farewell word and sweet good night on the door-step
Lingered long in Evangeline's heart, and filled it with gladness.
Carefully then were covered the embers that glowed on the hearth-stone;
And on the oaken stairs resounded the tread of the farmer.
Soon with a soundless step the foot of Evangeline followed.
Up the staircase moved a luminous space in the darkness,
Lighted less by the lamp than the shining face of the maiden.
Silent she passed the hall, and entered the door of her chamber.
Simple that chamber was, with its curtains of white, and its clothes-press
Ample and high, on whose spacious shelves were carefully folded
Linen and woollen stuffs, by the hand of Evangeline woven.
This was the precious dower she would bring to her husband in marriage,
Better than flocks and herds, being proofs of her skill as a housewife.
Soon she extinguished her lamp, for the mellow and radiant moonlight
Streamed through the windows, and lighted the room, till the heart of the
    maiden
Swelled and obeyed its power, like the tremulous tides of the ocean.
Ah! she was fair, exceeding fair to behold, as she stood with
Naked snow-white feet on the gleaming floor of her chamber!
Little she dreamed that below, among the trees of the orchard,
Waited her lover and watched for the gleam of her lamp and her shadow.
Yet were her thoughts of him, and at times a feeling of sadness
Passed o'er her soul, as the sailing shade of clouds in the moonlight
Flitted across the floor and darkened the room for a moment.
And, as she gazed from the window, she saw serenely the moon pass
Forth from the folds of a cloud, and one star follow her footsteps,
As out of Abraham's tent young Ishmael wandered with Hagar!

IV.

PLEASANTLY rose next morn the sun on the village of Grand-Pré.
   Pleasantly gleamed in the soft, sweet air the Basin of Minas,
   Where the ships, with their wavering shadows, were riding at anchor.
   Life had long been astir in the village, and clamorous labor
   Knocked with its hundred hands at the golden gates of the morning.

Now from the country around, from the farms and neighboring hamlets,
Came in their holiday dresses the blithe Acadian peasants.
Many a glad good morrow and jocund laugh from the young folk
Made the bright air brighter, as up from the numerous meadows,
Where no path could be seen but the track of wheels in the greensward,
Group after group appeared, and joined, or passed on the highway.
Long ere noon, in the village all sounds of labor were silenced.
Thronged were the streets with people; and noisy groups at the house-doors
Sat in the cheerful sun, and rejoiced and gossiped together,
Every house was an inn, where all were welcomed and feasted;
For with this simple people, who lived like brothers together,
All things were held in common, and what one had was another's.
Yet under Benedict's roof hospitality seemed more abundant:
For Evangeline stood among the guests of her father;
Bright was her face with smiles, and words of welcome and gladness
Fell from her beautiful lips, and blessed the cup as she gave it.

  Under the open sky, in the odorous air of the orchard,
Bending with golden fruit, was spread the feast of betrothal.
There in the shade of the porch were the priest and the notary seated;
There good Benedict sat, and sturdy Basil the blacksmith.
Not far withdrawn from these, by the cider-press and the beehives,
Michael the fiddler was placed, with the gayest of hearts and of waistcoats.
Shadow and light from the leaves alternately played on his snow-white
Hair, as it waved in the wind; and the jolly face of the fiddler
Glowed like a living coal when the ashes are blown from the embers.
Gayly the old man sang to the vibrant sound of his fiddle,
Tous les Bourgeois de Chartres, and Le Carillon de Dunkerque,
And anon with his wooden shoes beat time to the music.
Merrily, merrily whirled the wheels of the dizzying dances
Under the orchard-trees and down the path to the meadows;
Old folk and young together, and children mingled among them.
Fairest of all the maids was Evangeline, Benedict's daughter!
Noblest of all the youths was Gabriel, son of the blacksmith!

  So passed the morning away. And lo! with a summons sonorous
Sounded the bell from its tower, and over the meadows a drum beat.
Thronged erelong was the church with men. Without, in the churchyard,
Waited the women. They stood by the graves, and hung on the headstones
Garlands of autumn-leaves and evergreens fresh from the forest.
Then came the guard from the ships, and marching proudly among them
Entered the sacred portal. With loud and dissonant clangor
Echoed the sound of their brazen drums from ceiling and casement,—
Echoed a moment only, and slowly the ponderous portal

Closed, and in silence the crowd awaited the will of the soldiers.
Then uprose their commander, and spake from the steps of the altar,
Holding aloft in his hands, with its seals, the royal commission.
"You are convened this day," he said, "by his Majesty's orders.
Clement and kind has he been; but how you have answered his kindness,
Let your own hearts reply! To my natural make and my temper
Painful the task is I do, which to you I know must be grievous.
Yet must I bow and obey, and deliver the will of our monarch;
Namely, that all your lands, and dwellings, and cattle of all kinds
Forfeited be to the crown; and that you yourselves from this province
Be transported to other lands. God grant you may dwell there
Ever as faithful subjects, a happy and peaceable people!
Prisoners now I declare you; for such is his Majesty's pleasure!"
As, when the air is serene in the sultry solstice of summer,
Suddenly gathers a storm, and the deadly sling of the hailstones
Beats down the farmer's corn in the field and shatters his windows,
Hiding the sun, and strewing the ground with thatch from the house-roofs,
Bellowing fly the herds, and seek to break their enclosures;
So on the hearts of the people descended the words of the speaker.
Silent a moment they stood in speechless wonder, and then rose
Louder and ever louder a wail of sorrow and anger,
And, by one impulse moved, they madly rushed to the door-way.
Vain was the hope of escape; and cries and fierce imprecations
Rang through the house of prayer; and high o'er the heads of the others
Rose, with his arms uplifted, the figure of Basil the blacksmith,
As, on a stormy sea, a spar is tossed by the billows.
Flushed was his face and distorted with passion; and wildly he shouted,—
"Down with the tyrants of England! we never have sworn them allegiance!
Death to these foreign soldiers, who seize on our homes and our harvests!"
More he fain would have said, but the merciless hand of a soldier
Smote him upon the mouth, and dragged him down to the pavement.

  In the midst of the strife and tumult of angry contention,
Lo! the door of the chancel opened, and Father Felician
Entered, with serious mien, and ascended the steps of the altar.
Raising his reverend hand, with a gesture he awed into silence
All that clamorous throng; and thus he spake to his people;
Deep were his tones and solemn; in accents measured and mournful
Spake he, as, after the tocsin's alarum, distinctly the clock strikes.
"What is this that ye do, my children? what madness has seized you?
Forty years of my life have I labored among you, and taught you,
Not in word alone, but in deed, to love one another!
Is this the fruit of my toils, of my vigils and prayers and privations?
Have you so soon forgotten all lessons of love and forgiveness?

This is the house of the Prince of Peace, and would you profane it
Thus with violent deeds and hearts overflowing with hatred?
Lo! where the crucified Christ from his cross is gazing upon you!
See! in those sorrowful eyes what meekness and holy compassion!
Hark! how those lips still repeat the prayer, 'O Father, forgive them!'
Let us repeat that prayer in the hour when the wicked assail us,
Let us repeat it now, and say, 'O Father, forgive them!'"
Few were his words of rebuke, but deep in the hearts of his people
Sank they, and sobs of contrition succeeded the passionate outbreak,
And they repeated his prayer, and said, "O Father, forgive them!"

Then came the evening service. The tapers gleamed from the altar.
Fervent and deep was the voice of the priest, and the people responded,
Not with their lips alone, but their hearts; and the Ave Maria
Sang they, and fell on their knees, and their souls, with devotion translated,
Rose on the ardor of prayer, like Elijah ascending to heaven.

Meanwhile had spread in the village the tidings of ill, and on all sides
Wandered, wailing, from house to house the women and children.
Long at her father's door Evangeline stood, with her right hand
Shielding her eyes from the level rays of the sun, that, descending,
Lighted the village street with mysterious splendor, and roofed each
Peasant's cottage with golden thatch, and emblazoned its windows.
Long within had been spread the snow-white cloth on the table;
There stood the wheaten loaf, and the honey fragrant with wild-flowers;
There stood the tankard of ale, and the cheese fresh brought from the dairy,
And, at the head of the board, the great arm-chair of the farmer.
Thus did Evangeline wait at her father's door, as the sunset
Threw the long shadows of trees o'er the broad ambrosial meadows.
Ah! on her spirit within a deeper shadow had fallen,
And from the fields of her soul a fragrance celestial ascended,—
Charity, meekness, love, and hope, and forgiveness, and patience!
Then, all-forgetful of self, she wandered into the village,
Cheering with looks and words the disconsolate hearts of the women,
As o'er the darkening fields with lingering steps they departed,
Urged by their household cares, and the weary feet of their children.
Down sank the great red sun, and in golden, glimmering vapors
Veiled the light of his face, like the Prophet descending from Sinai.
Sweetly over the village the bell of the Angelus sounded.

Meanwhile, amid the gloom, by the church Evangeline lingered.
All was silent within; and in vain at the door and the windows
Stood she, and listened and looked, till, overcome by emotion,
"Gabriel!" cried she aloud with tremulous voice; but no answer

Came from the graves of the dead, nor the gloomier grave of the living.
Slowly at length she returned to the tenantless house of her father.
Smouldered the fire on the hearth, on the board stood the supper untasted,
Empty and drear was each room, and haunted with phantoms of terror.
Sadly echoed her step on the stair and the floor of her chamber.
In the dead of the night she heard the whispering rain fall
Loud on the withered leaves of the sycamore-tree by the window.
Keenly the lightning flashed; and the voice of the echoing thunder
Told her that God was in heaven, and governed the world he created!
Then she remembered the tale she had heard of the justice of Heaven;
Soothed was her troubled soul, and she peacefully slumbered till morning.

V.

FOUR times the sun had risen and set; and now on the fifth day
  Cheerily called the cock to the sleeping maids of the farm-house.
  Soon o'er the yellow fields, in silent and mournful procession,
  Came from the neighboring hamlets and farms the Acadian women,
  Driving in ponderous wains their household goods to the sea-shore,
  Pausing and looking back to gaze once more on their dwellings,
  Ere they were shut from sight by the winding road and the woodland.
  Close at their sides their children ran, and urged on the oxen,
  While in their little hands they clasped some fragments of playthings.

   Thus to the Gaspereau's mouth they hurried; and there on the sea-beach
  Piled in confusion lay the household goods of the peasants.
  All day long between the shore and the ships did the boats ply;
  All day long the wains came laboring down from the village.
  Late in the afternoon, when the sun was near to his setting,
  Echoed far o'er the fields came the roll of drums from the churchyard.
  Thither the women and children thronged. On a sudden the church-doors
  Opened, and forth came the guard, and marching in gloomy procession
  Followed the long-imprisoned, but patient, Acadian farmers.
  Even as pilgrims, who journey afar from their homes and their country,
  Sing as they go, and in singing forget they are weary and wayworn,
  So with songs on their lips the Acadian peasants descended
  Down from the church to the shore, amid their wives and their daughters.
  Foremost the young men came; and, raising together their voices,
  Sang they with tremulous lips a chant of the Catholic Missions:—
  "Sacred heart of the Saviour! O inexhaustible fountain!
  Fill our hearts this day with strength and submission and patience!"
  Then the old men, as they marched, and the women that stood by the
     wayside

Joined in the sacred psalm, and the birds in the sunshine above them
Mingled their notes therewith, like voices of spirits departed.

Half-way down to the shore Evangeline waited in silence,
Not overcome with grief, but strong in the hour of affliction,—
Calmly and sadly she waited, until the procession approached her,
And she beheld the face of Gabriel pale with emotion.
Tears then filled her eyes, and, eagerly running to meet him,
Clasped she his hands, and laid her head on his shoulder and whispered,—
"Gabriel! be of good cheer! for if we love one another,
Nothing, in truth, can harm us, whatever mischances may happen!"
Smiling she spake these words; then suddenly paused, for her father
Saw she slowly advancing. Alas! how changed was his aspect!
Gone was the glow from his cheek, and the fire from his eye, and his footstep
Heavier seemed with the weight of the heavy heart in his bosom.
But with a smile and a sigh, she clasped his neck and embraced him,
Speaking words of endearment where words of comfort availed not.
Thus to the Gaspereau's mouth moved on that mournful procession.

There disorder prevailed, and the tumult and stir of embarking.
Busily plied the freighted boats; and in the confusion
Wives were torn from their husbands, and mothers, too late, saw their
    children
Left on the land, extending their arms, with wildest entreaties.
So unto separate ships were Basil and Gabriel carried,
While in despair on the shore Evangeline stood with her father.
Half the task was not done when the sun went down, and the twilight
Deepened and darkened around; and in haste the refluent ocean
Fled away from the shore, and left the line of the sand-beach
Covered with waifs of the tide, with kelp and the slippery sea-weed.
Farther back in the midst of the household goods and the wagons,
Like to a gypsy camp, or a leaguer after a battle,
All escape cut off by the sea, and the sentinels near them,
Lay encamped for the night the houseless Acadian farmers.
Back to its nethermost caves retreated the bellowing ocean,
Dragging adown the beach the rattling pebbles, and leaving
Inland and far up the shore the stranded boats of the sailors.
Then, as the night descended, the herds returned from their pastures;
Sweet was the moist still air with the odor of milk from their udders;
Lowing they waited, and long, at the well-known bars of the farm-yard,—
Waited and looked in vain for the voice and the hand of the milkmaid.
Silence reigned in the streets; from the church no Angelus sounded,
Rose no smoke from the roofs, and gleamed no lights from the windows.

But on the shores meanwhile the evening fires had been kindled,
Built of the drift-wood thrown on the sands from wrecks in the tempest.
Round them shapes of gloom and sorrowful faces were gathered,
Voices of women were heard, and of men, and the crying of children.
Onward from fire to fire, as from hearth to hearth in his parish,
Wandered the faithful priest, consoling and blessing and cheering,
Like unto shipwrecked Paul on Melita's desolate sea-shore.
Thus he approached the place where Evangeline sat with her father,
And in the flickering light beheld the face of the old man,
Haggard and hollow and wan, and without either thought or emotion,
E'en as the face of a clock from which the hands have been taken.
Vainly Evangeline strove with words and caresses to cheer him,
Vainly offered him food; yet he moved not, he looked not, he spake not,
But, with a vacant stare, ever gazed at the flickering fire-light.
"Benedicite!" murmured the priest; in tones of compassion.
More he fain would have said, but his heart was full, and his accents
Faltered and paused on his lips, as the feet of a child on a threshold,
Hushed by the scene he beholds, and the awful presence of sorrow.
Silently, therefore, he laid his hand on the head of the maiden,
Raising his eyes full of tears to the silent stars that above them
Moved on their way, unperturbed by the wrongs and sorrows of mortals.
Then sat he down at her side, and they wept together in silence.

Suddenly rose from the south a light, as in autumn the blood-red
Moon climbs the crystal walls of heaven, and o'er the horizon
Titan-like stretches its hundred hands upon mountain and meadow,
Seizing the rocks and the rivers, and piling huge shadows together.
Broader and ever broader it gleamed on the roofs of the village,
Gleamed on the sky and the sea, and the ships that lay in the roadstead.
Columns of shining smoke uprose, and flashes of flame were
Thrust through their folds and withdrawn, like the quivering hands of a
     martyr.
Then as the wind seized the gleeds and the burning thatch, and, uplifting,
Whirled them aloft through the air, at once from a hundred house-tops
Started the sheeted smoke with flashes of flame intermingled.

These things beheld in dismay the crowd on the shore and on shipboard.
Speechless at first they stood, then cried aloud in their anguish,
"We shall behold no more our homes in the village of Grand-Pré!"
Loud on a sudden the cocks began to crow in the farm-yards,
Thinking the day had dawned; and anon the lowing of cattle
Came on the evening breeze, by the barking of dogs interrupted.
Then rose a sound of dread, such as startles the sleeping encampments
Far in the western prairies or forests that skirt the Nebraska,

When the wild horses affrighted sweep by with the speed of the whirlwind,
Or the loud bellowing herds of buffaloes rush to the river.
Such was the sound that arose on the night, as the herds and the horses
Broke through their folds and fences, and madly rushed o'er the meadows.

  Overwhelmed with the sight, yet speechless, the priest and the maiden
Gazed on the scene of terror that reddened and widened before them;
And as they turned at length to speak to their silent companion,
Lo! from his seat he had fallen, and stretched abroad on the sea-shore
Motionless lay his form, from which the soul had departed.
Slowly the priest uplifted the lifeless head, and the maiden
Knelt at her father's side, and wailed aloud in her terror.
Then in a swoon she sank, and lay with her head on his bosom.
Through the long night she lay in deep, oblivious slumber;
And when she woke from the trance, she beheld a multitude near her.
Faces of friends she beheld, that were mournfully gazing upon her,
Pallid, with tearful eyes, and looks of saddest compassion.
Still the blaze of the burning village illumined the landscape,
Reddened the sky overhead, and gleamed on the faces around her,
And like the day of doom it seemed to her wavering senses.
Then a familiar voice she heard, as it said to the people,—
"Let us bury him here by the sea. When a happier season
Brings us again to our homes from the unknown land of our exile,
Then shall his sacred dust be piously laid in the churchyard."
Such were the words of the priest. And there in haste by the seaside,
Having the glare of the burning village for funeral torches,
But without bell or book, they buried the farmer of Grand-Pré.
And as the voice of the priest repeated the service of sorrow,
Lo! with a mournful sound, like the voice of a vast congregation,
Solemnly answered the sea, and mingled its roar with the dirges.
'Twas the returning tide, that afar from the waste of the ocean,
With the first dawn of the day, came heaving and hurrying landward.
Then recommenced once more the stir and noise of embarking;
And with the ebb of the tide the ships sailed out of the harbor,
Leaving behind them the dead on the shore, and the village in ruins.

PART THE SECOND

I.

  MANY a weary year had passed since the burning of Grand-Pré,
When on the falling tide the freighted vessels departed,
Bearing a nation, with all its household gods, into exile,

Exile without an end, and without an example in story.
Far asunder, on separate coasts, the Acadians landed;
Scattered were they, like flakes of snow, when the wind from the northeast
Strikes aslant through the fogs that darken the Banks of Newfoundland.
Friendless, homeless, hopeless, they wandered from city to city,
From the cold lakes of the North to sultry Southern savannas,—
From the bleak shores of the sea to the lands where the Father of Waters
Seizes the hills in his hands, and drags them down to the ocean,
Deep in their sands to bury the scattered bones of the mammoth.
Friends they sought and homes; and many, despairing, heart-broken,
Asked of the earth but a grave, and no longer a friend nor a fireside.
Written their history stands on tablets of stone in the churchyards.
Long among them was seen a maiden who waited and wandered,
Lowly and meek in spirit, and patiently suffering all things.
Fair was she and young; but, alas! before her extended,
Dreary and vast and silent, the desert of life, with its pathway
Marked by the graves of those who had sorrowed and suffered before her,
Passions long extinguished, and hopes long dead and abandoned,
As the emigrant's way o'er the Western desert is marked by
Camp-fires long consumed, and bones that bleach in the sunshine.
Something there was in her life incomplete, imperfect, unfinished;
As if a morning of June, with all its music and sunshine,
Suddenly paused in the sky, and, fading, slowly descended
Into the east again, from whence it late had arisen.
Sometimes she lingered in towns, till, urged by the fever within her,
Urged by a restless longing, the hunger and thirst of the spirit,
She would commence again her endless search and endeavor;
Sometimes in churchyards strayed, and gazed on the crosses and tombstones,
Sat by some nameless grave, and thought that perhaps in its bosom
He was already at rest, and she longed to slumber beside him.
Sometimes a rumor, a hearsay, an inarticulate whisper,
Came with its airy hand to point and beckon her forward.
Sometimes she spake with those who had seen her beloved and known him,
But it was long ago, in some far-off place or forgotten.
"Gabriel Lajeunesse!" they said; "O yes! we have seen him.
He was with Basil the blacksmith, and both have gone to the prairies;
Coureurs-des-Bois are they, and famous hunters and trappers,"
"Gabriel Lajeunesse!" said others; "O yes! we have seen him.
He is a Voyageur in the lowlands of Louisiana."
Then would they say: "Dear child! why dream and wait for him longer?
Are there not other youths as fair as Gabriel? others
Who have hearts as tender and true, and spirits as loyal?
Here is Baptiste Leblanc, the notary's son, who has loved thee
Many a tedious year; come, give him thy hand and be happy!

Thou art too fair to be left to braid St. Catherine's tresses."
Then would Evangeline answer, serenely but sadly, "I cannot!
Whither my heart has gone, there follows my hand, and not elsewhere.
For when the heart goes before, like a lamp, and illumines the pathway,
Many things are made clear, that else lie hidden in darkness."
Thereupon the priest, her friend and father-confessor,
Said, with a smile, "O daughter! thy God thus speaketh within thee!
Talk not of wasted affection, affection never was wasted;
If it enrich not the heart of another, its waters, returning
Back to their springs, like the rain, shall fill them full of refreshment;
That which the fountain sends forth returns again to the fountain.
Patience; accomplish thy labor; accomplish thy work of affection!
Sorrow and silence are strong, and patient endurance is godlike.
Therefore accomplish thy labor of love, till the heart is made godlike,
Purified, strengthened, perfected, and rendered more worthy of heaven!"
Cheered by the good man's words, Evangeline labored and waited.
Still in her heart she heard the funeral dirge of the ocean,
But with its sound there was mingled a voice that whispered, "Despair not!"
Thus did that poor soul wander in want and cheerless discomfort,
Bleeding, barefooted, over the shards and thorns of existence.
Let me essay, O Muse! to follow the wanderer's footsteps;—
Not through each devious path, each changeful year of existence;
But as a traveller follows a streamlet's course through the valley:
Far from its margin at times, and seeing the gleam of its water
Here and there, in some open space, and at intervals only;
Then drawing nearer its banks, through sylvan glooms that conceal it,
Though he behold it not, he can hear its continuous murmur;
Happy, at length, if he find the spot where it reaches an outlet.

II.

IT was the month of May. Far down the Beautiful River,
Past the Ohio shore and past the mouth of the Wabash,
Into the golden stream of the broad and swift Mississippi,
Floated a cumbrous boat, that was rowed by Acadian boatmen.
It was a band of exiles: a raft, as it were, from the shipwrecked
Nation, scattered along the coast, now floating together,
Bound by the bonds of a common belief and a common misfortune;
Men and women and children, who, guided by hope or by hearsay,
Sought for their kith and their kin among the few-acred farmers
On the Acadian coast, and the prairies of fair Opelousas.
With them Evangeline went, and her guide, the Father Felician.
Onward o'er sunken sands, through a wilderness somber with forests,

Day after day they glided adown the turbulent river;
Night after night, by their blazing fires, encamped on its borders.
Now through rushing chutes, among green islands, where plumelike
Cotton-trees nodded their shadowy crests, they swept with the current,
Then emerged into broad lagoons, where silvery sand-bars
Lay in the stream, and along the wimpling waves of their margin,
Shining with snow-white plumes, large flocks of pelicans waded.
Level the landscape grew, and along the shores of the river,
Shaded by china-trees, in the midst of luxuriant gardens,
Stood the houses of planters, with negro-cabins and dove-cots.
They were approaching the region where reigns perpetual summer,
Where through the Golden Coast, and groves of orange and citron,
Sweeps with majestic curve the river away to the eastward.
They, too, swerved from their course; and, entering the Bayou of Plaquemine,
Soon were lost in a maze of sluggish and devious waters,
Which, like a network of steel, extended in every direction.
Over their heads the towering and tenebrous boughs of the cypress
Met in a dusky arch, and trailing mosses in mid-air
Waved like banners that hang on the walls of ancient cathedrals.
Deathlike the silence seemed, and unbroken, save by the herons
Home to their roosts in the cedar-trees returning at sunset,
Or by the owl, as he greeted the moon with demoniac laughter.
Lovely the moonlight was as it glanced and gleamed on the water,
Gleamed on the columns of cypress and cedar sustaining the arches,
Down through whose broken vaults it fell as through chinks in a ruin.
Dreamlike, and indistinct, and strange were all things around them;
And o'er their spirits there came a feeling of wonder and sadness,—
Strange forebodings of ill, unseen and that cannot be compassed.
As, at the tramp of a horse's hoof on the turf of the prairies,
Far in advance are closed the leaves of the shrinking mimosa,
So, at the hoof-beats of fate, with sad forebodings of evil,
Shrinks and closes the heart, ere the stroke of doom has attained it.
But Evangeline's heart was sustained by a vision, that faintly
Floated before her eyes, and beckoned her on through the moonlight.
It was the thought of her brain that assumed the shape of a phantom.
Through those shadowy aisles had Gabriel wandered before her,
And every stroke of the oar now brought him nearer and nearer.

  Then in his place, at the prow of the boat, rose one of the oarsmen,
And, as a signal sound, if others like them peradventure
Sailed on those gloomy and midnight streams, blew a blast on his bugle.
Wild through the dark colonnades and corridors leafy the blast rang,
Breaking the seal of silence, and giving tongues to the forest.
Soundless above them the banners of moss just stirred to the music.

Multitudinous echoes awoke and died in the distance,
Over the watery floor, and beneath the reverberant branches;
But not a voice replied; no answer came from the darkness;
And, when the echoes had ceased, like a sense of pain was the silence.
Then Evangeline slept; but the boatmen rowed through the midnight,
Silent at times, then singing familiar Canadian boat-songs,
Such as they sang of old on their own Acadian rivers,
And through the night were heard the mysterious sounds of the desert,
Far off,—indistinct,—as of wave or wind in the forest,
Mixed with the whoop of the crane and the roar of the grim alligator.

Thus ere another noon they emerged from the shades; and before them
Lay, in the golden sun, the lakes of the Atchafalaya.
Water-lilies in myriads rocked on the slight undulations
Made by the passing oars, and, resplendent in beauty, the lotus
Lifted her golden crown above the heads of the boatmen.
Faint was the air with the odorous breath of magnolia blossoms,
And with the heat of noon; and numberless sylvan islands,
Fragrant and thickly embowered with blossoming hedges of roses,
Near to whose shores they glided along, invited to slumber.
Soon by the fairest of these their weary oars were suspended.
Under the boughs of Wachita willows, that grew by the margin,
Safely their boat was moored; and scattered about on the greensward,
Tired with their midnight toil, the weary travellers slumbered.
Over them vast and high extended the cope of a cedar.
Swinging from its great arms, the trumpet-flower and the grape-vine
Hung their ladder of ropes aloft like the ladder of Jacob,
On whose pendulous stairs the angels ascending, descending,
Were the swift humming-birds, that flitted from blossom to blossom.
Such was the vision Evangeline saw as she slumbered beneath it.
Filled was her heart with love, and the dawn of an opening heaven
Lighted her soul in sleep with the glory of regions celestial.

Nearer and ever nearer, among the numberless islands,
Darted a light, swift boat, that sped away o'er the water,
Urged on its course by the sinewy arms of hunters and trappers.
Northward its prow was turned, to the land of the bison and beaver.
At the helm sat a youth, with countenance thoughtful and care-worn.
Dark and neglected locks overshadowed his brow, and a sadness
Somewhat beyond his years on his face was legibly written.
Gabriel was it, who, weary with waiting, unhappy and restless,
Sought in the Western wilds oblivion of self and of sorrow.
Swiftly they glided along, close under the lee of the island,
But by the opposite bank, and behind a screen of palmettos,

So that they saw not the boat, where it lay concealed in the willows,
And undisturbed by the dash of their oars, and unseen, were the sleepers,
Angel of God was there none to awaken the slumbering maiden.
Swiftly they glided away, like the shade of a cloud on the prairie.
After the sound of their oars on the tholes had died in the distance,
As from a magic trance the sleepers awoke, and the maiden
Said with a sigh to the friendly priest, "O Father Felician!
Something says in my heart that near me Gabriel wanders.
Is it a foolish dream, an idle and vague superstition?
Or has an angel passed, and revealed the truth to my spirit?"
Then, with a blush, she added, "Alas for my credulous fancy!
Unto ears like thine such words as these have no meaning."
But made answer the reverend man, and he smiled as he answered,—
"Daughter, thy words are not idle; nor are they to me without meaning.
Feeling is deep and still; and the word that floats on the surface
Is as the tossing buoy, that betrays where the anchor is hidden.
Therefore trust to thy heart, and to what the world calls illusions.
Gabriel truly is near thee; for not far away to the southward,
On the banks of the Têche are the towns of St. Maur and St. Martin.
There the long-wandering bride shall be given again to her bridegroom,
There the long-absent pastor regain his flock and his sheepfold.
Beautiful is the land, with its prairies and forests of fruit-trees;
Under the feet a garden of flowers, and the bluest of heavens
Bending above, and resting its dome on the walls of the forest.
They who dwell there have named it the Eden of Louisiana."

  With these words of cheer they arose and continued their journey.
Softly the evening came. The sun from the western horizon
Like a magician extended his golden wand o'er the landscape;
Twinkling vapors arose; and sky and water and forest
Seemed all on fire at the touch, and melted and mingled together.
Hanging between two skies, a cloud with edges of silver,
Floated the boat, with its dripping oars, on the motionless water.
Filled was Evangeline's heart with inexpressible sweetness.
Touched by the magic spell, the sacred fountains of feeling
Glowed with the light of love, as the skies and waters around her.
Then from a neighboring thicket the mockingbird, wildest of singers,
Swinging aloft on a willow spray that hung o'er the water,
Shook from his little throat such floods of delirious music,
That the whole air and the woods and the waves seemed silent to listen.
Plaintive at first were the tones and sad; then soaring to madness
Seemed they to follow or guide the revel of frenzied Bacchantes.
Single notes were then heard, in sorrowful, low lamentation;
Till, having gathered them all, he flung them abroad in derision,

As when, after a storm, a gust of wind through the tree tops
Shakes down the rattling rain in a crystal shower on the branches.
With such a prelude as this, and hearts that throbbed with emotion,
Slowly they entered the Têche, where it flows through the green Opelousas,
And, through the amber air, above the crest of the woodland,
Saw the column of smoke that arose from a neighboring dwelling;—
Sounds of a horn they heard, and the distant lowing of cattle.

III.

  NEAR to the bank of the river, o'ershadowed by oaks, from whose branches
    Garlands of Spanish moss and of mystic mistletoe flaunted,
    Such as the Druids cut down with golden hatchets at Yule-tide,
    Stood, secluded and still, the house of the herdsman. A garden
    Girdled it round about with a belt of luxuriant blossoms,
    Filling the air with fragrance. The house itself was of timbers
    Hewn from the cypress-tree, and carefully fitted together.
    Large and low was the roof; and on slender columns supported,
    Rose-wreathed, vine-encircled, a broad and spacious veranda,
    Haunt of the humming-bird and the bee, extended around it.
    At each end of the house, amid the flowers of the garden,
    Stationed the dove-cots were, as love's perpetual symbol,
    Scenes of endless wooing, and endless contentions of rivals.
    Silence reigned o'er the place. The line of shadow and sunshine
    Ran near the tops of the trees; but the house itself was in shadow,
    And from its chimney-top, ascending and slowly expanding
    Into the evening air, a thin blue column of smoke rose.
    In the rear of the house, from the garden gate, ran a pathway
    Through the great groves of oak to the skirts of the limitless prairie,
    Into whose sea of flowers the sun was slowly descending.
    Full in his track of light, like ships with shadowy canvas
    Hanging loose from their spars in a motionless calm in the tropics,
    Stood a cluster of trees, with tangled cordage of grape-vines.

  Just where the woodlands met the flowery surf of the prairie,
    Mounted upon his horse, with Spanish saddle and stirrups,
    Sat a herdsman, arrayed in gaiters and doublet of deerskin.
    Broad and brown was the face that from under the Spanish sombrero
    Gazed on the peaceful scene, with the lordly look of its master.
    Round about him were numberless herds of kine, that were grazing
    Quietly in the meadows, and breathing the vapory freshness
    That uprose from the river, and spread itself over the landscape.
    Slowly lifting the horn that hung at his side, and expanding

Fully his broad, deep chest, he blew a blast, that resounded
Wildly and sweet and far, through the still damp air of the evening.
Suddenly out of the grass the long white horns of the cattle
Rose like flakes of foam on the adverse currents of ocean.
Silent a moment they gazed, then bellowing rushed o'er the prairie,
And the whole mass became a cloud, a shade in the distance.
Then as the herdsman turned to the house, through the gate of the garden
Saw he the forms of the priest and the maiden advancing to meet him.
Suddenly down from his horse he sprang in amazement, and forward
Rushed with extended arms and exclamations of wonder;
When they beheld his face, they recognized Basil the blacksmith.
Hearty his welcome was, as he led his guests to the garden.
There in an arbor of roses with endless question and answer
Gave they vent to their hearts, and renewed their friendly embraces,
Laughing and weeping by turns, or sitting silent and thoughtful.
Thoughtful, for Gabriel came not; and now dark doubts and misgivings
Stole o'er the maiden's heart; and Basil, somewhat embarrassed,
Broke the silence and said, "If you came by the Atchafalaya,
How have you nowhere encountered my Gabriel's boat on the bayous?"
Over Evangeline's face at the words of Basil a shade passed.
Tears came into her eyes, and she said, with a tremulous accent,
"Gone? is Gabriel gone?" and, concealing her face on his shoulder,
All her o'erburdened heart gave way, and she wept and lamented.
Then the good Basil said,—and his voice grew blithe as he said it,—
"Be of good cheer, my child; it is only to-day he departed.
Foolish boy! he has left me alone with my herds and my horses.
Moody and restless grown, and tried and troubled, his spirit
Could no longer endure the calm of this quiet existence.
Thinking ever of thee, uncertain and sorrowful ever,
Ever silent, or speaking only of thee and his troubles,
He at length had become so tedious to men and to maidens,
Tedious even to me, that at length I bethought me, and sent him
Unto the town of Adayes to trade for mules with the Spaniards.
Thence he will follow the Indian trails to the Ozark Mountains,
Hunting for furs in the forests, on rivers trapping the beaver.
Therefore be of good cheer; we will follow the fugitive lover;
He is not far on his way, and the Fates and the streams are against him.
Up and away to-morrow, and through the red dew of the morning
We will follow him fast and bring him back to his prison."

Then glad voices were heard, and up from the banks of the river,
Borne aloft on his comrades' arms, came Michael the fiddler.
Long under Basil's roof had he lived like a god on Olympus,
Having no other care than dispensing music to mortals.

Far renowned was he for his silver locks and his fiddle.
"Long live Michael," they cried, "our brave Acadian minstrel!"
As they bore him aloft in triumphal procession; and straightway
Father Felician advanced with Evangeline, greeting the old man
Kindly and oft, and recalling the past, while Basil, enraptured,
Hailed with hilarious joy his old companions and gossips,
Laughing loud and long, and embracing mothers and daughters.
Much they marvelled to see the wealth of the ci-devant blacksmith,
All his domains and his herds, and his patriarchal demeanor;
Much they marvelled to hear his tales of the soil and the climate,
And of the prairies, whose numberless herds were his who would take them;
Each one thought in his heart, that he, too, would go and do likewise.
Thus they ascended the steps, and, crossing the airy veranda,
Entered the hall of the house, where already the supper of Basil
Waited his late return; and they rested and feasted together.

Over the joyous feast the sudden darkness descended.
All was silent without, and, illuming the landscape with silver,
Fair rose the dewy moon and the myriad stars; but within doors,
Brighter than these, shone the faces of friends in the glimmering lamplight.
Then from his station aloft, at the head of the table, the herdsman
Poured forth his heart and his wine together in endless profusion.
Lighting his pipe, that was filled with sweet Natchitoches tobacco,
Thus he spake to his guests, who listened, and smiled as they listened:—
"Welcome once more, my friends, who long have been friendless and
    homeless,
Welcome once more to a home, that is better perchance than the old one!
Here no hungry winter congeals our blood like the rivers;
Here no stony ground provokes the wrath of the farmer.
Smoothly the ploughshare runs through the soil, as a keel through the water.
All the year round the orange-groves are in blossom; and grass grows
More in a single night than a whole Canadian summer.
Here, too, numberless herds run wild and unclaimed in the prairies;
Here, too, lands may be had for the asking, and forests of timber
With a few blows of the axe are hewn and framed into houses.
After your houses are built, and your fields are yellow with harvests,
No King George of England shall drive you away from your homesteads,
Burning your dwellings and barns, and stealing your farms and your cattle."
Speaking these words, he blew a wrathful cloud from his nostrils,
While his huge, brown hand came thundering down on the table,
So that the guests all started; and Father Felician, astounded,
Suddenly paused, with a pinch of snuff halfway to his nostrils.
But the brave Basil resumed, and his words were milder and gayer:
"Only beware of the fever, my friends, beware of the fever!

For it is not like that of our cold Acadian climate,
Cured by wearing a spider hung round one's neck in a nutshell!"
Then there were voices heard at the door, and footsteps approaching
Sounded upon the stairs and the floor of the breezy veranda.
It was the neighboring Creoles and small Acadian planters,
Who had been summoned all to the house of Basil the Herdsman.
Merry the meeting was of ancient comrades and neighbors:
Friend clasped friend in his arms; and they who before were as strangers,
Meeting in exile, became straightway as friends to each other,
Drawn by the gentle bond of a common country together.
But in the neighboring hall a strain of music, proceeding
From the accordant strings of Michael's melodious fiddle,
Broke up all further speech. Away, like children delighted,
All things forgotten beside, they gave themselves to the maddening
Whirl of the dizzy dance, as it swept and swayed to the music,
Dreamlike, with beaming eyes and the rush of fluttering garments.

  Meanwhile, apart, at the head of the hall, the priest and the herdsman
Sat, conversing together of past and present and future;
While Evangeline stood like one entranced, for within her
Olden memories rose, and loud in the midst of the music
Heard she the sound of the sea, and an irrepressible sadness
Came o'er her heart, and unseen she stole forth into the garden.
Beautiful was the night. Behind the black wall of the forest,
Tipping its summit with silver, arose the moon. On the river
Fell here and there through the branches a tremulous gleam of the moonlight,
Like the sweet thoughts of love on a darkened and devious spirit.
Nearer and round about her, the manifold flowers of the garden
Poured out their souls in odors, that were their prayers and confessions
Unto the night, as it went its way, like a silent Carthusian.
Fuller of fragrance than they, and as heavy with shadows and night-dews,
Hung the heart of the maiden. The calm and the magical moonlight
Seemed to inundate her soul with indefinable longings,
As, through the garden gate, beneath the shade of the oak-trees,
Passed she along the path to the edge of the measureless prairie.
Silent it lay, with a silvery haze upon it, and the fire-flies
Gleaming and floating away in mingled and infinite numbers.
Over her head the stars, the thoughts of God in the heavens,
Shone on the eyes of man, who had ceased to marvel and worship,
Save when a blazing comet was seen on the walls of that temple,
As if a hand had appeared and written upon them, "Upharsin."
And the soul of the maiden, between the stars and the fire-flies,
Wandered alone, and she cried, "O Gabriel! O my beloved!
Art thou so near unto me, and yet I cannot behold thee?

Art thou so near unto me, and yet thy voice does not reach me?
Ah! how often thy feet have trod this path to the prairie!
Ah! how often thine eyes have looked on the woodlands around me!
Ah! how often beneath this oak, returning from labor,
Thou hast lain down to rest, and to dream of me in thy slumbers!
When shall these eyes behold, these arms be folded about thee?"
Loud and sudden and near the note of a whippoorwill sounded
Like a flute in the woods; and anon, through the neighboring thickets,
Farther and farther away it floated and dropped into silence.
"Patience!" whispered the oaks from oracular caverns of darkness;
And, from the moonlit meadow, a sigh responded, "To-morrow!"

  Bright rose the sun next day; and all the flowers of the garden
Bathed his shining feet with their tears, and anointed his tresses
With the delicious balm that they bore in their vases of crystal.
"Farewell!" said the priest, as he stood at the shadowy threshold;
"See that you bring us the Prodigal Son from his fasting and famine,
And, too, the Foolish Virgin, who slept when the bridegroom was coming."
"Farewell!" answered the maiden, and, smiling, with Basil descended
Down to the river's brink, where the boatmen already were waiting.
Thus beginning their journey with morning, and sunshine, and gladness,
Swiftly they followed the flight of him who was speeding before them,
Blown by the blast of fate like a dead leaf over the desert.
Not that day, nor the next, nor yet the day that succeeded,
Found they trace of his course, in lake or forest or river,
Nor, after many days, had they found him; but vague and uncertain
Rumors alone were their guides through a wild and desolate country;
Till, at the little inn of the Spanish town of Adayes,
Weary and worn, they alighted, and learned from the garrulous landlord,
That on the day before, with horses and guides and companions,
Gabriel left the village, and took the road of the prairies.

IV.

  FAR in the West there lies a desert land, where the mountains
  Lift, through perpetual snows, their lofty and luminous summits.
  Down from their jagged, deep ravines, where the gorge, like a gateway,
  Opens a passage rude to the wheels of the emigrant's wagon,
  Westward the Oregon flows and the Walleway and Owyhee.
  Eastward, with devious course, among the Windriver Mountains,
  Through the Sweet-water Valley precipitate leaps the Nebraska;
  And to the south, from Fontaine-qui-bout and the Spanish sierras,
  Fretted with sands and rocks, and swept by the wind of the desert,

Numberless torrents, with ceaseless sound, descend to the ocean,
Like the great chords of a harp, in loud and solemn vibrations.
Spreading between these streams are the wondrous, beautiful prairies,
Billowy bays of grass ever rolling in shadow and sunshine,
Bright with luxuriant clusters of roses and purple amorphas.
Over them wandered the buffalo herds, and the elk and the roebuck;
Over them wandered the wolves, and herds of riderless horses;
Fires that blast and blight, and winds that are weary with travel;
Over them wander the scattered tribes of Ishmael's children,
Staining the desert with blood; and above their terrible war-trails
Circles and sails aloft, on pinions majestic, the vulture,
Like the implacable soul of a chieftain slaughtered in battle,
By invisible stairs ascending and scaling the heavens.
Here and there rise smokes from the camps of these savage marauders;
Here and there rise groves from the margins of swift-running rivers;
And the grim, taciturn bear, the anchorite monk of the desert,
Climbs down their dark ravines to dig for roots by the brookside,
And over all is the sky, the clear and crystalline heaven,
Like the protecting hand of God inverted above them.

Into this wonderful land, at the base of the Ozark Mountains,
Gabriel far had entered, with hunters and trappers behind him.
Day after day, with their Indian guides, the maiden and Basil
Followed his flying steps, and thought each day to o'ertake him.
Sometimes they saw, or thought they saw, the smoke of his camp-fire
Rise in the morning air from the distant plain; but at nightfall,
When they had reached the place, they found only embers and ashes.
And, though their hearts were sad at times and their bodies were weary,
Hope still guided them on, as the magic Fata Morgana
Showed them her lakes of light, that retreated and vanished before them.

Once, as they sat by their evening fire, there silently entered
Into the little camp an Indian woman, whose features
Wore deep traces of sorrow, and patience as great as her sorrow.
She was a Shawnee woman returning home to her people,
From the far-off hunting-grounds of the cruel Camanches,
Where her Canadian husband, a Coureur-des-Bois, had been murdered.
Touched were their hearts at her story, and warmest and friendliest welcome
Gave they, with words of cheer, and she sat and feasted among them
On the buffalo-meat and the venison cooked on the embers.
But when their meal was done, and Basil and all his companions,
Worn with the long day's march and the chase of the deer and the bison,
Stretched themselves on the ground, and slept where the quivering fire-
    light

Flashed on their swarthy cheeks, and their forms wrapped up in their
   blankets,
Then at the door of Evangeline's tent she sat and repeated
Slowly, with soft, low voice, and the charm of her Indian accent,
All the tale of her love, with its pleasures, and pains, and reverses.
Much Evangeline wept at the tale, and to know that another
Hapless heart like her own had loved and had been disappointed.
Moved to the depths of her soul by pity and woman's compassion,
Yet in her sorrow pleased that one who had suffered was near her,
She in turn related her love and all its disasters.
Mute with wonder the Shawnee sat, and when she had ended
Still was mute; but at length, as if a mysterious horror
Passed through her brain, she spake, and repeated the tale of the Mowis;
Mowis, the bridegroom of snow, who won and wedded a maiden,
But, when the morning came, arose and passed from the wigwam,
Fading and melting away and dissolving into the sunshine,
Till she beheld him no more, though she followed far into the forest.
Then, in those sweet, low tones, that seemed like a weird incantation,
Told she the tale of the fair Lilinau, who was wooed by a phantom,
That, through the pines o'er her father's lodge, in the hush of the twilight,
Breathed like the evening wind, and whispered love to the maiden,
Till she followed his green and waving plume through the forest,
And never more returned, nor was seen again by her people.
Silent with wonder and strange surprise, Evangeline listened
To the soft flow of her magical words, till the region around her
Seemed like enchanted ground, and her swarthy guest the enchantress.
Slowly over the tops of the Ozark Mountains the moon rose,
Lighting the little tent, and with a mysterious splendor
Touching the sombre leaves, and embracing and filling the woodland.
With a delicious sound the brook rushed by, and the branches
Swayed and sighed overhead in scarcely audible whispers.
Filled with the thoughts of love was Evangeline's heart, but a secret,
Subtile sense crept in of pain and indefinite terror,
As the cold, poisonous snake creeps into the nest of the swallow.
It was no earthly fear. A breath from the region of spirits
Seemed to float in the air of night; and she felt for a moment
That, like the Indian maid, she, too, was pursuing a phantom.
With this thought she slept, and the fear and the phantom had vanished.

  Early upon the morrow the march was resumed; and the Shawnee
Said, as they journeyed along, "On the western slope of these mountains
Dwells in his little village the Black Robe chief of the Mission.
Much he teaches the people, and tells them of Mary and Jesus;
Loud laugh their hearts with joy, and weep with pain, as they hear him."

Then, with a sudden and secret emotion, Evangeline answered,
"Let us go to the Mission, for there good tidings await us!"
Thither they turned their steeds; and behind a spur of the mountains,
Just as the sun went down, they heard a murmur of voices,
And in a meadow green and broad, by the bank of a river,
Saw the tents of the Christians, the tents of the Jesuit Mission.
Under a towering oak, that stood in the midst of the village,
Knelt the Black Robe chief with his children. A crucifix fastened
High on the trunk of the tree, and overshadowed by grape-vines,
Looked with its agonized face on the multitude kneeling beneath it.
This was their rural chapel. Aloft, through the intricate arches
Of its aerial roof, arose the chant of their vespers,
Mingling its notes with the soft susurrus and sighs of the branches.
Silent, with heads uncovered, the travellers, nearer approaching,
Knelt on the swarded floor, and joined in the evening devotions.
But when the service was done, and the benediction had fallen
Forth from the hands of the priest, like seed from the hands of the sower,
Slowly the reverend man advanced to the strangers and bade them
Welcome; and when they replied, he smiled with benignant expression,
Hearing the homelike sounds of his mother-tongue in the forest,
And, with words of kindness, conducted them into his wigwam.
There upon mats and skins they reposed, and on cakes of the maize-ear
Feasted, and slaked their thirst from the water-gourd of the teacher.
Soon was their story told; and the priest with solemnity answered:—
"Not six suns have risen and set since Gabriel, seated
On this mat by my side, where now the maiden reposes,
Told me this same sad tale; then arose and continued his journey!"
Soft was the voice of the priest, and he spake with an accent of kindness;
But on Evangeline's heart fell his words as in winter the snow-flakes
Fall into some lone nest from which the birds have departed.
"Far to the north he has gone," continued the priest; "but in autumn,
When the chase is done, will return again to the Mission."
Then Evangeline said, and her voice was meek and submissive,
"Let me remain with thee, for my soul is sad and afflicted."
So seemed it wise and well unto all; and betimes on the morrow,
Mounting his Mexican steed, with his Indian guides and companions,
Homeward Basil returned, and Evangeline stayed at the Mission.

   Slowly, slowly, slowly the days succeeded each other,—
Days and weeks and months; and the fields of maize that were springing
Green from the ground when a stranger she came, now waving above her,
Lifted their slender shafts, with leaves interlacing, and forming
Cloisters for mendicant crows and granaries pillaged by squirrels.
Then in the golden weather the maize was husked, and the maidens

Blushed at each blood-red ear, for that betokened a lover,
But at the crooked laughed, and called it a thief in the cornfield.
Even the blood-red ear to Evangeline brought not her lover.
"Patience!" the priest would say; "have faith, and thy prayer will be
    answered!
Look at this delicate plant that lifts its head from the meadow,
See how its leaves all point to the north, as true as the magnet;
This is the compass-flower, that the finger of God has suspended
Here on its fragile stock, to direct the traveller's journey
Over the sea-like, pathless, limitless waste of the desert.
Such in the soul of man is faith. The blossoms of passion,
Gay and luxuriant flowers, are brighter and fuller of fragrance,
But they beguile us, and lead us astray, and their odor is deadly.
Only this humble plant can guide us here, and hereafter
Crown us with asphodel flowers, that are wet with the dews of nepenthe."

  So came the autumn, and passed, and the winter,—yet Gabriel came not;
Blossomed the opening spring, and the notes of the robin and bluebird
Sounded sweet upon wold and in wood, yet Gabriel came not.
But on the breath of the summer winds a rumor was wafted
Sweeter than song of bird, or hue or odor of blossom.
Far to the north and east, it said, in the Michigan forests,
Gabriel had his lodge by the banks of the Saginaw river.
And, with returning guides, that sought the lakes of St. Lawrence,
Saying a sad farewell, Evangeline went from the Mission.
When over weary ways, by long and perilous marches,
She had attained at length the depths of the Michigan forests,
Found she the hunter's lodge deserted and fallen to ruin!

  Thus did the long sad years glide on, and in seasons and places
Divers and distant far was seen the wandering maiden;—
Now in the Tents of Grace of the meek Moravian Missions,
Now in the noisy camps and the battle-fields of the army,
Now in secluded hamlets, in towns and populous cities.
Like a phantom she came, and passed away unremembered.
Fair was she and young, when in hope began the long journey;
Faded was she and old, when in disappointment it ended.
Each succeeding year stole something away from her beauty.
Leaving behind it, broader and deeper, the gloom and the shadow.
Then there appeared and spread faint streaks of gray o'er her forehead,
Dawn of another life, that broke o'er her earthly horizon,
As in the eastern sky the first faint streaks of the morning.

V.

IN that delightful land, which is washed by the Delaware's waters,
  Guarding in sylvan shades the name of Penn the apostle.
Stands on the banks of its beautiful stream the city he founded.
There all the air is balm, and the peach is the emblem of beauty,
And the streets still re-echo the names of the trees of the forest,
As if they fain would appease the Dryads whose haunts they molested.
There from the troubled sea had Evangeline landed, an exile,
Finding among the children of Penn a home and a country.
There old René Leblanc had died; and when he departed,
Saw at his side only one of all his hundred descendants.
Something at least there was in the friendly streets of the city,
Something that spake to her heart, and made her no longer a stranger;
And her ear was pleased with the Thee and Thou of the Quakers,
For it recalled the past, the old Acadian country,
Where all men were equal, and all were brothers and sisters.
So, when the fruitless search, the disappointed endeavor,
Ended, to recommence no more upon earth, uncomplaining,
Thither, as leaves to the light, were turned her thoughts and her footsteps.
As from a mountain's top the rainy mists of the morning
Roll away, and afar we behold the landscape below us,
Sun-illumined, with shining rivers and cities and hamlets,
So fell the mists from her mind, and she saw the world far below her,
Dark no longer, but all illumined with love; and the pathway
Which she had climbed so far, lying smooth and fair in the distance.
Gabriel was not forgotten. Within her heart was his image,
Clothed in the beauty of love and youth, as last she beheld him,
Only more beautiful made by his deathlike silence and absence.
Into her thoughts of him time entered not, for it was not.
Over him years had no power; he was not changed, but transfigured;
He had become to her heart as one who is dead, and not absent;
Patience and abnegation of self, and devotion to others,
This was the lesson a life of trial and sorrow had taught her.
So was her love diffused, but, like to some odorous spices,
Suffered no waste nor loss, though filling the air with aroma.
Other hope had she none, nor wish in life, but to follow
Meekly, with reverent steps, the sacred feet of her Saviour.
Thus many years she lived as a Sister of Mercy; frequenting
Lonely and wretched roofs in the crowded lanes of the city,
Where distress and want concealed themselves from the sunlight,
Where disease and sorrow in garrets languished neglected.
Night after night, when the world was asleep, as the watchman repeated

Loud, through the gusty streets, that all was well in the city,
High at some lonely window he saw the light of her taper.
Day after day, in the gray of the dawn, as slow through the suburbs
Plodded the German farmer, with flowers and fruits for the market,
Met he that meek, pale face, returning home from its watchings.

  Then it came to pass that a pestilence fell on the city,
Presaged by wondrous signs, and mostly by flocks of wild pigeons,
Darkening the sun in their flight, with naught in their craws but an acorn.
And, as the tides of the sea arise in the month of September,
Flooding some silver stream, till it spreads to a lake in the meadow,
So death flooded life, and, o'erflowing its natural margin,
Spread to a brackish lake, the silver stream of existence.
Wealth had no power to bribe, nor beauty to charm, the oppressor;
But all perished alike beneath the scourge of his anger;—
Only, alas! the poor, who had neither friends nor attendants,
Crept away to die in the almshouse, home of the homeless.
Then in the suburbs it stood, in the midst of meadows and woodlands;—
Now the city surrounds it; but still, with its gateway and wicket
Meek, in the midst of splendor, its humble walls seem to echo
Softly the words of the Lord:—"The poor ye always have with you."
Thither, by night and by day, came the Sister of Mercy. The dying
Looked up into her face, and thought, indeed, to behold there
Gleams of celestial light encircle her forehead with splendor,
Such as the artist paints o'er the brows of saints and apostles,
Or such as hangs by night o'er a city seen at a distance.
Unto their eyes it seemed the lamps of the city celestial,
Into whose shining gates erelong their spirits would enter.

  Thus, on a Sabbath morn, through the streets, deserted and silent,
Wending her quiet way, she entered the door of the almshouse.
Sweet on the summer air was the odor of flowers in the garden;
And she paused on her way to gather the fairest among them,
That the dying once more might rejoice in their fragrance and beauty.
Then, as she mounted the stairs to the corridors, cooled by the east wind,
Distant and soft on her ear fell the chimes from the belfry of Christ Church,
While, intermingled with these, across the meadows were wafted
Sounds of psalms, that were sung by the Swedes in their church at Wicaco.
Soft as descending wings fell the calm of the hour on her spirit;
Something within her said, "At length thy trials are ended";
And, with light in her looks, she entered the chambers of sickness.
Noiselessly moved about the assiduous, careful attendants,
Moistening the feverish lip, and the aching brow, and in silence
Closing the sightless eyes of the dead, and concealing their faces,

Where on their pallets they lay, like drifts of snow by the roadside.
Many a languid head, upraised as Evangeline entered,
Turned on its pillow of pain to gaze while she passed, for her presence
Fell on their hearts like a ray of the sun on the walls of a prison.
And, as she looked around, she saw how Death, the consoler,
Laying his hand upon many a heart, had healed it forever.
Many familiar forms had disappeared in the night-time;
Vacant their places were, or filled already by strangers.

  Suddenly, as if arrested by fear or a feeling of wonder,
Still she stood, with her colorless lips apart, while a shudder
Ran through her frame, and, forgotten, the flowerets dropped from her
    fingers,
And from her eyes and cheeks the light and bloom of the morning.
Then there escaped from her lips a cry of such terrible anguish,
That the dying heard it, and started up from their pillows.
On the pallet before her was stretched the form of an old man.
Long, and thin, and gray were the locks that shaded his temples;
But, as he lay in the morning light, his face for a moment
Seemed to assume once more the forms of its earlier manhood;
So are wont to be changed the faces of those who are dying.
Hot and red on his lips still burned the flush of the fever,
As if life, like the Hebrew, with blood had besprinkled its portals,
That the Angel of Death might see the sign, and pass over.
Motionless, senseless, dying, he lay, and his spirit exhausted
Seemed to be sinking down through infinite depths in the darkness,
Darkness of slumber and death, forever sinking and sinking.
Then through those realms of shade, in multiplied reverberations,
Heard he that cry of pain, and through the hush that succeeded
Whispered a gentle voice, in accents tender and saint-like,
"Gabriel! O my beloved!" and died away into silence.
Then he beheld, in a dream, once more the home of his childhood;
Green Acadian meadows, with sylvan rivers among them,
Village, and mountain, and woodlands; and, walking under their shadow,
As in the days of her youth, Evangeline rose in his vision.
Tears came into his eyes; and as slowly he lifted his eyelids,
Vanished the vision away, but Evangeline knelt by his bedside.
Vainly he strove to whisper her name, for the accents unuttered
Died on his lips, and their motion revealed what his tongue would have
    spoken.
Vainly he strove to rise; and Evangeline, kneeling beside him,
Kissed his dying lips, and laid his head on her bosom.
Sweet was the light of his eyes; but it suddenly sank into darkness,
As when a lamp is blown out by a gust of wind at a casement.

All was ended now, the hope, and the fear, and the sorrow,
All the aching of heart, the restless, unsatisfied longing,
All the dull, deep pain, and constant anguish of patience!
And, as she pressed once more the lifeless head to her bosom,
Meekly she bowed her own, and murmured, "Father, I thank thee!"

STILL stands the forest primeval; but far away from its shadow,
Side by side, in their nameless graves, the lovers are sleeping.
Under the humble walls of the little Catholic churchyard,
In the heart of the city, they lie, unknown and unnoticed.
Daily the tides of life go ebbing and flowing beside them,
Thousands of throbbing hearts, where theirs are at rest and forever,
Thousands of aching brains, where theirs no longer are busy,
Thousands of toiling hands, where theirs have ceased from their labors,
Thousands of weary feet, where theirs have completed their journey!

Still stands the forest primeval; but under the shade of its branches
Dwells another race, with other customs and language.
Only along the shore of the mournful and misty Atlantic
Linger a few Acadian peasants, whose fathers from exile
Wandered back to their native land to die in its bosom.
In the fisherman's cot the wheel and the loom are still busy;
Maidens still wear their Norman caps and their kirtles of homespun,
And by the evening fire repeat Evangeline's story.
While from its rocky caverns the deep-voiced, neighboring ocean
Speaks, and in accents disconsolate answers the wail of the forest.

THE SONG OF HIAWATHA

THE SONG OF HIAWATHA

INTRODUCTION

Should you ask me, whence these stories?
Whence these legends and traditions,
With the odors of the forest
With the dew and damp of meadows,
With the curling smoke of wigwams,
With the rushing of great rivers,
With their frequent repetitions,
And their wild reverberations
As of thunder in the mountains?

I should answer, I should tell you,
"From the forests and the prairies,
From the great lakes of the Northland,
From the land of the Ojibways,
From the land of the Dacotahs,
From the mountains, moors, and fen-lands
Where the heron, the Shuh-shuh-gah,
Feeds among the reeds and rushes.
I repeat them as I heard them
From the lips of Nawadaha,
The musician, the sweet singer."

Should you ask where Nawadaha

Found these songs so wild and wayward,
Found these legends and traditions,
I should answer, I should tell you,
"In the bird's-nests of the forest,
In the lodges of the beaver,
In the hoofprint of the bison,
In the eyry of the eagle!

"All the wild-fowl sang them to him,
In the moorlands and the fen-lands,
In the melancholy marshes;
Chetowaik, the plover, sang them,
Mahng, the loon, the wild-goose, Wawa,
The blue heron, the Shuh-shuh-gah,
And the grouse, the Mushkodasa!"

If still further you should ask me,
Saying, "Who was Nawadaha?
Tell us of this Nawadaha,"
I should answer your inquiries
Straightway in such words as follow.

"In the vale of Tawasentha,
In the green and silent valley,
By the pleasant water-courses,
Dwelt the singer Nawadaha.
Round about the Indian village
Spread the meadows and the corn-fields,
And beyond them stood the forest,
Stood the groves of singing pine-trees,
Green in Summer, white in Winter,
Ever sighing, ever singing.

"And the pleasant water-courses,
You could trace them through the valley,
By the rushing in the Spring-time,
By the alders in the Summer,
By the white fog in the Autumn,
By the black line in the Winter;
And beside them dwelt the singer,
In the vale of Tawasentha,
In the green and silent valley.

"There he sang of Hiawatha,

Sang the Song of Hiawatha,
Sang his wondrous birth and being,
How he prayed and how be fasted,
How he lived, and toiled, and suffered,
That the tribes of men might prosper,
That he might advance his people!"

Ye who love the haunts of Nature,
Love the sunshine of the meadow,
Love the shadow of the forest,
Love the wind among the branches,
And the rain-shower and the snow-storm,
And the rushing of great rivers
Through their palisades of pine-trees,
And the thunder in the mountains,
Whose innumerable echoes
Flap like eagles in their eyries;--
Listen to these wild traditions,
To this Song of Hiawatha!

Ye who love a nation's legends,
Love the ballads of a people,
That like voices from afar off
Call to us to pause and listen,
Speak in tones so plain and childlike,
Scarcely can the ear distinguish
Whether they are sung or spoken;--
Listen to this Indian Legend,
To this Song of Hiawatha!

Ye whose hearts are fresh and simple,
Who have faith in God and Nature,
Who believe that in all ages
Every human heart is human,
That in even savage bosoms
There are longings, yearnings, strivings
For the good they comprehend not,
That the feeble hands and helpless,
Groping blindly in the darkness,
Touch God's right hand in that darkness
And are lifted up and strengthened;--
Listen to this simple story,
To this Song of Hiawatha!

Ye, who sometimes, in your rambles
Through the green lanes of the country,
Where the tangled barberry-bushes
Hang their tufts of crimson berries
Over stone walls gray with mosses,
Pause by some neglected graveyard,
For a while to muse, and ponder
On a half-effaced inscription,
Written with little skill of song-craft,
Homely phrases, but each letter
Full of hope and yet of heart-break,
Full of all the tender pathos
Of the Here and the Hereafter;
Stay and read this rude inscription,
Read this Song of Hiawatha!

I. THE PEACE-PIPE

On the Mountains of the Prairie,
On the great Red Pipe-stone Quarry,
Gitche Manito, the mighty,
He the Master of Life, descending,
On the red crags of the quarry
Stood erect, and called the nations,
Called the tribes of men together.

From his footprints flowed a river,
Leaped into the light of morning,
O'er the precipice plunging downward
Gleamed like Ishkoodah, the comet.
And the Spirit, stooping earthward,
With his finger on the meadow
Traced a winding pathway for it,
Saying to it, "Run in this way!"

From the red stone of the quarry
With his hand he broke a fragment,
Moulded it into a pipe-head,
Shaped and fashioned it with figures;
From the margin of the river
Took a long reed for a pipe-stem,
With its dark green leaves upon it;
Filled the pipe with bark of willow,

With the bark of the red willow;
Breathed upon the neighboring forest,
Made its great boughs chafe together,
Till in flame they burst and kindled;
And erect upon the mountains,
Gitche Manito, the mighty,
Smoked the calumet, the Peace-Pipe,
As a signal to the nations.

And the smoke rose slowly, slowly,
Through the tranquil air of morning,
First a single line of darkness,
Then a denser, bluer vapor,
Then a snow-white cloud unfolding,
Like the tree-tops of the forest,
Ever rising, rising, rising,
Till it touched the top of heaven,
Till it broke against the heaven,
And rolled outward all around it.

From the Vale of Tawasentha,
From the Valley of Wyoming,
From the groves of Tuscaloosa,
From the far-off Rocky Mountains,
From the Northern lakes and rivers
All the tribes beheld the signal,
Saw the distant smoke ascending,
The Pukwana of the Peace-Pipe.

And the Prophets of the nations
Said: "Behold it, the Pukwana!
By the signal of the Peace-Pipe,
Bending like a wand of willow,
Waving like a hand that beckons,
Gitche Manito, the mighty,
Calls the tribes of men together,
Calls the warriors to his council!"

Down the rivers, o'er the prairies,
Came the warriors of the nations,
Came the Delawares and Mohawks,
Came the Choctaws and Camanches,
Came the Shoshonies and Blackfeet,
Came the Pawnees and Omahas,

Came the Mandans and Dacotahs,
Came the Hurons and Ojibways,
All the warriors drawn together
By the signal of the Peace-Pipe,
To the Mountains of the Prairie,
To the great Red Pipe-stone Quarry,

And they stood there on the meadow,
With their weapons and their war-gear,
Painted like the leaves of Autumn,
Painted like the sky of morning,
Wildly glaring at each other;
In their faces stern defiance,
In their hearts the feuds of ages,
The hereditary hatred,
The ancestral thirst of vengeance.

Gitche Manito, the mighty,
The creator of the nations,
Looked upon them with compassion,
With paternal love and pity;
Looked upon their wrath and wrangling
But as quarrels among children,
But as feuds and fights of children!

Over them he stretched his right hand,
To subdue their stubborn natures,
To allay their thirst and fever,
By the shadow of his right hand;
Spake to them with voice majestic
As the sound of far-off waters,
Falling into deep abysses,
Warning, chiding, spake in this wise:

"O my children! my poor children!
Listen to the words of wisdom,
Listen to the words of warning,
From the lips of the Great Spirit,
From the Master of Life, who made you!

"I have given you lands to hunt in,
I have given you streams to fish in,
I have given you bear and bison,
I have given you roe and reindeer,

I have given you brant and beaver,
Filled the marshes full of wild-fowl,
Filled the rivers full of fishes:
Why then are you not contented?
Why then will you hunt each other?

"I am weary of your quarrels,
Weary of your wars and bloodshed,
Weary of your prayers for vengeance,
Of your wranglings and dissensions;
All your strength is in your union,
All your danger is in discord;
Therefore be at peace henceforward,
And as brothers live together.

"I will send a Prophet to you,
A Deliverer of the nations,
Who shall guide you and shall teach you,
Who shall toil and suffer with you.
If you listen to his counsels,
You will multiply and prosper;
If his warnings pass unheeded,
You will fade away and perish!

"Bathe now in the stream before you,
Wash the war-paint from your faces,
Wash the blood-stains from your fingers,
Bury your war-clubs and your weapons,
Break the red stone from this quarry,
Mould and make it into Peace-Pipes,
Take the reeds that grow beside you,
Deck them with your brightest feathers,
Smoke the calumet together,
And as brothers live henceforward!"

Then upon the ground the warriors
Threw their cloaks and shirts of deer-skin,
Threw their weapons and their war-gear,
Leaped into the rushing river,
Washed the war-paint from their faces.
Clear above them flowed the water,
Clear and limpid from the footprints
Of the Master of Life descending;
Dark below them flowed the water,

Soiled and stained with streaks of crimson,
As if blood were mingled with it!

From the river came the warriors,
Clean and washed from all their war-paint;
On the banks their clubs they buried,
Buried all their warlike weapons.
Gitche Manito, the mighty,
The Great Spirit, the creator,
Smiled upon his helpless children!

And in silence all the warriors
Broke the red stone of the quarry,
Smoothed and formed it into Peace-Pipes,
Broke the long reeds by the river,
Decked them with their brightest feathers,
And departed each one homeward,
While the Master of Life, ascending,
Through the opening of cloud-curtains,
Through the doorways of the heaven,
Vanished from before their faces,
In the smoke that rolled around him,
The Pukwana of the Peace-Pipe!

II. THE FOUR WINDS

"Honor be to Mudjekeewis!"
Cried the warriors, cried the old men,
When he came in triumph homeward
With the sacred Belt of Wampum,
From the regions of the North-Wind,
From the kingdom of Wabasso,
From the land of the White Rabbit.

He had stolen the Belt of Wampum
From the neck of Mishe-Mokwa,
From the Great Bear of the mountains,
From the terror of the nations,
As he lay asleep and cumbrous
On the summit of the mountains,
Like a rock with mosses on it,
Spotted brown and gray with mosses.

Silently he stole upon him
Till the red nails of the monster
Almost touched him, almost scared him,
Till the hot breath of his nostrils
Warmed the hands of Mudjekeewis,
As he drew the Belt of Wampum
Over the round ears, that heard not,
Over the small eyes, that saw not,
Over the long nose and nostrils,
The black muffle of the nostrils,
Out of which the heavy breathing
Warmed the hands of Mudjekeewis.

Then he swung aloft his war-club,
Shouted loud and long his war-cry,
Smote the mighty Mishe-Mokwa
In the middle of the forehead,
Right between the eyes he smote him.

With the heavy blow bewildered,
Rose the Great Bear of the mountains;
But his knees beneath him trembled,
And he whimpered like a woman,
As he reeled and staggered forward,
As he sat upon his haunches;
And the mighty Mudjekeewis,
Standing fearlessly before him,
Taunted him in loud derision,
Spake disdainfully in this wise:

"Hark you, Bear! you are a coward;
And no Brave, as you pretended;
Else you would not cry and whimper
Like a miserable woman!
Bear! you know our tribes are hostile,
Long have been at war together;
Now you find that we are strongest,
You go sneaking in the forest,
You go hiding in the mountains!
Had you conquered me in battle
Not a groan would I have uttered;
But you, Bear! sit here and whimper,
And disgrace your tribe by crying,
Like a wretched Shaugodaya,

Like a cowardly old woman!"

Then again he raised his war-club,
Smote again the Mishe-Mokwa
In the middle of his forehead,
Broke his skull, as ice is broken
When one goes to fish in Winter.
Thus was slain the Mishe-Mokwa,
He the Great Bear of the mountains,
He the terror of the nations.

"Honor be to Mudjekeewis!"
With a shout exclaimed the people,
"Honor be to Mudjekeewis!
Henceforth he shall be the West-Wind,
And hereafter and forever
Shall he hold supreme dominion
Over all the winds of heaven.
Call him no more Mudjekeewis,
Call him Kabeyun, the West-Wind!"

Thus was Mudjekeewis chosen
Father of the Winds of Heaven.
For himself he kept the West-Wind,
Gave the others to his children;
Unto Wabun gave the East-Wind,
Gave the South to Shawondasee,
And the North-Wind, wild and cruel,
To the fierce Kabibonokka.

Young and beautiful was Wabun;
He it was who brought the morning,
He it was whose silver arrows
Chased the dark o'er hill and valley;
He it was whose cheeks were painted
With the brightest streaks of crimson,
And whose voice awoke the village,
Called the deer, and called the hunter.

Lonely in the sky was Wabun;
Though the birds sang gayly to him,
Though the wild-flowers of the meadow
Filled the air with odors for him;
Though the forests and the rivers

Sang and shouted at his coming,
Still his heart was sad within him,
For he was alone in heaven.

But one morning, gazing earthward,
While the village still was sleeping,
And the fog lay on the river,
Like a ghost, that goes at sunrise,
He beheld a maiden walking
All alone upon a meadow,
Gathering water-flags and rushes
By a river in the meadow.

Every morning, gazing earthward,
Still the first thing he beheld there
Was her blue eyes looking at him,
Two blue lakes among the rushes.
And he loved the lonely maiden,
Who thus waited for his coming;
For they both were solitary,
She on earth and he in heaven.

And he wooed her with caresses,
Wooed her with his smile of sunshine,
With his flattering words he wooed her,
With his sighing and his singing,
Gentlest whispers in the branches,
Softest music, sweetest odors,
Till he drew her to his bosom,
Folded in his robes of crimson,
Till into a star he changed her,
Trembling still upon his bosom;
And forever in the heavens
They are seen together walking,
Wabun and the Wabun-Annung,
Wabun and the Star of Morning.

But the fierce Kabibonokka
Had his dwelling among icebergs,
In the everlasting snow-drifts,
In the kingdom of Wabasso,
In the land of the White Rabbit.
He it was whose hand in Autumn
Painted all the trees with scarlet,

Stained the leaves with red and yellow;
He it was who sent the snow-flake,
Sifting, hissing through the forest,
Froze the ponds, the lakes, the rivers,
Drove the loon and sea-gull southward,
Drove the cormorant and curlew
To their nests of sedge and sea-tang
In the realms of Shawondasee.

Once the fierce Kabibonokka
Issued from his lodge of snow-drifts
From his home among the icebergs,
And his hair, with snow besprinkled,
Streamed behind him like a river,
Like a black and wintry river,
As he howled and hurried southward,
Over frozen lakes and moorlands.

There among the reeds and rushes
Found he Shingebis, the diver,
Trailing strings of fish behind him,
O'er the frozen fens and moorlands,
Lingering still among the moorlands,
Though his tribe had long departed
To the land of Shawondasee.

Cried the fierce Kabibonokka,
"Who is this that dares to brave me?
Dares to stay in my dominions,
When the Wawa has departed,
When the wild-goose has gone southward,
And the heron, the Shuh-shuh-gah,
Long ago departed southward?
I will go into his wigwam,
I will put his smouldering fire out!"

And at night Kabibonokka,
To the lodge came wild and wailing,
Heaped the snow in drifts about it,
Shouted down into the smoke-flue,
Shook the lodge-poles in his fury,
Flapped the curtain of the door-way.
Shingebis, the diver, feared not,
Shingebis, the diver, cared not;

Four great logs had he for firewood,
One for each moon of the winter,
And for food the fishes served him.
By his blazing fire he sat there,
Warm and merry, eating, laughing,
Singing, "O Kabibonokka,
You are but my fellow-mortal!"

Then Kabibonokka entered,
And though Shingebis, the diver,
Felt his presence by the coldness,
Felt his icy breath upon him,
Still he did not cease his singing,
Still he did not leave his laughing,
Only turned the log a little,
Only made the fire burn brighter,
Made the sparks fly up the smoke-flue.

From Kabibonokka's forehead,
From his snow-besprinkled tresses,
Drops of sweat fell fast and heavy,
Making dints upon the ashes,
As along the eaves of lodges,
As from drooping boughs of hemlock,
Drips the melting snow in spring-time,
Making hollows in the snow-drifts.

Till at last he rose defeated,
Could not bear the heat and laughter,
Could not bear the merry singing,
But rushed headlong through the door-way,
Stamped upon the crusted snow-drifts,
Stamped upon the lakes and rivers,
Made the snow upon them harder,
Made the ice upon them thicker,
Challenged Shingebis, the diver,
To come forth and wrestle with him,
To come forth and wrestle naked
On the frozen fens and moorlands.

Forth went Shingebis, the diver,
Wrestled all night with the North-Wind,
Wrestled naked on the moorlands
With the fierce Kabibonokka,

Till his panting breath grew fainter,
Till his frozen grasp grew feebler,
Till he reeled and staggered backward,
And retreated, baffled, beaten,
To the kingdom of Wabasso,
To the land of the White Rabbit,
Hearing still the gusty laughter,
Hearing Shingebis, the diver,
Singing, "O Kabibonokka,
You are but my fellow-mortal!"

Shawondasee, fat and lazy,
Had his dwelling far to southward,
In the drowsy, dreamy sunshine,
In the never-ending Summer.
He it was who sent the wood-birds,
Sent the robin, the Opechee,
Sent the bluebird, the Owaissa,
Sent the Shawshaw, sent the swallow,
Sent the wild-goose, Wawa, northward,
Sent the melons and tobacco,
And the grapes in purple clusters.

From his pipe the smoke ascending
Filled the sky with haze and vapor,
Filled the air with dreamy softness,
Gave a twinkle to the water,
Touched the rugged hills with smoothness,
Brought the tender Indian Summer
To the melancholy north-land,
In the dreary Moon of Snow-shoes.

Listless, careless Shawondasee!
In his life he had one shadow,
In his heart one sorrow had he.
Once, as he was gazing northward,
Far away upon a prairie
He beheld a maiden standing,
Saw a tall and slender maiden
All alone upon a prairie;
Brightest green were all her garments,
And her hair was like the sunshine.

Day by day he gazed upon her,

Day by day he sighed with passion,
Day by day his heart within him
Grew more hot with love and longing
For the maid with yellow tresses.
But he was too fat and lazy
To bestir himself and woo her.
Yes, too indolent and easy
To pursue her and persuade her;
So he only gazed upon her,
Only sat and sighed with passion
For the maiden of the prairie.

Till one morning, looking northward,
He beheld her yellow tresses
Changed and covered o'er with whiteness,
Covered as with whitest snow-flakes.
"Ah! my brother from the North-land,
From the kingdom of Wabasso,
From the land of the White Rabbit!
You have stolen the maiden from me,
You have laid your hand upon her,
You have wooed and won my maiden,
With your stories of the North-land!"

Thus the wretched Shawondasee
Breathed into the air his sorrow;
And the South-Wind o'er the prairie
Wandered warm with sighs of passion,
With the sighs of Shawondasee,
Till the air seemed full of snow-flakes,
Full of thistle-down the prairie,
And the maid with hair like sunshine
Vanished from his sight forever;
Never more did Shawondasee
See the maid with yellow tresses!

Poor, deluded Shawondasee!
'T was no woman that you gazed at,
'T was no maiden that you sighed for,
'T was the prairie dandelion
That through all the dreamy Summer
You had gazed at with such longing,
You had sighed for with such passion,
And had puffed away forever,

Blown into the air with sighing.
Ah! deluded Shawondasee!

Thus the Four Winds were divided
Thus the sons of Mudjekeewis
Had their stations in the heavens,
At the corners of the heavens;
For himself the West-Wind only
Kept the mighty Mudjekeewis.

III. HIAWATHA'S CHILDHOOD

Downward through the evening twilight,
In the days that are forgotten,
In the unremembered ages,
From the full moon fell Nokomis,
Fell the beautiful Nokomis,
She a wife, but not a mother.

She was sporting with her women,
Swinging in a swing of grape-vines,
When her rival the rejected,
Full of jealousy and hatred,
Cut the leafy swing asunder,
Cut in twain the twisted grape-vines,
And Nokomis fell affrighted
Downward through the evening twilight,
On the Muskoday, the meadow,
On the prairie full of blossoms.
"See! a star falls!" said the people;
"From the sky a star is falling!"

There among the ferns and mosses,
There among the prairie lilies,
On the Muskoday, the meadow,
In the moonlight and the starlight,
Fair Nokomis bore a daughter.
And she called her name Wenonah,
As the first-born of her daughters.
And the daughter of Nokomis
Grew up like the prairie lilies,
Grew a tall and slender maiden,
With the beauty of the moonlight,

With the beauty of the starlight.

And Nokomis warned her often,
Saying oft, and oft repeating,
"Oh, beware of Mudjekeewis,
Of the West-Wind, Mudjekeewis;
Listen not to what he tells you;
Lie not down upon the meadow,
Stoop not down among the lilies,
Lest the West-Wind come and harm you!"

But she heeded not the warning,
Heeded not those words of wisdom,
And the West-Wind came at evening,
Walking lightly o'er the prairie,
Whispering to the leaves and blossoms,
Bending low the flowers and grasses,
Found the beautiful Wenonah,
Lying there among the lilies,
Wooed her with his words of sweetness,
Wooed her with his soft caresses,
Till she bore a son in sorrow,
Bore a son of love and sorrow.

Thus was born my Hiawatha,
Thus was born the child of wonder;
But the daughter of Nokomis,
Hiawatha's gentle mother,
In her anguish died deserted
By the West-Wind, false and faithless,
By the heartless Mudjekeewis.

For her daughter long and loudly
Wailed and wept the sad Nokomis;
"Oh that I were dead!" she murmured,
"Oh that I were dead, as thou art!
No more work, and no more weeping,
Wahonowin! Wahonowin!"

By the shores of Gitche Gumee,
By the shining Big-Sea-Water,
Stood the wigwam of Nokomis,
Daughter of the Moon, Nokomis.
Dark behind it rose the forest,

Rose the black and gloomy pine-trees,
Rose the firs with cones upon them;
Bright before it beat the water,
Beat the clear and sunny water,
Beat the shining Big-Sea-Water.

There the wrinkled old Nokomis
Nursed the little Hiawatha,
Rocked him in his linden cradle,
Bedded soft in moss and rushes,
Safely bound with reindeer sinews;
Stilled his fretful wail by saying,
"Hush! the Naked Bear will hear thee!"
Lulled him into slumber, singing,
"Ewa-yea! my little owlet!
Who is this, that lights the wigwam?
With his great eyes lights the wigwam?
Ewa-yea! my little owlet!"

Many things Nokomis taught him
Of the stars that shine in heaven;
Showed him Ishkoodah, the comet,
Ishkoodah, with fiery tresses;
Showed the Death-Dance of the spirits,
Warriors with their plumes and war-clubs,
Flaring far away to northward
In the frosty nights of Winter;
Showed the broad white road in heaven,
Pathway of the ghosts, the shadows,
Running straight across the heavens,
Crowded with the ghosts, the shadows.

At the door on summer evenings
Sat the little Hiawatha;
Heard the whispering of the pine-trees,
Heard the lapping of the waters,
Sounds of music, words of wonder;
"Minne-wawa!" said the Pine-trees,
"Mudway-aushka!" said the water.

Saw the fire-fly, Wah-wah-taysee,
Flitting through the dusk of evening,
With the twinkle of its candle
Lighting up the brakes and bushes,

And he sang the song of children,
Sang the song Nokomis taught him:
"Wah-wah-taysee, little fire-fly,
Little, flitting, white-fire insect,
Little, dancing, white-fire creature,
Light me with your little candle,
Ere upon my bed I lay me,
Ere in sleep I close my eyelids!"

Saw the moon rise from the water
Rippling, rounding from the water,
Saw the flecks and shadows on it,
Whispered, "What is that, Nokomis?"
And the good Nokomis answered:
"Once a warrior, very angry,
Seized his grandmother, and threw her
Up into the sky at midnight;
Right against the moon he threw her;
'T is her body that you see there."

Saw the rainbow in the heaven,
In the eastern sky, the rainbow,
Whispered, "What is that, Nokomis?"
And the good Nokomis answered:
"'T is the heaven of flowers you see there;
All the wild-flowers of the forest,
All the lilies of the prairie,
When on earth they fade and perish,
Blossom in that heaven above us."

When he heard the owls at midnight,
Hooting, laughing in the forest,
"What is that?" he cried in terror,
"What is that," he said, "Nokomis?"
And the good Nokomis answered:
"That is but the owl and owlet,
Talking in their native language,
Talking, scolding at each other."

Then the little Hiawatha
Learned of every bird its language,
Learned their names and all their secrets,
How they built their nests in Summer,
Where they hid themselves in Winter,

Talked with them whene'er he met them,
Called them "Hiawatha's Chickens."

Of all beasts he learned the language,
Learned their names and all their secrets,
How the beavers built their lodges,
Where the squirrels hid their acorns,
How the reindeer ran so swiftly,
Why the rabbit was so timid,
Talked with them whene'er he met them,
Called them "Hiawatha's Brothers."

Then Iagoo, the great boaster,
He the marvellous story-teller,
He the traveller and the talker,
He the friend of old Nokomis,
Made a bow for Hiawatha;
From a branch of ash he made it,
From an oak-bough made the arrows,
Tipped with flint, and winged with feathers,
And the cord he made of deer-skin.

Then he said to Hiawatha:
"Go, my son, into the forest,
Where the red deer herd together,
Kill for us a famous roebuck,
Kill for us a deer with antlers!"

Forth into the forest straightway
All alone walked Hiawatha
Proudly, with his bow and arrows;
And the birds sang round him, o'er him,
"Do not shoot us, Hiawatha!"
Sang the robin, the Opechee,
Sang the bluebird, the Owaissa,
"Do not shoot us, Hiawatha!"

Up the oak-tree, close beside him,
Sprang the squirrel, Adjidaumo,
In and out among the branches,
Coughed and chattered from the oak-tree,
Laughed, and said between his laughing,
"Do not shoot me, Hiawatha!"

And the rabbit from his pathway
Leaped aside, and at a distance
Sat erect upon his haunches,
Half in fear and half in frolic,
Saying to the little hunter,
"Do not shoot me, Hiawatha!"

But he heeded not, nor heard them,
For his thoughts were with the red deer;
On their tracks his eyes were fastened,
Leading downward to the river,
To the ford across the river,
And as one in slumber walked he.

Hidden in the alder-bushes,
There he waited till the deer came,
Till he saw two antlers lifted,
Saw two eyes look from the thicket,
Saw two nostrils point to windward,
And a deer came down the pathway,
Flecked with leafy light and shadow.
And his heart within him fluttered,
Trembled like the leaves above him,
Like the birch-leaf palpitated,
As the deer came down the pathway.

Then, upon one knee uprising,
Hiawatha aimed an arrow;
Scarce a twig moved with his motion,
Scarce a leaf was stirred or rustled,
But the wary roebuck started,
Stamped with all his hoofs together,
Listened with one foot uplifted,
Leaped as if to meet the arrow;
Ah! the singing, fatal arrow,
Like a wasp it buzzed and stung him!

Dead he lay there in the forest,
By the ford across the river;
Beat his timid heart no longer,
But the heart of Hiawatha
Throbbed and shouted and exulted,
As he bore the red deer homeward,
And Iagoo and Nokomis

Hailed his coming with applauses.

From the red deer's hide Nokomis
Made a cloak for Hiawatha,
From the red deer's flesh Nokomis
Made a banquet to his honor.
All the village came and feasted,
All the guests praised Hiawatha,
Called him Strong-Heart, Soan-ge-taha!
Called him Loon-Heart, Mahn-go-taysee!

IV. HIAWATHA AND MUDJEKEEWLS

Out of childhood into manhood
Now had grown my Hiawatha,
Skilled in all the craft of hunters,
Learned in all the lore of old men,
In all youthful sports and pastimes,
In all manly arts and labors.

Swift of foot was Hiawatha;
He could shoot an arrow from him,
And run forward with such fleetness,
That the arrow fell behind him!
Strong of arm was Hiawatha;
He could shoot ten arrows upward,
Shoot them with such strength and swiftness,
That the tenth had left the bow-string
Ere the first to earth had fallen!

He had mittens, Minjekahwun,
Magic mittens made of deer-skin;
When upon his hands he wore them,
He could smite the rocks asunder,
He could grind them into powder.
He had moccasins enchanted,
Magic moccasins of deer-skin;
When he bound them round his ankles,
When upon his feet he tied them,
At each stride a mile he measured!

Much he questioned old Nokomis
Of his father Mudjekeewis;

Learned from her the fatal secret
Of the beauty of his mother,
Of the falsehood of his father;
And his heart was hot within him,
Like a living coal his heart was.

Then he said to old Nokomis,
"I will go to Mudjekeewis,
See how fares it with my father,
At the doorways of the West-Wind,
At the portals of the Sunset!"

From his lodge went Hiawatha,
Dressed for travel, armed for hunting;
Dressed in deer-skin shirt and leggings,
Richly wrought with quills and wampum;
On his head his eagle-feathers,
Round his waist his belt of wampum,
In his hand his bow of ash-wood,
Strung with sinews of the reindeer;
In his quiver oaken arrows,
Tipped with jasper, winged with feathers;
With his mittens, Minjekahwun,
With his moccasins enchanted.

Warning said the old Nokomis,
"Go not forth, O Hiawatha!
To the kingdom of the West-Wind,
To the realms of Mudjekeewis,
Lest he harm you with his magic,
Lest he kill you with his cunning!"

But the fearless Hiawatha
Heeded not her woman's warning;
Forth he strode into the forest,
At each stride a mile he measured;
Lurid seemed the sky above him,
Lurid seemed the earth beneath him,
Hot and close the air around him,
Filled with smoke and fiery vapors,
As of burning woods and prairies,
For his heart was hot within him,
Like a living coal his heart was.

So he journeyed westward, westward,
Left the fleetest deer behind him,
Left the antelope and bison;
Crossed the rushing Esconaba,
Crossed the mighty Mississippi,
Passed the Mountains of the Prairie,
Passed the land of Crows and Foxes,
Passed the dwellings of the Blackfeet,
Came unto the Rocky Mountains,
To the kingdom of the West-Wind,
Where upon the gusty summits
Sat the ancient Mudjekeewis,
Ruler of the winds of heaven.

Filled with awe was Hiawatha
At the aspect of his father.
On the air about him wildly
Tossed and streamed his cloudy tresses,
Gleamed like drifting snow his tresses,
Glared like Ishkoodah, the comet,
Like the star with fiery tresses.

Filled with joy was Mudjekeewis
When he looked on Hiawatha,
Saw his youth rise up before him
In the face of Hiawatha,
Saw the beauty of Wenonah
From the grave rise up before him.

"Welcome!" said he, "Hiawatha,
To the kingdom of the West-Wind
Long have I been waiting for you
Youth is lovely, age is lonely,
Youth is fiery, age is frosty;
You bring back the days departed,
You bring back my youth of passion,
And the beautiful Wenonah!"

Many days they talked together,
Questioned, listened, waited, answered;
Much the mighty Mudjekeewis
Boasted of his ancient prowess,
Of his perilous adventures,
His indomitable courage,

His invulnerable body.

Patiently sat Hiawatha,
Listening to his father's boasting;
With a smile he sat and listened,
Uttered neither threat nor menace,
Neither word nor look betrayed him,
But his heart was hot within him,
Like a living coal his heart was.

Then he said, "O Mudjekeewis,
Is there nothing that can harm you?
Nothing that you are afraid of?"
And the mighty Mudjekeewis,
Grand and gracious in his boasting,
Answered, saying, "There is nothing,
Nothing but the black rock yonder,
Nothing but the fatal Wawbeek!"

And he looked at Hiawatha
With a wise look and benignant,
With a countenance paternal,
Looked with pride upon the beauty
Of his tall and graceful figure,
Saying, "O my Hiawatha!
Is there anything can harm you?
Anything you are afraid of?"

But the wary Hiawatha
Paused awhile, as if uncertain,
Held his peace, as if resolving,
And then answered, "There is nothing,
Nothing but the bulrush yonder,
Nothing but the great Apukwa!"

And as Mudjekeewis, rising,
Stretched his hand to pluck the bulrush,
Hiawatha cried in terror,
Cried in well-dissembled terror,
"Kago! kago! do not touch it!"
"Ah, kaween!" said Mudjekeewis,
"No indeed, I will not touch it!"

Then they talked of other matters;

First of Hiawatha's brothers,
First of Wabun, of the East-Wind,
Of the South-Wind, Shawondasee,
Of the North, Kabibonokka;
Then of Hiawatha's mother,
Of the beautiful Wenonah,
Of her birth upon the meadow,
Of her death, as old Nokomis
Had remembered and related.

And he cried, "O Mudjekeewis,
It was you who killed Wenonah,
Took her young life and her beauty,
Broke the Lily of the Prairie,
Trampled it beneath your footsteps;
You confess it! you confess it!"
And the mighty Mudjekeewis
Tossed upon the wind his tresses,
Bowed his hoary head in anguish,
With a silent nod assented.

Then up started Hiawatha,
And with threatening look and gesture
Laid his hand upon the black rock,
On the fatal Wawbeek laid it,
With his mittens, Minjekahwun,
Rent the jutting crag asunder,
Smote and crushed it into fragments,
Hurled them madly at his father,
The remorseful Mudjekeewis,
For his heart was hot within him,
Like a living coal his heart was.

But the ruler of the West-Wind
Blew the fragments backward from him,
With the breathing of his nostrils,
With the tempest of his anger,
Blew them back at his assailant;
Seized the bulrush, the Apukwa,
Dragged it with its roots and fibres
From the margin of the meadow,
From its ooze the giant bulrush;
Long and loud laughed Hiawatha!

Then began the deadly conflict,
Hand to hand among the mountains;
From his eyry screamed the eagle,
The Keneu, the great war-eagle,
Sat upon the crags around them,
Wheeling flapped his wings above them.

Like a tall tree in the tempest
Bent and lashed the giant bulrush;
And in masses huge and heavy
Crashing fell the fatal Wawbeek;
Till the earth shook with the tumult
And confusion of the battle,
And the air was full of shoutings,
And the thunder of the mountains,
Starting, answered, "Baim-wawa!"

Back retreated Mudjekeewis,
Rushing westward o'er the mountains,
Stumbling westward down the mountains,
Three whole days retreated fighting,
Still pursued by Hiawatha
To the doorways of the West-Wind,
To the portals of the Sunset,
To the earth's remotest border,
Where into the empty spaces
Sinks the sun, as a flamingo
Drops into her nest at nightfall
In the melancholy marshes.

"Hold!" at length cried Mudjekeewis,
"Hold, my son, my Hiawatha!
'T is impossible to kill me,
For you cannot kill the immortal
I have put you to this trial,
But to know and prove your courage;
Now receive the prize of valor!

"Go back to your home and people,
Live among them, toil among them,
Cleanse the earth from all that harms it,
Clear the fishing-grounds and rivers,
Slay all monsters and magicians,
All the Wendigoes, the giants,

All the serpents, the Kenabeeks,
As I slew the Mishe-Mokwa,
Slew the Great Bear of the mountains.

"And at last when Death draws near you,
When the awful eyes of Pauguk
Glare upon you in the darkness,
I will share my kingdom with you,
Ruler shall you be thenceforward
Of the Northwest-Wind, Keewaydin,
Of the home-wind, the Keewaydin."

Thus was fought that famous battle
In the dreadful days of Shah-shah,
In the days long since departed,
In the kingdom of the West-Wind.
Still the hunter sees its traces
Scattered far o'er hill and valley;
Sees the giant bulrush growing
By the ponds and water-courses,
Sees the masses of the Wawbeek
Lying still in every valley.

Homeward now went Hiawatha;
Pleasant was the landscape round him,
Pleasant was the air above him,
For the bitterness of anger
Had departed wholly from him,
From his brain the thought of vengeance,
From his heart the burning fever.

Only once his pace he slackened,
Only once he paused or halted,
Paused to purchase heads of arrows
Of the ancient Arrow-maker,
In the land of the Dacotahs,
Where the Falls of Minnehaha
Flash and gleam among the oak-trees,
Laugh and leap into the valley.

There the ancient Arrow-maker
Made his arrow-heads of sandstone,
Arrow-heads of chalcedony,
Arrow-heads of flint and jasper,

Smoothed and sharpened at the edges,
Hard and polished, keen and costly.

With him dwelt his dark-eyed daughter,
Wayward as the Minnehaha,
With her moods of shade and sunshine,
Eyes that smiled and frowned alternate,
Feet as rapid as the river,
Tresses flowing like the water,
And as musical a laughter:
And he named her from the river,
From the water-fall he named her,
Minnehaha, Laughing Water.

Was it then for heads of arrows,
Arrow-heads of chalcedony,
Arrow-heads of flint and jasper,
That my Hiawatha halted
In the land of the Dacotahs?

Was it not to see the maiden,
See the face of Laughing Water
Peeping from behind the curtain,
Hear the rustling of her garments
From behind the waving curtain,
As one sees the Minnehaha
Gleaming, glancing through the branches,
As one hears the Laughing Water
From behind its screen of branches?

Who shall say what thoughts and visions
Fill the fiery brains of young men?
Who shall say what dreams of beauty
Filled the heart of Hiawatha?
All he told to old Nokomis,
When he reached the lodge at sunset,
Was the meeting with his father,
Was his fight with Mudjekeewis;
Not a word he said of arrows,
Not a word of Laughing Water.

V. HIAWATHA'S FASTING

You shall hear how Hiawatha
Prayed and fasted in the forest,
Not for greater skill in hunting,
Not for greater craft in fishing,
Not for triumphs in the battle,
And renown among the warriors,
But for profit of the people,
For advantage of the nations.

First he built a lodge for fasting,
Built a wigwam in the forest,
By the shining Big-Sea-Water,
In the blithe and pleasant Spring-time,
In the Moon of Leaves he built it,
And, with dreams and visions many,
Seven whole days and nights he fasted.

On the first day of his fasting
Through the leafy woods he wandered;
Saw the deer start from the thicket,
Saw the rabbit in his burrow,
Heard the pheasant, Bena, drumming,
Heard the squirrel, Adjidaumo,
Rattling in his hoard of acorns,
Saw the pigeon, the Omeme,
Building nests among the pinetrees,
And in flocks the wild-goose, Wawa,
Flying to the fen-lands northward,
Whirring, wailing far above him.
"Master of Life!" he cried, desponding,
"Must our lives depend on these things?"

On the next day of his fasting
By the river's brink he wandered,
Through the Muskoday, the meadow,
Saw the wild rice, Mahnomonee,
Saw the blueberry, Meenahga,
And the strawberry, Odahmin,
And the gooseberry, Shahbomin,
And the grape-vine, the Bemahgut,
Trailing o'er the alder-branches,

Filling all the air with fragrance!
"Master of Life!" he cried, desponding,
"Must our lives depend on these things?"

On the third day of his fasting
By the lake he sat and pondered,
By the still, transparent water;
Saw the sturgeon, Nahma, leaping,
Scattering drops like beads of wampum,
Saw the yellow perch, the Sahwa,
Like a sunbeam in the water,
Saw the pike, the Maskenozha,
And the herring, Okahahwis,
And the Shawgashee, the crawfish!
"Master of Life!" he cried, desponding,
"Must our lives depend on these things?"

On the fourth day of his fasting
In his lodge he lay exhausted;
From his couch of leaves and branches
Gazing with half-open eyelids,
Full of shadowy dreams and visions,
On the dizzy, swimming landscape,
On the gleaming of the water,
On the splendor of the sunset.

And he saw a youth approaching,
Dressed in garments green and yellow,
Coming through the purple twilight,
Through the splendor of the sunset;
Plumes of green bent o'er his forehead,
And his hair was soft and golden.

Standing at the open doorway,
Long he looked at Hiawatha,
Looked with pity and compassion
On his wasted form and features,
And, in accents like the sighing
Of the South-Wind in the tree-tops,
Said he, "O my Hiawatha!
All your prayers are heard in heaven,
For you pray not like the others;
Not for greater skill in hunting,
Not for greater craft in fishing,

Not for triumph in the battle,
Nor renown among the warriors,
But for profit of the people,
For advantage of the nations.

"From the Master of Life descending,
I, the friend of man, Mondamin,
Come to warn you and instruct you,
How by struggle and by labor
You shall gain what you have prayed for.
Rise up from your bed of branches,
Rise, O youth, and wrestle with me!"

Faint with famine, Hiawatha
Started from his bed of branches,
From the twilight of his wigwam
Forth into the flush of sunset
Came, and wrestled with Mondamin;
At his touch he felt new courage
Throbbing in his brain and bosom,
Felt new life and hope and vigor
Run through every nerve and fibre.

So they wrestled there together
In the glory of the sunset,
And the more they strove and struggled,
Stronger still grew Hiawatha;
Till the darkness fell around them,
And the heron, the Shuh-shuh-gah,
From her nest among the pine-trees,
Gave a cry of lamentation,
Gave a scream of pain and famine.

"'T is enough!" then said Mondamin,
Smiling upon Hiawatha,
"But tomorrow, when the sun sets,
I will come again to try you."
And he vanished, and was seen not;
Whether sinking as the rain sinks,
Whether rising as the mists rise,
Hiawatha saw not, knew not,
Only saw that he had vanished,
Leaving him alone and fainting,
With the misty lake below him,

And the reeling stars above him.

On the morrow and the next day,
When the sun through heaven descending,
Like a red and burning cinder
From the hearth of the Great Spirit,
Fell into the western waters,
Came Mondamin for the trial,
For the strife with Hiawatha;
Came as silent as the dew comes,
From the empty air appearing,
Into empty air returning,
Taking shape when earth it touches,
But invisible to all men
In its coming and its going.

Thrice they wrestled there together
In the glory of the sunset,
Till the darkness fell around them,
Till the heron, the Shuh-shuh-gah,
From her nest among the pine-trees,
Uttered her loud cry of famine,
And Mondamin paused to listen.

Tall and beautiful he stood there,
In his garments green and yellow;
To and fro his plumes above him,
Waved and nodded with his breathing,
And the sweat of the encounter
Stood like drops of dew upon him.

And he cried, "O Hiawatha!
Bravely have you wrestled with me,
Thrice have wrestled stoutly with me,
And the Master of Life, who sees us,
He will give to you the triumph!"

Then he smiled, and said: "To-morrow
Is the last day of your conflict,
Is the last day of your fasting.
You will conquer and o'ercome me;
Make a bed for me to lie in,
Where the rain may fall upon me,
Where the sun may come and warm me;

Strip these garments, green and yellow,
Strip this nodding plumage from me,
Lay me in the earth, and make it
Soft and loose and light above me.

"Let no hand disturb my slumber,
Let no weed nor worm molest me,
Let not Kahgahgee, the raven,
Come to haunt me and molest me,
Only come yourself to watch me,
Till I wake, and start, and quicken,
Till I leap into the sunshine"

And thus saying, he departed;
Peacefully slept Hiawatha,
But he heard the Wawonaissa,
Heard the whippoorwill complaining,
Perched upon his lonely wigwam;
Heard the rushing Sebowisha,
Heard the rivulet rippling near him,
Talking to the darksome forest;
Heard the sighing of the branches,
As they lifted and subsided
At the passing of the night-wind,
Heard them, as one hears in slumber
Far-off murmurs, dreamy whispers:
Peacefully slept Hiawatha.

On the morrow came Nokomis,
On the seventh day of his fasting,
Came with food for Hiawatha,
Came imploring and bewailing,
Lest his hunger should o'ercome him,
Lest his fasting should be fatal.

But he tasted not, and touched not,
Only said to her, "Nokomis,
Wait until the sun is setting,
Till the darkness falls around us,
Till the heron, the Shuh-shuh-gah,
Crying from the desolate marshes,
Tells us that the day is ended."

Homeward weeping went Nokomis,

Sorrowing for her Hiawatha,
Fearing lest his strength should fail him,
Lest his fasting should be fatal.
He meanwhile sat weary waiting
For the coming of Mondamin,
Till the shadows, pointing eastward,
Lengthened over field and forest,
Till the sun dropped from the heaven,
Floating on the waters westward,
As a red leaf in the Autumn
Falls and floats upon the water,
Falls and sinks into its bosom.

And behold! the young Mondamin,
With his soft and shining tresses,
With his garments green and yellow,
With his long and glossy plumage,
Stood and beckoned at the doorway.
And as one in slumber walking,
Pale and haggard, but undaunted,
From the wigwam Hiawatha
Came and wrestled with Mondamin.

Round about him spun the landscape,
Sky and forest reeled together,
And his strong heart leaped within him,
As the sturgeon leaps and struggles
In a net to break its meshes.
Like a ring of fire around him
Blazed and flared the red horizon,
And a hundred suns seemed looking
At the combat of the wrestlers.

Suddenly upon the greensward
All alone stood Hiawatha,
Panting with his wild exertion,
Palpitating with the struggle;
And before him breathless, lifeless,
Lay the youth, with hair dishevelled,
Plumage torn, and garments tattered,
Dead he lay there in the sunset.

And victorious Hiawatha
Made the grave as he commanded,

Stripped the garments from Mondamin,
Stripped his tattered plumage from him,
Laid him in the earth, and made it
Soft and loose and light above him;
And the heron, the Shuh-shuh-gah,
From the melancholy moorlands,
Gave a cry of lamentation,
Gave a cry of pain and anguish!

Homeward then went Hiawatha
To the lodge of old Nokomis,
And the seven days of his fasting
Were accomplished and completed.
But the place was not forgotten
Where he wrestled with Mondamin;
Nor forgotten nor neglected
Was the grave where lay Mondamin,
Sleeping in the rain and sunshine,
Where his scattered plumes and garments
Faded in the rain and sunshine.

Day by day did Hiawatha
Go to wait and watch beside it;
Kept the dark mould soft above it,
Kept it clean from weeds and insects,
Drove away, with scoffs and shoutings,
Kahgahgee, the king of ravens.

Till at length a small green feather
From the earth shot slowly upward,
Then another and another,
And before the Summer ended
Stood the maize in all its beauty,
With its shining robes about it,
And its long, soft, yellow tresses;
And in rapture Hiawatha
Cried aloud, "It is Mondamin!
Yes, the friend of man, Mondamin!"

Then he called to old Nokomis
And Iagoo, the great boaster,
Showed them where the maize was growing,
Told them of his wondrous vision,
Of his wrestling and his triumph,

Of this new gift to the nations,
Which should be their food forever.

And still later, when the Autumn
Changed the long, green leaves to yellow,
And the soft and juicy kernels
Grew like wampum hard and yellow,
Then the ripened ears he gathered,
Stripped the withered husks from off them,
As he once had stripped the wrestler,
Gave the first Feast of Mondamin,
And made known unto the people
This new gift of the Great Spirit.

VI. HIAWATHA'S FRIENDS

Two good friends had Hiawatha,
Singled out from all the others,
Bound to him in closest union,
And to whom he gave the right hand
Of his heart, in joy and sorrow;
Chibiabos, the musician,
And the very strong man, Kwasind.

Straight between them ran the pathway,
Never grew the grass upon it;
Singing birds, that utter falsehoods,
Story-tellers, mischief-makers,
Found no eager ear to listen,
Could not breed ill-will between them,
For they kept each other's counsel,
Spake with naked hearts together,
Pondering much and much contriving
How the tribes of men might prosper.

Most beloved by Hiawatha
Was the gentle Chibiabos,
He the best of all musicians,
He the sweetest of all singers.
Beautiful and childlike was he,
Brave as man is, soft as woman,
Pliant as a wand of willow,
Stately as a deer with antlers.

When he sang, the village listened;
All the warriors gathered round him,
All the women came to hear him;
Now he stirred their souls to passion,
Now he melted them to pity.

From the hollow reeds he fashioned
Flutes so musical and mellow,
That the brook, the Sebowisha,
Ceased to murmur in the woodland,
That the wood-birds ceased from singing,
And the squirrel, Adjidaumo,
Ceased his chatter in the oak-tree,
And the rabbit, the Wabasso,
Sat upright to look and listen.

Yes, the brook, the Sebowisha,
Pausing, said, "O Chibiabos,
Teach my waves to flow in music,
Softly as your words in singing!"

Yes, the bluebird, the Owaissa,
Envious, said, "O Chibiabos,
Teach me tones as wild and wayward,
Teach me songs as full of frenzy!"

Yes, the robin, the Opechee,
Joyous, said, "O Chibiabos,
Teach me tones as sweet and tender,
Teach me songs as full of gladness!"

And the whippoorwill, Wawonaissa,
Sobbing, said, "O Chibiabos,
Teach me tones as melancholy,
Teach me songs as full of sadness!"

All the many sounds of nature
Borrowed sweetness from his singing;
All the hearts of men were softened
By the pathos of his music;
For he sang of peace and freedom,
Sang of beauty, love, and longing;
Sang of death, and life undying
In the Islands of the Blessed,

In the kingdom of Ponemah,
In the land of the Hereafter.

Very dear to Hiawatha
Was the gentle Chibiabos,
He the best of all musicians,
He the sweetest of all singers;
For his gentleness he loved him,
And the magic of his singing.

Dear, too, unto Hiawatha
Was the very strong man, Kwasind,
He the strongest of all mortals,
He the mightiest among many;
For his very strength he loved him,
For his strength allied to goodness.

Idle in his youth was Kwasind,
Very listless, dull, and dreamy,
Never played with other children,
Never fished and never hunted,
Not like other children was he;
But they saw that much he fasted,
Much his Manito entreated,
Much besought his Guardian Spirit.

"Lazy Kwasind!" said his mother,
"In my work you never help me!
In the Summer you are roaming
Idly in the fields and forests;
In the Winter you are cowering
O'er the firebrands in the wigwam!
In the coldest days of Winter
I must break the ice for fishing;
With my nets you never help me!
At the door my nets are hanging,
Dripping, freezing with the water;
Go and wring them, Yenadizze!
Go and dry them in the sunshine!"

Slowly, from the ashes, Kwasind
Rose, but made no angry answer;
From the lodge went forth in silence,
Took the nets, that hung together,

Dripping, freezing at the doorway;
Like a wisp of straw he wrung them,
Like a wisp of straw he broke them,
Could not wring them without breaking,
Such the strength was in his fingers.

"Lazy Kwasind!" said his father,
"In the hunt you never help me;
Every bow you touch is broken,
Snapped asunder every arrow;
Yet come with me to the forest,
You shall bring the hunting homeward."

Down a narrow pass they wandered,
Where a brooklet led them onward,
Where the trail of deer and bison
Marked the soft mud on the margin,
Till they found all further passage
Shut against them, barred securely
By the trunks of trees uprooted,
Lying lengthwise, lying crosswise,
And forbidding further passage.

"We must go back," said the old man,
"O'er these logs we cannot clamber;
Not a woodchuck could get through them,
Not a squirrel clamber o'er them!"
And straightway his pipe he lighted,
And sat down to smoke and ponder.
But before his pipe was finished,
Lo! the path was cleared before him;
All the trunks had Kwasind lifted,
To the right hand, to the left hand,
Shot the pine-trees swift as arrows,
Hurled the cedars light as lances.

"Lazy Kwasind!" said the young men,
As they sported in the meadow:
"Why stand idly looking at us,
Leaning on the rock behind you?
Come and wrestle with the others,
Let us pitch the quoit together!"

Lazy Kwasind made no answer,

To their challenge made no answer,
Only rose, and slowly turning,
Seized the huge rock in his fingers,
Tore it from its deep foundation,
Poised it in the air a moment,
Pitched it sheer into the river,
Sheer into the swift Pauwating,
Where it still is seen in Summer.

Once as down that foaming river,
Down the rapids of Pauwating,
Kwasind sailed with his companions,
In the stream he saw a beaver,
Saw Ahmeek, the King of Beavers,
Struggling with the rushing currents,
Rising, sinking in the water.

Without speaking, without pausing,
Kwasind leaped into the river,
Plunged beneath the bubbling surface,
Through the whirlpools chased the beaver,
Followed him among the islands,
Stayed so long beneath the water,
That his terrified companions
Cried, "Alas! good-by to Kwasind!
We shall never more see Kwasind!"
But he reappeared triumphant,
And upon his shining shoulders
Brought the beaver, dead and dripping,
Brought the King of all the Beavers.

And these two, as I have told you,
Were the friends of Hiawatha,
Chibiabos, the musician,
And the very strong man, Kwasind.
Long they lived in peace together,
Spake with naked hearts together,
Pondering much and much contriving
How the tribes of men might prosper.

VII. HIAWATHA'S SAILING

"Give me of your bark, O Birch-tree!

Of your yellow bark, O Birch-tree!
Growing by the rushing river,
Tall and stately in the valley!
I a light canoe will build me,
Build a swift Cheemaun for sailing,
That shall float upon the river,
Like a yellow leaf in Autumn,
Like a yellow water-lily!

"Lay aside your cloak, O Birch-tree!
Lay aside your white-skin wrapper,
For the Summer-time is coming,
And the sun is warm in heaven,
And you need no white-skin wrapper!"

Thus aloud cried Hiawatha
In the solitary forest,
By the rushing Taquamenaw,
When the birds were singing gayly,
In the Moon of Leaves were singing,
And the sun, from sleep awaking,
Started up and said, "Behold me!
Gheezis, the great Sun, behold me!"

And the tree with all its branches
Rustled in the breeze of morning,
Saying, with a sigh of patience,
"Take my cloak, O Hiawatha!"

With his knife the tree he girdled;
Just beneath its lowest branches,
Just above the roots, he cut it,
Till the sap came oozing outward;
Down the trunk, from top to bottom,
Sheer he cleft the bark asunder,
With a wooden wedge he raised it,
Stripped it from the trunk unbroken.

"Give me of your boughs, O Cedar!
Of your strong and pliant branches,
My canoe to make more steady,
Make more strong and firm beneath me!"

Through the summit of the Cedar

Went a sound, a cry of horror,
Went a murmur of resistance;
But it whispered, bending downward,
"Take my boughs, O Hiawatha!"

Down he hewed the boughs of cedar,
Shaped them straightway to a frame-work,
Like two bows he formed and shaped them,
Like two bended bows together.

"Give me of your roots, O Tamarack!
Of your fibrous roots, O Larch-tree!
My canoe to bind together,
So to bind the ends together
That the water may not enter,
That the river may not wet me!"

And the Larch, with all its fibres,
Shivered in the air of morning,
Touched his forehead with its tassels,
Slid, with one long sigh of sorrow.
"Take them all, O Hiawatha!"

From the earth he tore the fibres,
Tore the tough roots of the Larch-tree,
Closely sewed the bark together,
Bound it closely to the frame-work.

"Give me of your balm, O Fir-tree!
Of your balsam and your resin,
So to close the seams together
That the water may not enter,
That the river may not wet me!"

And the Fir-tree, tall and sombre,
Sobbed through all its robes of darkness,
Rattled like a shore with pebbles,
Answered wailing, answered weeping,
"Take my balm, O Hiawatha!"

And he took the tears of balsam,
Took the resin of the Fir-tree,
Smeared therewith each seam and fissure,
Made each crevice safe from water.

"Give me of your quills, O Hedgehog!
All your quills, O Kagh, the Hedgehog!
I will make a necklace of them,
Make a girdle for my beauty,
And two stars to deck her bosom!"

From a hollow tree the Hedgehog
With his sleepy eyes looked at him,
Shot his shining quills, like arrows,
Saying with a drowsy murmur,
Through the tangle of his whiskers,
"Take my quills, O Hiawatha!"

From the ground the quills he gathered,
All the little shining arrows,
Stained them red and blue and yellow,
With the juice of roots and berries;
Into his canoe he wrought them,
Round its waist a shining girdle,
Round its bows a gleaming necklace,
On its breast two stars resplendent.

Thus the Birch Canoe was builded
In the valley, by the river,
In the bosom of the forest;
And the forest's life was in it,
All its mystery and its magic,
All the lightness of the birch-tree,
All the toughness of the cedar,
All the larch's supple sinews;
And it floated on the river
Like a yellow leaf in Autumn,
Like a yellow water-lily.

Paddles none had Hiawatha,
Paddles none he had or needed,
For his thoughts as paddles served him,
And his wishes served to guide him;
Swift or slow at will he glided,
Veered to right or left at pleasure.

Then he called aloud to Kwasind,
To his friend, the strong man, Kwasind,
Saying, "Help me clear this river

Of its sunken logs and sand-bars."

Straight into the river Kwasind
Plunged as if he were an otter,
Dived as if he were a beaver,
Stood up to his waist in water,
To his arm-pits in the river,
Swam and scouted in the river,
Tugged at sunken logs and branches,
With his hands he scooped the sand-bars,
With his feet the ooze and tangle.

And thus sailed my Hiawatha
Down the rushing Taquamenaw,
Sailed through all its bends and windings,
Sailed through all its deeps and shallows,
While his friend, the strong man, Kwasind,
Swam the deeps, the shallows waded.

Up and down the river went they,
In and out among its islands,
Cleared its bed of root and sand-bar,
Dragged the dead trees from its channel,
Made its passage safe and certain,
Made a pathway for the people,
From its springs among the mountains,
To the waters of Pauwating,
To the bay of Taquamenaw.

VIII. HIAWATHA'S FISHING

Forth upon the Gitche Gumee,
On the shining Big-Sea-Water,
With his fishing-line of cedar,
Of the twisted bark of cedar,
Forth to catch the sturgeon Nahma,
Mishe-Nahma, King of Fishes,
In his birch canoe exulting
All alone went Hiawatha.

Through the clear, transparent water
He could see the fishes swimming
Far down in the depths below him;

See the yellow perch, the Sahwa,
Like a sunbeam in the water,
See the Shawgashee, the craw-fish,
Like a spider on the bottom,
On the white and sandy bottom.

At the stern sat Hiawatha,
With his fishing-line of cedar;
In his plumes the breeze of morning
Played as in the hemlock branches;
On the bows, with tail erected,
Sat the squirrel, Adjidaumo;
In his fur the breeze of morning
Played as in the prairie grasses.

On the white sand of the bottom
Lay the monster Mishe-Nahma,
Lay the sturgeon, King of Fishes;
Through his gills he breathed the water,
With his fins he fanned and winnowed,
With his tail he swept the sand-floor.

There he lay in all his armor;
On each side a shield to guard him,
Plates of bone upon his forehead,
Down his sides and back and shoulders
Plates of bone with spines projecting
Painted was he with his war-paints,
Stripes of yellow, red, and azure,
Spots of brown and spots of sable;
And he lay there on the bottom,
Fanning with his fins of purple,
As above him Hiawatha
In his birch canoe came sailing,
With his fishing-line of cedar.

"Take my bait," cried Hiawatha,
Dawn into the depths beneath him,
"Take my bait, O Sturgeon, Nahma!
Come up from below the water,
Let us see which is the stronger!"
And he dropped his line of cedar
Through the clear, transparent water,
Waited vainly for an answer,

Long sat waiting for an answer,
And repeating loud and louder,
"Take my bait, O King of Fishes!"

Quiet lay the sturgeon, Nahma,
Fanning slowly in the water,
Looking up at Hiawatha,
Listening to his call and clamor,
His unnecessary tumult,
Till he wearied of the shouting;
And he said to the Kenozha,
To the pike, the Maskenozha,
"Take the bait of this rude fellow,
Break the line of Hiawatha!"

In his fingers Hiawatha
Felt the loose line jerk and tighten,
As he drew it in, it tugged so
That the birch canoe stood endwise,
Like a birch log in the water,
With the squirrel, Adjidaumo,
Perched and frisking on the summit.

Full of scorn was Hiawatha
When he saw the fish rise upward,
Saw the pike, the Maskenozha,
Coming nearer, nearer to him,
And he shouted through the water,
"Esa! esa! shame upon you!
You are but the pike, Kenozha,
You are not the fish I wanted,
You are not the King of Fishes!"

Reeling downward to the bottom
Sank the pike in great confusion,
And the mighty sturgeon, Nahma,
Said to Ugudwash, the sun-fish,
To the bream, with scales of crimson,
"Take the bait of this great boaster,
Break the line of Hiawatha!"

Slowly upward, wavering, gleaming,
Rose the Ugudwash, the sun-fish,
Seized the line of Hiawatha,

Swung with all his weight upon it,
Made a whirlpool in the water,
Whirled the birch canoe in circles,
Round and round in gurgling eddies,
Till the circles in the water
Reached the far-off sandy beaches,
Till the water-flags and rushes
Nodded on the distant margins.

But when Hiawatha saw him
Slowly rising through the water,
Lifting up his disk refulgent,
Loud he shouted in derision,
"Esa! esa! shame upon you!
You are Ugudwash, the sun-fish,
You are not the fish I wanted,
You are not the King of Fishes!"

Slowly downward, wavering, gleaming,
Sank the Ugudwash, the sun-fish,
And again the sturgeon, Nahma,
Heard the shout of Hiawatha,
Heard his challenge of defiance,
The unnecessary tumult,
Ringing far across the water.

From the white sand of the bottom
Up he rose with angry gesture,
Quivering in each nerve and fibre,
Clashing all his plates of armor,
Gleaming bright with all his war-paint;
In his wrath he darted upward,
Flashing leaped into the sunshine,
Opened his great jaws, and swallowed
Both canoe and Hiawatha.

Down into that darksome cavern
Plunged the headlong Hiawatha,
As a log on some black river
Shoots and plunges down the rapids,
Found himself in utter darkness,
Groped about in helpless wonder,
Till he felt a great heart beating,
Throbbing in that utter darkness.

And he smote it in his anger,
With his fist, the heart of Nahma,
Felt the mighty King of Fishes
Shudder through each nerve and fibre,
Heard the water gurgle round him
As he leaped and staggered through it,
Sick at heart, and faint and weary.

Crosswise then did Hiawatha
Drag his birch-canoe for safety,
Lest from out the jaws of Nahma,
In the turmoil and confusion,
Forth he might be hurled and perish.
And the squirrel, Adjidaumo,
Frisked and chatted very gayly,
Toiled and tugged with Hiawatha
Till the labor was completed.

Then said Hiawatha to him,
"O my little friend, the squirrel,
Bravely have you toiled to help me;
Take the thanks of Hiawatha,
And the name which now he gives you;
For hereafter and forever
Boys shall call you Adjidaumo,
Tail-in-air the boys shall call you!"

And again the sturgeon, Nahma,
Gasped and quivered in the water,
Then was still, and drifted landward
Till he grated on the pebbles,
Till the listening Hiawatha
Heard him grate upon the margin,
Felt him strand upon the pebbles,
Knew that Nahma, King of Fishes,
Lay there dead upon the margin.

Then he heard a clang and flapping,
As of many wings assembling,
Heard a screaming and confusion,
As of birds of prey contending,
Saw a gleam of light above him,
Shining through the ribs of Nahma,
Saw the glittering eyes of sea-gulls,

Of Kayoshk, the sea-gulls, peering,
Gazing at him through the opening,
Heard them saying to each other,
"'T is our brother, Hiawatha!"

And he shouted from below them,
Cried exulting from the caverns:
"O ye sea-gulls! O my brothers!
I have slain the sturgeon, Nahma;
Make the rifts a little larger,
With your claws the openings widen,
Set me free from this dark prison,
And henceforward and forever
Men shall speak of your achievements,
Calling you Kayoshk, the sea-gulls,
Yes, Kayoshk, the Noble Scratchers!"

And the wild and clamorous sea-gulls
Toiled with beak and claws together,
Made the rifts and openings wider
In the mighty ribs of Nahma,
And from peril and from prison,
From the body of the sturgeon,
From the peril of the water,
They released my Hiawatha.

He was standing near his wigwam,
On the margin of the water,
And he called to old Nokomis,
Called and beckoned to Nokomis,
Pointed to the sturgeon, Nahma,
Lying lifeless on the pebbles,
With the sea-gulls feeding on him.

"I have slain the Mishe-Nahma,
Slain the King of Fishes!" said he;
"Look! the sea-gulls feed upon him,
Yes, my friends Kayoshk, the sea-gulls;
Drive them not away, Nokomis,
They have saved me from great peril
In the body of the sturgeon,
Wait until their meal is ended,
Till their craws are full with feasting,
Till they homeward fly, at sunset,

To their nests among the marshes;
Then bring all your pots and kettles,
And make oil for us in Winter."

And she waited till the sun set,
Till the pallid moon, the Night-sun,
Rose above the tranquil water,
Till Kayoshk, the sated sea-gulls,
From their banquet rose with clamor,
And across the fiery sunset
Winged their way to far-off islands,
To their nests among the rushes.

To his sleep went Hiawatha,
And Nokomis to her labor,
Toiling patient in the moonlight,
Till the sun and moon changed places,
Till the sky was red with sunrise,
And Kayoshk, the hungry sea-gulls,
Came back from the reedy islands,
Clamorous for their morning banquet.

Three whole days and nights alternate
Old Nokomis and the sea-gulls
Stripped the oily flesh of Nahma,
Till the waves washed through the rib-bones,
Till the sea-gulls came no longer,
And upon the sands lay nothing
But the skeleton of Nahma.

IX. HIAWATHA AND THE PEARL-FEATHER

On the shores of Gitche Gumee,
Of the shining Big-Sea-Water,
Stood Nokomis, the old woman,
Pointing with her finger westward,
O'er the water pointing westward,
To the purple clouds of sunset.

Fiercely the red sun descending
Burned his way along the heavens,
Set the sky on fire behind him,
As war-parties, when retreating,

Burn the prairies on their war-trail;
And the moon, the Night-sun, eastward,
Suddenly starting from his ambush,
Followed fast those bloody footprints,
Followed in that fiery war-trail,
With its glare upon his features.

And Nokomis, the old woman,
Pointing with her finger westward,
Spake these words to Hiawatha:
"Yonder dwells the great Pearl-Feather,
Megissogwon, the Magician,
Manito of Wealth and Wampum,
Guarded by his fiery serpents,
Guarded by the black pitch-water.
You can see his fiery serpents,
The Kenabeek, the great serpents,
Coiling, playing in the water;
You can see the black pitch-water
Stretching far away beyond them,
To the purple clouds of sunset!

"He it was who slew my father,
By his wicked wiles and cunning,
When he from the moon descended,
When he came on earth to seek me.
He, the mightiest of Magicians,
Sends the fever from the marshes,
Sends the pestilential vapors,
Sends the poisonous exhalations,
Sends the white fog from the fen-lands,
Sends disease and death among us!

"Take your bow, O Hiawatha,
Take your arrows, jasper-headed,
Take your war-club, Puggawaugun,
And your mittens, Minjekahwun,
And your birch-canoe for sailing,
And the oil of Mishe-Nahma,
So to smear its sides, that swiftly
You may pass the black pitch-water;
Slay this merciless magician,
Save the people from the fever
That he breathes across the fen-lands,

And avenge my father's murder!"

Straightway then my Hiawatha
Armed himself with all his war-gear,
Launched his birch-canoe for sailing;
With his palm its sides he patted,
Said with glee, "Cheemaun, my darling,
O my Birch-canoe! leap forward,
Where you see the fiery serpents,
Where you see the black pitch-water!"

Forward leaped Cheemaun exulting,
And the noble Hiawatha
Sang his war-song wild and woful,
And above him the war-eagle,
The Keneu, the great war-eagle,
Master of all fowls with feathers,
Screamed and hurtled through the heavens.

Soon he reached the fiery serpents,
The Kenabeek, the great serpents,
Lying huge upon the water,
Sparkling, rippling in the water,
Lying coiled across the passage,
With their blazing crests uplifted,
Breathing fiery fogs and vapors,
So that none could pass beyond them.

But the fearless Hiawatha
Cried aloud, and spake in this wise,
"Let me pass my way, Kenabeek,
Let me go upon my journey!"
And they answered, hissing fiercely,
With their fiery breath made answer:
"Back, go back! O Shaugodaya!
Back to old Nokomis, Faint-heart!"

Then the angry Hiawatha
Raised his mighty bow of ash-tree,
Seized his arrows, jasper-headed,
Shot them fast among the serpents;
Every twanging of the bow-string
Was a war-cry and a death-cry,
Every whizzing of an arrow

Was a death-song of Kenabeek.

Weltering in the bloody water,
Dead lay all the fiery serpents,
And among them Hiawatha
Harmless sailed, and cried exulting:
"Onward, O Cheemaun, my darling!
Onward to the black pitch-water!"

Then he took the oil of Nahma,
And the bows and sides anointed,
Smeared them well with oil, that swiftly
He might pass the black pitch-water.

All night long he sailed upon it,
Sailed upon that sluggish water,
Covered with its mould of ages,
Black with rotting water-rushes,
Rank with flags and leaves of lilies,
Stagnant, lifeless, dreary, dismal,
Lighted by the shimmering moonlight,
And by will-o'-the-wisps illumined,
Fires by ghosts of dead men kindled,
In their weary night-encampments.

All the air was white with moonlight,
All the water black with shadow,
And around him the Suggema,
The mosquito, sang his war-song,
And the fire-flies, Wah-wah-taysee,
Waved their torches to mislead him;
And the bull-frog, the Dahinda,
Thrust his head into the moonlight,
Fixed his yellow eyes upon him,
Sobbed and sank beneath the surface;
And anon a thousand whistles,
Answered over all the fen-lands,
And the heron, the Shuh-shuh-gah,
Far off on the reedy margin,
Heralded the hero's coming.

Westward thus fared Hiawatha,
Toward the realm of Megissogwon,
Toward the land of the Pearl-Feather,

Till the level moon stared at him
In his face stared pale and haggard,
Till the sun was hot behind him,
Till it burned upon his shoulders,
And before him on the upland
He could see the Shining Wigwam
Of the Manito of Wampum,
Of the mightiest of Magicians.

Then once more Cheemaun he patted,
To his birch-canoe said, "Onward!"
And it stirred in all its fibres,
And with one great bound of triumph
Leaped across the water-lilies,
Leaped through tangled flags and rushes,
And upon the beach beyond them
Dry-shod landed Hiawatha.

Straight he took his bow of ash-tree,
On the sand one end he rested,
With his knee he pressed the middle,
Stretched the faithful bow-string tighter,
Took an arrow, jasperheaded,
Shot it at the Shining Wigwam,
Sent it singing as a herald,
As a bearer of his message,
Of his challenge loud and lofty:
"Come forth from your lodge, Pearl-Feather!
Hiawatha waits your coming!"

Straightway from the Shining Wigwam
Came the mighty Megissogwon,
Tall of stature, broad of shoulder,
Dark and terrible in aspect,
Clad from head to foot in wampum,
Armed with all his warlike weapons,
Painted like the sky of morning,
Streaked with crimson, blue, and yellow,
Crested with great eagle-feathers,
Streaming upward, streaming outward.

"Well I know you, Hiawatha!"
Cried he in a voice of thunder,
In a tone of loud derision.

"Hasten back, O Shaugodaya!
Hasten back among the women,
Back to old Nokomis, Faint-heart!
I will slay you as you stand there,
As of old I slew her father!"

But my Hiawatha answered,
Nothing daunted, fearing nothing:
"Big words do not smite like war-clubs,
Boastful breath is not a bow-string,
Taunts are not so sharp as arrows,
Deeds are better things than words are,
Actions mightier than boastings!"

Then began the greatest battle
That the sun had ever looked on,
That the war-birds ever witnessed.
All a Summer's day it lasted,
From the sunrise to the sunset;
For the shafts of Hiawatha
Harmless hit the shirt of wampum,
Harmless fell the blows he dealt it
With his mittens, Minjekahwun,
Harmless fell the heavy war-club;
It could dash the rocks asunder,
But it could not break the meshes
Of that magic shirt of wampum.

Till at sunset Hiawatha,
Leaning on his bow of ash-tree,
Wounded, weary, and desponding,
With his mighty war-club broken,
With his mittens torn and tattered,
And three useless arrows only,
Paused to rest beneath a pine-tree,
From whose branches trailed the mosses,
And whose trunk was coated over
With the Dead-man's Moccasin-leather,
With the fungus white and yellow.

Suddenly from the boughs above him
Sang the Mama, the woodpecker:
"Aim your arrows, Hiawatha,
At the head of Megissogwon,

Strike the tuft of hair upon it,
At their roots the long black tresses;
There alone can he be wounded!"

Winged with feathers, tipped with jasper,
Swift flew Hiawatha's arrow,
Just as Megissogwon, stooping,
Raised a heavy stone to throw it.
Full upon the crown it struck him,
At the roots of his long tresses,
And he reeled and staggered forward,
Plunging like a wounded bison,
Yes, like Pezhekee, the bison,
When the snow is on the prairie.

Swifter flew the second arrow,
In the pathway of the other,
Piercing deeper than the other,
Wounding sorer than the other;
And the knees of Megissogwon
Shook like windy reeds beneath him,
Bent and trembled like the rushes.

But the third and latest arrow
Swiftest flew, and wounded sorest,
And the mighty Megissogwon
Saw the fiery eyes of Pauguk,
Saw the eyes of Death glare at him,
Heard his voice call in the darkness;
At the feet of Hiawatha
Lifeless lay the great Pearl-Feather,
Lay the mightiest of Magicians.

Then the grateful Hiawatha
Called the Mama, the woodpecker,
From his perch among the branches
Of the melancholy pine-tree,
And, in honor of his service,
Stained with blood the tuft of feathers
On the little head of Mama;
Even to this day he wears it,
Wears the tuft of crimson feathers,
As a symbol of his service.

Then he stripped the shirt of wampum
From the back of Megissogwon,
As a trophy of the battle,
As a signal of his conquest.
On the shore he left the body,
Half on land and half in water,
In the sand his feet were buried,
And his face was in the water.
And above him, wheeled and clamored
The Keneu, the great war-eagle,
Sailing round in narrower circles,
Hovering nearer, nearer, nearer.

From the wigwam Hiawatha
Bore the wealth of Megissogwon,
All his wealth of skins and wampum,
Furs of bison and of beaver,
Furs of sable and of ermine,
Wampum belts and strings and pouches,
Quivers wrought with beads of wampum,
Filled with arrows, silver-headed.

Homeward then he sailed exulting,
Homeward through the black pitch-water,
Homeward through the weltering serpents,
With the trophies of the battle,
With a shout and song of triumph.

On the shore stood old Nokomis,
On the shore stood Chibiabos,
And the very strong man, Kwasind,
Waiting for the hero's coming,
Listening to his songs of triumph.
And the people of the village
Welcomed him with songs and dances,
Made a joyous feast, and shouted:
"Honor be to Hiawatha!
He has slain the great Pearl-Feather,
Slain the mightiest of Magicians,
Him, who sent the fiery fever,
Sent the white fog from the fen-lands,
Sent disease and death among us!"

Ever dear to Hiawatha

Was the memory of Mama!
And in token of his friendship,
As a mark of his remembrance,
He adorned and decked his pipe-stem
With the crimson tuft of feathers,
With the blood-red crest of Mama.
But the wealth of Megissogwon,
All the trophies of the battle,
He divided with his people,
Shared it equally among them.

X. HIAWATHA'S WOOING

"As unto the bow the cord is,
So unto the man is woman;
Though she bends him, she obeys him,
Though she draws him, yet she follows;
Useless each without the other!"

Thus the youthful Hiawatha
Said within himself and pondered,
Much perplexed by various feelings,
Listless, longing, hoping, fearing,
Dreaming still of Minnehaha,
Of the lovely Laughing Water,
In the land of the Dacotahs.

"Wed a maiden of your people,"
Warning said the old Nokomis;
"Go not eastward, go not westward,
For a stranger, whom we know not!
Like a fire upon the hearth-stone
Is a neighbor's homely daughter,
Like the starlight or the moonlight
Is the handsomest of strangers!"

Thus dissuading spake Nokomis,
And my Hiawatha answered
Only this: "Dear old Nokomis,
Very pleasant is the firelight,
But I like the starlight better,
Better do I like the moonlight!"

Gravely then said old Nokomis:
"Bring not here an idle maiden,
Bring not here a useless woman,
Hands unskilful, feet unwilling;
Bring a wife with nimble fingers,
Heart and hand that move together,
Feet that run on willing errands!"

Smiling answered Hiawatha:
"In the land of the Dacotahs
Lives the Arrow-maker's daughter,
Minnehaha, Laughing Water,
Handsomest of all the women.
I will bring her to your wigwam,
She shall run upon your errands,
Be your starlight, moonlight, firelight,
Be the sunlight of my people!"

Still dissuading said Nokomis:
"Bring not to my lodge a stranger
From the land of the Dacotahs!
Very fierce are the Dacotahs,
Often is there war between us,
There are feuds yet unforgotten,
Wounds that ache and still may open!"

Laughing answered Hiawatha:
"For that reason, if no other,
Would I wed the fair Dacotah,
That our tribes might be united,
That old feuds might be forgotten,
And old wounds be healed forever!"

Thus departed Hiawatha
To the land of the Dacotahs,
To the land of handsome women;
Striding over moor and meadow,
Through interminable forests,
Through uninterrupted silence.

With his moccasins of magic,
At each stride a mile he measured;
Yet the way seemed long before him,
And his heart outran his footsteps;

And he journeyed without resting,
Till he heard the cataract's laughter,
Heard the Falls of Minnehaha
Calling to him through the silence.
"Pleasant is the sound!" he murmured,
"Pleasant is the voice that calls me!"

On the outskirts of the forests,
'Twixt the shadow and the sunshine,
Herds of fallow deer were feeding,
But they saw not Hiawatha;
To his bow he whispered, "Fail not!"
To his arrow whispered, "Swerve not!"
Sent it singing on its errand,
To the red heart of the roebuck;
Threw the deer across his shoulder,
And sped forward without pausing.

At the doorway of his wigwam
Sat the ancient Arrow-maker,
In the land of the Dacotahs,
Making arrow-heads of jasper,
Arrow-heads of chalcedony.
At his side, in all her beauty,
Sat the lovely Minnehaha,
Sat his daughter, Laughing Water,
Plaiting mats of flags and rushes
Of the past the old man's thoughts were,
And the maiden's of the future.

He was thinking, as he sat there,
Of the days when with such arrows
He had struck the deer and bison,
On the Muskoday, the meadow;
Shot the wild goose, flying southward
On the wing, the clamorous Wawa;
Thinking of the great war-parties,
How they came to buy his arrows,
Could not fight without his arrows.
Ah, no more such noble warriors
Could be found on earth as they were!
Now the men were all like women,
Only used their tongues for weapons!

She was thinking of a hunter,
From another tribe and country,
Young and tall and very handsome,
Who one morning, in the Spring-time,
Came to buy her father's arrows,
Sat and rested in the wigwam,
Lingered long about the doorway,
Looking back as he departed.
She had heard her father praise him,
Praise his courage and his wisdom;
Would he come again for arrows
To the Falls of Minnehaha?
On the mat her hands lay idle,
And her eyes were very dreamy.

Through their thoughts they heard a footstep,
Heard a rustling in the branches,
And with glowing cheek and forehead,
With the deer upon his shoulders,
Suddenly from out the woodlands
Hiawatha stood before them.

Straight the ancient Arrow-maker
Looked up gravely from his labor,
Laid aside the unfinished arrow,
Bade him enter at the doorway,
Saying, as he rose to meet him,
"Hiawatha, you are welcome!"

At the feet of Laughing Water
Hiawatha laid his burden,
Threw the red deer from his shoulders;
And the maiden looked up at him,
Looked up from her mat of rushes,
Said with gentle look and accent,
"You are welcome, Hiawatha!"

Very spacious was the wigwam,
Made of deer-skins dressed and whitened,
With the Gods of the Dacotahs
Drawn and painted on its curtains,
And so tall the doorway, hardly
Hiawatha stooped to enter,
Hardly touched his eagle-feathers

As he entered at the doorway.

Then uprose the Laughing Water,
From the ground fair Minnehaha,
Laid aside her mat unfinished,
Brought forth food and set before them,
Water brought them from the brooklet,
Gave them food in earthen vessels,
Gave them drink in bowls of bass-wood,
Listened while the guest was speaking,
Listened while her father answered,
But not once her lips she opened,
Not a single word she uttered.

Yes, as in a dream she listened
To the words of Hiawatha,
As he talked of old Nokomis,
Who had nursed him in his childhood,
As he told of his companions,
Chibiabos, the musician,
And the very strong man, Kwasind,
And of happiness and plenty
In the land of the Ojibways,
In the pleasant land and peaceful.

"After many years of warfare,
Many years of strife and bloodshed,
There is peace between the Ojibways
And the tribe of the Dacotahs."
Thus continued Hiawatha,
And then added, speaking slowly,
"That this peace may last forever,
And our hands be clasped more closely,
And our hearts be more united,
Give me as my wife this maiden,
Minnehaha, Laughing Water,
Loveliest of Dacotah women!"

And the ancient Arrow-maker
Paused a moment ere he answered,
Smoked a little while in silence,
Looked at Hiawatha proudly,
Fondly looked at Laughing Water,
And made answer very gravely:

"Yes, if Minnehaha wishes;
Let your heart speak, Minnehaha!"

And the lovely Laughing Water
Seemed more lovely as she stood there,
Neither willing nor reluctant,
As she went to Hiawatha,
Softly took the seat beside him,
While she said, and blushed to say it,
"I will follow you, my husband!"

This was Hiawatha's wooing!
Thus it was he won the daughter
Of the ancient Arrow-maker,
In the land of the Dacotahs!

From the wigwam he departed,
Leading with him Laughing Water;
Hand in hand they went together,
Through the woodland and the meadow,
Left the old man standing lonely
At the doorway of his wigwam,
Heard the Falls of Minnehaha
Calling to them from the distance,
Crying to them from afar off,
"Fare thee well, O Minnehaha!"

And the ancient Arrow-maker
Turned again unto his labor,
Sat down by his sunny doorway,
Murmuring to himself, and saying:
"Thus it is our daughters leave us,
Those we love, and those who love us!
Just when they have learned to help us,
When we are old and lean upon them,
Comes a youth with flaunting feathers,
With his flute of reeds, a stranger
Wanders piping through the village,
Beckons to the fairest maiden,
And she follows where he leads her,
Leaving all things for the stranger!"

Pleasant was the journey homeward,
Through interminable forests,

Over meadow, over mountain,
Over river, hill, and hollow.
Short it seemed to Hiawatha,
Though they journeyed very slowly,
Though his pace he checked and slackened
To the steps of Laughing Water.

Over wide and rushing rivers
In his arms he bore the maiden;
Light he thought her as a feather,
As the plume upon his head-gear;
Cleared the tangled pathway for her,
Bent aside the swaying branches,
Made at night a lodge of branches,
And a bed with boughs of hemlock,
And a fire before the doorway
With the dry cones of the pine-tree.

All the travelling winds went with them,
O'er the meadows, through the forest;
All the stars of night looked at them,
Watched with sleepless eyes their slumber;
From his ambush in the oak-tree
Peeped the squirrel, Adjidaumo,
Watched with eager eyes the lovers;
And the rabbit, the Wabasso,
Scampered from the path before them,
Peering, peeping from his burrow,
Sat erect upon his haunches,
Watched with curious eyes the lovers.

Pleasant was the journey homeward!
All the birds sang loud and sweetly
Songs of happiness and heart's-ease;
Sang the bluebird, the Owaissa,
"Happy are you, Hiawatha,
Having such a wife to love you!"
Sang the robin, the Opechee,
"Happy are you, Laughing Water,
Having such a noble husband!"

From the sky the sun benignant
Looked upon them through the branches,
Saying to them, "O my children,

Love is sunshine, hate is shadow,
Life is checkered shade and sunshine,
Rule by love, O Hiawatha!"

From the sky the moon looked at them,
Filled the lodge with mystic splendors,
Whispered to them, "O my children,
Day is restless, night is quiet,
Man imperious, woman feeble;
Half is mine, although I follow;
Rule by patience, Laughing Water!"

Thus it was they journeyed homeward;
Thus it was that Hiawatha
To the lodge of old Nokomis
Brought the moonlight, starlight, firelight,
Brought the sunshine of his people,
Minnehaha, Laughing Water,
Handsomest of all the women
In the land of the Dacotahs,
In the land of handsome women.

XI. HIAWATHA'S WEDDING-FEAST

You shall hear how Pau-Puk-Keewis,
How the handsome Yenadizze
Danced at Hiawatha's wedding;
How the gentle Chibiabos,
He the sweetest of musicians,
Sang his songs of love and longing;
How Iagoo, the great boaster,
He the marvellous story-teller,
Told his tales of strange adventure,
That the feast might be more joyous,
That the time might pass more gayly,
And the guests be more contented.

Sumptuous was the feast Nokomis
Made at Hiawatha's wedding;
All the bowls were made of bass-wood,
White and polished very smoothly,
All the spoons of horn of bison,
Black and polished very smoothly.

She had sent through all the village
Messengers with wands of willow,
As a sign of invitation,
As a token of the feasting;
And the wedding guests assembled,
Clad in all their richest raiment,
Robes of fur and belts of wampum,
Splendid with their paint and plumage,
Beautiful with beads and tassels.

First they ate the sturgeon, Nahma,
And the pike, the Maskenozha,
Caught and cooked by old Nokomis;
Then on pemican they feasted,
Pemican and buffalo marrow,
Haunch of deer and hump of bison,
Yellow cakes of the Mondamin,
And the wild rice of the river.

But the gracious Hiawatha,
And the lovely Laughing Water,
And the careful old Nokomis,
Tasted not the food before them,
Only waited on the others
Only served their guests in silence.

And when all the guests had finished,
Old Nokomis, brisk and busy,
From an ample pouch of otter,
Filled the red-stone pipes for smoking
With tobacco from the South-land,
Mixed with bark of the red willow,
And with herbs and leaves of fragrance.

Then she said, "O Pau-Puk-Keewis,
Dance for us your merry dances,
Dance the Beggar's Dance to please us,
That the feast may be more joyous,
That the time may pass more gayly,
And our guests be more contented!"

Then the handsome Pau-Puk-Keewis,
He the idle Yenadizze,
He the merry mischief-maker,

Whom the people called the Storm-Fool,
Rose among the guests assembled.

Skilled was he in sports and pastimes,
In the merry dance of snow-shoes,
In the play of quoits and ball-play;
Skilled was he in games of hazard,
In all games of skill and hazard,
Pugasaing, the Bowl and Counters,
Kuntassoo, the Game of Plum-stones.
Though the warriors called him Faint-Heart,
Called him coward, Shaugodaya,
Idler, gambler, Yenadizze,
Little heeded he their jesting,
Little cared he for their insults,
For the women and the maidens
Loved the handsome Pau-Puk-Keewis.

He was dressed in shirt of doeskin,
White and soft, and fringed with ermine,
All inwrought with beads of wampum;
He was dressed in deer-skin leggings,
Fringed with hedgehog quills and ermine,
And in moccasins of buck-skin,
Thick with quills and beads embroidered.
On his head were plumes of swan's down,
On his heels were tails of foxes,
In one hand a fan of feathers,
And a pipe was in the other.

Barred with streaks of red and yellow,
Streaks of blue and bright vermilion,
Shone the face of Pau-Puk-Keewis.
From his forehead fell his tresses,
Smooth, and parted like a woman's,
Shining bright with oil, and plaited,
Hung with braids of scented grasses,
As among the guests assembled,
To the sound of flutes and singing,
To the sound of drums and voices,
Rose the handsome Pau-Puk-Keewis,
And began his mystic dances.

First he danced a solemn measure,

Very slow in step and gesture,
In and out among the pine-trees,
Through the shadows and the sunshine,
Treading softly like a panther.
Then more swiftly and still swifter,
Whirling, spinning round in circles,
Leaping o'er the guests assembled,
Eddying round and round the wigwam,
Till the leaves went whirling with him,
Till the dust and wind together
Swept in eddies round about him.

Then along the sandy margin
Of the lake, the Big-Sea-Water,
On he sped with frenzied gestures,
Stamped upon the sand, and tossed it
Wildly in the air around him;
Till the wind became a whirlwind,
Till the sand was blown and sifted
Like great snowdrifts o'er the landscape,
Heaping all the shores with Sand Dunes,
Sand Hills of the Nagow Wudjoo!

Thus the merry Pau-Puk-Keewis
Danced his Beggar's Dance to please them,
And, returning, sat down laughing
There among the guests assembled,
Sat and fanned himself serenely
With his fan of turkey-feathers.

Then they said to Chibiabos,
To the friend of Hiawatha,
To the sweetest of all singers,
To the best of all musicians,
"Sing to us, O Chibiabos!
Songs of love and songs of longing,
That the feast may be more joyous,
That the time may pass more gayly,
And our guests be more contented!"

And the gentle Chibiabos
Sang in accents sweet and tender,
Sang in tones of deep emotion,
Songs of love and songs of longing;

Looking still at Hiawatha,
Looking at fair Laughing Water,
Sang he softly, sang in this wise:

"Onaway! Awake, beloved!
Thou the wild-flower of the forest!
Thou the wild-bird of the prairie!
Thou with eyes so soft and fawn-like!

"If thou only lookest at me,
I am happy, I am happy,
As the lilies of the prairie,
When they feel the dew upon them!

"Sweet thy breath is as the fragrance
Of the wild-flowers in the morning,
As their fragrance is at evening,
In the Moon when leaves are falling.

"Does not all the blood within me
Leap to meet thee, leap to meet thee,
As the springs to meet the sunshine,
In the Moon when nights are brightest?

"Onaway! my heart sings to thee,
Sings with joy when thou art near me,
As the sighing, singing branches
In the pleasant Moon of Strawberries!

"When thou art not pleased, beloved,
Then my heart is sad and darkened,
As the shining river darkens
When the clouds drop shadows on it!

"When thou smilest, my beloved,
Then my troubled heart is brightened,
As in sunshine gleam the ripples
That the cold wind makes in rivers.

"Smiles the earth, and smile the waters,
Smile the cloudless skies above us,
But I lose the way of smiling
When thou art no longer near me!

"I myself, myself! behold me!
Blood of my beating heart, behold me!
Oh awake, awake, beloved!
Onaway! awake, beloved!"

Thus the gentle Chibiabos
Sang his song of love and longing;
And Iagoo, the great boaster,
He the marvellous story-teller,
He the friend of old Nokomis,
Jealous of the sweet musician,
Jealous of the applause they gave him,
Saw in all the eyes around him,
Saw in all their looks and gestures,
That the wedding guests assembled
Longed to hear his pleasant stories,
His immeasurable falsehoods.

Very boastful was Iagoo;
Never heard he an adventure
But himself had met a greater;
Never any deed of daring
But himself had done a bolder;
Never any marvellous story
But himself could tell a stranger.

Would you listen to his boasting,
Would you only give him credence,
No one ever shot an arrow
Half so far and high as he had;
Ever caught so many fishes,
Ever killed so many reindeer,
Ever trapped so many beaver!

None could run so fast as he could,
None could dive so deep as he could,
None could swim so far as he could;
None had made so many journeys,
None had seen so many wonders,
As this wonderful Iagoo,
As this marvellous story-teller!
Thus his name became a by-word
And a jest among the people;
And whene'er a boastful hunter

Praised his own address too highly,
Or a warrior, home returning,
Talked too much of his achievements,
All his hearers cried, "Iagoo!
Here's Iagoo come among us!"

He it was who carved the cradle
Of the little Hiawatha,
Carved its framework out of linden,
Bound it strong with reindeer sinews;
He it was who taught him later
How to make his bows and arrows,
How to make the bows of ash-tree,
And the arrows of the oak-tree.
So among the guests assembled
At my Hiawatha's wedding
Sat Iagoo, old and ugly,
Sat the marvellous story-teller.

And they said, "O good Iagoo,
Tell us now a tale of wonder,
Tell us of some strange adventure,
That the feast may be more joyous,
That the time may pass more gayly,
And our guests be more contented!"

And Iagoo answered straightway,
"You shall hear a tale of wonder,
You shall hear the strange adventures
Of Osseo, the Magician,
From the Evening Star descending."

XII. THE SON OF THE EVENING STAR

Can it be the sun descending
O'er the level plain of water?
Or the Red Swan floating, flying,
Wounded by the magic arrow,
Staining all the waves with crimson,
With the crimson of its life-blood,
Filling all the air with splendor,
With the splendor of its plumage?

Yes; it is the sun descending,
Sinking down into the water;
All the sky is stained with purple,
All the water flushed with crimson!
No; it is the Red Swan floating,
Diving down beneath the water;
To the sky its wings are lifted,
With its blood the waves are reddened!

Over it the Star of Evening
Melts and trembles through the purple,
Hangs suspended in the twilight.
No; it is a bead of wampum
On the robes of the Great Spirit
As he passes through the twilight,
Walks in silence through the heavens.

This with joy beheld Iagoo
And he said in haste: "Behold it!
See the sacred Star of Evening!
You shall hear a tale of wonder,
Hear the story of Osseo,
Son of the Evening Star, Osseo!

"Once, in days no more remembered,
Ages nearer the beginning,
When the heavens were closer to us,
And the Gods were more familiar,
In the North-land lived a hunter,
With ten young and comely daughters,
Tall and lithe as wands of willow;
Only Oweenee, the youngest,
She the wilful and the wayward,
She the silent, dreamy maiden,
Was the fairest of the sisters.

"All these women married warriors,
Married brave and haughty husbands;
Only Oweenee, the youngest,
Laughed and flouted all her lovers,
All her young and handsome suitors,
And then married old Osseo,
Old Osseo, poor and ugly,
Broken with age and weak with coughing,

Always coughing like a squirrel.

"Ah, but beautiful within him
Was the spirit of Osseo,
From the Evening Star descended,
Star of Evening, Star of Woman,
Star of tenderness and passion!
All its fire was in his bosom,
All its beauty in his spirit,
All its mystery in his being,
All its splendor in his language!

"And her lovers, the rejected,
Handsome men with belts of wampum,
Handsome men with paint and feathers,
Pointed at her in derision,
Followed her with jest and laughter.
But she said: 'I care not for you,
Care not for your belts of wampum,
Care not for your paint and feathers,
Care not for your jests and laughter;
I am happy with Osseo!'

"Once to some great feast invited,
Through the damp and dusk of evening,
Walked together the ten sisters,
Walked together with their husbands;
Slowly followed old Osseo,
With fair Oweenee beside him;
All the others chatted gayly,
These two only walked in silence.

"At the western sky Osseo
Gazed intent, as if imploring,
Often stopped and gazed imploring
At the trembling Star of Evening,
At the tender Star of Woman;
And they heard him murmur softly,
'Ah, showain nemeshin, Nosa!
Pity, pity me, my father!'

"'Listen!' said the eldest sister,
'He is praying to his father!
What a pity that the old man

Does not stumble in the pathway,
Does not break his neck by falling!'
And they laughed till all the forest
Rang with their unseemly laughter.

"On their pathway through the woodlands
Lay an oak, by storms uprooted,
Lay the great trunk of an oak-tree,
Buried half in leaves and mosses,
Mouldering, crumbling, huge and hollow.
And Osseo, when he saw it,
Gave a shout, a cry of anguish,
Leaped into its yawning cavern,
At one end went in an old man,
Wasted, wrinkled, old, and ugly;
From the other came a young man,
Tall and straight and strong and handsome.

"Thus Osseo was transfigured,
Thus restored to youth and beauty;
But, alas for good Osseo,
And for Oweenee, the faithful!
Strangely, too, was she transfigured.
Changed into a weak old woman,
With a staff she tottered onward,
Wasted, wrinkled, old, and ugly!
And the sisters and their husbands
Laughed until the echoing forest
Rang with their unseemly laughter.

"But Osseo turned not from her,
Walked with slower step beside her,
Took her hand, as brown and withered
As an oak-leaf is in Winter,
Called her sweetheart, Nenemoosha,
Soothed her with soft words of kindness,
Till they reached the lodge of feasting,
Till they sat down in the wigwam,
Sacred to the Star of Evening,
To the tender Star of Woman.

"Wrapt in visions, lost in dreaming,
At the banquet sat Osseo;
All were merry, all were happy,

All were joyous but Osseo.
Neither food nor drink he tasted,
Neither did he speak nor listen;
But as one bewildered sat he,
Looking dreamily and sadly,
First at Oweenee, then upward
At the gleaming sky above them.

"Then a voice was heard, a whisper,
Coming from the starry distance,
Coming from the empty vastness,
Low, and musical, and tender;
And the voice said: 'O Osseo!
O my son, my best beloved!
Broken are the spells that bound you,
All the charms of the magicians,
All the magic powers of evil;
Come to me; ascend, Osseo!

"'Taste the food that stands before you:
It is blessed and enchanted,
It has magic virtues in it,
It will change you to a spirit.
All your bowls and all your kettles
Shall be wood and clay no longer;
But the bowls be changed to wampum,
And the kettles shall be silver;
They shall shine like shells of scarlet,
Like the fire shall gleam and glimmer.

"'And the women shall no longer
Bear the dreary doom of labor,
But be changed to birds, and glisten
With the beauty of the starlight,
Painted with the dusky splendors
Of the skies and clouds of evening!'

"What Osseo heard as whispers,
What as words he comprehended,
Was but music to the others,
Music as of birds afar off,
Of the whippoorwill afar off,
Of the lonely Wawonaissa
Singing in the darksome forest.

"Then the lodge began to tremble,
Straight began to shake and tremble,
And they felt it rising, rising,
Slowly through the air ascending,
From the darkness of the tree-tops
Forth into the dewy starlight,
Till it passed the topmost branches;
And behold! the wooden dishes
All were changed to shells of scarlet!
And behold! the earthen kettles
All were changed to bowls of silver!
And the roof-poles of the wigwam
Were as glittering rods of silver,
And the roof of bark upon them
As the shining shards of beetles.

"Then Osseo gazed around him,
And he saw the nine fair sisters,
All the sisters and their husbands,
Changed to birds of various plumage.
Some were jays and some were magpies,
Others thrushes, others blackbirds;
And they hopped, and sang, and twittered,
Perked and fluttered all their feathers,
Strutted in their shining plumage,
And their tails like fans unfolded.

"Only Oweenee, the youngest,
Was not changed, but sat in silence,
Wasted, wrinkled, old, and ugly,
Looking sadly at the others;
Till Osseo, gazing upward,
Gave another cry of anguish,
Such a cry as he had uttered
By the oak-tree in the forest.
"Then returned her youth and beauty,
And her soiled and tattered garments
Were transformed to robes of ermine,
And her staff became a feather,
Yes, a shining silver feather!

"And again the wigwam trembled,
Swayed and rushed through airy currents,
Through transparent cloud and vapor,

And amid celestial splendors
On the Evening Star alighted,
As a snow-flake falls on snow-flake,
As a leaf drops on a river,
As the thistledown on water.

"Forth with cheerful words of welcome
Came the father of Osseo,
He with radiant locks of silver,
He with eyes serene and tender.
And he said: `My son, Osseo,
Hang the cage of birds you bring there,
Hang the cage with rods of silver,
And the birds with glistening feathers,
At the doorway of my wigwam.'

"At the door he hung the bird-cage,
And they entered in and gladly
Listened to Osseo's father,
Ruler of the Star of Evening,
As he said: `O my Osseo!
I have had compassion on you,
Given you back your youth and beauty,
Into birds of various plumage
Changed your sisters and their husbands;
Changed them thus because they mocked you
In the figure of the old man,
In that aspect sad and wrinkled,
Could not see your heart of passion,
Could not see your youth immortal;
Only Oweenee, the faithful,
Saw your naked heart and loved you.

"`In the lodge that glimmers yonder,
In the little star that twinkles
Through the vapors, on the left hand,
Lives the envious Evil Spirit,
The Wabeno, the magician,
Who transformed you to an old man.
Take heed lest his beams fall on you,
For the rays he darts around him
Are the power of his enchantment,
Are the arrows that he uses.'

"Many years, in peace and quiet,
On the peaceful Star of Evening
Dwelt Osseo with his father;
Many years, in song and flutter,
At the doorway of the wigwam,
Hung the cage with rods of silver,
And fair Oweenee, the faithful,
Bore a son unto Osseo,
With the beauty of his mother,
With the courage of his father.

"And the boy grew up and prospered,
And Osseo, to delight him,
Made him little bows and arrows,
Opened the great cage of silver,
And let loose his aunts and uncles,
All those birds with glossy feathers,
For his little son to shoot at.

"Round and round they wheeled and darted,
Filled the Evening Star with music,
With their songs of joy and freedom
Filled the Evening Star with splendor,
With the fluttering of their plumage;
Till the boy, the little hunter,
Bent his bow and shot an arrow,
Shot a swift and fatal arrow,
And a bird, with shining feathers,
At his feet fell wounded sorely.

"But, O wondrous transformation!
'T was no bird he saw before him,
'T was a beautiful young woman,
With the arrow in her bosom!

"When her blood fell on the planet,
On the sacred Star of Evening,
Broken was the spell of magic,
Powerless was the strange enchantment,
And the youth, the fearless bowman,
Suddenly felt himself descending,
Held by unseen hands, but sinking
Downward through the empty spaces,
Downward through the clouds and vapors,

Till he rested on an island,
On an island, green and grassy,
Yonder in the Big-Sea-Water.

"After him he saw descending
All the birds with shining feathers,
Fluttering, falling, wafted downward,
Like the painted leaves of Autumn;
And the lodge with poles of silver,
With its roof like wings of beetles,
Like the shining shards of beetles,
By the winds of heaven uplifted,
Slowly sank upon the island,
Bringing back the good Osseo,
Bringing Oweenee, the faithful.

"Then the birds, again transfigured,
Reassumed the shape of mortals,
Took their shape, but not their stature;
They remained as Little People,
Like the pygmies, the Puk-Wudjies,
And on pleasant nights of Summer,
When the Evening Star was shining,
Hand in hand they danced together
On the island's craggy headlands,
On the sand-beach low and level.

"Still their glittering lodge is seen there,
On the tranquil Summer evenings,
And upon the shore the fisher
Sometimes hears their happy voices,
Sees them dancing in the starlight !"

When the story was completed,
When the wondrous tale was ended,
Looking round upon his listeners,
Solemnly Iagoo added:
"There are great men, I have known such,
Whom their people understand not,
Whom they even make a jest of,
Scoff and jeer at in derision.
From the story of Osseo
Let us learn the fate of jesters!"

All the wedding guests delighted
Listened to the marvellous story,
Listened laughing and applauding,
And they whispered to each other:
"Does he mean himself, I wonder?
And are we the aunts and uncles?"

Then again sang Chibiabos,
Sang a song of love and longing,
In those accents sweet and tender,
In those tones of pensive sadness,
Sang a maiden's lamentation
For her lover, her Algonquin.

"When I think of my beloved,
Ah me! think of my beloved,
When my heart is thinking of him,
O my sweetheart, my Algonquin!

"Ah me! when I parted from him,
Round my neck he hung the wampum,
As a pledge, the snow-white wampum,
O my sweetheart, my Algonquin!

"'I will go with you,' he whispered,
'Ah me! to your native country;
Let me go with you,' he whispered,
'O my sweetheart, my Algonquin!'
'Far away, away,' I answered,
'Very far away,' I answered,
'Ah me! is my native country,
O my sweetheart, my Algonquin!'

"When I looked back to behold him,
Where we parted, to behold him,
After me he still was gazing,
O my sweetheart, my Algonquin!

"By the tree he still was standing,
By the fallen tree was standing,
That had dropped into the water,
O my sweetheart, my Algonquin!
"When I think of my beloved,
Ah me! think of my beloved,

When my heart is thinking of him,
O my sweetheart, my Algonquin!"
Such was Hiawatha's Wedding,
Such the dance of Pau-Puk-Keewis,
Such the story of Iagoo,
Such the songs of Chibiabos;
Thus the wedding banquet ended,
And the wedding guests departed,
Leaving Hiawatha happy
With the night and Minnehaha.

XIII. BLESSING THE CORNFIELDS

Sing, O Song of Hiawatha,
Of the happy days that followed,
In the land of the Ojibways,
In the pleasant land and peaceful!
Sing the mysteries of Mondamin,
Sing the Blessing of the Cornfields!

Buried was the bloody hatchet,
Buried was the dreadful war-club,
Buried were all warlike weapons,
And the war-cry was forgotten.
There was peace among the nations;
Unmolested roved the hunters,
Built the birch canoe for sailing,
Caught the fish in lake and river,
Shot the deer and trapped the beaver;
Unmolested worked the women,
Made their sugar from the maple,
Gathered wild rice in the meadows,
Dressed the skins of deer and beaver.

All around the happy village
Stood the maize-fields, green and shining,
Waved the green plumes of Mondamin,
Waved his soft and sunny tresses,
Filling all the land with plenty.
`T was the women who in Spring-time
Planted the broad fields and fruitful,
Buried in the earth Mondamin;
`T was the women who in Autumn

Stripped the yellow husks of harvest,
Stripped the garments from Mondamin,
Even as Hiawatha taught them.

Once, when all the maize was planted,
Hiawatha, wise and thoughtful,
Spake and said to Minnehaha,
To his wife, the Laughing Water:
"You shall bless to-night the cornfields,
Draw a magic circle round them,
To protect them from destruction,
Blast of mildew, blight of insect,
Wagemin, the thief of cornfields,
Paimosaid, who steals the maize-ear.

"In the night, when all is silence,'
In the night, when all is darkness,
When the Spirit of Sleep, Nepahwin,
Shuts the doors of all the wigwams,
So that not an ear can hear you,
So that not an eye can see you,
Rise up from your bed in silence,
Lay aside your garments wholly,
Walk around the fields you planted,
Round the borders of the cornfields,
Covered by your tresses only,
Robed with darkness as a garment.

"Thus the fields shall be more fruitful,
And the passing of your footsteps
Draw a magic circle round them,
So that neither blight nor mildew,
Neither burrowing worm nor insect,
Shall pass o'er the magic circle;
Not the dragon-fly, Kwo-ne-she,
Nor the spider, Subbekashe,
Nor the grasshopper, Pah-puk-keena;
Nor the mighty caterpillar,
Way-muk-kwana, with the bear-skin,
King of all the caterpillars!"

On the tree-tops near the cornfields
Sat the hungry crows and ravens,
Kahgahgee, the King of Ravens,

With his band of black marauders.
And they laughed at Hiawatha,
Till the tree-tops shook with laughter,
With their melancholy laughter,
At the words of Hiawatha.
"Hear him!" said they; "hear the Wise Man,
Hear the plots of Hiawatha!"

When the noiseless night descended
Broad and dark o'er field and forest,
When the mournful Wawonaissa
Sorrowing sang among the hemlocks,
And the Spirit of Sleep, Nepahwin,
Shut the doors of all the wigwams,
From her bed rose Laughing Water,
Laid aside her garments wholly,
And with darkness clothed and guarded,
Unashamed and unaffrighted,
Walked securely round the cornfields,
Drew the sacred, magic circle
Of her footprints round the cornfields.

No one but the Midnight only
Saw her beauty in the darkness,
No one but the Wawonaissa
Heard the panting of her bosom
Guskewau, the darkness, wrapped her
Closely in his sacred mantle,
So that none might see her beauty,
So that none might boast, "I saw her!"

On the morrow, as the day dawned,
Kahgahgee, the King of Ravens,
Gathered all his black marauders,
Crows and blackbirds, jays and ravens,
Clamorous on the dusky tree-tops,
And descended, fast and fearless,
On the fields of Hiawatha,
On the grave of the Mondamin.

"We will drag Mondamin," said they,
"From the grave where he is buried,
Spite of all the magic circles
Laughing Water draws around it,

Spite of all the sacred footprints
Minnehaha stamps upon it!"

But the wary Hiawatha,
Ever thoughtful, careful, watchful,
Had o'erheard the scornful laughter
When they mocked him from the tree-tops.
"Kaw!" he said, "my friends the ravens!
Kahgahgee, my King of Ravens!
I will teach you all a lesson
That shall not be soon forgotten!"

He had risen before the daybreak,
He had spread o'er all the cornfields
Snares to catch the black marauders,
And was lying now in ambush
In the neighboring grove of pine-trees,
Waiting for the crows and blackbirds,
Waiting for the jays and ravens.

Soon they came with caw and clamor,
Rush of wings and cry of voices,
To their work of devastation,
Settling down upon the cornfields,
Delving deep with beak and talon,
For the body of Mondamin.
And with all their craft and cunning,
All their skill in wiles of warfare,
They perceived no danger near them,
Till their claws became entangled,
Till they found themselves imprisoned
In the snares of Hiawatha.

From his place of ambush came he,
Striding terrible among them,
And so awful was his aspect
That the bravest quailed with terror.
Without mercy he destroyed them
Right and left, by tens and twenties,
And their wretched, lifeless bodies
Hung aloft on poles for scarecrows
Round the consecrated cornfields,
As a signal of his vengeance,
As a warning to marauders.

Only Kahgahgee, the leader,
Kahgahgee, the King of Ravens,
He alone was spared among them
As a hostage for his people.
With his prisoner-string he bound him,
Led him captive to his wigwam,
Tied him fast with cords of elm-bark
To the ridge-pole of his wigwam.

"Kahgahgee, my raven!" said he,
"You the leader of the robbers,
You the plotter of this mischief,
The contriver of this outrage,
I will keep you, I will hold you,
As a hostage for your people,
As a pledge of good behavior!"

And he left him, grim and sulky,
Sitting in the morning sunshine
On the summit of the wigwam,
Croaking fiercely his displeasure,
Flapping his great sable pinions,
Vainly struggling for his freedom,
Vainly calling on his people!

Summer passed, and Shawondasee
Breathed his sighs o'er all the landscape,
From the South-land sent his ardor,
Wafted kisses warm and tender;
And the maize-field grew and ripened,
Till it stood in all the splendor
Of its garments green and yellow,
Of its tassels and its plumage,
And the maize-ears full and shining
Gleamed from bursting sheaths of verdure.

Then Nokomis, the old woman,
Spake, and said to Minnehaha:

"'T is the Moon when, leaves are falling;
All the wild rice has been gathered,
And the maize is ripe and ready;
Let us gather in the harvest,
Let us wrestle with Mondamin,

Strip him of his plumes and tassels,
Of his garments green and yellow!"

And the merry Laughing Water
Went rejoicing from the wigwam,
With Nokomis, old and wrinkled,
And they called the women round them,
Called the young men and the maidens,
To the harvest of the cornfields,
To the husking of the maize-ear.

On the border of the forest,
Underneath the fragrant pine-trees,
Sat the old men and the warriors
Smoking in the pleasant shadow.
In uninterrupted silence
Looked they at the gamesome labor
Of the young men and the women;
Listened to their noisy talking,
To their laughter and their singing,
Heard them chattering like the magpies,
Heard them laughing like the blue-jays,
Heard them singing like the robins.

And whene'er some lucky maiden
Found a red ear in the husking,
Found a maize-ear red as blood is,
"Nushka!" cried they all together,
"Nushka! you shall have a sweetheart,
You shall have a handsome husband!"
"Ugh!" the old men all responded
From their seats beneath the pine-trees.

And whene'er a youth or maiden
Found a crooked ear in husking,
Found a maize-ear in the husking
Blighted, mildewed, or misshapen,
Then they laughed and sang together,
Crept and limped about the cornfields,
Mimicked in their gait and gestures
Some old man, bent almost double,
Singing singly or together:
"Wagemin, the thief of cornfields!
Paimosaid, who steals the maize-ear!"

Till the cornfields rang with laughter,
Till from Hiawatha's wigwam
Kahgahgee, the King of Ravens,
Screamed and quivered in his anger,
And from all the neighboring tree-tops
Cawed and croaked the black marauders.
"Ugh!" the old men all responded,
From their seats beneath the pine-trees!

XIV. PICTURE-WRITING

In those days said Hiawatha,
"Lo! how all things fade and perish!
From the memory of the old men
Pass away the great traditions,
The achievements of the warriors,
The adventures of the hunters,
All the wisdom of the Medas,
All the craft of the Wabenos,
All the marvellous dreams and visions
Of the Jossakeeds, the Prophets!

"Great men die and are forgotten,
Wise men speak; their words of wisdom
Perish in the ears that hear them,
Do not reach the generations
That, as yet unborn, are waiting
In the great, mysterious darkness
Of the speechless days that shall be!

"On the grave-posts of our fathers
Are no signs, no figures painted;
Who are in those graves we know not,
Only know they are our fathers.
Of what kith they are and kindred,
From what old, ancestral Totem,
Be it Eagle, Bear, or Beaver,
They descended, this we know not,
Only know they are our fathers.

"Face to face we speak together,
But we cannot speak when absent,
Cannot send our voices from us

To the friends that dwell afar off;
Cannot send a secret message,
But the bearer learns our secret,
May pervert it, may betray it,
May reveal it unto others."
Thus said Hiawatha, walking
In the solitary forest,
Pondering, musing in the forest,
On the welfare of his people.

From his pouch he took his colors,
Took his paints of different colors,
On the smooth bark of a birch-tree
Painted many shapes and figures,
Wonderful and mystic figures,
And each figure had a meaning,
Each some word or thought suggested.

Gitche Manito the Mighty,
He, the Master of Life, was painted
As an egg, with points projecting
To the four winds of the heavens.
Everywhere is the Great Spirit,
Was the meaning of this symbol.

Mitche Manito the Mighty,
He the dreadful Spirit of Evil,
As a serpent was depicted,
As Kenabeek, the great serpent.
Very crafty, very cunning,
Is the creeping Spirit of Evil,
Was the meaning of this symbol.

Life and Death he drew as circles,
Life was white, but Death was darkened;
Sun and moon and stars he painted,
Man and beast, and fish and reptile,
Forests, mountains, lakes, and rivers.

For the earth he drew a straight line,
For the sky a bow above it;
White the space between for daytime,
Filled with little stars for night-time;
On the left a point for sunrise,

On the right a point for sunset,
On the top a point for noontide,
And for rain and cloudy weather
Waving lines descending from it.

Footprints pointing towards a wigwam
Were a sign of invitation,
Were a sign of guests assembling;
Bloody hands with palms uplifted
Were a symbol of destruction,
Were a hostile sign and symbol.

All these things did Hiawatha
Show unto his wondering people,
And interpreted their meaning,
And he said: "Behold, your grave-posts
Have no mark, no sign, nor symbol,
Go and paint them all with figures;
Each one with its household symbol,
With its own ancestral Totem;
So that those who follow after
May distinguish them and know them."

And they painted on the grave-posts
On the graves yet unforgotten,
Each his own ancestral Totem,
Each the symbol of his household;
Figures of the Bear and Reindeer,
Of the Turtle, Crane, and Beaver,
Each inverted as a token
That the owner was departed,
That the chief who bore the symbol
Lay beneath in dust and ashes.

And the Jossakeeds, the Prophets,
The Wabenos, the Magicians,
And the Medicine-men, the Medas,
Painted upon bark and deer-skin
Figures for the songs they chanted,
For each song a separate symbol,
Figures mystical and awful,
Figures strange and brightly colored;
And each figure had its meaning,
Each some magic song suggested.

The Great Spirit, the Creator,
Flashing light through all the heaven;
The Great Serpent, the Kenabeek,
With his bloody crest erected,
Creeping, looking into heaven;
In the sky the sun, that listens,
And the moon eclipsed and dying;
Owl and eagle, crane and hen-hawk,
And the cormorant, bird of magic;
Headless men, that walk the heavens,
Bodies lying pierced with arrows,
Bloody hands of death uplifted,
Flags on graves, and great war-captains
Grasping both the earth and heaven!

Such as these the shapes they painted
On the birch-bark and the deer-skin;
Songs of war and songs of hunting,
Songs of medicine and of magic,
All were written in these figures,
For each figure had its meaning,
Each its separate song recorded.

Nor forgotten was the Love-Song,
The most subtle of all medicines,
The most potent spell of magic,
Dangerous more than war or hunting!
Thus the Love-Song was recorded,
Symbol and interpretation.

First a human figure standing,
Painted in the brightest scarlet;
`T is the lover, the musician,
And the meaning is, "My painting
Makes me powerful over others."

Then the figure seated, singing,
Playing on a drum of magic,
And the interpretation, "Listen!
`T is my voice you hear, my singing!"

Then the same red figure seated
In the shelter of a wigwam,
And the meaning of the symbol,

"I will come and sit beside you
In the mystery of my passion!"

Then two figures, man and woman,
Standing hand in hand together
With their hands so clasped together
That they seemed in one united,
And the words thus represented
Are, "I see your heart within you,
And your cheeks are red with blushes!"

Next the maiden on an island,
In the centre of an Island;
And the song this shape suggested
Was, "Though you were at a distance,
Were upon some far-off island,
Such the spell I cast upon you,
Such the magic power of passion,
I could straightway draw you to me!"

Then the figure of the maiden
Sleeping, and the lover near her,
Whispering to her in her slumbers,
Saying, "Though you were far from me
In the land of Sleep and Silence,
Still the voice of love would reach you!"

And the last of all the figures
Was a heart within a circle,
Drawn within a magic circle;
And the image had this meaning:
"Naked lies your heart before me,
To your naked heart I whisper!"

Thus it was that Hiawatha,
In his wisdom, taught the people
All the mysteries of painting,
All the art of Picture-Writing,
On the smooth bark of the birch-tree,
On the white skin of the reindeer,
On the grave-posts of the village.

XV. HIAWATHA'S LAMENTATION

In those days the Evil Spirits,
All the Manitos of mischief,
Fearing Hiawatha's wisdom,
And his love for Chibiabos,
Jealous of their faithful friendship,
And their noble words and actions,
Made at length a league against them,
To molest them and destroy them.

Hiawatha, wise and wary,
Often said to Chibiabos,
"O my brother! do not leave me,
Lest the Evil Spirits harm you!"
Chibiabos, young and heedless,
Laughing shook his coal-black tresses,
Answered ever sweet and childlike,
"Do not fear for me, O brother!
Harm and evil come not near me!"

Once when Peboan, the Winter,
Roofed with ice the Big-Sea-Water,
When the snow-flakes, whirling downward,
Hissed among the withered oak-leaves,
Changed the pine-trees into wigwams,
Covered all the earth with silence,
Armed with arrows, shod with snow-shoes,
Heeding not his brother's warning,
Fearing not the Evil Spirits,
Forth to hunt the deer with antlers
All alone went Chibiabos.

Right across the Big-Sea-Water
Sprang with speed the deer before him.
With the wind and snow he followed,
O'er the treacherous ice he followed,
Wild with all the fierce commotion
And the rapture of the hunting.

But beneath, the Evil Spirits
Lay in ambush, waiting for him,
Broke the treacherous ice beneath him,

Dragged him downward to the bottom,
Buried in the sand his body.
Unktahee, the god of water,
He the god of the Dacotahs,
Drowned him in the deep abysses
Of the lake of Gitche Gumee.

From the headlands Hiawatha
Sent forth such a wail of anguish,
Such a fearful lamentation,
That the bison paused to listen,
And the wolves howled from the prairies,
And the thunder in the distance
Starting answered "Baim-wawa!"

Then his face with black he painted,
With his robe his head he covered,
In his wigwam sat lamenting,
Seven long weeks he sat lamenting,
Uttering still this moan of sorrow:

"He is dead, the sweet musician!
He the sweetest of all singers!
He has gone from us forever,
He has moved a little nearer
To the Master of all music,
To the Master of all singing!
O my brother, Chibiabos!"

And the melancholy fir-trees
Waved their dark green fans above him,
Waved their purple cones above him,
Sighing with him to console him,
Mingling with his lamentation
Their complaining, their lamenting.

Came the Spring, and all the forest
Looked in vain for Chibiabos;
Sighed the rivulet, Sebowisha,
Sighed the rushes in the meadow.

From the tree-tops sang the bluebird,
Sang the bluebird, the Owaissa,
"Chibiabos! Chibiabos!

He is dead, the sweet musician!"

From the wigwam sang the robin,
Sang the robin, the Opechee,
"Chibiabos! Chibiabos!
He is dead, the sweetest singer!"

And at night through all the forest
Went the whippoorwill complaining,
Wailing went the Wawonaissa,
"Chibiabos! Chibiabos!
He is dead, the sweet musician!
He the sweetest of all singers!"

Then the Medicine-men, the Medas,
The magicians, the Wabenos,
And the Jossakeeds, the Prophets,
Came to visit Hiawatha;
Built a Sacred Lodge beside him,
To appease him, to console him,
Walked in silent, grave procession,
Bearing each a pouch of healing,
Skin of beaver, lynx, or otter,
Filled with magic roots and simples,
Filled with very potent medicines.

When he heard their steps approaching,
Hiawatha ceased lamenting,
Called no more on Chibiabos;
Naught he questioned, naught he answered,
But his mournful head uncovered,
From his face the mourning colors
Washed he slowly and in silence,
Slowly and in silence followed
Onward to the Sacred Wigwam.

There a magic drink they gave him,
Made of Nahma-wusk, the spearmint,
And Wabeno-wusk, the yarrow,
Roots of power, and herbs of healing;
Beat their drums, and shook their rattles;
Chanted singly and in chorus,
Mystic songs like these, they chanted.

"I myself, myself! behold me!
`T is the great Gray Eagle talking;
Come, ye white crows, come and hear him!
The loud-speaking thunder helps me;
All the unseen spirits help me;
I can hear their voices calling,
All around the sky I hear them!
I can blow you strong, my brother,
I can heal you, Hiawatha!"

"Hi-au-ha!" replied the chorus,
"Wayha-way!" the mystic chorus.

Friends of mine are all the serpents!
Hear me shake my skin of hen-hawk!
Mahng, the white loon, I can kill him;
I can shoot your heart and kill it!
I can blow you strong, my brother,
I can heal you, Hiawatha !"

"Hi-au-ha!" replied the chorus,
"Wayhaway!" the mystic chorus.

"I myself, myself! the prophet!
When I speak the wigwam trembles,
Shakes the Sacred Lodge with terror,
Hands unseen begin to shake it!
When I walk, the sky I tread on
Bends and makes a noise beneath me!
I can blow you strong, my brother!
Rise and speak, O Hiawatha!"

"Hi-au-ha!" replied the chorus,
"Way-ha-way!" the mystic chorus.

Then they shook their medicine-pouches
O'er the head of Hiawatha,
Danced their medicine-dance around him;
And upstarting wild and haggard,
Like a man from dreams awakened,
He was healed of all his madness.
As the clouds are swept from heaven,
Straightway from his brain departed
All his moody melancholy;

As the ice is swept from rivers,
Straightway from his heart departed
All his sorrow and affliction.

Then they summoned Chibiabos
From his grave beneath the waters,
From the sands of Gitche Gumee
Summoned Hiawatha's brother.
And so mighty was the magic
Of that cry and invocation,
That he heard it as he lay there
Underneath the Big-Sea-Water;
From the sand he rose and listened,
Heard the music and the singing,
Came, obedient to the summons,
To the doorway of the wigwam,
But to enter they forbade him.

Through a chink a coal they gave him,
Through the door a burning fire-brand;
Ruler in the Land of Spirits,
Ruler o'er the dead, they made him,
Telling him a fire to kindle
For all those that died thereafter,
Camp-fires for their night encampments
On their solitary journey
To the kingdom of Ponemah,
To the land of the Hereafter.

From the village of his childhood,
From the homes of those who knew him,
Passing silent through the forest,
Like a smoke-wreath wafted sideways,
Slowly vanished Chibiabos!
Where he passed, the branches moved not,
Where he trod, the grasses bent not,
And the fallen leaves of last year
Made no sound beneath his footstep.

Four whole days he journeyed onward
Down the pathway of the dead men;
On the dead-man's strawberry feasted,
Crossed the melancholy river,
On the swinging log he crossed it,

Came unto the Lake of Silver,
In the Stone Canoe was carried
To the Islands of the Blessed,
To the land of ghosts and shadows.

On that journey, moving slowly,
Many weary spirits saw he,
Panting under heavy burdens,
Laden with war-clubs, bows and arrows,
Robes of fur, and pots and kettles,
And with food that friends had given
For that solitary journey.

"Ay! why do the living," said they,
"Lay such heavy burdens on us!
Better were it to go naked,
Better were it to go fasting,
Than to bear such heavy burdens
On our long and weary journey!"
Forth then issued Hiawatha,
Wandered eastward, wandered westward,
Teaching men the use of simples
And the antidotes for poisons,
And the cure of all diseases.
Thus was first made known to mortals
All the mystery of Medamin,
All the sacred art of healing.

XVI. PAU-PUK-KEEWIS

You shall hear how Pau-Puk-Keewis,
He, the handsome Yenadizze,
Whom the people called the Storm-Fool,
Vexed the village with disturbance;
You shall hear of all his mischief,
And his flight from Hiawatha,
And his wondrous transmigrations,
And the end of his adventures.

On the shores of Gitche Gumee,
On the dunes of Nagow Wudjoo,
By the shining Big-Sea-Water
Stood the lodge of Pau-Puk-Keewis.

It was he who in his frenzy
Whirled these drifting sands together,
On the dunes of Nagow Wudjoo,
When, among the guests assembled,
He so merrily and madly
Danced at Hiawatha's wedding,
Danced the Beggar's Dance to please them.

Now, in search of new adventures,
From his lodge went Pau-Puk-Keewis,
Came with speed into the village,
Found the young men all assembled
In the lodge of old Iagoo,
Listening to his monstrous stories,
To his wonderful adventures.

He was telling them the story
Of Ojeeg, the Summer-Maker,
How he made a hole in heaven,
How he climbed up into heaven,
And let out the summer-weather,
The perpetual, pleasant Summer;
How the Otter first essayed it;
How the Beaver, Lynx, and Badger
Tried in turn the great achievement,
From the summit of the mountain
Smote their fists against the heavens,
Smote against the sky their foreheads,
Cracked the sky, but could not break it;
How the Wolverine, uprising,
Made him ready for the encounter,
Bent his knees down, like a squirrel,
Drew his arms back, like a cricket.

"Once he leaped," said old Iagoo,
"Once he leaped, and lo! above him
Bent the sky, as ice in rivers
When the waters rise beneath it;
Twice he leaped, and lo! above him
Cracked the sky, as ice in rivers
When the freshet is at highest!
Thrice he leaped, and lo! above him
Broke the shattered sky asunder,
And he disappeared within it,

And Ojeeg, the Fisher Weasel,
With a bound went in behind him!"

"Hark you!" shouted Pau-Puk-Keewis
As he entered at the doorway;
"I am tired of all this talking,
Tired of old Iagoo's stories,
Tired of Hiawatha's wisdom.
Here is something to amuse you,
Better than this endless talking."

Then from out his pouch of wolf-skin
Forth he drew, with solemn manner,
All the game of Bowl and Counters,
Pugasaing, with thirteen pieces.
White on one side were they painted,
And vermilion on the other;
Two Kenabeeks or great serpents,
Two Ininewug or wedge-men,
One great war-club, Pugamaugun,
And one slender fish, the Keego,
Four round pieces, Ozawabeeks,
And three Sheshebwug or ducklings.
All were made of bone and painted,
All except the Ozawabeeks;
These were brass, on one side burnished,
And were black upon the other.

In a wooden bowl he placed them,
Shook and jostled them together,
Threw them on the ground before him,
Thus exclaiming and explaining:
"Red side up are all the pieces,
And one great Kenabeek standing
On the bright side of a brass piece,
On a burnished Ozawabeek;
Thirteen tens and eight are counted."

Then again he shook the pieces,
Shook and jostled them together,
Threw them on the ground before him,
Still exclaiming and explaining:
"White are both the great Kenabeeks,
White the Ininewug, the wedge-men,

Red are all the other pieces;
Five tens and an eight are counted."

Thus he taught the game of hazard,
Thus displayed it and explained it,
Running through its various chances,
Various changes, various meanings:
Twenty curious eyes stared at him,
Full of eagerness stared at him.

"Many games," said old Iagoo,
"Many games of skill and hazard
Have I seen in different nations,
Have I played in different countries.
He who plays with old Iagoo
Must have very nimble fingers;
Though you think yourself so skilful,
I can beat you, Pau-Puk-Keewis,
I can even give you lessons
In your game of Bowl and Counters!"

So they sat and played together,
All the old men and the young men,
Played for dresses, weapons, wampum,
Played till midnight, played till morning,
Played until the Yenadizze,
Till the cunning Pau-Puk-Keewis,
Of their treasures had despoiled them,
Of the best of all their dresses,
Shirts of deer-skin, robes of ermine,
Belts of wampum, crests of feathers,
Warlike weapons, pipes and pouches.
Twenty eyes glared wildly at him,
Like the eyes of wolves glared at him.

Said the lucky Pau-Puk-Keewis:
"In my wigwam I am lonely,
In my wanderings and adventures
I have need of a companion,
Fain would have a Meshinauwa,
An attendant and pipe-bearer.
I will venture all these winnings,
All these garments heaped about me,
All this wampum, all these feathers,

On a single throw will venture
All against the young man yonder!"
`T was a youth of sixteen summers,
`T was a nephew of Iagoo;
Face-in-a-Mist, the people called him.

As the fire burns in a pipe-head
Dusky red beneath the ashes,
So beneath his shaggy eyebrows
Glowed the eyes of old Iagoo.
"Ugh!" he answered very fiercely;
"Ugh!" they answered all and each one.

Seized the wooden bowl the old man,
Closely in his bony fingers
Clutched the fatal bowl, Onagon,
Shook it fiercely and with fury,
Made the pieces ring together
As he threw them down before him.

Red were both the great Kenabeeks,
Red the Ininewug, the wedge-men,
Red the Sheshebwug, the ducklings,
Black the four brass Ozawabeeks,
White alone the fish, the Keego;
Only five the pieces counted!

Then the smiling Pau-Puk-Keewis
Shook the bowl and threw the pieces;
Lightly in the air he tossed them,
And they fell about him scattered;
Dark and bright the Ozawabeeks,
Red and white the other pieces,
And upright among the others
One Ininewug was standing,
Even as crafty Pau-Puk-Keewis
Stood alone among the players,
Saying, "Five tens! mine the game is,"

Twenty eyes glared at him fiercely,
Like the eyes of wolves glared at him,
As he turned and left the wigwam,
Followed by his Meshinauwa,
By the nephew of Iagoo,

By the tall and graceful stripling,
Bearing in his arms the winnings,
Shirts of deer-skin, robes of ermine,
Belts of wampum, pipes and weapons.

"Carry them," said Pau-Puk-Keewis,
Pointing with his fan of feathers,
"To my wigwam far to eastward,
On the dunes of Nagow Wudjoo!"

Hot and red with smoke and gambling
Were the eyes of Pau-Puk-Keewis
As he came forth to the freshness
Of the pleasant Summer morning.
All the birds were singing gayly,
All the streamlets flowing swiftly,
And the heart of Pau-Puk-Keewis
Sang with pleasure as the birds sing,
Beat with triumph like the streamlets,
As he wandered through the village,
In the early gray of morning,
With his fan of turkey-feathers,
With his plumes and tufts of swan's down,
Till he reached the farthest wigwam,
Reached the lodge of Hiawatha.

Silent was it and deserted;
No one met him at the doorway,
No one came to bid him welcome;
But the birds were singing round it,
In and out and round the doorway,
Hopping, singing, fluttering, feeding,
And aloft upon the ridge-pole
Kahgahgee, the King of Ravens,
Sat with fiery eyes, and, screaming,
Flapped his wings at Pau-Puk-Keewis.

"All are gone! the lodge is empty!"
Thus it was spake Pau-Puk-Keewis,
In his heart resolving mischief
"Gone is wary Hiawatha,
Gone the silly Laughing Water,
Gone Nokomis, the old woman,
And the lodge is left unguarded!"

By the neck he seized the raven,
Whirled it round him like a rattle,
Like a medicine-pouch he shook it,
Strangled Kahgahgee, the raven,
From the ridge-pole of the wigwam
Left its lifeless body hanging,
As an insult to its master,
As a taunt to Hiawatha.

With a stealthy step he entered,
Round the lodge in wild disorder
Threw the household things about him,
Piled together in confusion
Bowls of wood and earthen kettles,
Robes of buffalo and beaver,
Skins of otter, lynx, and ermine,
As an insult to Nokomis,
As a taunt to Minnehaha.

Then departed Pau-Puk-Keewis,
Whistling, singing through the forest,
Whistling gayly to the squirrels,
Who from hollow boughs above him
Dropped their acorn-shells upon him,
Singing gayly to the wood birds,
Who from out the leafy darkness
Answered with a song as merry.

Then he climbed the rocky headlands,
Looking o'er the Gitche Gumee,
Perched himself upon their summit,
Waiting full of mirth and mischief
The return of Hiawatha.

Stretched upon his back he lay there;
Far below him splashed the waters,
Plashed and washed the dreamy waters;
Far above him swam the heavens,
Swam the dizzy, dreamy heavens;
Round him hovered, fluttered, rustled
Hiawatha's mountain chickens,
Flock-wise swept and wheeled about him,
Almost brushed him with their pinions.

And he killed them as he lay there,
Slaughtered them by tens and twenties,
Threw their bodies down the headland,
Threw them on the beach below him,
Till at length Kayoshk, the sea-gull,
Perched upon a crag above them,
Shouted: "It is Pau-Puk-Keewis!
He is slaying us by hundreds!
Send a message to our brother,
Tidings send to Hiawatha!"

XVII. THE HUNTING OF PAU-PUK-KEEWIS

Full of wrath was Hiawatha
When he came into the village,
Found the people in confusion,
Heard of all the misdemeanors,
All the malice and the mischief,
Of the cunning Pau-Puk-Keewis.

Hard his breath came through his nostrils,
Through his teeth he buzzed and muttered
Words of anger and resentment,
Hot and humming, like a hornet.
"I will slay this Pau-Puk-Keewis,
Slay this mischief-maker!" said he.
"Not so long and wide the world is,
Not so rude and rough the way is,
That my wrath shall not attain him,
That my vengeance shall not reach him!"

Then in swift pursuit departed
Hiawatha and the hunters
On the trail of Pau-Puk-Keewis,
Through the forest, where he passed it,
To the headlands where he rested;
But they found not Pau-Puk-Keewis,
Only in the trampled grasses,
In the whortleberry-bushes,
Found the couch where he had rested,
Found the impress of his body.

From the lowlands far beneath them,

From the Muskoday, the meadow,
Pau-Puk-Keewis, turning backward,
Made a gesture of defiance,
Made a gesture of derision;
And aloud cried Hiawatha,
From the summit of the mountains:
"Not so long and wide the world is,
Not so rude and rough the way is,
But my wrath shall overtake you,
And my vengeance shall attain you!"

Over rock and over river,
Through bush, and brake, and forest,
Ran the cunning Pau-Puk-Keewis;
Like an antelope he bounded,
Till he came unto a streamlet
In the middle of the forest,
To a streamlet still and tranquil,
That had overflowed its margin,
To a dam made by the beavers,
To a pond of quiet water,
Where knee-deep the trees were standing,
Where the water lilies floated,
Where the rushes waved and whispered.

On the dam stood Pau-Puk-Keewis,
On the dam of trunks and branches,
Through whose chinks the water spouted,
O'er whose summit flowed the streamlet.
From the bottom rose the beaver,
Looked with two great eyes of wonder,
Eyes that seemed to ask a question,
At the stranger, Pau-Puk-Keewis.

On the dam stood Pau-Puk-Keewis,
O'er his ankles flowed the streamlet,
Flowed the bright and silvery water,
And he spake unto the beaver,
With a smile he spake in this wise:

"O my friend Ahmeek, the beaver,
Cool and pleasant is the water;
Let me dive into the water,
Let me rest there in your lodges;

Change me, too, into a beaver!"

Cautiously replied the beaver,
With reserve he thus made answer:
"Let me first consult the others,
Let me ask the other beavers."
Down he sank into the water,
Heavily sank he, as a stone sinks,
Down among the leaves and branches,
Brown and matted at the bottom.

On the dam stood Pau-Puk-Keewis,
O'er his ankles flowed the streamlet,
Spouted through the chinks below him,
Dashed upon the stones beneath him,
Spread serene and calm before him,
And the sunshine and the shadows
Fell in flecks and gleams upon him,
Fell in little shining patches,
Through the waving, rustling branches.

From the bottom rose the beavers,
Silently above the surface
Rose one head and then another,
Till the pond seemed full of beavers,
Full of black and shining faces.

To the beavers Pau-Puk-Keewis
Spake entreating, said in this wise:
"Very pleasant is your dwelling,
O my friends! and safe from danger;
Can you not, with all your cunning,
All your wisdom and contrivance,
Change me, too, into a beaver?"

"Yes!" replied Ahmeek, the beaver,
He the King of all the beavers,
"Let yourself slide down among us,
Down into the tranquil water."

Down into the pond among them
Silently sank Pau-Puk-Keewis;
Black became his shirt of deer-skin,
Black his moccasins and leggings,

In a broad black tail behind him
Spread his fox-tails and his fringes;
He was changed into a beaver.

"Make me large," said Pau-Puk-Keewis,
"Make me large and make me larger,
Larger than the other beavers."
"Yes," the beaver chief responded,
"When our lodge below you enter,
In our wigwam we will make you
Ten times larger than the others."

Thus into the clear, brown water
Silently sank Pau-Puk-Keewis:
Found the bottom covered over
With the trunks of trees and branches,
Hoards of food against the winter,
Piles and heaps against the famine;
Found the lodge with arching doorway,
Leading into spacious chambers.

Here they made him large and larger,
Made him largest of the beavers,
Ten times larger than the others.
"You shall be our ruler," said they;
"Chief and King of all the beavers."

But not long had Pau-Puk-Keewis
Sat in state among the beavers,
When there came a voice, of warning
From the watchman at his station
In the water-flags and lilies,
Saying, "Here is Hiawatha!
Hiawatha with his hunters!"

Then they heard a cry above them,
Heard a shouting and a tramping,
Heard a crashing and a rushing,
And the water round and o'er them
Sank and sucked away in eddies,
And they knew their dam was broken.

On the lodge's roof the hunters
Leaped, and broke it all asunder;

Streamed the sunshine through the crevice,
Sprang the beavers through the doorway,
Hid themselves in deeper water,
In the channel of the streamlet;
But the mighty Pau-Puk-Keewis
Could not pass beneath the doorway;
He was puffed with pride and feeding,
He was swollen like a bladder.

Through the roof looked Hiawatha,
Cried aloud, "O Pau-Puk-Keewis
Vain are all your craft and cunning,
Vain your manifold disguises!
Well I know you, Pau-Puk-Keewis!"
With their clubs they beat and bruised him,
Beat to death poor Pau-Puk-Keewis,
Pounded him as maize is pounded,
Till his skull was crushed to pieces.

Six tall hunters, lithe and limber,
Bore him home on poles and branches,
Bore the body of the beaver;
But the ghost, the Jeebi in him,
Thought and felt as Pau-Puk-Keewis,
Still lived on as Pau-Puk-Keewis.

And it fluttered, strove, and struggled,
Waving hither, waving thither,
As the curtains of a wigwam
Struggle with their thongs of deer-skin,
When the wintry wind is blowing;
Till it drew itself together,
Till it rose up from the body,
Till it took the form and features
Of the cunning Pau-Puk-Keewis
Vanishing into the forest.

But the wary Hiawatha
Saw the figure ere it vanished,
Saw the form of Pau-Puk-Keewis
Glide into the soft blue shadow
Of the pine-trees of the forest;
Toward the squares of white beyond it,
Toward an opening in the forest.

Like a wind it rushed and panted,
Bending all the boughs before it,
And behind it, as the rain comes,
Came the steps of Hiawatha.

To a lake with many islands
Came the breathless Pau-Puk-Keewis,
Where among the water-lilies
Pishnekuh, the brant, were sailing;
Through the tufts of rushes floating,
Steering through the reedy Islands.
Now their broad black beaks they lifted,
Now they plunged beneath the water,
Now they darkened in the shadow,
Now they brightened in the sunshine.

"Pishnekuh!" cried Pau-Puk-Keewis,
"Pishnekuh! my brothers!" said he,
"Change me to a brant with plumage,
With a shining neck and feathers,
Make me large, and make me larger,
Ten times larger than the others."

Straightway to a brant they changed him,
With two huge and dusky pinions,
With a bosom smooth and rounded,
With a bill like two great paddles,
Made him larger than the others,
Ten times larger than the largest,
Just as, shouting from the forest,
On the shore stood Hiawatha.

Up they rose with cry and clamor,
With a whir and beat of pinions,
Rose up from the reedy Islands,
From the water-flags and lilies.
And they said to Pau-Puk-Keewis:
"In your flying, look not downward,
Take good heed and look not downward,
Lest some strange mischance should happen,
Lest some great mishap befall you!"

Fast and far they fled to northward,
Fast and far through mist and sunshine,

Fed among the moors and fen-lands,
Slept among the reeds and rushes.

On the morrow as they journeyed,
Buoyed and lifted by the South-wind,
Wafted onward by the South-wind,
Blowing fresh and strong behind them,
Rose a sound of human voices,
Rose a clamor from beneath them,
From the lodges of a village,
From the people miles beneath them.

For the people of the village
Saw the flock of brant with wonder,
Saw the wings of Pau-Puk-Keewis
Flapping far up in the ether,
Broader than two doorway curtains.

Pau-Puk-Keewis heard the shouting,
Knew the voice of Hiawatha,
Knew the outcry of Iagoo,
And, forgetful of the warning,
Drew his neck in, and looked downward,
And the wind that blew behind him
Caught his mighty fan of feathers,
Sent him wheeling, whirling downward!

All in vain did Pau-Puk-Keewis
Struggle to regain his balance!
Whirling round and round and downward,
He beheld in turn the village
And in turn the flock above him,
Saw the village coming nearer,
And the flock receding farther,
Heard the voices growing louder,
Heard the shouting and the laughter;
Saw no more the flocks above him,
Only saw the earth beneath him;
Dead out of the empty heaven,
Dead among the shouting people,
With a heavy sound and sullen,
Fell the brant with broken pinions.

But his soul, his ghost, his shadow,

Still survived as Pau-Puk-Keewis,
Took again the form and features
Of the handsome Yenadizze,
And again went rushing onward,
Followed fast by Hiawatha,
Crying: "Not so wide the world is,
Not so long and rough the way is,
But my wrath shall overtake you,
But my vengeance shall attain you!"

And so near he came, so near him,
That his hand was stretched to seize him,
His right hand to seize and hold him,
When the cunning Pau-Puk-Keewis
Whirled and spun about in circles,
Fanned the air into a whirlwind,
Danced the dust and leaves about him,
And amid the whirling eddies
Sprang into a hollow oak-tree,
Changed himself into a serpent,
Gliding out through root and rubbish.

With his right hand Hiawatha
Smote amain the hollow oak-tree,
Rent it into shreds and splinters,
Left it lying there in fragments.
But in vain; for Pau-Puk-Keewis,
Once again in human figure,
Full in sight ran on before him,
Sped away in gust and whirlwind,
On the shores of Gitche Gumee,
Westward by the Big-Sea-Water,
Came unto the rocky headlands,
To the Pictured Rocks of sandstone,
Looking over lake and landscape.

And the Old Man of the Mountain,
He the Manito of Mountains,
Opened wide his rocky doorways,
Opened wide his deep abysses,
Giving Pau-Puk-Keewis shelter
In his caverns dark and dreary,
Bidding Pau-Puk-Keewis welcome
To his gloomy lodge of sandstone.

There without stood Hiawatha,
Found the doorways closed against him,
With his mittens, Minjekahwun,
Smote great caverns in the sandstone,
Cried aloud in tones of thunder,
"Open! I am Hiawatha!"
But the Old Man of the Mountain
Opened not, and made no answer
From the silent crags of sandstone,
From the gloomy rock abysses.

Then he raised his hands to heaven,
Called imploring on the tempest,
Called Waywassimo, the lightning,
And the thunder, Annemeekee;
And they came with night and darkness,
Sweeping down the Big-Sea-Water
From the distant Thunder Mountains;
And the trembling Pau-Puk-Keewis
Heard the footsteps of the thunder,
Saw the red eyes of the lightning,
Was afraid, and crouched and trembled.

Then Waywassimo, the lightning,
Smote the doorways of the caverns,
With his war-club smote the doorways,
Smote the jutting crags of sandstone,
And the thunder, Annemeekee,
Shouted down into the caverns,
Saying, "Where is Pau-Puk-Keewis!"
And the crags fell, and beneath them
Dead among the rocky ruins
Lay the cunning Pau-Puk-Keewis,
Lay the handsome Yenadizze,
Slain in his own human figure.

Ended were his wild adventures,
Ended were his tricks and gambols,
Ended all his craft and cunning,
Ended all his mischief-making,
All his gambling and his dancing,
All his wooing of the maidens.

Then the noble Hiawatha

Took his soul, his ghost, his shadow,
Spake and said: "O Pau-Puk-Keewis,
Never more in human figure
Shall you search for new adventures;
Never more with jest and laughter
Dance the dust and leaves in whirlwinds;
But above there in the heavens
You shall soar and sail in circles;
I will change you to an eagle,
To Keneu, the great war-eagle,
Chief of all the fowls with feathers,
Chief of Hiawatha's chickens."

And the name of Pau-Puk-Keewis
Lingers still among the people,
Lingers still among the singers,
And among the story-tellers;
And in Winter, when the snow-flakes
Whirl in eddies round the lodges,
When the wind in gusty tumult
O'er the smoke-flue pipes and whistles,
"There," they cry, "comes Pau-Puk-Keewis,
He is dancing through the village,
He is gathering in his harvest!"

XVIII. THE DEATH OF KWASIND

Far and wide among the nations
Spread the name and fame of Kwasind;
No man dared to strive with Kwasind,
No man could compete with Kwasind.
But the mischievous Puk-Wudjies,
They the envious Little People,
They the fairies and the pygmies,
Plotted and conspired against him.

"If this hateful Kwasind," said they,
"If this great, outrageous fellow
Goes on thus a little longer,
Tearing everything he touches,
Rending everything to pieces,
Filling all the world with wonder,
What becomes of the Puk-Wudjies?

Who will care for the Puk-Wudjies?
He will tread us down like mushrooms,
Drive us all into the water,
Give our bodies to be eaten
By the wicked Nee-ba-naw-baigs,
By the Spirits of the water!"

So the angry Little People
All conspired against the Strong Man,
All conspired to murder Kwasind,
Yes, to rid the world of Kwasind,
The audacious, overbearing,
Heartless, haughty, dangerous Kwasind!

Now this wondrous strength of Kwasind
In his crown alone was seated;
In his crown too was his weakness;
There alone could he be wounded,
Nowhere else could weapon pierce him,
Nowhere else could weapon harm him.

Even there the only weapon
That could wound him, that could slay him,
Was the seed-cone of the pine-tree,
Was the blue cone of the fir-tree.
This was Kwasind's fatal secret,
Known to no man among mortals;
But the cunning Little People,
The Puk-Wudjies, knew the secret,
Knew the only way to kill him.

So they gathered cones together,
Gathered seed-cones of the pine-tree,
Gathered blue cones of the fir-tree,
In the woods by Taquamenaw,
Brought them to the river's margin,
Heaped them in great piles together,
Where the red rocks from the margin
Jutting overhang the river.
There they lay in wait for Kwasind,
The malicious Little People.

`T was an afternoon in Summer;
Very hot and still the air was,

Very smooth the gliding river,
Motionless the sleeping shadows:
Insects glistened in the sunshine,
Insects skated on the water,
Filled the drowsy air with buzzing,
With a far resounding war-cry.

Down the river came the Strong Man,
In his birch canoe came Kwasind,
Floating slowly down the current
Of the sluggish Taquamenaw,
Very languid with the weather,
Very sleepy with the silence.

From the overhanging branches,
From the tassels of the birch-trees,
Soft the Spirit of Sleep descended;
By his airy hosts surrounded,
His invisible attendants,
Came the Spirit of Sleep, Nepahwin;
Like a burnished Dush-kwo-ne-she,
Like a dragon-fly, he hovered
O'er the drowsy head of Kwasind.

To his ear there came a murmur
As of waves upon a sea-shore,
As of far-off tumbling waters,
As of winds among the pine-trees;
And he felt upon his forehead
Blows of little airy war-clubs,
Wielded by the slumbrous legions
Of the Spirit of Sleep, Nepahwin,
As of some one breathing on him.

At the first blow of their war-clubs,
Fell a drowsiness on Kwasind;
At the second blow they smote him,
Motionless his paddle rested;
At the third, before his vision
Reeled the landscape Into darkness,
Very sound asleep was Kwasind.

So he floated down the river,
Like a blind man seated upright,

Floated down the Taquamenaw,
Underneath the trembling birch-trees,
Underneath the wooded headlands,
Underneath the war encampment
Of the pygmies, the Puk-Wudjies.

There they stood, all armed and waiting,
Hurled the pine-cones down upon him,
Struck him on his brawny shoulders,
On his crown defenceless struck him.
"Death to Kwasind!" was the sudden
War-cry of the Little People.

And he sideways swayed and tumbled,
Sideways fell into the river,
Plunged beneath the sluggish water
Headlong, as an otter plunges;
And the birch canoe, abandoned,
Drifted empty down the river,
Bottom upward swerved and drifted:
Nothing more was seen of Kwasind.

But the memory of the Strong Man
Lingered long among the people,
And whenever through the forest
Raged and roared the wintry tempest,
And the branches, tossed and troubled,
Creaked and groaned and split asunder,
"Kwasind!" cried they; "that is Kwasind!
He is gathering in his fire-wood!"

XIX. THE GHOSTS

Never stoops the soaring vulture
On his quarry in the desert,
On the sick or wounded bison,
But another vulture, watching
From his high aerial look-out,
Sees the downward plunge, and follows;
And a third pursues the second,
Coming from the invisible ether,
First a speck, and then a vulture,
Till the air is dark with pinions.

So disasters come not singly;
But as if they watched and waited,
Scanning one another's motions,
When the first descends, the others
Follow, follow, gathering flock-wise
Round their victim, sick and wounded,
First a shadow, then a sorrow,
Till the air is dark with anguish.

Now, o'er all the dreary North-land,
Mighty Peboan, the Winter,
Breathing on the lakes and rivers,
Into stone had changed their waters.
From his hair he shook the snow-flakes,
Till the plains were strewn with whiteness,
One uninterrupted level,
As if, stooping, the Creator
With his hand had smoothed them over.

Through the forest, wide and wailing,
Roamed the hunter on his snow-shoes;
In the village worked the women,
Pounded maize, or dressed the deer-skin;
And the young men played together
On the ice the noisy ball-play,
On the plain the dance of snow-shoes.

One dark evening, after sundown,
In her wigwam Laughing Water
Sat with old Nokomis, waiting
For the steps of Hiawatha
Homeward from the hunt returning.

On their faces gleamed the firelight,
Painting them with streaks of crimson,
In the eyes of old Nokomis
Glimmered like the watery moonlight,
In the eyes of Laughing Water
Glistened like the sun in water;
And behind them crouched their shadows
In the corners of the wigwam,
And the smoke in wreaths above them
Climbed and crowded through the smoke-flue.

Then the curtain of the doorway
From without was slowly lifted;
Brighter glowed the fire a moment,
And a moment swerved the smoke-wreath,
As two women entered softly,
Passed the doorway uninvited,
Without word of salutation,
Without sign of recognition,
Sat down in the farthest corner,
Crouching low among the shadows.

From their aspect and their garments,
Strangers seemed they in the village;
Very pale and haggard were they,
As they sat there sad and silent,
Trembling, cowering with the shadows.

Was it the wind above the smoke-flue,
Muttering down into the wigwam?
Was it the owl, the Koko-koho,
Hooting from the dismal forest?
Sure a voice said in the silence:
"These are corpses clad in garments,
These are ghosts that come to haunt you,
From the kingdom of Ponemah,
From the land of the Hereafter!"

Homeward now came Hiawatha
From his hunting in the forest,
With the snow upon his tresses,
And the red deer on his shoulders.
At the feet of Laughing Water
Down he threw his lifeless burden;
Nobler, handsomer she thought him,
Than when first he came to woo her,
First threw down the deer before her,
As a token of his wishes,
As a promise of the future.

Then he turned and saw the strangers,
Cowering, crouching with the shadows;
Said within himself, "Who are they?
What strange guests has Minnehaha?"
But he questioned not the strangers,

Only spake to bid them welcome
To his lodge, his food, his fireside.

When the evening meal was ready,
And the deer had been divided,
Both the pallid guests, the strangers,
Springing from among the shadows,
Seized upon the choicest portions,
Seized the white fat of the roebuck,
Set apart for Laughing Water,
For the wife of Hiawatha;
Without asking, without thanking,
Eagerly devoured the morsels,
Flitted back among the shadows
In the corner of the wigwam.

Not a word spake Hiawatha,
Not a motion made Nokomis,
Not a gesture Laughing Water;
Not a change came o'er their features;
Only Minnehaha softly
Whispered, saying, "They are famished;
Let them do what best delights them;
Let them eat, for they are famished."

Many a daylight dawned and darkened,
Many a night shook off the daylight
As the pine shakes off the snow-flakes
From the midnight of its branches;
Day by day the guests unmoving
Sat there silent in the wigwam;
But by night, in storm or starlight,
Forth they went into the forest,
Bringing fire-wood to the wigwam,
Bringing pine-cones for the burning,
Always sad and always silent.

And whenever Hiawatha
Came from fishing or from hunting,
When the evening meal was ready,
And the food had been divided,
Gliding from their darksome corner,
Came the pallid guests, the strangers,
Seized upon the choicest portions

Set aside for Laughing Water,
And without rebuke or question
Flitted back among the shadows.

Never once had Hiawatha
By a word or look reproved them;
Never once had old Nokomis
Made a gesture of impatience;
Never once had Laughing Water
Shown resentment at the outrage.
All had they endured in silence,
That the rights of guest and stranger,
That the virtue of free-giving,
By a look might not be lessened,
By a word might not be broken.

Once at midnight Hiawatha,
Ever wakeful, ever watchful,
In the wigwam, dimly lighted
By the brands that still were burning,
By the glimmering, flickering firelight
Heard a sighing, oft repeated,

From his couch rose Hiawatha,
From his shaggy hides of bison,
Pushed aside the deer-skin curtain,
Saw the pallid guests, the shadows,
Sitting upright on their couches,
Weeping in the silent midnight.

And he said: "O guests! why is it
That your hearts are so afflicted,
That you sob so in the midnight?
Has perchance the old Nokomis,
Has my wife, my Minnehaha,
Wronged or grieved you by unkindness,
Failed in hospitable duties?"

Then the shadows ceased from weeping,
Ceased from sobbing and lamenting,
And they said, with gentle voices:
"We are ghosts of the departed,
Souls of those who once were with you.
From the realms of Chibiabos

Hither have we come to try you,
Hither have we come to warn you.

"Cries of grief and lamentation
Reach us in the Blessed Islands;
Cries of anguish from the living,
Calling back their friends departed,
Sadden us with useless sorrow.
Therefore have we come to try you;
No one knows us, no one heeds us.
We are but a burden to you,
And we see that the departed
Have no place among the living.

"Think of this, O Hiawatha!
Speak of it to all the people,
That henceforward and forever
They no more with lamentations
Sadden the souls of the departed
In the Islands of the Blessed.

"Do not lay such heavy burdens
In the graves of those you bury,
Not such weight of furs and wampum,
Not such weight of pots and kettles,
For the spirits faint beneath them.
Only give them food to carry,
Only give them fire to light them.

"Four days is the spirit's journey
To the land of ghosts and shadows,
Four its lonely night encampments;
Four times must their fires be lighted.
Therefore, when the dead are buried,
Let a fire, as night approaches,
Four times on the grave be kindled,
That the soul upon its journey
May not lack the cheerful firelight,
May not grope about in darkness.

"Farewell, noble Hiawatha!
We have put you to the trial,
To the proof have put your patience,
By the insult of our presence,

By the outrage of our actions.
We have found you great and noble.
Fail not in the greater trial,
Faint not in the harder struggle."

When they ceased, a sudden darkness
Fell and filled the silent wigwam.
Hiawatha heard a rustle
As of garments trailing by him,
Heard the curtain of the doorway
Lifted by a hand he saw not,
Felt the cold breath of the night air,
For a moment saw the starlight;
But he saw the ghosts no longer,
Saw no more the wandering spirits
From the kingdom of Ponemah,
From the land of the Hereafter.

XX. THE FAMINE

Oh the long and dreary Winter!
Oh the cold and cruel Winter!
Ever thicker, thicker, thicker
Froze the ice on lake and river,
Ever deeper, deeper, deeper
Fell the snow o'er all the landscape,
Fell the covering snow, and drifted
Through the forest, round the village.
Hardly from his buried wigwam
Could the hunter force a passage;
With his mittens and his snow-shoes
Vainly walked he through the forest,
Sought for bird or beast and found none,
Saw no track of deer or rabbit,
In the snow beheld no footprints,
In the ghastly, gleaming forest
Fell, and could not rise from weakness,
Perished there from cold and hunger.

Oh the famine and the fever!
Oh the wasting of the famine!
Oh the blasting of the fever!
Oh the wailing of the children!

Oh the anguish of the women!

All the earth was sick and famished;
Hungry was the air around them,
Hungry was the sky above them,
And the hungry stars in heaven
Like the eyes of wolves glared at them!

Into Hiawatha's wigwam
Came two other guests, as silent
As the ghosts were, and as gloomy,
Waited not to be invited
Did not parley at the doorway
Sat there without word of welcome
In the seat of Laughing Water;
Looked with haggard eyes and hollow
At the face of Laughing Water.

And the foremost said: "Behold me!
I am Famine, Bukadawin!"
And the other said: "Behold me!
I am Fever, Ahkosewin!"

And the lovely Minnehaha
Shuddered as they looked upon her,
Shuddered at the words they uttered,
Lay down on her bed in silence,
Hid her face, but made no answer;
Lay there trembling, freezing, burning
At the looks they cast upon her,
At the fearful words they uttered.

Forth into the empty forest
Rushed the maddened Hiawatha;
In his heart was deadly sorrow,
In his face a stony firmness;
On his brow the sweat of anguish
Started, but it froze and fell not.

Wrapped in furs and armed for hunting,
With his mighty bow of ash-tree,
With his quiver full of arrows,
With his mittens, Minjekahwun,
Into the vast and vacant forest

On his snow-shoes strode he forward.

"Gitche Manito, the Mighty!"
Cried he with his face uplifted
In that bitter hour of anguish,
"Give your children food, O father!
Give us food, or we must perish!
Give me food for Minnehaha,
For my dying Minnehaha!"

Through the far-resounding forest,
Through the forest vast and vacant
Rang that cry of desolation,
But there came no other answer
Than the echo of his crying,
Than the echo of the woodlands,
"Minnehaha! Minnehaha!"

All day long roved Hiawatha
In that melancholy forest,
Through the shadow of whose thickets,
In the pleasant days of Summer,
Of that ne'er forgotten Summer,
He had brought his young wife homeward
From the land of the Dacotahs;
When the birds sang in the thickets,
And the streamlets laughed and glistened,
And the air was full of fragrance,
And the lovely Laughing Water
Said with voice that did not tremble,
"I will follow you, my husband!"

In the wigwam with Nokomis,
With those gloomy guests that watched her,
With the Famine and the Fever,
She was lying, the Beloved,
She, the dying Minnehaha.

"Hark!" she said; "I hear a rushing,
Hear a roaring and a rushing,
Hear the Falls of Minnehaha
Calling to me from a distance!"
"No, my child!" said old Nokomis,
"'T is the night-wind in the pine-trees!"

"Look!" she said; "I see my father
Standing lonely at his doorway,
Beckoning to me from his wigwam
In the land of the Dacotahs!"
"No, my child!" said old Nokomis.
"'T is the smoke, that waves and beckons!"
"Ah!" said she, "the eyes of Pauguk
Glare upon me in the darkness,
I can feel his icy fingers
Clasping mine amid the darkness!
Hiawatha! Hiawatha!"

And the desolate Hiawatha,
Far away amid the forest,
Miles away among the mountains,
Heard that sudden cry of anguish,
Heard the voice of Minnehaha
Calling to him in the darkness,
"Hiawatha! Hiawatha!"

Over snow-fields waste and pathless,
Under snow-encumbered branches,
Homeward hurried Hiawatha,
Empty-handed, heavy-hearted,
Heard Nokomis moaning, wailing:
"Wahonowin! Wahonowin!
Would that I had perished for you,
Would that I were dead as you are!
Wahonowin! Wahonowin!"

And he rushed into the wigwam,
Saw the old Nokomis slowly
Rocking to and fro and moaning,
Saw his lovely Minnehaha
Lying dead and cold before him,
And his bursting heart within him
Uttered such a cry of anguish,
That the forest moaned and shuddered,
That the very stars in heaven
Shook and trembled with his anguish.

Then he sat down, still and speechless,
On the bed of Minnehaha,
At the feet of Laughing Water,

At those willing feet, that never
More would lightly run to meet him,
Never more would lightly follow.

With both hands his face he covered,
Seven long days and nights he sat there,
As if in a swoon he sat there,
Speechless, motionless, unconscious
Of the daylight or the darkness.

Then they buried Minnehaha;
In the snow a grave they made her
In the forest deep and darksome
Underneath the moaning hemlocks;
Clothed her in her richest garments
Wrapped her in her robes of ermine,
Covered her with snow, like ermine;
Thus they buried Minnehaha.

And at night a fire was lighted,
On her grave four times was kindled,
For her soul upon its journey
To the Islands of the Blessed.
From his doorway Hiawatha
Saw it burning in the forest,
Lighting up the gloomy hemlocks;
From his sleepless bed uprising,
From the bed of Minnehaha,
Stood and watched it at the doorway,
That it might not be extinguished,

Might not leave her in the darkness.
"Farewell!" said he, "Minnehaha!
Farewell, O my Laughing Water!
All my heart is buried with you,
All my thoughts go onward with you!
Come not back again to labor,
Come not back again to suffer,
Where the Famine and the Fever
Wear the heart and waste the body.
Soon my task will be completed,
Soon your footsteps I shall follow
To the Islands of the Blessed,
To the Kingdom of Ponemah,

To the Land of the Hereafter!"

XXI. THE WHITE MAN'S FOOT

In his lodge beside a river,
Close beside a frozen river,
Sat an old man, sad and lonely.
White his hair was as a snow-drift;
Dull and low his fire was burning,
And the old man shook and trembled,
Folded in his Waubewyon,
In his tattered white-skin-wrapper,
Hearing nothing but the tempest
As it roared along the forest,
Seeing nothing but the snow-storm,
As it whirled and hissed and drifted.

All the coals were white with ashes,
And the fire was slowly dying,
As a young man, walking lightly,
At the open doorway entered.
Red with blood of youth his cheeks were,
Soft his eyes, as stars in Spring-time,
Bound his forehead was with grasses;
Bound and plumed with scented grasses,
On his lips a smile of beauty,
Filling all the lodge with sunshine,
In his hand a bunch of blossoms
Filling all the lodge with sweetness.

"Ah, my son!" exclaimed the old man,
"Happy are my eyes to see you.
Sit here on the mat beside me,
Sit here by the dying embers,
Let us pass the night together,
Tell me of your strange adventures,
Of the lands where you have travelled;
I will tell you of my prowess,
Of my many deeds of wonder."

From his pouch he drew his peace-pipe,
Very old and strangely fashioned;
Made of red stone was the pipe-head,

And the stem a reed with feathers;
Filled the pipe with bark of willow,
Placed a burning coal upon it,
Gave it to his guest, the stranger,
And began to speak in this wise:
"When I blow my breath about me,
When I breathe upon the landscape,
Motionless are all the rivers,
Hard as stone becomes the water!"

And the young man answered, smiling:
"When I blow my breath about me,
When I breathe upon the landscape,
Flowers spring up o'er all the meadows,
Singing, onward rush the rivers!"

"When I shake my hoary tresses,"
Said the old man darkly frowning,
"All the land with snow is covered;
All the leaves from all the branches
Fall and fade and die and wither,
For I breathe, and lo! they are not.
From the waters and the marshes,
Rise the wild goose and the heron,
Fly away to distant regions,
For I speak, and lo! they are not.
And where'er my footsteps wander,
All the wild beasts of the forest
Hide themselves in holes and caverns,
And the earth becomes as flintstone!"

"When I shake my flowing ringlets,"
Said the young man, softly laughing,
"Showers of rain fall warm and welcome,
Plants lift up their heads rejoicing,
Back unto their lakes and marshes
Come the wild goose and the heron,
Homeward shoots the arrowy swallow,
Sing the bluebird and the robin,
And where'er my footsteps wander,
All the meadows wave with blossoms,
All the woodlands ring with music,
All the trees are dark with foliage!"

While they spake, the night departed:
From the distant realms of Wabun,
From his shining lodge of silver,
Like a warrior robed and painted,
Came the sun, and said, "Behold me
Gheezis, the great sun, behold me!"

Then the old man's tongue was speechless
And the air grew warm and pleasant,
And upon the wigwam sweetly
Sang the bluebird and the robin,
And the stream began to murmur,
And a scent of growing grasses
Through the lodge was gently wafted.

And Segwun, the youthful stranger,
More distinctly in the daylight
Saw the icy face before him;
It was Peboan, the Winter!

From his eyes the tears were flowing,
As from melting lakes the streamlets,
And his body shrunk and dwindled
As the shouting sun ascended,
Till into the air it faded,
Till into the ground it vanished,
And the young man saw before him,
On the hearth-stone of the wigwam,
Where the fire had smoked and smouldered,
Saw the earliest flower of Spring-time,
Saw the Beauty of the Spring-time,
Saw the Miskodeed in blossom.

Thus it was that in the North-land
After that unheard-of coldness,
That intolerable Winter,
Came the Spring with all its splendor,
All its birds and all its blossoms,
All its flowers and leaves and grasses.

Sailing on the wind to northward,
Flying in great flocks, like arrows,
Like huge arrows shot through heaven,
Passed the swan, the Mahnahbezee,

Speaking almost as a man speaks;
And in long lines waving, bending
Like a bow-string snapped asunder,
Came the white goose, Waw-be-wawa;
And in pairs, or singly flying,
Mahng the loon, with clangorous pinions,
The blue heron, the Shuh-shuh-gah,
And the grouse, the Mushkodasa.

In the thickets and the meadows
Piped the bluebird, the Owaissa,
On the summit of the lodges
Sang the robin, the Opechee,
In the covert of the pine-trees
Cooed the pigeon, the Omemee;
And the sorrowing Hiawatha,
Speechless in his infinite sorrow,
Heard their voices calling to him,
Went forth from his gloomy doorway,
Stood and gazed into the heaven,
Gazed upon the earth and waters.

From his wanderings far to eastward,
From the regions of the morning,
From the shining land of Wabun,
Homeward now returned Iagoo,
The great traveller, the great boaster,
Full of new and strange adventures,
Marvels many and many wonders.

And the people of the village
Listened to him as he told them
Of his marvellous adventures,
Laughing answered him in this wise:
"Ugh! it is indeed Iagoo!
No one else beholds such wonders!"

He had seen, he said, a water
Bigger than the Big-Sea-Water,
Broader than the Gitche Gumee,
Bitter so that none could drink it!
At each other looked the warriors,
Looked the women at each other,
Smiled, and said, "It cannot be so!"

Kaw!" they said, "it cannot be so!"

O'er it, said he, o'er this water
Came a great canoe with pinions,
A canoe with wings came flying,
Bigger than a grove of pine-trees,
Taller than the tallest tree-tops!
And the old men and the women
Looked and tittered at each other;
"Kaw!" they said, "we don't believe it!"

From its mouth, he said, to greet him,
Came Waywassimo, the lightning,
Came the thunder, Annemeekee!
And the warriors and the women
Laughed aloud at poor Iagoo;
"Kaw!" they said, "what tales you tell us!"

In it, said he, came a people,
In the great canoe with pinions
Came, he said, a hundred warriors;
Painted white were all their faces
And with hair their chins were covered!
And the warriors and the women
Laughed and shouted in derision,
Like the ravens on the tree-tops,
Like the crows upon the hemlocks.
"Kaw!" they said, "what lies you tell us!
Do not think that we believe them!"

Only Hiawatha laughed not,
But he gravely spake and answered
To their jeering and their jesting:
"True is all Iagoo tells us;
I have seen it in a vision,
Seen the great canoe with pinions,
Seen the people with white faces,
Seen the coming of this bearded
People of the wooden vessel
From the regions of the morning,
From the shining land of Wabun.

"Gitche Manito, the Mighty,
The Great Spirit, the Creator,

Sends them hither on his errand.
Sends them to us with his message.
Wheresoe'er they move, before them
Swarms the stinging fly, the Ahmo,
Swarms the bee, the honey-maker;
Wheresoe'er they tread, beneath them
Springs a flower unknown among us,
Springs the White-man's Foot in blossom.

"Let us welcome, then, the strangers,
Hail them as our friends and brothers,
And the heart's right hand of friendship
Give them when they come to see us.
Gitche Manito, the Mighty,
Said this to me in my vision.

"I beheld, too, in that vision
All the secrets of the future,
Of the distant days that shall be.
I beheld the westward marches
Of the unknown, crowded nations.
All the land was full of people,
Restless, struggling, toiling, striving,
Speaking many tongues, yet feeling
But one heart-beat in their bosoms.
In the woodlands rang their axes,
Smoked their towns in all the valleys,
Over all the lakes and rivers
Rushed their great canoes of thunder.

"Then a darker, drearier vision
Passed before me, vague and cloud-like;
I beheld our nation scattered,
All forgetful of my counsels,
Weakened, warring with each other:
Saw the remnants of our people
Sweeping westward, wild and woful,
Like the cloud-rack of a tempest,
Like the withered leaves of Autumn!"

XXII. HIAWATHA'S DEPARTURE

By the shore of Gitche Gumee,

By the shining Big-Sea-Water,
At the doorway of his wigwam,
In the pleasant Summer morning,
Hiawatha stood and waited.
All the air was full of freshness,
All the earth was bright and joyous,
And before him, through the sunshine,
Westward toward the neighboring forest
Passed in golden swarms the Ahmo,
Passed the bees, the honey-makers,
Burning, singing in the sunshine.

Bright above him shone the heavens,
Level spread the lake before him;
From its bosom leaped the sturgeon,
Sparkling, flashing in the sunshine;
On its margin the great forest
Stood reflected in the water,
Every tree-top had its shadow,
Motionless beneath the water.

From the brow of Hiawatha
Gone was every trace of sorrow,
As the fog from off the water,
As the mist from off the meadow.
With a smile of joy and triumph,
With a look of exultation,
As of one who in a vision
Sees what is to be, but is not,
Stood and waited Hiawatha.

Toward the sun his hands were lifted,
Both the palms spread out against it,
And between the parted fingers
Fell the sunshine on his features,
Flecked with light his naked shoulders,
As it falls and flecks an oak-tree
Through the rifted leaves and branches.

O'er the water floating, flying,
Something in the hazy distance,
Something in the mists of morning,
Loomed and lifted from the water,
Now seemed floating, now seemed flying,

Coming nearer, nearer, nearer.

Was it Shingebis the diver?
Or the pelican, the Shada?
Or the heron, the Shuh-shuh-gah?
Or the white goose, Waw-be-wawa,
With the water dripping, flashing,
From its glossy neck and feathers?

It was neither goose nor diver,
Neither pelican nor heron,
O'er the water floating, flying,
Through the shining mist of morning,
But a birch canoe with paddles,
Rising, sinking on the water,
Dripping, flashing in the sunshine;
And within it came a people
From the distant land of Wabun,
From the farthest realms of morning
Came the Black-Robe chief, the Prophet,
He the Priest of Prayer, the Pale-face,
With his guides and his companions.

And the noble Hiawatha,
With his hands aloft extended,
Held aloft in sign of welcome,
Waited, full of exultation,
Till the birch canoe with paddles
Grated on the shining pebbles,
Stranded on the sandy margin,
Till the Black-Robe chief, the Pale-face,
With the cross upon his bosom,
Landed on the sandy margin.

Then the joyous Hiawatha
Cried aloud and spake in this wise:
"Beautiful is the sun, O strangers,
When you come so far to see us!
All our town in peace awaits you,
All our doors stand open for you;
You shall enter all our wigwams,
For the heart's right hand we give you.

"Never bloomed the earth so gayly,

Never shone the sun so brightly,
As to-day they shine and blossom
When you come so far to see us!
Never was our lake so tranquil,
Nor so free from rocks, and sand-bars;
For your birch canoe in passing
Has removed both rock and sand-bar.
"Never before had our tobacco
Such a sweet and pleasant flavor,
Never the broad leaves of our cornfields
Were so beautiful to look on,
As they seem to us this morning,
When you come so far to see us!'

And the Black-Robe chief made answer,
Stammered in his speech a little,
Speaking words yet unfamiliar:
"Peace be with you, Hiawatha,
Peace be with you and your people,
Peace of prayer, and peace of pardon,
Peace of Christ, and joy of Mary!"

Then the generous Hiawatha
Led the strangers to his wigwam,
Seated them on skins of bison,
Seated them on skins of ermine,
And the careful old Nokomis
Brought them food in bowls of basswood,
Water brought in birchen dippers,
And the calumet, the peace-pipe,
Filled and lighted for their smoking.

All the old men of the village,
All the warriors of the nation,
All the Jossakeeds, the Prophets,
The magicians, the Wabenos,
And the Medicine-men, the Medas,
Came to bid the strangers welcome;
"It is well", they said, "O brothers,
That you come so far to see us!"

In a circle round the doorway,
With their pipes they sat in silence,
Waiting to behold the strangers,

Waiting to receive their message;
Till the Black-Robe chief, the Pale-face,
From the wigwam came to greet them,
Stammering in his speech a little,
Speaking words yet unfamiliar;
"It is well," they said, "O brother,
That you come so far to see us!"

Then the Black-Robe chief, the Prophet,
Told his message to the people,
Told the purport of his mission,
Told them of the Virgin Mary,
And her blessed Son, the Saviour,
How in distant lands and ages
He had lived on earth as we do;
How he fasted, prayed, and labored;
How the Jews, the tribe accursed,
Mocked him, scourged him, crucified him;
How he rose from where they laid him,
Walked again with his disciples,
And ascended into heaven.

And the chiefs made answer, saying:
"We have listened to your message,
We have heard your words of wisdom,
We will think on what you tell us.
It is well for us, O brothers,
That you come so far to see us!"

Then they rose up and departed
Each one homeward to his wigwam,
To the young men and the women
Told the story of the strangers
Whom the Master of Life had sent them
From the shining land of Wabun.

Heavy with the heat and silence
Grew the afternoon of Summer;
With a drowsy sound the forest
Whispered round the sultry wigwam,
With a sound of sleep the water
Rippled on the beach below it;
From the cornfields shrill and ceaseless
Sang the grasshopper, Pah-puk-keena;

And the guests of Hiawatha,
Weary with the heat of Summer,
Slumbered in the sultry wigwam.

Slowly o'er the simmering landscape
Fell the evening's dusk and coolness,
And the long and level sunbeams
Shot their spears into the forest,
Breaking through its shields of shadow,
Rushed into each secret ambush,
Searched each thicket, dingle, hollow;
Still the guests of Hiawatha
Slumbered in the silent wigwam.

From his place rose Hiawatha,
Bade farewell to old Nokomis,
Spake in whispers, spake in this wise,
Did not wake the guests, that slumbered.

"I am going, O Nokomis,
On a long and distant journey,
To the portals of the Sunset.
To the regions of the home-wind,
Of the Northwest-Wind, Keewaydin.
But these guests I leave behind me,
In your watch and ward I leave them;
See that never harm comes near them,
See that never fear molests them,
Never danger nor suspicion,
Never want of food or shelter,
In the lodge of Hiawatha!"

Forth into the village went he,
Bade farewell to all the warriors,
Bade farewell to all the young men,
Spake persuading, spake in this wise:

"I am going, O my people,
On a long and distant journey;
Many moons and many winters
Will have come, and will have vanished,
Ere I come again to see you.
But my guests I leave behind me;
Listen to their words of wisdom,

Listen to the truth they tell you,
For the Master of Life has sent them
From the land of light and morning!"

On the shore stood Hiawatha,
Turned and waved his hand at parting;
On the clear and luminous water
Launched his birch canoe for sailing,
From the pebbles of the margin
Shoved it forth into the water;
Whispered to it, "Westward! westward!"
And with speed it darted forward.

And the evening sun descending
Set the clouds on fire with redness,
Burned the broad sky, like a prairie,
Left upon the level water
One long track and trail of splendor,
Down whose stream, as down a river,
Westward, westward Hiawatha
Sailed into the fiery sunset,
Sailed into the purple vapors,
Sailed into the dusk of evening:

And the people from the margin
Watched him floating, rising, sinking,
Till the birch canoe seemed lifted
High into that sea of splendor,
Till it sank into the vapors
Like the new moon slowly, slowly
Sinking in the purple distance.

And they said, "Farewell forever!"
Said, "Farewell, O Hiawatha!"
And the forests, dark and lonely,
Moved through all their depths of darkness,
Sighed, "Farewell, O Hiawatha!"
And the waves upon the margin
Rising, rippling on the pebbles,
Sobbed, "Farewell, O Hiawatha!"
And the heron, the Shuh-shuh-gah,
From her haunts among the fen-lands,
Screamed, "Farewell, O Hiawatha!"

Thus departed Hiawatha,
Hiawatha the Beloved,
In the glory of the sunset,
In the purple mists of evening,
To the regions of the home-wind,
Of the Northwest-Wind, Keewaydin,
To the Islands of the Blessed,
To the Kingdom of Ponemah,
To the Land of the Hereafter!

THE COURTSHIP OF MILES STANDISH

THE COURTSHIP OF MILES STANDISH

I. MILES STANDISH

In the Old Colony days, in Plymouth the land of the Pilgrims,
To and fro in a room of his simple and primitive dwelling,
Clad in doublet and hose, and boots of Cordovan leather,
Strode, with martial air, Miles Standish the Puritan Captain.
Buried in thought he seemed, with his hands behind him, and pausing 5
Ever and anon to behold his glittering weapons of warfare,
Hanging in shining array along the walls of his chamber,—
Cutlass and corselet of steel, and his trusty sword of Damascus,
Curved at the point and inscribed with its mystical Arabic sentence,
While underneath, in a corner, were fowling-piece, musket and matchlock. 10
Short of stature he was, but strongly built and athletic,
Broad in the shoulders, deep-chested, with muscles and sinews of iron;
Brown as a nut was his face, but his russet beard was already
Flaked with patches of snow, as hedges sometimes in November.
Near him was seated John Alden, his friend and household companion, 15
Writing with diligent speed at a table of pine by the window;
Fair-haired, azure-eyed, with delicate Saxon complexion,
Having the dew of his youth, and the beauty thereof, as the captives
Whom Saint Gregory saw, and exclaimed, "Not Angles but Angels."
Youngest of all was he of the men who came in the Mayflower. 20

Suddenly breaking the silence, the diligent scribe interrupting,
Spake, in the pride of his heart, Miles Standish the Captain of Plymouth.

"Look at these arms," he said, "the warlike weapons that hang here
Burnished and bright and clean, as if for parade or inspection!
This is the sword of Damascus I fought with in Flanders; this breastplate,— 25
Well I remember the day!—once saved my life in a skirmish;
Here in front you can see the very dint of the bullet
Fired point-blank at my heart by a Spanish arcabucero.
Had it not been of sheer steel, the forgotten bones of Miles Standish
Would at this moment be mold, in their grave in the Flemish morasses." 30
Thereupon answered John Alden, but looked not up from his writing:
"Truly the breath of the Lord hath slackened the speed of the bullet;
He in his mercy preserved you, to be our shield and our weapon!"
Still the Captain continued, unheeding the words of the stripling:
"See, how bright they are burnished, as if in an arsenal hanging; 35
That is because I have done it myself, and not left it to others.
Serve yourself, would you be well served, is an excellent adage;
So I take care of my arms, as you of your pens and your inkhorn.
Then, too, there are my soldiers, my great, invincible army,
Twelve men, all equipped, having each his rest and his matchlock, 40
Eighteen shillings a month, together with diet and pillage,
And, like Cæsar, I know the name of each of my soldiers!"
This he said with a smile, that danced in his eyes, as the sunbeams
Dance on the waves of the sea, and vanish again in a moment.
Alden laughed as he wrote, and still the Captain continued: 45

"Look! you can see from this window my brazen howitzer planted
High on the roof of the church, a preacher who speaks to the purpose,
Steady, straightforward, and strong, with irresistible logic,
Orthodox, flashing conviction right into the hearts of the heathen.
Now we are ready, I think, for any assault of the Indians: 50
And the sooner they try it the better,—
Let them come if they like, be it sagamore, sachem, or pow-wow,
Aspinet, Samoset, Corbitant, Squanto, or Tokamahamon!"

Long at the window he stood, and wistfully gazed on the landscape,
Washed with a cold gray mist, the vapory breath of the east-wind, 55
Forest and meadow and hill, and the steel-blue rim of the ocean,
Lying silent and sad, in the afternoon shadows and sunshine.
Over his countenance flitted a shadow like those on the landscape,
Gloom intermingled with light; and his voice was subdued with emotion,
Tenderness, pity, regret, as after a pause he proceeded: 60
"Yonder there, on the hill by the sea, lies buried Rose Standish;
Beautiful rose of love, that bloomed for me by the wayside!
She was the first to die of all who came in the Mayflower!
Green above her is growing the field of wheat we have sown there,

Better to hide from the Indian scouts the graves of our people, 65
Lest they should count them and see how many already have perished!"
Sadly his face he averted, and strode up and down, and was thoughtful.

Fixed to the opposite wall was a shelf of books, and among them
Prominent three, distinguished alike for bulk and for binding:
Barriffe's Artillery Guide, and the Commentaries of Cæsar, 70
Out of the Latin translated by Arthur Goldinge of London,
And, as if guarded by these, between them was standing the Bible.
Musing a moment before them, Miles Standish paused, as if doubtful
Which of the three he should choose for his consolation and comfort,
Whether the wars of the Hebrews, the famous campaigns of the Romans, 75
Or the Artillery practice, designed for belligerent Christians.
Finally down from its shelf he dragged the ponderous Roman,
Seated himself at the window, and opened the book, and in silence
Turned o'er the well-worn leaves, where thumb-marks thick on the margin,
Like the trample of feet, proclaimed the battle was hottest. 80
Nothing was heard in the room but the hurrying pen of the stripling,
Busily writing epistles important, to go by the Mayflower,
Ready to sail on the morrow, or next day at latest, God willing!
Homeward bound with the tidings of all that terrible winter,
Letters written by Alden, and full of the name of Priscilla, 85
Full of the name and the fame of the Puritan maiden Priscilla!

II. LOVE AND FRIENDSHIP

Nothing was heard in the room but the hurrying pen of the stripling,
Or an occasional sigh from the laboring heart of the Captain,
Reading the marvelous words and achievements of Julius Cæsar.
After a while he exclaimed, as he smote with his hand, palm downwards, 90
Heavily on the page: "A wonderful man was this Cæsar!
You are a writer, and I am a fighter, but here is a fellow
Who could both write and fight, and in both was equally skillful!"
Straightway answered and spake John Alden, the comely, the youthful:
"Yes, he was equally skilled, as you say, with his pen and his weapons. 95
Somewhere have I read, but where I forget, he could dictate
Seven letters at once, at the same time writing his memoirs."
"Truly," continued the Captain, not heeding or hearing the other,
"Truly a wonderful man was this Caius Julius Cæsar!
'Better be first,' he said, 'in a little Iberian village, 100
Than be second in Rome,' and I think he was right when he said it.
Twice was he married before he was twenty, and many times after;
Battles five hundred he fought, and a thousand cities he conquered;

He, too, fought in Flanders, as he himself has recorded;
Finally he was stabbed by his friend, the orator Brutus! 105
Now, do you know what he did on a certain occasion in Flanders,
When the rear guard of his army retreated, the front giving way too,
And the immortal Twelfth Legion was crowded so closely together
There was no room for their swords? Why, he seized a shield from a soldier,
Put himself straight at the head of his troops, and commanded the captains, 110
Calling on each by his name, to order forward the ensigns;
Then to widen the ranks, and give more room for their weapons;
So he won the day, the battle of something-or-other.
That's what I always say; if you wish a thing to be well done,
You must do it yourself, you must not leave it to others!" 115

All was silent again; the Captain continued his reading.
Nothing was heard in the room but the hurrying pen of the stripling
Writing epistles important to go next day by the Mayflower,
Filled with the name and the fame of the Puritan maiden Priscilla;
Every sentence began or closed with the name of Priscilla, 120
Till the treacherous pen, to which he confided the secret,
Strove to betray it by singing and shouting the name of Priscilla!
Finally closing his book, with a bang of the ponderous cover,
Sudden and loud as the sound of a soldier grounding his musket,
Thus to the young man spake Miles Standish the Captain of Plymouth: 125
"When you have finished your work, I have something important to tell you.
Be not, however, in haste; I can wait; I shall not be impatient!"
Straightway Alden replied, as he folded the last of his letters,
Pushing his papers aside, and giving respectful attention:
"Speak; for whenever you speak, I am always ready to listen, 130
Always ready to hear whatever pertains to Miles Standish."
Thereupon answered the Captain, embarrassed, and culling his phrases:
"'Tis not good for a man to be alone, say the Scriptures.
This I have said before, and again and again I repeat it;
Every hour in the day, I think it, and feel it, and say it. 135
Since Rose Standish died, my life has been weary and dreary;
Sick at heart have I been, beyond the healing of friendship.
Oft in my lonely hours have I thought of the maiden Priscilla.
She is alone in the world; her father and mother and brother
Died in the winter together; I saw her going and coming, 140
Now to the grave of the dead, and now to the bed of the dying,
Patient, courageous, and strong, and said to myself, that if ever
There were angels on earth, as there are angels in heaven,
Two have I seen and known; and the angel whose name is Priscilla
Holds in my desolate life the place which the other abandoned. 145
Long have I cherished the thought, but never have dared to reveal it,

Being a coward in this, though valiant enough for the most part.
Go to the damsel Priscilla, the loveliest maiden of Plymouth,
Say that a blunt old Captain, a man not of words but of actions,
Offers his hand and his heart, the hand and heart of a soldier. 150
Not in these words, you know, but this in short is my meaning;
I am a maker of war, and not a maker of phrases.
You, who are bred as a scholar, can say it in elegant language,
Such as you read in your books of the pleadings and wooings of lovers,
Such as you think best adapted to win the heart of a maiden." 155

When he had spoken, John Alden, the fair-haired, taciturn stripling,
All aghast at his words, surprised, embarrassed, bewildered,
Trying to mask his dismay by treating the subject with lightness,
Trying to smile, and yet feeling his heart stand still in his bosom,
Just as a timepiece stops in a house that is stricken by lightning, 160
Thus made answer and spake, or rather stammered than answered:
"Such a message as that, I am sure I should mangle and mar it;
If you would have it well done,—I am only repeating your maxim,—
You must do it yourself, you must not leave it to others!"
But with the air of a man whom nothing can turn from his purpose, 165
Gravely shaking his head, made answer the Captain of Plymouth:
"Truly the maxim is good, and I do not mean to gainsay it;
But we must use it discreetly, and not waste powder for nothing.
Now, as I said before, I was never a maker of phrases.
I can march up to a fortress and summon the place to surrender, 170
But march up to a woman with such a proposal, I dare not.
I'm not afraid of bullets, nor shot from the mouth of a cannon,
But of a thundering 'No!' point-blank from the mouth of a woman,
That, I confess, I'm afraid of, nor am I ashamed to confess it!
So you must grant my request, for you are an elegant scholar, 175
Having the graces of speech, and skill in the turning of phrases."
Taking the hand of his friend, who still was reluctant and doubtful,
Holding it long in his own, and pressing it kindly, he added:
"Though I have spoken thus lightly, yet deep is the feeling that prompts me;
Surely you cannot refuse what I ask in the name of our friendship!" 180
Then made answer John Alden: "The name of friendship is sacred;
What you demand in that name, I have not the power to deny you!"
So the strong will prevailed, subduing and molding the gentler,
Friendship prevailed over love, and Alden went on his errand.

III. THE LOVER'S ERRAND

So the strong will prevailed, and Alden went on his errand, 185

Out of the street of the village, and into the paths of the forest.
Into the tranquil woods, where bluebirds and robins were building
Towns in the populous trees, with hanging gardens of verdure,
Peaceful, aerial cities of joy and affection and freedom.
All around him was calm, but within him commotion and conflict, 190
Love contending with friendship, and self with each generous impulse.
To and fro in his breast his thoughts were heaving and dashing,
As in a foundering ship, with every roll of the vessel,
Washes the bitter sea, the merciless surge of the ocean!
"Must I relinquish it all," he cried with a wild lamentation,—195
"Must I relinquish it all, the joy, the hope, the illusion?
Was it for this I have loved, and waited, and worshiped in silence?
Was it for this I have followed the flying feet and the shadow
Over the wintry sea, to the desolate shores of New England?
Truly the heart is deceitful, and out of its depths of corruption 200
Rise, like an exhalation, the misty phantoms of passion;
Angels of light they seem, but are only delusions of Satan.
All is clear to me now; I feel it, I see it distinctly!
This is the hand of the Lord; it is laid upon me in anger,
For I have followed too much the heart's desires and devices, 205
Worshiping Astaroth blindly, and impious idols of Baal.
This is the cross I must bear; the sin and the swift retribution."

So through the Plymouth woods John Alden went on his errand;
Crossing the brook at the ford, where it brawled over pebble and shallow,
Gathering still, as he went, the mayflowers blooming around him, 210
Fragrant, filling the air with a strange and wonderful sweetness,
Children lost in the woods, and covered with leaves in their slumber.
"Puritan flowers," he said, "and the type of Puritan maidens,
Modest and simple and sweet, the very type of Priscilla!
So I will take them to her; to Priscilla the mayflower of Plymouth, 215
Modest and simple and sweet, as a parting gift will I take them;
Breathing their silent farewells, as they fade and wither and perish,
Soon to be thrown away as is the heart of the giver."
So through the Plymouth woods John Alden went on his errand;
Came to an open space, and saw the disk of the ocean, 220
sailless, somber and cold with the comfortless breath of the east-wind;
Saw the new-built house, and people at work in a meadow;
Heard, as he drew near the door, the musical voice of Priscilla
Singing the hundredth Psalm, the grand old Puritan anthem,
Music that Luther sang to the sacred words of the Psalmist, 225
Full of the breath of the Lord, consoling and comforting many.
Then, as he opened the door, he beheld the form of the maiden
Seated beside her wheel, and the carded wool like a snow-drift

Piled at her knee, her white hands feeding the ravenous spindle,
While with her foot on the treadle she guided the wheel in its motion. $_{230}$
Open wide on her lap lay the well-worn psalm-book of Ainsworth,
Printed in Amsterdam, the words and the music together.
Rough-hewn, angular notes, like stones in the Avail of a churchyard,
Darkened and overhung by the running vine of the verses.
Such was the book from whose pages she sang the old Puritan anthem, $_{235}$
She, the Puritan girl, in the solitude of the forest,
Making the humble house and the modest apparel of homespun
Beautiful with her beauty, and rich with the wealth of her being!
Over him rushed, like a wind that is keen and cold and relentless,
Thoughts of what might have been, and the weight and woe of his errand; $_{240}$
All the dreams that had faded, and all the hopes that had vanished,
All his life henceforth a dreary and tenantless mansion,
Haunted by vain regrets, and pallid, sorrowful faces.
Still he said to himself, and almost fiercely he said it,
"Let not him that putteth his hand to the plow look backwards; $_{245}$
Though the plowshare cut through the flowers of life to its fountains,
Though it pass o'er the graves of the dead and the hearths of the living,
It is the will of the Lord; and his mercy endureth forever!"

So he entered the house; and the hum of the wheel and the singing
Suddenly ceased; for Priscilla, aroused by his step on the threshold, $_{250}$
Rose as he entered, and gave him her hand, in signal of welcome,
Saying, "I knew it was you, when I heard your step in the passage;
For I was thinking of you, as I sat there singing and spinning."
Awkward and dumb with delight, that a thought of him had been mingled
Thus in the sacred psalm, that came from the heart of the maiden, $_{255}$
Silent before her he stood, and gave her the flowers for an answer,
Finding no words for his thought. He remembered that day in the winter,
After the first great snow, when he broke a path from the village,
Reeling and plunging along through the drifts that encumbered the doorway,
Stamping the snow from his feet as he entered the house, and Priscilla $_{260}$
Laughed at his snowy locks, and gave him a seat by the fireside,
Grateful and pleased to know he had thought of her in the snow-storm.
Had he but spoken then, perhaps not in vain had he spoken!
Now it was all too late; the golden moment had vanished!
So he stood there abashed, and gave her the flowers for an answer. $_{265}$
Then they sat down and talked of the birds and the beautiful springtime;
Talked of their friends at home, and the Mayflower that sailed on the morrow.
"I have been thinking all day," said gently the Puritan maiden,
"Dreaming all night, and thinking all day, of the hedgerows of England,—
They are in blossom now, and the country is all like a garden; $_{270}$
Thinking of lanes and fields, and the song of the lark and the linnet,

Seeing the village street, and familiar faces of neighbors
Going about as of old, and stopping to gossip together,
And, at the end of the street, the village church, with the ivy
Climbing the old gray tower, and the quiet graves in the churchyard. 275
Kind are the people I live with, and dear to me my religion;
Still my heart is so sad, that I wish myself back in Old England.
You will say it is wrong, but I cannot help it: I almost
Wish myself back in Old England, I feel so lonely and wretched."

Thereupon answered the youth: "Indeed I do not condemn you; 280
Stouter hearts than a woman's have quailed in this terrible winter.
Yours is tender and trusting, and needs a stronger to lean on;
So I have come to you now, with an offer and proffer of marriage
Made by a good man and true, Miles Standish the Captain of Plymouth!"

Thus he delivered his message, the dexterous writer of letters,—285
Did not embellish the theme, nor array it in beautiful phrases,
But came straight to the point, and blurted it out like a schoolboy;
Even the Captain himself could hardly have said it more bluntly.
Mute with amazement and sorrow, Priscilla the Puritan maiden
Looked into Alden's face, her eyes dilated with wonder,290
Feeling his words like a blow, that stunned her and rendered her speechless;
Till at length she exclaimed, interrupting the ominous silence:
"If the great Captain of Plymouth is so very eager to wed me,
Why does he not come himself, and take the trouble to woo me?
If I am not worth the wooing, I surely am not worth the winning!" 295
Then John Alden began explaining and smoothing the matter,
Making it worse as he went, by saying the Captain was busy,—
Had no time for such things;—such things! the words grating harshly
Fell on the ear of Priscilla; and swift as a flash she made answer:
"Has he no time for such things, as you call it, before he is married, 300
Would he be likely to find it, or make it, after the wedding?
That is the way with you men; you don't understand us, you cannot.
When you have made up your minds, after thinking of this one and that one,
Choosing, selecting, rejecting, comparing one with another,
Then you make known your desire, with abrupt and sudden avowal, 305
And are offended and hurt, and indignant perhaps, that a woman
Does not respond at once to a love that she never suspected,
Does not attain at a bound to the height to which you have been climbing.
This is not right nor just; for surely a woman's affection
Is not a thing to be asked for, and had for only the asking. 310
When one is truly in love, one not only says it, but shows it.
Had he but waited a while, had he only showed that he loved me,
Even this Captain of yours—who knows?—at last might have won me,

Old and rough as he is; but now it never can happen."

Still John Alden went on, unheeding the words of Priscilla,315
Urging the suit of his friend, explaining, persuading, expanding;
Spoke of his courage and skill, and of all his battles in Flanders,
How with the people of God he had chosen to suffer affliction,
How, in return for his zeal, they had made him Captain of Plymouth;
He was a gentleman born, could trace his pedigree plainly 320
Back to Hugh Standish of Duxbury Hall, in Lancashire, England,
Who was the son of Ralph, and the grandson of Thurston de Standish;
Heir unto vast estates, of which he was basely defrauded,
Still bore the family arms, and had for his crest a cock argent
Combed and wattled gules, and all the rest of the blazon. 325
He was a man of honor, of noble and generous nature;
Though he was rough, he was kindly; she knew how during the winter
He had attended the sick, with a hand as gentle as woman's;
Somewhat hasty and hot, he could not deny it, and headstrong,
Stern as a soldier might be, but hearty, and placable always, 330
Not to be laughed at and scorned, because he was little of stature;
For he was great of heart, magnanimous, courtly, courageous;
Any woman in Plymouth, nay, any woman in England,
Might be happy and proud to be called the wife of Miles Standish!

But as he warmed and glowed, in his simple and eloquent language, 335
Quite forgetful of self, and full of the praise of his rival,
Archly the maiden smiled, and, with eyes overrunning with laughter,
Said, in a tremulous voice, "Why don't you speak for yourself, John?"

IV. JOHN ALDEN

Into the open air John Alden, perplexed and bewildered,
Rushed like a man insane, and wandered alone by the seaside; 340
Paced up and down the sands, and bared his head to the east-wind,
Cooling his heated brow, and the fire and fever within him.
Slowly, as out of the heavens, with apocalyptical splendors,
Sank the City of God, in the vision of John the Apostle;
So, with its cloudy walls of chrysolite, jasper, and sapphire, 345
Sank the broad red sun, and over its turrets uplifted
Glimmered the golden reed of the angel who measured the city.

"Welcome, O wind of the East!" he exclaimed in his wild exultation,
"Welcome, O wind of the East, from the caves of the misty Atlantic!
Blowing o'er fields of dulse, and measureless meadows of seagrass, 350

Blowing o'er rocky wastes, and the grottoes and gardens of ocean!
Lay thy cold, moist hand on my burning forehead, and wrap me
Close in thy garments of mist, to allay the fever within me!"
Like an awakened conscience, the sea was moaning and tossing,
Beating remorseful and loud the mutable sands of the seashore. 355
Fierce in his soul was the struggle and tumult of passions contending;
Love triumphant and crowned, and friendship wounded and bleeding,
Passionate cries of desire, and importunate pleadings of duty!
"Is it my fault," he said, "that the maiden has chosen between us?
Is it my fault that he failed,—my fault that I am the victor?" 360
Then within him there thundered a voice, like the voice of the Prophet:
"It hath displeased the Lord!"—and he thought of David's transgression,
Bathsheba's beautiful face, and his friend in the front of the battle!
Shame and confusion of guilt, and abasement and self-condemnation,
Overwhelmed him at once; and he cried in the deepest contrition: 365
"It hath displeased the Lord! It is the temptation of Satan!"

Then, uplifting his head, he looked at the sea, and beheld there
Dimly the shadowy form of the Mayflower riding at anchor,
Rocked on the rising tide, and ready to sail on the morrow;
Heard the voices of men through the mist, the rattle of cordage 370
Thrown on the deck, the shouts of the mate, and the sailors' "Aye, aye, sir!"
Clear and distinct, but not loud, in the dripping air of the twilight.
Still for a moment he stood, and listened, and stared at the vessel,
Then went hurriedly on, as one who, seeing a phantom,
Stops, then quickens his pace, and follows the beckoning shadow. 375
"Yes, it is plain to me now," he murmured, "the hand of the Lord is
Leading me out of the land of darkness, the bondage of error,
Through the sea, that shall lift the walls of its waters around me,
Hiding me, cutting me off, from the cruel thoughts that pursue me.
Back will I go o'er the ocean, this dreary land will abandon, 380
Her whom I may not love, and him whom my heart has offended.
Better to be in my grave in the green old churchyard in England,
Close by my mother's side, and among the dust of my kindred;
Better be dead and forgotten, than living in shame and dishonor!
Sacred and safe and unseen, in the dark of the narrow chamber 385
With me my secret shall lie, like a buried jewel that glimmers
Bright on the hand that is dust, in the chambers of silence and darkness,—
Yes, as the marriage ring of the great espousal hereafter!"

Thus as he spake, he turned, in the strength of his strong resolution,
Leaving behind him the shore, and hurried along in the twilight, 390
Through the congenial gloom of the forest silent and somber,
Till he beheld the lights in the seven houses of Plymouth,

Shining like seven stars in the dusk and mist of the evening.
Soon he entered his door, and found the redoubtable Captain
Sitting alone, and absorbed in the martial pages of Cæsar, 395
Fighting some great campaign in Hainault or Brabant or Flanders.
"Long have you been on your errand," he said with a cheery demeanor,
Even as one who is waiting an answer, and fears not the issue.
"Not far off is the house, although the woods are between us;
But you have lingered so long, that while you were going and coming 400
I have fought ten battles and sacked and demolished a city.
Come, sit down, and in order relate to me all that has happened."

Then John Alden spake, and related the wondrous adventure
From beginning to end, minutely, just as it happened;
How he had seen Priscilla, and how he had sped in his courtship, 405
Only smoothing a little, and softening down her refusal,
But when he came at length to the words Priscilla had spoken,
Words so tender and cruel: "Why don't you speak for yourself, John?"
Up leaped the Captain of Plymouth, and stamped on the floor, till his armor
Clanged on the wall, where it hung, with a sound of sinister omen. 410
All his pent-up wrath burst forth in a sudden explosion,
E'en as a hand-grenade, that scatters destruction around it.
Wildly he shouted, and loud: "John Alden! you have betrayed me!
Me, Miles Standish, your friend! have supplanted, defrauded, betrayed me!
One of my ancestors ran his sword through the heart of Wat Tyler; 415
Who shall prevent me from running my own through the heart of a traitor?
Yours is the greater treason, for yours is a treason to friendship!
You, who lived under my roof, whom I cherished and loved as a brother;
You, who have fed at my board, and drunk at my cup, to whose keeping
I have intrusted my honor, my thoughts the most sacred and secret,— 420
You too, Brutus! ah, woe to the name of friendship hereafter!
Brutus was Cæsar's friend, and you were mine, but henceforward
Let there be nothing between us save war, and implacable hatred!"

So spake the Captain of Plymouth, and strode about in the chamber,
Chafing and choking with rage; like cords were the veins on his temples. 425
But in the midst of his anger a man appeared at the doorway,
Bringing in uttermost haste a message of urgent importance,
Rumors of danger and war and hostile incursions of Indians!
Straightway the Captain paused, and, without further question or parley,
Took from the nail on the wall his sword with its scabbard of iron, 430
Buckled the belt round his waist, and, frowning fiercely, departed.
Alden was left alone. He heard the clank of the scabbard
Growing fainter and fainter, and dying away in the distance.
Then he arose from his seat, and looked forth into the darkness,

Felt the cool air blow on his cheek, that was hot with the insult, 435
Lifted his eyes to the heavens, and, folding his hands as in childhood,
Prayed in the silence of night to the Father who seeth in secret.

Meanwhile the choleric Captain strode wrathful away to the council,
Found it already assembled, impatiently waiting his coming;
Men in the middle of life, austere and grave in deportment, 440
Only one of them old, the hill that was nearest to heaven,
Covered with snow, but erect, the excellent Elder of Plymouth.
God had sifted three kingdoms to find the wheat for this planting,
Then had sifted the wheat, as the living seed of a nation;
So say the chronicles old, and such is the faith of the people! 445
Near them was standing an Indian, in attitude stern and defiant,
Naked down to the waist, and grim and ferocious in aspect;
While on the table before them was lying unopened a Bible,
Ponderous, bound in leather, brass-studded, printed in Holland,
And beside it outstretched the skin of a rattlesnake glittered, 450
Filled, like a quiver, with arrows: a signal and challenge of warfare,
Brought by the Indian, and speaking with arrowy tongues of defiance.
This Miles Standish beheld, as he entered, and heard them debating
What were an answer befitting the hostile message and menace,
Talking of this and of that, contriving, suggesting, objecting; 455
One voice only for peace, and that the voice of the Elder,
Judging it wise and well that some at least were converted,
Rather than any were slain, for this was but Christian behavior!
Then out spake Miles Standish, the stalwart Captain of Plymouth,
Muttering deep in his throat, for his voice was husky with anger, 460
"What! do you mean to make war with milk and the water of roses?
Is it to shoot red squirrels you have your howitzer planted
There on the roof of the church, or is it to shoot red devils?
Truly the only tongue that is understood by a savage
Must be the tongue of fire that speaks from the mouth of the cannon!" 465
Thereupon answered and said the excellent Elder of Plymouth,
Somewhat amazed and alarmed at this irreverent language:
"Not so thought St. Paul, nor yet the other Apostles;
Not from the cannon's mouth were the tongues of fire they spake with!"
But unheeded fell this mild rebuke on the Captain, 470
Who had advanced to the table, and thus continued discoursing:
"Leave this matter to me, for to me by right it pertaineth.
War is a terrible trade; but in the cause that is righteous,
Sweet is the smell of powder; and thus I answer the challenge!"

Then from the rattlesnake's skin, with a sudden, contemptuous gesture, 475
Jerking the Indian arrows, he filled it with powder and bullets

Full to the very jaws, and handed it back to the savage,
Saying, in thundering tones: "Here, take it! this is your answer!"
Silently out of the room then glided the glistening savage,
Bearing the serpent's skin, and seeming himself like a serpent, 480
Winding his sinuous way in the dark to the depths of the forest.

V. THE SAILING OF THE MAYFLOWER

Just in the gray of the dawn, as the mists uprose from the meadows,
There was a stir and a sound in the slumbering village of Plymouth;
Clanging and clicking of arms, and the order imperative, "Forward!"
Given in tone suppressed, a tramp of feet, and then silence. 485
Figures ten, in the mist, marched slowly out of the village.
Standish the stalwart it was, with eight of his valorous army,
Led by their Indian guide, by Hobomok, friend of the white men,
Northward marching to quell the sudden revolt of the savage.
Giants they seemed in the mist, or the mighty men of King David; 490
Giants in heart they were, who believed in God and the Bible,—
Aye, who believed in the smiting of Midianites and Philistines.
Over them gleamed far off the crimson banners of morning;
Under them loud on the sands, the serried billows, advancing,
Fired along the line, and in regular order retreated. 495

Many a mile had they marched, when at length the village of Plymouth
Woke from its sleep, and arose, intent on its manifold labors.
Sweet was the air and soft; and slowly the smoke from the chimneys
Rose over roofs of thatch, and pointed steadily eastward;
Men came forth from the doors, and paused and talked of the weather, 500
Said that the wind had changed, and was blowing fair for the Mayflower;
Talked of their Captain's departure, and all the dangers that menaced,
He being gone, the town, and what should be done in his absence.
Merrily sang the birds, and the tender voices of women
Consecrated with hymns the common cares of the household. 505
Out of the sea rose the sun, and the billows rejoiced at his coming:
Beautiful were his feet on the purple tops of the mountains;
Beautiful on the sails of the Mayflower riding at anchor,
Battered and blackened and worn by all the storms of the winter.
Loosely against her masts was hanging and flapping her canvas, 510
Rent by so many gales, and patched by the hands of the sailors.
Suddenly from her side, as the sun rose over the ocean,
Darted a puff of smoke, and floated seaward; anon rang
Loud over field and forest the cannon's roar, and the echoes
Heard and repeated the sound, the signal-gun of departure! 515

Ah! but with louder echoes replied the hearts of the people!
Meekly, in voices subdued, the chapter was read from the Bible,
Meekly the prayer was begun, but ended in fervent entreaty!
Then from their houses in haste came forth the Pilgrims of Plymouth,
Men and women and children, all hurrying down to the seashore, 520
Eager, with tearful eyes, to say farewell to the Mayflower,
Homeward bound o'er the sea, and leaving them here in the desert.

Foremost among them was Alden. All night he had lain without slumber,
Turning and tossing about in the heat and unrest of his fever.
He had beheld Miles Standish, who came back late from the council, 525
Stalking into the room, and heard him mutter and murmur,
Sometimes it seemed a prayer, and sometimes it sounded like swearing.
Once he had come to the bed, and stood there a moment in silence;
Then he had turned away, and said: "I will not awake him;
Let him sleep on, it is best; for what is the use of more talking!" 530
Then he extinguished the light, and threw himself down on his pallet,
Dressed as he was, and ready to start at the break of the morning,—
Covered himself with the cloak he had worn in his campaigns in Flanders,—
Slept as a soldier sleeps in his bivouac, ready for action.
But with the dawn he arose; in the twilight Alden beheld him 535
Put on his corselet of steel, and all the rest of his armor,
Buckle about his waist his trusty blade of Damascus,
Take from the corner his musket, and so stride out of the chamber.
Often the heart of the youth had burned and yearned to embrace him,
Often his lips had essayed to speak, imploring for pardon; 540
All the old friendship came back with its tender and grateful emotions;
But his pride overmastered the nobler nature within him,—
Pride, and the sense of his wrong, and the burning fire of the insult.
So he beheld his friend departing in anger, but spake not,
Saw him go forth to danger, perhaps to death, and he spake not! 545
Then he arose from his bed, and heard what the people were saying,
Joined in the talk at the door, with Stephen and Richard and Gilbert,
Joined in the morning prayer, and in the reading of Scripture,
And, with the others, in haste went hurrying down to the seashore,
Down to the Plymouth Rock, that had been to their feet as a doorstep 550
Into a world unknown,—the corner-stone of a nation!

There with his boat was the Master, already a little impatient
Lest he should lose the tide, or the wind might shift to the eastward,
Square-built, hearty, and strong, with an odor of ocean about him,
Speaking with this one and that, and cramming letters and parcels 555
Into his pockets capacious, and messages mingled together
Into his narrow brain, till at last he was wholly bewildered.

Nearer the boat stood Alden, with one foot placed on the gunwale,
One still firm on the rock, and talking at times with the sailors,
Seated erect on the thwarts, all ready and eager for starting. 560
He too was eager to go, and thus put an end to his anguish,
Thinking to fly from despair, that swifter than keel is or canvas,
Thinking to drown in the sea the ghost that would rise and pursue him.
But as he gazed on the crowd, he beheld the form of Priscilla
Standing dejected, among them, unconscious of all that was passing. 565
Fixed were her eyes upon his, as if she divined his intention,
Fixed with a look so sad, so reproachful, imploring, and patient,
That with a sudden revulsion his heart recoiled from its purpose,
As from the verge of a crag, where one step more is destruction.
Strange is the heart of man, with its quick, mysterious instincts! 570
Strange is the life of man, and fatal or fated are moments,
Whereupon turn, as on hinges, the gates of the wall adamantine!
"Here I remain!" he exclaimed, as he looked at the heavens above him,
Thanking the Lord whose breath had scattered the mist and the madness,
Wherein, blind and lost, to death he was staggering headlong. 575
"Yonder snow-white cloud, that floats in the ether above me,
Seems like a hand that is pointing and beckoning over the ocean.
There is another hand, that is not so spectral and ghostlike,
Holding me, drawing me back, and clasping mine for protection.
Float, O hand of cloud, and vanish away in the ether! 580

Roll thyself up like a fist, to threaten and daunt me; I heed not
Either your warning or menace, or any omen of evil!
There is no land so sacred, no air so pure and so wholesome,
As is the air she breathes, and the soil that is pressed by her footsteps.
Here for her sake will I stay, and like an invisible presence. 585
Hover around her forever, protecting, supporting her weakness;
Yes! as my foot was the first that stepped on this rock at the landing,
So, with the blessing of God, shall it be the last at the leaving!"

Meanwhile the Master alert, but with dignified air and important,
Scanning with watchful eye the tide and the wind and the weather, 590
Walked about on the sands, and the people crowded around him
Saying a few last words, and enforcing his careful remembrance.
Then, taking each by the hand, as if he were grasping a tiller,
Into the boat he sprang, and in haste shoved off to his vessel.
Glad in his heart to get rid of all this worry and flurry, 595
Glad to be gone from a land of sand and sickness and sorrow,
Short allowance of victual, and plenty of nothing but Gospel!
Lost in the sound of oars was the last farewell of the Pilgrims.
O strong hearts and true! not one went back in the Mayflower!

No, not one looked back, who had set his hand to this plowing! 600

Soon were heard on board the shouts and songs of the sailors
Heaving the windlass round, and hoisting the ponderous anchor.
Then the yards were braced, and all sails set to the west-wind,
Blowing steady and strong; and the Mayflower sailed from the harbor,
Rounded the point of the Gurnet, and leaving far to the southward 605
Island and cape of sand, and the Field of the First Encounter,
Took the wind on her quarter, and stood for the open Atlantic,
Borne on the send of the sea, and the swelling hearts of the Pilgrims.

Long in silence they watched the receding sail of the vessel,
Much endeared to them all, as something living and human; 610
Then, as if tilled with the spirit, and wrapt in a vision prophetic,
Baring his hoary head, the excellent Elder of Plymouth
Said, "Let us pray!" and they prayed, and thanked the Lord and took courage.
Mournfully sobbed the waves at the base of the rock, and above them
Bowed and whispered the wheat on the hill of death, and their kindred 615
Seemed to awake in their graves, and to join in the prayer that they uttered.
Sun-illumined and white, on the eastern verge of the ocean
Gleamed the departing sail, like a marble slab in a graveyard;
Buried beneath it lay forever all hope of escaping.
Lo! as they turned to depart, they saw the form of an Indian, 620
Watching them from the hill; but while they spake with each other,
Pointing with outstretched hands, and saying, "Look!" he had vanished.
So they returned to their homes; but Alden lingered a little,
Musing alone on the shore, and watching the wash of the billows
Round the base of the rock, and the sparkle and flash of the sunshine, 625
Like the spirit of God, moving visibly over the waters.

VI. PRISCILLA

Thus for a while he stood, and mused by the shore of the ocean,
Thinking of many things, and most of all of Priscilla;
And as if thought had the power to draw to itself, like the loadstone,
Whatsoever it touches, by subtle laws of its nature, 630
Lo! as he turned to depart, Priscilla was standing beside him.

"Are you so much offended, you will not speak to me?" said she.
"Am I so much to blame, that yesterday, when you were pleading
Warmly the cause of another, my heart, impulsive and wayward,
Pleaded your own, and spake out, forgetful perhaps of decorum? 635
Certainly you can forgive me for speaking so frankly, for saying

What I ought not to have said, yet now I can never unsay it;
For there are moments in life, when the heart is so full of emotion,
That if by chance it be shaken, or into its depths like a pebble
Drops some careless word, it overflows, and its secret, 640
Spilt on the ground like water, can never be gathered together.
Yesterday I was shocked, when I heard you speak of Miles Standish,
Praising his virtues, transforming his very defects into virtues,
Praising his courage and strength, and even his fighting in Flanders,
As if by fighting alone you could win the heart of a woman, 645
Quite overlooking yourself and the rest, in exalting your hero.
Therefore I spake as I did, by an irresistible impulse.
You will forgive me, I hope, for the sake of the friendship between us,
Which is too true and too sacred to be so easily broken!"
Thereupon answered John Alden, the scholar, the friend of Miles Standish: 650
"I was not angry with you, with myself alone I was angry,
Seeing how badly I managed the matter I had in my keeping."
"No!" interrupted the maiden, with answer prompt and decisive;
"No; you were angry with me, for speaking so frankly and freely.
It was wrong, I acknowledge; for it is the fate of a woman 655
Long to be patient and silent, to wait like a ghost that is speechless,
Till some questioning voice dissolves the spell of its silence.
Hence is the inner life of so many suffering women
Sunless and silent and deep, like subterranean rivers
Running through caverns of darkness, unheard, unseen, and unfruitful, 660
Chafing their channels of stone, with endless and profitless murmurs."
Thereupon answered John Alden, the young man, the lover of women:
"Heaven forbid it, Priscilla; and truly they seem to me always
More like the beautiful rivers that watered the garden of Eden,
More like the river Euphrates, through deserts of Havilah flowing, 665
Filling the land with delight, and memories sweet of the garden!"
"All, by these words, I can see," again interrupted the maiden,
"How very little you prize me, or care for what I am saying.
When from the depths of my heart, in pain and with secret misgiving,
Frankly I speak to you, asking for sympathy only and kindness, 670
Straightway you take up my words, that are plain and direct and in earnest,
Turn them away from their meaning, and answer with flattering phrases.
This is not right, is not just, is not true to the best that is in you;
For I know and esteem you, and feel that your nature is noble,
Lifting mine up to a higher, a more ethereal level. 675
Therefore I value your friendship, and feel it perhaps the more keenly
If you say aught that implies I am only as one among many,
If you make use of those common and complimentary phrases
Most men think so fine, in dealing and speaking with women,
But which women reject as insipid, if not as insulting." 680

Mute and amazed was Alden; and listened and looked at Priscilla,
Thinking he never had seen her more fair, more divine in her beauty.
He who but yesterday pleaded so glibly the cause of another,
Stood there embarrassed and silent, and seeking in vain for an answer.
So the maiden went on, and little divined or imagined 685
What was at work in his heart, that made him so awkward and speechless.
"Let us, then, be what we are, and speak what we think, and in all things
Keep ourselves loyal to truth, and the sacred professions of friendship.
It is no secret I tell you, nor am I ashamed to declare it:
I have liked to be with you, to see you, to speak with you always. 690
So I was hurt at your words, and a little affronted to hear you
Urge me to marry your friend, though he were the Captain Miles Standish.
For I must tell you the truth: much more to me is your friendship
Than all the love he could give, were he twice the hero you think him."
Then she extended her hand, and Alden, who eagerly grasped it, 695
Felt all the wounds in his heart, that were aching and bleeding so sorely,
Healed by the touch of that hand, and he said, with a voice full of feeling:
"Yes, we must ever be friends; and of all who offer you friendship
Let me be ever the first, the truest, the nearest, and dearest!"

Casting a farewell look at the glimmering sail of the Mayflower 700
Distant, but still in sight, and sinking below the horizon,
Homeward together they walked, with a strange, indefinite feeling,
That all the rest had departed and left them alone in the desert.
But, as they went through the fields in the blessing and smile of the sunshine,
Lighter grew their hearts, and Priscilla said very archly: 705
"Now that our terrible Captain has gone in pursuit of the Indians,
Where he is happier far than he would be commanding a household,
You may speak boldly, and tell me of all that happened between you,
When you returned last night, and said how ungrateful you found me."
Thereupon answered John Alden, and told her the whole of the story,— 710
Told her his own despair, and the direful wrath of Miles Standish.
Whereat the maiden smiled, and said between laughing and earnest,
"He is a little chimney, and heated hot in a moment!"
But as he gently rebuked her, and told her how much he had suffered,—
How he had even determined to sail that day in the Mayflower, 715
And had remained for her sake, on hearing the dangers that threatened,—
All her manner was changed, and she said with a faltering accent,
"Truly I thank you for this: how good you have been to me always!"

Thus, as a pilgrim devout, who toward Jerusalem journeys,
Taking three steps in advance, and one reluctantly backward, 720
Urged by importunate zeal, and withheld by pangs of contrition;
Slowly but steadily onward, receding yet ever advancing,

Journeyed this Puritan youth to the Holy Land of his longings,
Urged by the fervor of love, and withheld by remorseful misgivings.

VII. THE MARCH OF MILES STANDISH

Meanwhile the stalwart Miles Standish was marching steadily northward,
725
Winding through forest and swamp, and along the trend of the seashore,
All day long, with hardly a halt, the fire of his anger
Burning and crackling within, and the sulphurous odor of powder
Seeming more sweet to his nostrils than all the scents of the forest.
Silent and moody he went, and much he revolved his discomfort; 730
He who was used to success, and to easy victories always,
Thus to be flouted, rejected, and laughed to scorn by a maiden,
Thus to be mocked and betrayed by the friend whom most he had trusted!
Ah! 'twas too much to be borne, and he fretted and chafed in his armor!
"I alone am to blame," he muttered, "for mine was the folly. 735

What has a rough old soldier, grown grim and gray in the harness,
Used to the camp and its ways, to do with the wooing of maidens?
'Twas but a dream,—let it pass,—let it vanish like so many others!
What I thought was a flower, is only a weed, and is worthless;
Out of my heart will I pluck it, and throw it away, and henceforward 740
Be but a fighter of battles, a lover and wooer of dangers!"
Thus he revolved in his mind his sorry defeat and discomfort,
While he was marching by day or lying at night in the forest,
Looking up at the trees and the constellations beyond them.

After a three days' march he came to an Indian encampment 745
Pitched on the edge of a meadow, between the sea and the forest;
Women at work by the tents, and the warriors, horrid with warpaint,
Seated about a fire, and smoking and talking together;
Who, when they saw from afar the sudden approach of the white men,
Saw the flash of the sun on breastplate and saber and musket, 750
Straightway leaped to their feet, and two, from among them advancing,
Came to parley with Standish, and offer him furs as a present;
Friendship was in their looks, but in their hearts there was hatred.
Braves of the tribe were these, and brothers, gigantic in stature,
Huge as Goliath of Gath, or the terrible Og, king of Bashan; 755
One was Pecksuot named, and the other was called Wattawamat.
Round their necks were suspended their knives in scabbards of wampum,
Two-edged trenchant knives, with points as sharp as a needle.
Other arms had they none, for they were cunning and crafty.

"Welcome, English!" they said,—these words they had learned from the
    traders 760
Touching at times on the coast, to barter and chaffer for peltries.
Then in their native tongue they begun to parley with Standish,
Through his guide and interpreter, Hobomok, friend of the white man,
Begging for blankets and knives, but mostly for muskets and powder,
Kept by the white man, they said, concealed, with the plague, in his cellars, 765
Ready to be let loose, and destroy his brother the red man!
But when Standish refused, and said he would give them the Bible,
Suddenly changing their tone, they began to boast and to bluster.
Then Wattawamat advanced with a stride in front of the other,
And, with a lofty demeanor, thus vauntingly spake to the Captain: 770
"Now Wattawamat can see, by the fiery eyes of the Captain,
Angry is he in his heart; but the heart of the brave Wattawamat
Is not afraid at the sight. He was not born of a woman,
But on a mountain, at night, from an oak-tree riven by lightning,
Forth he sprang at a bound, with all his weapons about him, 775
Shouting, 'Who is there here to fight with the brave Wattawamat?'"
Then he unsheathed his knife, and, whetting the blade on his left hand,
Held it aloft and displayed a woman's face on the handle,
Saying, with bitter expression and look of sinister meaning:
"I have another at home, with the face of a man on the handle; 780
By-and-by they shall marry; and there will be plenty of children!"

Then stood Pecksuot forth, self-vaunting, insulting Miles Standish;
While with his fingers he patted the knife that hung at his bosom,
Drawing it half from its sheath, and plunging it back, as he muttered,
"By-and-by it shall see; it shall eat; ah, ha! but shall speak not! 785
This is the mighty Captain the white men have sent to destroy us!
He is a little man; let him go and work with the women!"

Meanwhile Standish had noted the faces and figures of Indians
Peeping and creeping about from bush to tree in the forest,
Feigning to look for game, with arrows set on their bowstrings, 790
Drawing about him still closer and closer the net of their ambush.
But undaunted he stood, and dissembled and treated them smoothly;
So the old chronicles say, that were writ in the days of the fathers.
But when he heard their defiance, the boast, the taunt, and the insult,
All the hot blood of his race, of Sir Hugh and of Thurston de Standish, 795
Boiled and beat in his heart, and swelled in the veins of his temples.
Headlong he leaped on the boaster, and, snatching his knife from its scabbard,
Plunged it into his heart, and, reeling backward, the savage
Fell with his face to the sky, and a fiendlike fierceness upon it.
Straight there arose from the forest the awful sound of the war-whoop, 800

And, like a flurry of snow on the whistling wind of December,
Swift and sudden and keen came a flight of feathery arrows.
Then came a cloud of smoke, and out of the cloud came the lightning,
Out of the lightning thunder; and death unseen ran before it.
Frightened, the savages fled for shelter in swamp and in thicket, 805
Hotly pursued and beset; but their sachem, the brave Wattawamat,
Fled not; he was dead. Unswerving and swift had a bullet
Passed through his brain, and he fell with both hands clutching the
    greensward,
Seeming in death to hold back from his foe the land of his fathers.

There on the flowers of the meadow the warriors lay, and above them 810
Silent, with folded arms, stood Hobomok, friend of the white man.
Smiling at length he exclaimed to the stalwart Captain of Plymouth:
"Pecksuot bragged very loud, of his courage, his strength, and his stature,—
Mocked the great Captain, and called him a little man; but I see now
Big enough have you been to lay him speechless before you!" 815

Thus the first battle was fought and won by the stalwart Miles Standish.
When the tidings thereof were brought to the village of Plymouth,
And as a trophy of war the head of the brave Wattawamat
Scowled from the roof of the fort, which at once was a church and a fortress,
All who beheld it rejoiced, and praised the Lord, and took courage. 820
Only Priscilla averted her face from this specter of terror,
Thanking God in her heart that she had not married Miles Standish;
Shrinking, fearing almost, lest, coming home from his battles,
He should lay claim to her hand, as the prize and reward of his valor.

VIII. THE SPINNING-WHEEL

Month after month passed away, and in autumn the ships of the merchants 825
Came with kindred and friends, with cattle and corn for the Pilgrims.
All in the village was peace; the men were intent on their labors,
Busy with hewing and building, with garden plot and with merestead,
Busy with breaking the glebe, and mowing the grass in the meadows,
Searching the sea for its fish, and hunting the deer in the forest. 830
All in the village was peace; but at times the rumor of warfare
Filled the air with alarm, and the apprehension of danger.
Bravely the stalwart Miles Standish was scouring the land with his forces,
Waxing valiant in fight and defeating the alien armies,
Till his name had become a sound of fear to the nations. 835
Anger was still in his heart, but at times the remorse and contrition
Which in all noble natures succeed the passionate outbreak,

Came like a rising tide, that encounters the rush of a river,
Staying its current a while, but making it bitter and brackish.

Meanwhile Alden at home had built him a new habitation, 840
Solid, substantial, of timber rough-hewn from the firs of the forest.
Wooden-barred was the door, and the roof was covered with rushes;
Latticed the windows were, and the window-panes were of paper,
Oiled to admit the light, while wind and rain were excluded.
There too he dug a well, and around it planted an orchard: 845
Still may be seen to this day some trace of the well and the orchard.
Close to the house was the stall, where, safe and secure from annoyance,
Raghorn, the snow-white bull, that had fallen to Alden's allotment
In the division of cattle, might ruminate in the nighttime
Over the pastures he cropped, made fragrant by sweet pennyroyal. 850

Oft when his labor was finished, with eager feet would the dreamer
Follow the pathway that ran through the woods to the house of Priscilla,
Led by illusions romantic and subtile deceptions of fancy,
Pleasure disguised as duty, and love in the semblance of friendship.
Ever of her he thought, when he fashioned the walls of his dwelling; 855
Ever of her he thought, when he delved in the soil of his garden;
Ever of her he thought, when he read in his Bible on Sunday
Praise of the virtuous woman, as she is described in the Proverbs,—
How the heart of her husband doth safely trust in her always,
How all the days of her life she will do him good, and not evil, 860
How she seeketh the wool and the flax and worketh with gladness,
How she layeth her hand to the spindle and holdeth the distaff,
How she is not afraid of the snow for herself or her household,
Knowing her household are clothed with the scarlet cloth of her weaving!

So as she sat at her wheel one afternoon in the autumn, 865
Alden, who opposite sat, and was watching her dexterous fingers,
As if the thread she was spinning were that of his life and his fortune,
After a pause in their talk, thus spake to the sound of the spindle:
"Truly, Priscilla," he said, "when I see you spinning and spinning,
Never idle a moment, but thrifty and thoughtful of others, 870
Suddenly you are transformed, are visibly changed in a moment;
You are no longer Priscilla, but Bertha the Beautiful Spinner."
Here the light foot on the treadle grew swifter and swifter; the spindle
Uttered an angry snarl, and the thread snapped short in her fingers;
While the impetuous speaker, not heeding the mischief, continued: 875
"You are the beautiful Bertha, the spinner, the queen of Helvetia;
She whose story I read at a stall in the streets of Southampton,
Who, as she rode on her palfrey, o'er valley and meadow and mountain,

Ever was spinning her thread from a distaff fixed to her saddle.
She was so thrifty and good, that her name passed into a proverb. 880
So shall it be with your own, when the spinning-wheel shall no longer
Hum in the house of the farmer, and fill its chambers with music.
Then shall the mothers, reproving, relate how it was in their childhood,
Praising the good old times, and the days of Priscilla the spinner!"
Straight uprose from her wheel the beautiful Puritan maiden, 885
Pleased with the praise of her thrift from him whose praise was the sweetest,
Drew from the reel on the table a snowy skein of her spinning,
Thus making answer, meanwhile, to the flattering praises of Alden:
"Come, you must not be idle; if I am a pattern for housewives,
Show yourself equally worthy of being the model of husbands. 890
Hold this skein on your hands, while I wind it, ready for knitting;
Then who knows but hereafter, when fashions have changed and the manners,
Fathers may talk to their sons of the good old times of John Alden!"
Thus, with a jest and a laugh, the skein on his hands she adjusted,
He sitting awkwardly there, with his arms extended before him, 895
She standing graceful, erect, and winding the thread from his fingers,
Sometimes chiding a little his clumsy manner of holding,
Sometimes touching his hands, as she disentangled expertly
Twist or knot in the yarn, unawares—for how could she help it?—
Sending electrical thrills through every nerve in his body. 900

Lo! in the midst of this scene, a breathless messenger entered,
Bringing in hurry and heat the terrible news from the village.
Yes; Miles Standish was dead!—an Indian had brought them the tidings,—
Slain by a poisoned arrow, shot down in the front of the battle,
Into an ambush beguiled, cut off with the whole of his forces; 905
All the town would be burned, and all the people be murdered!
Such were the tidings of evil that burst on the hearts of the hearers.
Silent and statue-like stood Priscilla, her face looking backward
Still at the face of the speaker, her arms uplifted in horror;
But John Alden, upstarting, as if the barb of the arrow 910
Piercing the heart of his friend had struck his own, and had sundered
Once and forever the bonds that held him bound as a captive,
Wild with excess of sensation, the awful delight of his freedom,
Mingled with pain and regret, unconscious of what he was doing,
Clasped, almost with a groan, the motionless form of Priscilla, 915
Pressing her close to his heart, as forever his own, and exclaiming:
"Those whom the Lord hath united, let no man put them asunder!"

Even as rivulets twain, from distant and separate sources,
Seeing each other afar, as they leap from the rocks, and pursuing
Each one its devious path, but drawing nearer and nearer, 920

Rush together at last, at their trysting-place in the forest;
So these lives that had run thus far in separate channels,
Coming in sight of each other, then swerving and flowing asunder,
Parted by barriers strong, but drawing nearer and nearer,
Rushed together at last, and one was lost in the other. 925

IX. THE WEDDING-DAY

Forth from the curtain of clouds, from the tent of purple and scarlet,
Issued the sun, the great High-Priest, in his garments resplendent,
Holiness unto the Lord, in letters of light, on his forehead,
Round the hem of his robe the golden bells and pomegranates.
Blessing the world he came, and the bars of vapor beneath him 930
Gleamed like a grate of brass, and the sea at his feet was a laver!

This was the wedding morn of Priscilla the Puritan maiden.
Friends were assembled together; the Elder and Magistrate also
Graced the scene with their presence, and stood like the Law and the Gospel,
One with the sanction of earth and one with the blessing of heaven. 935
Simple and brief was the wedding, as that of Ruth and of Boaz.
Softly the youth and the maiden repeated the words of betrothal,
Taking each other for husband and wife in the Magistrate's presence,
After the Puritan way, and the laudable custom of Holland.
Fervently then and devoutly, the excellent Elder of Plymouth 940
Prayed for the hearth and the home, that were founded that day in affection,
Speaking of life and of death, and imploring Divine benedictions.

Lo! when the service was ended, a form appeared on the threshold,
Clad in armor of steel, a somber and sorrowful figure!
Why does the bridegroom start and stare at the strange apparition? 945
Why does the bride turn pale, and hide her face on his shoulder?
Is it a phantom of air,—a bodiless, spectral illusion?
Is it a ghost from the grave, that has come to forbid the betrothal?
Long had it stood there unseen, a guest uninvited, unwelcomed;
Over its clouded eyes there had passed at times an expression 950
Softening the gloom and revealing the warm heart hidden beneath them,
As when across the sky the driving rack of the rain-cloud
Grows for a moment thin, and betrays the sun by its brightness.
Once it had lifted its hand, and moved its lips, but was silent,
As if an iron will had mastered the fleeting intention. 955
But when were ended the troth and the prayer and the last benediction,
Into the room it strode, and the people beheld with amazement
Bodily there in his armor Miles Standish, the Captain of Plymouth!

Grasping the bridegroom's hand, he said with emotion, "Forgive me!
I have been angry and hurt,—too long have I cherished the feeling; 960
I have been cruel and hard, but now, thank God! it is ended.
Mine is the same hot blood that leaped in the veins of Hugh Standish,
Sensitive, swift to resent, but as swift in atoning for error.
Never so much as now was Miles Standish the friend of John Alden."
Thereupon answered the bridegroom: "Let all be forgotten between us,— 965
All save the dear old friendship, and that shall grow older and dearer!"
Then the Captain advanced, and, bowing, saluted Priscilla,
Gravely, and after the manner of old-fashioned gentry in England,
Something of camp and of court, of town and of country, commingled,
Wishing her joy of her wedding, and loudly lauding her husband. 970
Then he said with a smile: "I should have remembered the adage,—
If you would be well served, you must serve yourself, and, moreover,
No man can gather cherries in Kent at the season of Christmas!"

Great was the people's amazement, and greater yet their rejoicing,
Thus to behold once more the sunburnt face of their Captain, 975
Whom they had mourned as dead; and they gathered and crowded about him,
Eager to see him and hear him, forgetful of bride and of bridegroom,
Questioning, answering, laughing, and each interrupting the other,
Till the good Captain declared, being quite overpowered and bewildered,
He had rather by far break into an Indian encampment, 980
Than come again to a wedding to which he had not been invited.

Meanwhile the bridegroom went forth and stood with the bride at the
    doorway,
Breathing the perfumed air of that warm and beautiful morning.
Touched with autumnal tints, but lonely and sad in the sunshine,
Lay extended before them the land of toil and privation; 985
There were the graves of the dead, and the barren waste of the seashore,
There the familiar fields, the groves of pine, and the meadows;
But to their eyes transfigured, it seemed as the Garden of Eden,
Filled with the presence of God, whose voice was the sound of the ocean.

Soon was their vision disturbed by the noise and stir of departure, 990
Friends coming forth from the house, and impatient of longer delaying,
Each with his plan for the day, and the work that was left uncompleted.
Then from a stall near at hand, amid exclamations of wonder,
Alden, the thoughtful, the careful, so happy, so proud of Priscilla,
Brought out the snow-white bull, obeying the hand of its master, 995
Led by a cord that was tied to an iron ring in its nostrils,
Covered with crimson cloth, and a cushion placed for a saddle.
She should not walk, he said, through the dust and heat of the noonday;

Nay, she should ride like a queen, not plod along like a peasant.
Somewhat alarmed at first, but reassured by the others, 1000
placing her hand on the cushion, her foot in the hand of her husband,
Gayly, with joyous laugh, Priscilla mounted her palfrey.
"Nothing is wanting now," he said with a smile, "but the distaff;
Then you would be in truth my queen, my beautiful Bertha!"

Onward the bridal procession now moved to their new habitation, 1005
Happy husband and wife, and friends conversing together.
Pleasantly murmured the brook, as they crossed the ford in the forest,
Pleased with the image that passed, like a dream of love through its bosom,
Tremulous, floating in air, o'er the depths of the azure abysses,
Down through the golden leaves the sun was pouring his splendors, 1010
Gleaming on purple grapes, that, from branches above them suspended,
Mingled their odorous breath with the balm of the pine and fir-tree,
Wild and sweet as the clusters that grew in the valley of Eshcol.
Like a picture it seemed of the primitive pastoral ages,
Fresh with the youth of the world, and recalling Rebecca and Isaac, 1015
Old and yet ever new, and simple and beautiful always,
Love immortal and young in the endless succession of lovers,
So through the Plymouth woods passed onward the bridal procession.

BIRDS OF PASSAGE

FLIGHT THE FIRST

BIRDS OF PASSAGE

Black shadows fall
From the lindens tall,
That lift aloft their massive wall
  Against the southern sky;
And from the realms
Of the shadowy elms
A tide-like darkness overwhelms
  The fields that round us lie.
But the night is fair,
And everywhere
A warm, soft vapor fills the air,
  And distant sounds seem near,
And above, in the light
Of the star-lit night,
Swift birds of passage wing their flight
  Through the dewy atmosphere.
I hear the beat
Of their pinions fleet,
As from the land of snow and sleet
  They seek a southern lea.
I hear the cry
Of their voices high
Falling dreamily through the sky,

But their forms I cannot see.
O, say not so!
Those sounds that flow
In murmurs of delight and woe
  Come not from wings of birds.
They are the throngs
Of the poet's songs,
Murmurs of pleasures, and pains, and wrongs,
  The sound of winged words.
This is the cry
Of souls, that high
On toiling, beating pinions, fly,
  Seeking a warmer clime,
From their distant flight
Through realms of light
It falls into our world of night,
  With the murmuring sound of rhyme.

PROMETHEUS OR THE POET'S FORETHOUGHT

Of Prometheus, how undaunted
  On Olympus' shining bastions
His audacious foot he planted,
Myths are told and songs are chanted,
  Full of promptings and suggestions.
Beautiful is the tradition
  Of that flight through heavenly portals,
The old classic superstition
Of the theft and the transmission
  Of the fire of the Immortals!
First the deed of noble daring,
  Born of heavenward aspiration,
Then the fire with mortals sharing,
Then the vulture,—the despairing
  Cry of pain on crags Caucasian.
All is but a symbol painted
  Of the Poet, Prophet, Seer;
Only those are crowned and sainted
Who with grief have been acquainted,
  Making nations nobler, freer.
In their feverish exultations,
  In their triumph and their yearning,
In their passionate pulsations,

In their words among the nations,
  The Promethean fire is burning.
Shall it, then, be unavailing,
  All this toil for human culture?
Through the cloud-rack, dark and trailing,
Must they see above them sailing
  O'er life's barren crags the vulture?
Such a fate as this was Dante's,
  By defeat and exile maddened;
Thus were Milton and Cervantes,
Nature's priests and Corybantes,
  By affliction touched and saddened.
But the glories so transcendent
  That around their memories cluster,
And, on all their steps attendant,
Make their darkened lives resplendent
  With such gleams of inward lustre!
All the melodies mysterious,
  Through the dreary darkness chanted;
Thoughts in attitudes imperious,
Voices soft, and deep, and serious,
  Words that whispered, songs that haunted!
All the soul in rapt suspension,
  All the quivering, palpitating
Chords of life in utmost tension,
With the fervor of invention,
  With the rapture of creating!
Ah, Prometheus! heaven-scaling!
  In such hours of exultation
Even the faintest heart, unquailing,
Might behold the vulture sailing
  Round the cloudy crags Caucasian!
Though to all there is not given
  Strength for such sublime endeavor,
Thus to scale the walls of heaven,
And to leaven with fiery leaven
  All the hearts of men for ever;
Yet all bards, whose hearts unblighted
  Honor and believe the presage,
Hold aloft their torches lighted,
Gleaming through the realms benighted,
  As they onward bear the message!

EPIMETHEUS OR THE POET'S AFTERTHOUGHT

Have I dreamed? or was it real,
  What I saw as in a vision,
When to marches hymeneal
In the land of the Ideal
  Moved my thought o'er Fields Elysian?
What! are these the guests whose glances
  Seemed like sunshine gleaming round me?
These the wild, bewildering fancies,
That with dithyrambic dances
  As with magic circles bound me?
Ah! how cold are their caresses!
  Pallid cheeks, and haggard bosoms!
Spectral gleam their snow-white dresses,
And from loose dishevelled tresses
  Fall the hyacinthine blossoms!
O my songs! whose winsome measures
  Filled my heart with secret rapture!
Children of my golden leisures!
Must even your delights and pleasures
  Fade and perish with the capture?
Fair they seemed, those songs sonorous,
  When they came to me unbidden;
Voices single, and in chorus,
Like the wild birds singing o'er us
  In the dark of branches hidden.
Disenchantment! Disillusion!
  Must each noble aspiration
Come at last to this conclusion,
Jarring discord, wild confusion,
  Lassitude, renunciation?
Not with steeper fall nor faster,
  From the sun's serene dominions,
Not through brighter realms nor vaster,
In swift ruin and disaster,
  Icarus fell with shattered pinions!
Sweet Pandora! dear Pandora!
  Why did mighty Jove create thee
Coy as Thetis, fair as Flora,
Beautiful as young Aurora,
  If to win thee is to hate thee?
No, not hate thee! for this feeling

Of unrest and long resistance
Is but passionate appealing,
A prophetic whisper stealing
  O'er the chords of our existence.
Him whom thou dost once enamour,
  Thou, beloved, never leavest;
In life's discord, strife, and clamor,
Still he feels thy spell of glamour;
  Him of Hope thou ne'er bereavest.
Weary hearts by thee are lifted,
  Struggling souls by thee are strengthened,
Clouds of fear asunder rifted,
Truth from falsehood cleansed and sifted,
  Lives, like days in summer, lengthened!
Therefore art thou ever clearer,
  O my Sibyl, my deceiver!
For thou makest each mystery clearer,
And the unattained seems nearer,
  When thou fillest my heart with fever!
Muse of all the Gifts and Graces!
  Though the fields around us wither,
There are ampler realms and spaces,
Where no foot has left its traces:
  Let us turn and wander thither!

THE LADDER OF ST. AUGUSTINE

Saint Augustine! well hast thou said,
  That of our vices we can frame
A ladder, if we will but tread
  Beneath our feet each deed of shame!
All common things, each day's events,
  That with the hour begin and end,
Our pleasures and our discontents,
  Are rounds by which we may ascend.
The low desire, the base design,
  That makes another's virtues less;
The revel of the ruddy wine,
  And all occasions of excess;
The longing for ignoble things;
  The strife for triumph more than truth;
The hardening of the heart, that brings
  Irreverence for the dreams of youth;

All thoughts of ill; all evil deeds,
  That have their root in thoughts of ill;
Whatever hinders or impedes
  The action of the nobler will;—
All these must first be trampled down
  Beneath our feet, if we would gain
In the bright fields of fair renown
  The right of eminent domain.
We have not wings, we cannot soar;
  But we have feet to scale and climb
By slow degrees, by more and more,
  The cloudy summits of our time.
The mighty pyramids of stone
  That wedge-like cleave the desert airs,
When nearer seen, and better known,
  Are but gigantic flights of stairs.
The distant mountains, that uprear
  Their solid bastions to the skies,
Are crossed by pathways, that appear
  As we to higher levels rise.
The heights by great men reached and kept
  Were not attained by sudden flight,
But they, while their companions slept,
  Were toiling upward in the night.
Standing on what too long we bore
  With shoulders bent and downcast eyes,
We may discern—unseen before—
  A path to higher destinies.
Nor deem the irrevocable Past,
  As wholly wasted, wholly vain,
If, rising on its wrecks, at last
  To something nobler we attain.

THE PHANTOM SHIP

In Mather's Magnalia Christi,
  Of the old colonial time,
May be found in prose the legend
  That is here set down in rhyme.
A ship sailed from New Haven,
  And the keen and frosty airs,
That filled her sails at parting,
  Were heavy with good men's prayers.

"O Lord! if it be thy pleasure"—
  Thus prayed the old divine—
"To bury our friends in the ocean,
  Take them, for they are thine!"
But Master Lamberton muttered,
  And under his breath said he,
"This ship is so crank and walty
  I fear our grave she will be!"
And the ships that came from England,
  When the winter months were gone,
Brought no tidings of this vessel
  Nor of Master Lamberton.
This put the people to praying
  That the Lord would let them hear
What in his greater wisdom
  He had done with friends so dear.
And at last their prayers were answered:—
  It was in the month of June,
An hour before the sunset
  Of a windy afternoon,
When, steadily steering landward,
  A ship was seen below,
And they knew it was Lamberton, Master,
  Who sailed so long ago.
On she came, with a cloud of canvas,
  Right against the wind that blew,
Until the eye could distinguish
  The faces of the crew.
Then fell her straining topmasts,
  Hanging tangled in the shrouds,
And her sails were loosened and lifted,
  And blown away like clouds.
And the masts, with all their rigging,
  Fell slowly, one by one,
And the hulk dilated and vanished,
  As a sea-mist in the sun!
And the people who saw this marvel
  Each said unto his friend,
That this was the mould of their vessel,
  And thus her tragic end.
And the pastor of the village
  Gave thanks to God in prayer,
That, to quiet their troubled spirits,
  He had sent this Ship of Air.

THE WARDEN OF THE CINQUE PORTS

A mist was driving down the British Channel,
    The day was just begun,
And through the window-panes, on floor and panel,
    Streamed the red autumn sun.

It glanced on flowing flag and rippling pennon,
    And the white sails of ships;
And, from the frowning rampart, the black cannon
    Hailed it with feverish lips.

Sandwich and Romney, Hastings, Hithe, and Dover
    Were all alert that day,
To see the French war-steamers speeding over,
    When the fog cleared away.

Sullen and silent, and like couchant lions,
    Their cannon, through the night,
Holding their breath, had watched, in grim defiance,
    The sea-coast opposite.

And now they roared at drum-beat from their stations
    On every citadel;
Each answering each, with morning salutations,
    That all was well.

And down the coast, all taking up the burden,
    Replied the distant forts,
As if to summon from his sleep the Warden
    And Lord of the Cinque Ports.

Him shall no sunshine from the fields of azure,
    No drum-beat from the wall,
No morning gun from the black fort's embrasure,
    Awaken with its call!

No more, surveying with an eye impartial
    The long line of the coast,
Shall the gaunt figure of the old Field Marshal
    Be seen upon his post!

For in the night, unseen, a single warrior,
    In sombre harness mailed,
Dreaded of man, and surnamed the Destroyer,
    The rampart wall has scaled.

He passed into the chamber of the sleeper,
    The dark and silent room,
And as he entered, darker grew, and deeper,
    The silence and the gloom.

He did not pause to parley or dissemble,

But smote the Warden hoar;
Ah! what a blow! that made all England tremble
　And groan from shore to shore.
Meanwhile, without, the surly cannon waited,
　The sun rose bright o'erhead;
Nothing in Nature's aspect intimated
　That a great man was dead.

HAUNTED HOUSES

All houses wherein men have lived and died
　Are haunted houses. Through the open doors
The harmless phantoms on their errands glide,
　With feet that make no sound upon the floors.
We meet them at the door-way, on the stair,
　Along the passages they come and go,
Impalpable impressions on the air,
　A sense of something moving to and fro.
There are more guests at table, than the hosts
　Invited; the illuminated hall
Is thronged with quiet, inoffensive ghosts,
　As silent as the pictures on the wall.
The stranger at my fireside cannot see
　The forms I see, nor hear the sounds I hear;
He but perceives what is; while unto me
　All that has been is visible and clear.
We have no title-deeds to house or lands;
　Owners and occupants of earlier dates
From graves forgotten stretch their dusty hands,
　And hold in mortmain still their old estates.
The spirit-world around this world of sense
　Floats like an atmosphere, and everywhere
Wafts through these earthly mists and vapors dense
　A vital breath of more ethereal air.
Our little lives are kept in equipoise
　By opposite attractions and desires;
The struggle of the instinct that enjoys,
　And the more noble instinct that aspires.
These perturbations, this perpetual jar
　Of earthly wants and aspirations high,
Come from the influence of an unseen star,
　An undiscovered planet in our sky.
And as the moon from some dark gate of cloud

Throws o'er the sea a floating bridge of light,
Across whose trembling planks our fancies crowd
   Into the realm of mystery and night,—
So from the world of spirits there descends
   A bridge of light, connecting it with this,
O'er whose unsteady floor, that sways and bends,
   Wander our thoughts above the dark abyss.

IN THE CHURCHYARD AT CAMBRIDGE

In the village churchyard she lies,
Dust is in her beautiful eyes,
   No more she breathes, nor feels, nor stirs;
At her feet and at her head
Lies a slave to attend the dead,
   But their dust is white as hers.
Was she a lady of high degree,
So much in love with the vanity
   And foolish pomp of this world of ours?
Or was it Christian charity,
And lowliness and humility,
   The richest and rarest of all dowers?
Who shall tell us? No one speaks;
No color shoots into those cheeks,
   Either of anger or of pride,
At the rude question we have asked;
Nor will the mystery be unmasked
   By those who are sleeping at her side.
Hereafter?—And do you think to look
On the terrible pages of that Book
   To find her failings, faults, and errors?
Ah, you will then have other cares,
In your own short-comings and despairs,
   In your own secret sins and terrors!

THE EMPEROR'S BIRD'S-NEST

Once the Emperor Charles of Spain,
   With his swarthy, grave commanders,
I forget in what campaign,
Long besieged, in mud and rain,
   Some old frontier town of Flanders.
Up and down the dreary camp,

In great boots of Spanish leather,
Striding with a measured tramp,
These Hidalgos, dull and damp,
  Cursed the Frenchmen, cursed the weather.
Thus as to and fro they went,
  Over upland and through hollow,
Giving their impatience vent,
Perched upon the Emperor's tent,
  In her nest, they spied a swallow.
Yes, it was a swallow's nest,
  Built of clay and hair of horses,
Mane, or tail, or dragoon's crest,
Found on hedge-rows east and west,
  After skirmish of the forces.
Then an old Hidalgo said,
  As he twirled his gray mustachio,
"Sure this swallow overhead
Thinks the Emperor's tent a shed,
  And the Emperor but a Macho!"
Hearing his imperial name
  Coupled with those words of malice,
Half in anger, half in shame,
Forth the great campaigner came
  Slowly from his canvas palace.
"Let no hand the bird molest,"
  Said he solemnly, "nor hurt her!"
Adding then, by way of jest,
"Golondrina is my guest,
  'Tis the wife of some deserter!"
Swift as bowstring speeds a shaft,
  Through the camp was spread the rumor,
And the soldiers, as they quaffed
Flemish beer at dinner, laughed
  At the Emperor's pleasant humor.
So unharmed and unafraid
  Sat the swallow still and brooded,
Till the constant cannonade
Through the walls a breach had made,
  And the siege was thus concluded.
Then the army, elsewhere bent,
  Struck its tents as if disbanding,
Only not the Emperor's tent,
For he ordered, ere he went,
  Very curtly, "Leave it standing!"

So it stood there all alone,
  Loosely flapping, torn and tattered,
Till the brood was fledged and flown,
Singing o'er those walls of stone
  Which the cannon-shot had shattered.

THE TWO ANGELS

Two angels, one of Life and one of Death,
  Passed o'er our village as the morning broke;
The dawn was on their faces, and beneath,
  The sombre houses hearsed with plumes of smoke.
Their attitude and aspect were the same,
  Alike their features and their robes of white;
But one was crowned with amaranth, as with flame,
  And one with asphodels, like flakes of light.
I saw them pause on their celestial way;
  Then said I, with deep fear and doubt oppressed,
"Beat not so loud, my heart, lest thou betray
  The place where thy beloved are at rest!"
And he who wore the crown of asphodels,
  Descending, at my door began to knock,
And my soul sank within me, as in wells
  The waters sink before an earthquake's shock.
I recognized the nameless agony,
  The terror and the tremor and the pain,
That oft before had filled or haunted me,
  And now returned with threefold strength again.
The door I opened to my heavenly guest,
  And listened, for I thought I heard God's voice;
And, knowing whatsoe'er he sent was best,
  Dared neither to lament nor to rejoice.
Then with a smile, that filled the house with light,
  "My errand is not Death, but Life," he said;
And ere I answered, passing out of sight,
  On his celestial embassy he sped.
'T was at thy door, O friend! and not at mine,
  The angel with the amaranthine wreath,
Pausing, descended, and with voice divine,
  Whispered a word that had a sound like Death.
Then fell upon the house a sudden gloom,
  A shadow on those features fair and thin;
And softly, from that hushed and darkened room,

Two angels issued, where but one went in.
All is of God! If he but wave his hand,
   The mists collect, the rain falls thick and loud,
Till, with a smile of light on sea and land,
   Lo! he looks back from the departing cloud.
Angels of Life and Death alike are his;
   Without his leave they pass no threshold o'er;
Who, then, would wish or dare, believing this,
   Against his messengers to shut the door?

DAYLIGHT AND MOONLIGHT

In broad daylight, and at noon, Yesterday I saw the moon Sailing high, but
   faint and white, As a school-boy's paper kite.
In broad daylight, yesterday, I read a Poet's mystic lay; And it seemed to me at
   most As a phantom, or a ghost.
But at length the feverish day Like a passion died away, And the night, serene
   and still, Fell on village, vale, and hill.
Then the moon, in all her pride, Like a spirit glorified, Filled and overflowed
   the night With revelations of her light.
And the Poet's song again Passed like music through my brain; Night
   interpreted to me All its grace and mystery.

THE JEWISH CEMETERY AT NEWPORT

How strange it seems! These Hebrews in their graves,
   Close by the street of this fair seaport town,
Silent beside the never-silent waves,
   At rest in all this moving up and down!
The trees are white with dust, that o'er their sleep
   Wave their broad curtains in the south-wind's breath,
While underneath such leafy tents they keep
   The long, mysterious Exodus of Death.
And these sepulchral stones, so old and brown,
   That pave with level flags their burial-place,
Seem like the tablets of the Law, thrown down
   And broken by Moses at the mountain's base.
The very names recorded here are strange,
   Of foreign accent, and of different climes;
Alvares and Rivera interchange
   With Abraham and Jacob of old times.
"Blessed be God! for he created Death!"
   The mourners said, "and Death is rest and peace";

Then added, in the certainty of faith,
  "And giveth Life that never more shall cease."
Closed are the portals of their Synagogue,
  No Psalms of David now the silence break,
No Rabbi reads the ancient Decalogue
  In the grand dialect the Prophets spake.
Gone are the living, but the dead remain,
  And not neglected; for a hand unseen,
Scattering its bounty, like a summer rain,
  Still keeps their graves and their remembrance green.
How came they here? What burst of Christian hate,
  What persecution, merciless and blind,
Drove o'er the sea—that desert desolate—
  These Ishmaels and Hagars of mankind?
They lived in narrow streets and lanes obscure,
  Ghetto and Judenstrass, in mirk and mire;
Taught in the school of patience to endure
  The life of anguish and the death of fire.
All their lives long, with the unleavened bread
  And bitter herbs of exile and its fears,
The wasting famine of the heart they fed,
  And slaked its thirst with marah of their tears.
Anathema maranatha! was the cry
  That rang from town to town, from street to street;
At every gate the accursed Mordecai
  Was mocked and jeered, and spurned by Christian feet.
Pride and humiliation hand in hand
  Walked with them through the world where'er they went;
Trampled and beaten were they as the sand,
  And yet unshaken as the continent.
For in the background figures vague and vast
  Of patriarchs and of prophets rose sublime,
And all the great traditions of the Past
  They saw reflected in the coming time.
And thus for ever with reverted look
  The mystic volume of the world they read,
Spelling it backward, like a Hebrew book,
  Till life became a Legend of the Dead.
But ah! what once has been shall be no more!
  The groaning earth in travail and in pain
Brings forth its races, but does not restore,
  And the dead nations never rise again.

OLIVER BASSELIN

In the Valley of the Vire
  Still is seen an ancient mill,
With its gables quaint and queer,
  And beneath the window-sill,
      On the stone,
      These words alone:
"Oliver Basselin lived here."
Far above it, on the steep,
  Ruined stands the old Chateau;
Nothing but the donjon-keep
  Left for shelter or for show.
      Its vacant eyes
      Stare at the skies,
Stare at the valley green and deep.
Once a convent, old and brown,
  Looked, but ah! it looks no more,
From the neighboring hillside down
  On the rushing and the roar
      Of the stream
      Whose sunny gleam
Cheers the little Norman town.
In that darksome mill of stone,
  To the water's dash and din,
Careless, humble, and unknown,
  Sang the poet Basselin
      Songs that fill
      That ancient mill
With a splendor of its own.
Never feeling of unrest
  Broke the pleasant dream he dreamed;
Only made to be his nest,
  All the lovely valley seemed;
      No desire
      Of soaring higher
Stirred or fluttered in his breast.
True, his songs were not divine;
  Were not songs of that high art,
Which, as winds do in the pine,
  Find an answer in each heart;
      But the mirth
      Of this green earth

Laughed and revelled in his line.
From the alehouse and the inn,
  Opening on the narrow street,
Came the loud, convivial din,
  Singing and applause of feet,
      The laughing lays
      That in those days
Sang the poet Basselin.
In the castle, cased in steel,
  Knights, who fought at Agincourt,
Watched and waited, spur on heel;
  But the poet sang for sport
      Songs that rang
      Another clang,
Songs that lowlier hearts could feel.
In the convent, clad in gray,
  Sat the monks in lonely cells,
Paced the cloisters, knelt to pray,
  And the poet heard their bells;
      But his rhymes
      Found other chimes,
Nearer to the earth than they.
Gone are all the barons bold,
  Gone are all the knights and squires,
Gone the abbot stern and cold,
  And the brotherhood of friars;
      Not a name
      Remains to fame,
From those mouldering days of old!
But the poet's memory here
  Of the landscape makes a part;
Like the river, swift and clear,
  Flows his song through many a heart;
      Haunting still
      That ancient mill,
In the Valley of the Vire.

VICTOR GALBRAITH

Under the walls of Monterey
At daybreak the bugles began to play,
    Victor Galbraith!
In the mist of the morning damp and gray,

These were the words they seemed to say:
    "Come forth to thy death,
    Victor Galbraith!"
Forth he came, with a martial tread;
Firm was his step, erect his head;
    Victor Galbraith,
He who so well the bugle played,
Could not mistake the words it said:
    "Come forth to thy death,
    Victor Galbraith!"

He looked at the earth, he looked at the sky,
He looked at the files of musketry,
    Victor Galbraith!
And he said, with a steady voice and eye,
"Take good aim; I am ready to die!"
    Thus challenges death
    Victor Galbraith.

Twelve fiery tongues flashed straight and red,
Six leaden balls on their errand sped;
    Victor Galbraith
Falls to the ground, but he is not dead;
His name was not stamped on those balls of lead,
    And they only scath
    Victor Galbraith.

Three balls are in his breast and brain,
But he rises out of the dust again,
    Victor Galbraith!
The water he drinks has a bloody stain;
"O kill me, and put me out of my pain!"
    In his agony prayeth
    Victor Galbraith.

Forth dart once more those tongues of flame,
And the bugler has died a death of shame,
    Victor Galbraith!
His soul has gone back to whence it came,
And no one answers to the name,
    When the Sergeant saith,
    "Victor Galbraith!"

Under the walls of Monterey
By night a bugle is heard to play,
    Victor Galbraith!
Through the mist of the valley damp and gray
The sentinels hear the sound, and say,
    "That is the wraith

    Of Victor Galbraith!"

MY LOST YOUTH

Often I think of the beautiful town
  That is seated by the sea;
Often in thought go up and down
The pleasant streets of that dear old town,
  And my youth comes back to me.
    And a verse of a Lapland song
    Is haunting my memory still:
  "A boy's will is the wind's will,
And the thoughts of youth are long, long thoughts."
I can see the shadowy lines of its trees,
  And catch, in sudden gleams,
The sheen of the far-surrounding seas,
And islands that were the Hersperides
  Of all my boyish dreams.
    And the burden of that old song,
    It murmurs and whispers still:
  "A boy's will is the wind's will,
And the thoughts of youth are long, long thoughts."
I remember the black wharves and the slips,
  And the sea-tides tossing free;
And Spanish sailors with bearded lips,
And the beauty and mystery of the ships,
  And the magic of the sea.
    And the voice of that wayward song
    Is singing and saying still:
  "A boy's will is the wind's will,
And the thoughts of youth are long, long thoughts."
I remember the bulwarks by the shore,
  And the fort upon the hill;
The sunrise gun, with its hollow roar,
The drum-beat repeated o'er and o'er,
  And the bugle wild and shrill.
    And the music of that old song
    Throbs in my memory still:
  "A boy's will is the wind's will,
And the thoughts of youth are long, long thoughts."
I remember the sea-fight far away,
  How it thundered o'er the tide!
And the dead captains, as they lay

In their graves, o'erlooking the tranquil bay,
  Where they in battle died.
    And the sound of that mournful song
    Goes through me with a thrill:
  "A boy's will is the wind's will,
And the thoughts of youth are long, long thoughts."
I can see the breezy dome of groves,
  The shadows of Deering's Woods;
And the friendships old and the early loves
Come back with a sabbath sound, as of doves
  In quiet neighborhoods.
    And the verse of that sweet old song,
    It flutters and murmurs still:
  "A boy's will is the wind's will,
And the thoughts of youth are long, long thoughts."
I remember the gleams and glooms that dart
  Across the schoolboy's brain;
The song and the silence in the heart,
That in part are prophecies, and in part
  Are longings wild and vain.
    And the voice of that fitful song
    Sings on, and is never still:
  "A boy's will is the wind's will,
And the thoughts of youth are long, long thoughts."
There are things of which I may not speak;
  There are dreams that cannot die;
There are thoughts that make the strong heart weak,
And bring a pallor into the cheek,
  And a mist before the eye.
    And the words of that fatal song
    Come over me like a chill:
  "A boy's will is the wind's will,
And the thoughts of youth are long, long thoughts."
Strange to me now are the forms I meet
  When I visit the dear old town;
But the native air is pure and sweet,
And the trees that o'ershadow each well-known street,
  As they balance up and down,
    Are singing the beautiful song,
    Are sighing and whispering still:
  "A boy's will is the wind's will,
And the thoughts of youth are long, long thoughts."
And Deering's Woods are fresh and fair,
  And with joy that is almost pain

My heart goes back to wander there,
And among the dreams of the days that were,
  I find my lost youth again.
    And the strange and beautiful song,
    The groves are repeating it still:
    "A boy's will is the wind's will,
And the thoughts of youth are long, long thoughts."

THE ROPEWALK

In that building, long and low,
With its windows all a-row,
  Like the port-holes of a hulk,
Human spiders spin and spin,
Backward down their threads so thin
  Dropping, each a hempen bulk.
At the end, an open door;
Squares of sunshine on the floor
  Light the long and dusky lane;
And the whirring of a wheel,
Dull and drowsy, makes me feel
  All its spokes are in my brain.
As the spinners to the end
Downward go and reascend,
  Gleam the long threads in the sun;
While within this brain of mine
Cobwebs brighter and more fine
  By the busy wheel are spun.
Two fair maidens in a swing,
Like white doves upon the wing,
  First before my vision pass;
Laughing, as their gentle hands
Closely clasp the twisted strands,
  At their shadow on the grass.
Then a booth of mountebanks,
With its smell of tan and planks,
  And a girl poised high in air
On a cord, in spangled dress,
With a faded loveliness,
  And a weary look of care.
Then a homestead among farms,
And a woman with bare arms
  Drawing water from a well;

As the bucket mounts apace,
With it mounts her own fair face,
    As at some magician's spell.
Then an old man in a tower,
Ringing loud the noontide hour,
    While the rope coils round and round
Like a serpent at his feet,
And again, in swift retreat,
    Nearly lifts him from the ground.
Then within a prison-yard,
Faces fixed, and stern, and hard,
    Laughter and indecent mirth;
Ah! it is the gallows-tree!
Breath of Christian charity,
    Blow, and sweep it from the earth!
Then a school-boy, with his kite
Gleaming in a sky of light,
    And an eager, upward look;
Steeds pursued through lane and field;
Fowlers with their snares concealed;
    And an angler by a brook.
Ships rejoicing in the breeze,
Wrecks that float o'er unknown seas,
    Anchors dragged through faithless sand;
Sea-fog drifting overhead,
And, with lessening line and lead,
    Sailors feeling for the land.
All these scenes do I behold,
These, and many left untold,
    In that building long and low;
While the wheel goes round and round,
With a drowsy, dreamy sound,
    And the spinners backward go.

THE GOLDEN MILE-STONE

Leafless are the trees; their purple branches
Spread themselves abroad, like reefs of coral,
    Rising silent
In the Red Sea of the Winter sunset.
From the hundred chimneys of the village,
Like the Afreet in the Arabian story,
    Smoky columns

Tower aloft into the air of amber.
At the window winks the flickering fire-light;
Here and there the lamps of evening glimmer,
    Social watch-fires
Answering one another through the darkness.
On the hearth the lighted logs are glowing,
And like Ariel in the cloven pine-tree
    For its freedom
Groans and sighs the air imprisoned in them.
By the fireside there are old men seated,
Seeing ruined cities in the ashes,
    Asking sadly
Of the Past what it can ne'er restore them.
By the fireside there are youthful dreamers,
Building castles fair, with stately stairways,
    Asking blindly
Of the Future what it cannot give them.
By the fireside tragedies are acted
In whose scenes appear two actors only,
    Wife and husband,
And above them God the sole spectator.
By the fireside there are peace and comfort,
Wives and children, with fair, thoughtful faces,
    Waiting, watching
For a well-known footstep in the passage.
Each man's chimney is his Golden Mile-stone;
Is the central point, from which he measures
    Every distance
Through the gateways of the world around him.
In his farthest wanderings still he sees it;
Hears the talking flame, the answering night-wind,
    As he heard them
When he sat with those who were, but are not.
Happy he whom neither wealth nor fashion,
Nor the march of the encroaching city,
    Drives an exile
From the hearth of his ancestral homestead.
We may build more splendid habitations,
Fill our rooms with paintings and with sculptures,
    But we cannot
Buy with gold the old associations!

CATAWBA WINE

This song of mine
    Is a Song of the Vine,
To be sung by the glowing embers
    Of wayside inns,
    When the rain begins
To darken the drear Novembers.

It is not a song
    Of the Scuppernong,
From warm Carolinian valleys,
    Nor the Isabel
    And the Muscadel
That bask in our garden alleys.

Nor the red Mustang,
    Whose clusters hang
O'er the waves of the Colorado,
    And the fiery flood
    Of whose purple blood
Has a dash of Spanish bravado.

For richest and best
    Is the wine of the West,
That grows by the Beautiful River;
    Whose sweet perfume
    Fills all the room
With a benison on the giver.

And as hollow trees
    Are the haunts of bees,
For ever going and coming;
    So this crystal hive
    Is all alive
With a swarming and buzzing and humming.

Very good in its way
    Is the Verzenay,
Or the Sillery soft and creamy;
    But Catawba wine
    Has a taste more divine,
More dulcet, delicious, and dreamy.

There grows no vine
   By the haunted Rhine,
By Danube or Guadalquivir,
   Nor on island or cape,
   That bears such a grape
As grows by the Beautiful River.

   Drugged is their juice
   For foreign use,
When shipped o'er the reeling Atlantic,
   To rack our brains
   With the fever pains,
That have driven the Old World frantic.

   To the sewers and sinks
   With all such drinks,
And after them tumble the mixer;
   For a poison malign
   Is such Borgia wine,
Or at best but a Devil's Elixir.

   While pure as a spring
   Is the wine I sing,
And to praise it, one needs but name it;
   For Catawba wine
   Has need of no sign,
No tavern-bush to proclaim it.

   And this Song of the Vine,
   This greeting of mine,
The winds and the birds shall deliver
   To the Queen of the West,
   In her garlands dressed,
On the banks of the Beautiful River.

SANTA FILOMENA

Whene'er a noble deed is wrought,
Whene'er is spoken a noble thought,
   Our hearts, in glad surprise,
   To higher levels rise.
The tidal wave of deeper souls
Into our inmost being rolls,

And lifts us unawares
Out of all meaner cares.
Honor to those whose words or deeds
Thus help us in our daily needs,
And by their overflow
Raise us from what is low!
Thus thought I, as by night I read
Of the great army of the dead,
The trenches cold and damp,
The starved and frozen camp,—
The wounded from the battle-plain,
In dreary hospitals of pain,
The cheerless corridors,
The cold and stony floors.
Lo! in that house of misery
A lady with a lamp I see
Pass through the glimmering gloom,
And flit from room to room.
And slow, as in a dream of bliss,
The speechless sufferer turns to kiss
Her shadow, as it falls
Upon the darkening walls.
As if a door in heaven should be
Opened and then closed suddenly,
The vision came and went,
The light shone and was spent.
On England's annals, through the long
Hereafter of her speech and song,
That light its rays shall cast
From portals of the past.
A Lady with a Lamp shall stand
In the great history of the land,
A noble type of good,
Heroic womanhood.
Nor even shall be wanting here
The palm, the lily, and the spear,
The symbols that of yore
Saint Filomena bore.

THE DISCOVERER OF THE NORTH CAPE A LEAF FROM KING
ALFRED'S OROSIUS

Othere, the old sea-captain,

Who dwelt in Helgoland,
To King Alfred, the Lover of Truth,
Brought a snow-white walrus-tooth,
　Which he held in his brown right hand.
His figure was tall and stately,
　Like a boy's his eye appeared;
His hair was yellow as hay,
But threads of a silvery gray
　Gleamed in his tawny beard.
Hearty and hale was Othere,
　His cheek had the color of oak;
With a kind of laugh in his speech,
Like the sea-tide on a beach,
　As unto the King he spoke.
And Alfred, King of the Saxons,
　Had a book upon his knees,
And wrote down the wondrous tale
Of him who was first to sail
　Into the Arctic seas.
"So far I live to the northward,
　No man lives north of me;
To the east are wild mountain-chains;
And beyond them meres and plains;
　To the westward all is sea.
"So far I live to the northward,
　From the harbor of Skeringes-hale,
If you only sailed by day,
With a fair wind all the way,
　More than a month would you sail.
"I own six hundred reindeer,
　With sheep and swine beside;
I have tribute from the Finns,
Whalebone and reindeer-skins,
　And ropes of walrus-hide.
"I ploughed the land with horses,
　But my heart was ill at ease,
For the old seafaring men
Came to me now and then,
　With their sagas of the seas;—
"Of Iceland and of Greenland,
　And the stormy Hebrides,
And the undiscovered deep;—
I could not eat nor sleep
　For thinking of those seas.

"To the northward stretched the desert,
　How far I fain would know;
So at last I sallied forth,
And three days sailed due north,
　As far as the whale-ships go.
"To the west of me was the ocean,
　To the right the desolate shore,
But I did not slacken sail
For the walrus or the whale,
　Till after three days more.
"The days grew longer and longer,
　Till they became as one,
And southward through the haze
I saw the sullen blaze
　Of the red midnight sun.
"And then uprose before me,
　Upon the water's edge,
The huge and haggard shape
Of that unknown North Cape,
　Whose form is like a wedge.
"The sea was rough and stormy,
　The tempest howled and wailed,
And the sea-fog, like a ghost,
Haunted that dreary coast,
　But onward still I sailed.
"Four days I steered to eastward,
　Four days without a night:
Round in a fiery ring
Went the great sun, O King,
　With red and lurid light."
Here Alfred, King of the Saxons,
　Ceased writing for a while;
And raised his eyes from his book,
With a strange and puzzled look,
　And an incredulous smile.
But Othere, the old sea-captain,
　He neither paused nor stirred,
Till the King listened, and then
Once more took up his pen,
　And wrote down every word.
"And now the land," said Othere,
　"Bent southward suddenly,
And I followed the curving shore
And ever southward bore

Into a nameless sea.
"And there we hunted the walrus,
　The narwhale, and the seal;
Ha! 't was a noble game!
And like the lightning's flame
　Flew our harpoons of steel.
"There were six of us all together,
　Norsemen of Helgoland;
In two days and no more
We killed of them threescore,
　And dragged them to the strand!"
Here Alfred the Truth-Teller
　Suddenly closed his book,
And lifted his blue eyes,
With doubt and strange surmise
　Depicted in their look.
And Othere the old sea-captain
　Stared at him wild and weird,
Then smiled, till his shining teeth
Gleamed white from underneath
　His tawny, quivering beard.
And to the King of the Saxons,
　In witness of the truth,
Raising his noble head,
He stretched his brown hand, and said,
　"Behold this walrus-tooth!"

DAYBREAK

A wind came up out of the sea, And said, "O mists, make room for me."
It hailed the ships, and cried, "Sail on, Ye mariners, the night is gone."
And hurried landward far away, Crying, "Awake! it is the day."
It said unto the forest, "Shout! Hang all your leafy banners out!"
It touched the wood-bird's folded wing, And said, "O bird, awake and sing."
And o'er the farms, "O chanticleer, Your clarion blow; the day is near."
It whispered to the fields of corn, "Bow down, and hail the coming morn."
It shouted through the belfry-tower, "Awake, O bell! proclaim the hour."
It crossed the churchyard with a sigh, And said, "Not yet! in quiet lie."

THE FIFTIETH BIRTHDAY OF AGASSIZ: MAY 28, 1857

It was fifty years ago
　In the pleasant month of May,

In the beautiful Pays de Vaud,
  A child in its cradle lay.
And Nature, the old nurse, took
  The child upon her knee,
Saying: "Here is a story-book
  Thy Father has written for thee."
"Come, wander with me," she said,
  "Into regions yet untrod;
And read what is still unread
  In the manuscripts of God."
And he wandered away and away
  With Nature, the dear old nurse,
Who sang to him night and day
  The rhymes of the universe.
And whenever the way seemed long,
  Or his heart began to fail,
She would sing a more wonderful song,
  Or tell a more marvellous tale.
So she keeps him still a child,
  And will not let him go,
Though at times his heart beats wild
  For the beautiful Pays de Vaud;
Though at times he hears in his dreams
  The Ranz des Vaches of old,
And the rush of mountain streams
  From glaciers clear and cold;
And the mother at home says, "Hark!
  For his voice I listen and yearn;
It is growing late and dark,
  And my boy does not return!"

CHILDREN

Come to me, O ye children!
  For I hear you at your play,
And the questions that perplexed me
  Have vanished quite away.
Ye open the eastern windows,
  That look towards the sun,
Where thoughts are singing swallows
  And the brooks of morning run.
In your hearts are the birds and the sunshine,
  In your thoughts the brooklet's flow,

But in mine is the wind of Autumn
　And the first fall of the snow.
Ah! what would the world be to us
　If the children were no more?
We should dread the desert behind us
　Worse than the dark before.
What the leaves are to the forest,
　With light and air for food,
Ere their sweet and tender juices
　Have been hardened into wood,—
That to the world are children;
　Through them it feels the glow
Of a brighter and sunnier climate
　Than reaches the trunks below.
Come to me, O ye children!
　And whisper in my ear
What the birds and the winds are singing
　In your sunny atmosphere.
For what are all our contrivings,
　And the wisdom of our books,
When compared with your caresses,
　And the gladness of your looks?
Ye are better than all the ballads
　That ever were sung or said;
For ye are living poems,
　And all the rest are dead.

SANDALPHON

Have you read in the Talmud of old,
In the Legends the Rabbins have told
　Of the limitless realms of the air,—
Have you read it,—the marvellous story
Of Sandalphon, the Angel of Glory,
　Sandalphon, the Angel of Prayer?
How, erect, at the outermost gates
Of the City Celestial he waits,
　With his feet on the ladder of light,
That, crowded with angels unnumbered,
By Jacob was seen, as he slumbered
　Alone in the desert at night?
The Angels of Wind and of Fire
Chant only one hymn, and expire

With the song's irresistible stress;
Expire in their rapture and wonder,
As harp-strings are broken asunder
  By music they throb to express.
But serene in the rapturous throng,
Unmoved by the rush of the song,
  With eyes unimpassioned and slow,
Among the dead angels, the deathless
Sandalphon stands listening breathless
  To sounds that ascend from below;—
From the spirits on earth that adore,
From the souls that entreat and implore
  In the fervor and passion of prayer;
From the hearts that are broken with losses,
And weary with dragging the crosses
  Too heavy for mortals to bear.
And he gathers the prayers as he stands,
And they change into flowers in his hands,
  Into garlands of purple and red;
And beneath the great arch of the portal,
Through the streets of the City Immortal
  Is wafted the fragrance they shed.
It is but a legend, I know,—
A fable, a phantom, a show,
  Of the ancient Rabbinical lore;
Yet the old mediaeval tradition,
The beautiful, strange superstition,
  But haunts me and holds me the more.
When I look from my window at night,
And the welkin above is all white,
  All throbbing and panting with stars,
Among them majestic is standing
Sandalphon the angel, expanding
  His pinions in nebulous bars.
And the legend, I feel, is a part
Of the hunger and thirst of the heart,
  The frenzy and fire of the brain,
That grasps at the fruitage forbidden,
The golden pomegranates of Eden,
  To quiet its fever and pain.

FLIGHT THE SECOND

THE CHILDREN'S HOUR

Between the dark and the daylight,
  When the night is beginning to lower,
Comes a pause in the day's occupations,
  That is known as the Children's Hour.
I hear in the chamber above me
  The patter of little feet,
The sound of a door that is opened,
  And voices soft and sweet.
From my study I see in the lamplight,
  Descending the broad hall stair,
Grave Alice, and laughing Allegra,
  And Edith with golden hair.
A whisper, and then a silence:
  Yet I know by their merry eyes
They are plotting and planning together
  To take me by surprise.
A sudden rush from the stairway,
  A sudden raid from the hall!
By three doors left unguarded
  They enter my castle wall!
They climb up into my turret
  O'er the arms and back of my chair;
If I try to escape, they surround me;

They seem to be everywhere.
They almost devour me with kisses,
  Their arms about me entwine,
Till I think of the Bishop of Bingen
  In his Mouse-Tower on the Rhine!
Do you think, o blue-eyed banditti,
  Because you have scaled the wall,
Such an old mustache as I am
  Is not a match for you all!
I have you fast in my fortress,
  And will not let you depart,
But put you down into the dungeon
  In the round-tower of my heart.
And there will I keep you forever,
  Yes, forever and a day,
Till the walls shall crumble to ruin,
  And moulder in dust away!

ENCELADUS

Under Mount Etna he lies,
  It is slumber, it is not death;
For he struggles at times to arise,
And above him the lurid skies
  Are hot with his fiery breath.
The crags are piled on his breast,
  The earth is heaped on his head;
But the groans of his wild unrest,
Though smothered and half suppressed,
  Are heard, and he is not dead.
And the nations far away
  Are watching with eager eyes;
They talk together and say,
"To-morrow, perhaps to-day,
  Euceladus will arise!"
And the old gods, the austere
  Oppressors in their strength,
Stand aghast and white with fear
At the ominous sounds they hear,
  And tremble, and mutter, "At length!"
Ah me! for the land that is sown
  With the harvest of despair!
Where the burning cinders, blown

From the lips of the overthrown
  Enceladus, fill the air.
Where ashes are heaped in drifts
  Over vineyard and field and town,
Whenever he starts and lifts
His head through the blackened rifts
  Of the crags that keep him down.
See, see! the red light shines!
  'T is the glare of his awful eyes!
And the storm-wind shouts through the pines
Of Alps and of Apennines,
  "Enceladus, arise!"

THE CUMBERLAND

At anchor in Hampton Roads we lay,
  On board of the cumberland, sloop-of-war;
And at times from the fortress across the bay
    The alarum of drums swept past,
    Or a bugle blast
  From the camp on the shore.
Then far away to the south uprose
  A little feather of snow-white smoke,
And we knew that the iron ship of our foes
    Was steadily steering its course
    To try the force
  Of our ribs of oak.
Down upon us heavily runs,
  Silent and sullen, the floating fort;
Then comes a puff of smoke from her guns,
    And leaps the terrible death,
    With fiery breath,
  From each open port.
We are not idle, but send her straight
  Defiance back in a full broadside!
As hail rebounds from a roof of slate,
    Rebounds our heavier hail
    From each iron scale
  Of the monster's hide.
"Strike your flag!" the rebel cries,
  In his arrogant old plantation strain.
"Never!" our gallant Morris replies;
    "It is better to sink than to yield!"

And the whole air pealed
  With the cheers of our men.
Then, like a kraken huge and black,
  She crushed our ribs in her iron grasp!
Down went the Cumberland all a wrack,
    With a sudden shudder of death,
    And the cannon's breath
  For her dying gasp.
Next morn, as the sun rose over the bay,
  Still floated our flag at the mainmast head.
Lord, how beautiful was Thy day!
    Every waft of the air
    Was a whisper of prayer,
  Or a dirge for the dead.
Ho! brave hearts that went down in the seas
  Ye are at peace in the troubled stream;
Ho! brave land! with hearts like these,
    Thy flag, that is rent in twain,
    Shall be one again,
    And without a seam!

SNOW-FLAKES

Out of the bosom of the Air,
  Out of the cloud-folds of her garments shaken,
Over the woodlands brown and bare,
  Over the harvest-fields forsaken,
    Silent, and soft, and slow
    Descends the snow.
Even as our cloudy fancies take
  Suddenly shape in some divine expression,
Even as the troubled heart doth make
  In the white countenance confession,
    The troubled sky reveals
    The grief it feels.
This is the poem of the air,
  Slowly in silent syllables recorded;
This is the secret of despair,
  Long in its cloudy bosom hoarded,
    Now whispered and revealed
    To wood and field.

A DAY OF SUNSHINE

O gift of God! O perfect day: Whereon shall no man work, but play; Whereon
    it is enough for me, Not to be doing, but to be!
Through every fibre of my brain, Through every nerve, through every vein, I
    feel the electric thrill, the touch Of life, that seems almost too much.
I hear the wind among the trees Playing celestial symphonies; I see the
    branches downward bent, Like keys of some great instrument.
And over me unrolls on high The splendid scenery of the sky, Where though a
    sapphire sea the sun Sails like a golden galleon,
Towards yonder cloud-land in the West, Towards yonder Islands of the Blest,
    Whose steep sierra far uplifts Its craggy summits white with drifts.
Blow, winds! and waft through all the rooms The snow-flakes of the cherry-
    blooms! Blow, winds! and bend within my reach The fiery blossoms of the
    peach!
O Life and Love! O happy throng Of thoughts, whose only speech is song! O
    heart of man! canst thou not be Blithe as the air is, and as free?

SOMETHING LEFT UNDONE

Labor with what zeal we will,
  Something still remains undone,
Something uncompleted still
  Waits the rising of the sun.
By the bedside, on the stair,
  At the threshold, near the gates,
With its menace or its prayer,
  Like a mendicant it waits;
Waits, and will not go away;
  Waits, and will not be gainsaid;
By the cares of yesterday
  Each to-day is heavier made;
Till at length the burden seems
  Greater than our strength can bear,
Heavy as the weight of dreams,
  Pressing on us everywhere.
And we stand from day to day,
  Like the dwarfs of times gone by,
Who, as Northern legends say,
  On their shoulders held the sky.

WEARINESS

O little feet! that such long years
Must wander on through hopes and fears,
  Must ache and bleed beneath your load;
I, nearer to the wayside inn
Where toil shall cease and rest begin,
  Am weary, thinking of your road!
O little hands! that, weak or strong,
Have still to serve or rule so long,
  Have still so long to give or ask;
I, who so much with book and pen
Have toiled among my fellow-men,
  Am weary, thinking of your task.
O little hearts! that throb and beat
With such impatient, feverish heat,
  Such limitless and strong desires;
Mine that so long has glowed and burned,
With passions into ashes turned
  Now covers and conceals its fires.
O little souls! as pure and white
And crystalline as rays of light
  Direct from heaven, their source divine;
Refracted through the mist of years,
How red my setting sun appears,
  How lurid looks this soul of mine!

FLIGHT THE THIRD

FATA MORGANA

O sweet illusions of Song,
  That tempt me everywhere,
In the lonely fields, and the throng
  Of the crowded thoroughfare!
I approach, and ye vanish away,
  I grasp you, and ye are gone;
But ever by nigh an day,
  The melody soundeth on.
As the weary traveller sees
  In desert or prairie vast,
Blue lakes, overhung with trees,
  That a pleasant shadow cast;
Fair towns with turrets high,
  And shining roofs of gold,
That vanish as he draws nigh,
  Like mists together rolled,—
So I wander and wander along,
  And forever before me gleams
The shining city of song,
  In the beautiful land of dreams.
But when I would enter the gate
  Of that golden atmosphere,
It is gone, and I wander and wait

For the vision to reappear.

THE HAUNTED CHAMBER

Each heart has its haunted chamber,
  Where the silent moonlight falls!
On the floor are mysterious footsteps,
  There are whispers along the walls!
And mine at times is haunted
  By phantoms of the Past
As motionless as shadows
  By the silent moonlight cast.
A form sits by the window,
  That is not seen by day,
For as soon as the dawn approaches
  It vanishes away.
It sits there in the moonlight
  Itself as pale and still,
And points with its airy finger
  Across the window-sill.
Without before the window,
  There stands a gloomy pine,
Whose boughs wave upward and downward
  As wave these thoughts of mine.
And underneath its branches
  Is the grave of a little child,
Who died upon life's threshold,
  And never wept nor smiled.
What are ye, O pallid phantoms!
  That haunt my troubled brain?
That vanish when day approaches,
  And at night return again?
What are ye, O pallid phantoms!
  But the statues without breath,
That stand on the bridge overarching
  The silent river of death?

THE MEETING

After so long an absence
  At last we meet again:
Does the meeting give us pleasure,
  Or does it give us pain?

The tree of life has been shaken,
  And but few of us linger now,
Like the Prophet's two or three berries
  In the top of the uppermost bough.
We cordially greet each other
  In the old, familiar tone;
And we think, though we do not say it,
  How old and gray he is grown!
We speak of a Merry Christmas
  And many a Happy New Year
But each in his heart is thinking
  Of those that are not here.
We speak of friends and their fortunes,
  And of what they did and said,
Till the dead alone seem living,
  And the living alone seem dead.
And at last we hardly distinguish
  Between the ghosts and the guests;
And a mist and shadow of sadness
  Steals over our merriest jests.

VOX POPULI

When Mazarvan the Magician,
  Journeyed westward through Cathay,
Nothing heard he but the praises
  Of Badoura on his way.
But the lessening rumor ended
  When he came to Khaledan,
There the folk were talking only
  Of Prince Camaralzaman,
So it happens with the poets:
  Every province hath its own;
Camaralzaman is famous
  Where Badoura is unknown.

THE CASTLE-BUILDER

A gentle boy, with soft and silken locks
  A dreamy boy, with brown and tender eyes,
A castle-builder, with his wooden blocks,
  And towers that touch imaginary skies.
A fearless rider on his father's knee,

An eager listener unto stories told
At the Round Table of the nursery,
  Of heroes and adventures manifold.
There will be other towers for thee to build;
  There will be other steeds for thee to ride;
There will be other legends, and all filled
  With greater marvels and more glorified.
Build on, and make thy castles high and fair,
  Rising and reaching upward to the skies;
Listen to voices in the upper air,
  Nor lose thy simple faith in mysteries.

CHANGED

From the outskirts of the town
  Where of old the mile-stone stood.
Now a stranger, looking down
I behold the shadowy crown
  Of the dark and haunted wood.
Is it changed, or am I changed?
  Ah! the oaks are fresh and green,
But the friends with whom I ranged
Through their thickets are estranged
  By the years that intervene.
Bright as ever flows the sea,
  Bright as ever shines the sun,
But alas! they seem to me
Not the sun that used to be,
  Not the tides that used to run.

THE CHALLENGE

I have a vague remembrance
  Of a story, that is told
In some ancient Spanish legend
  Or chronicle of old.
It was when brave King Sanchez
  Was before Zamora slain,
And his great besieging army
  Lay encamped upon the plain.
Don Diego de Ordonez
  Sallied forth in front of all,
And shouted loud his challenge

To the warders on the wall.
All the people of Zamora,
  Both the born and the unborn,
As traitors did he challenge
  With taunting words of scorn.
The living, in their houses,
  And in their graves, the dead!
And the waters of their rivers,
  And their wine, and oil, and bread!
There is a greater army,
  That besets us round with strife,
A starving, numberless army,
  At all the gates of life.
The poverty-stricken millions
  Who challenge our wine and bread,
And impeach us all as traitors,
  Both the living and the dead.
And whenever I sit at the banquet,
  Where the feast and song are high,
Amid the mirth and the music
  I can hear that fearful cry.
And hollow and haggard faces
  Look into the lighted hall,
And wasted hands are extended
  To catch the crumbs that fall.
For within there is light and plenty,
  And odors fill the air;
But without there is cold and darkness,
  And hunger and despair.
And there in the camp of famine,
  In wind and cold and rain,
Christ, the great Lord of the army,
  Lies dead upon the plain!

THE BROOK AND THE WAVE

The brooklet came from the mountain,
  As sang the bard of old,
Running with feet of silver
  Over the sands of gold!
Far away in the briny ocean
  There rolled a turbulent wave,
Now singing along the sea-beach,

Now howling along the cave.
And the brooklet has found the billow
  Though they flowed so far apart,
And has filled with its freshness and sweetness
  That turbulent bitter heart!

AFTERMATH

When the summer fields are mown,
When the birds are fledged and flown,
  And the dry leaves strew the path;
With the falling of the snow,
With the cawing of the crow,
Once again the fields we mow
  And gather in the aftermath.
Not the sweet, new grass with flowers
Is this harvesting of ours;
  Not the upland clover bloom;
But the rowen mired with weeds,
Tangled tufts from marsh and meads,
Where the poppy drops its seeds
  In the silence and the gloom.

FLIGHT THE FOURTH

CHARLES SUMNER

Garlands upon his grave,
  And flowers upon his hearse,
And to the tender heart and brave
  The tribute of this verse.

His was the troubled life,
  The conflict and the pain,
The grief, the bitterness of strife,
  The honor without stain.

Like Winkelried, he took
  Into his manly breast
The sheaf of hostile spears, and broke
  A path for the oppressed.

Then from the fatal field
  Upon a nation's heart
Borne like a warrior on his shield!—
  So should the brave depart.

Death takes us by surprise,
  And stays our hurrying feet;
The great design unfinished lies,

Our lives are incomplete.

But in the dark unknown
Perfect their circles seem,
Even as a bridge's arch of stone
Is rounded in the stream.

Alike are life and death,
When life in death survives,
And the uninterrupted breath
Inspires a thousand lives.

Were a star quenched on high,
For ages would its light,
Still travelling downward from the sky,
Shine on our mortal sight.

So when a great man dies,
For years beyond our ken,
The light he leaves behind him lies
Upon the paths of men.

TRAVELS BY THE FIRESIDE

The ceaseless rain is falling fast,
  And yonder gilded vane,
Immovable for three days past,
  Points to the misty main,
It drives me in upon myself
  And to the fireside gleams,
To pleasant books that crowd my shelf,
  And still more pleasant dreams,
I read whatever bards have sung
  Of lands beyond the sea,
And the bright days when I was young
  Come thronging back to me.
In fancy I can hear again
  The Alpine torrent's roar,
The mule-bells on the hills of Spain,
  The sea at Elsinore.
I see the convent's gleaming wall
  Rise from its groves of pine,
And towers of old cathedrals tall,

And castles by the Rhine.
I journey on by park and spire,
  Beneath centennial trees,
Through fields with poppies all on fire,
  And gleams of distant seas.
I fear no more the dust and heat,
  No more I feel fatigue,
While journeying with another's feet
  O'er many a lengthening league.
Let others traverse sea and land,
  And toil through various climes,
I turn the world round with my hand
  Reading these poets' rhymes.
From them I learn whatever lies
  Beneath each changing zone,
And see, when looking with their eyes,
  Better than with mine own.

CADENABBIA: LAKE OF COMO

No sound of wheels or hoof-beat breaks
  The silence of the summer day,
As by the loveliest of all lakes
  I while the idle hours away.
I pace the leafy colonnade
  Where level branches of the plane
Above me weave a roof of shade
  Impervious to the sun and rain.
At times a sudden rush of air
  Flutters the lazy leaves o'erhead,
And gleams of sunshine toss and flare
  Like torches down the path I tread.
By Somariva's garden gate
  I make the marble stairs my seat,
And hear the water, as I wait,
  Lapping the steps beneath my feet.
The undulation sinks and swells
  Along the stony parapets,
And far away the floating bells
  Tinkle upon the fisher's nets.
Silent and slow, by tower and town
  The freighted barges come and go,
Their pendent shadows gliding down

By town and tower submerged below.
The hills sweep upward from the shore,
  With villas scattered one by one
Upon their wooded spurs, and lower
  Bellaggio blazing in the sun.
And dimly seen, a tangled mass
  Of walls and woods, of light and shade,
Stands beckoning up the Stelvio Pass
  Varenna with its white cascade.
I ask myself, Is this a dream?
  Will it all vanish into air?
Is there a land of such supreme
  And perfect beauty anywhere?
Sweet vision! Do not fade away;
  Linger until my heart shall take
Into itself the summer day,
  And all the beauty of the lake.
Linger until upon my brain
  Is stamped an image of the scene,
Then fade into the air again,
  And be as if thou hadst not been.

MONTE CASSINO: TERRA DI LAVORO

Beautiful valley! through whose verdant meads
  Unheard the Garigliano glides along;—
The Liris, nurse of rushes and of reeds,
  The river taciturn of classic song.
The Land of Labor and the Land of Rest,
  Where mediaeval towns are white on all
The hillsides, and where every mountain's crest
  Is an Etrurian or a Roman wall.
There is Alagna, where Pope Boniface
  Was dragged with contumely from his throne;
Sciarra Colonna, was that day's disgrace
  The Pontiff's only, or in part thine own?
There is Ceprano, where a renegade
  Was each Apulian, as great Dante saith,
When Manfred by his men-at-arms betrayed
  Spurred on to Benevento and to death.
There is Aquinum, the old Volscian town,
  Where Juvenal was born, whose lurid light
Still hovers o'er his birthplace like the crown

Of splendor seen o'er cities in the night.
Doubled the splendor is, that in its streets
  The Angelic Doctor as a school-boy played,
And dreamed perhaps the dreams, that he repeats
  In ponderous folios for scholastics made.
And there, uplifted, like a passing cloud
  That pauses on a mountain summit high,
Monte Cassino's convent rears its proud
  And venerable walls against the sky.
Well I remember how on foot I climbed
  The stony pathway leading to its gate;
Above, the convent bells for vespers chimed,
  Below, the darkening town grew desolate.
Well I remember the low arch and dark,
  The court-yard with its well, the terrace wide,
From which, far down, the valley like a park
  Veiled in the evening mists, was dim descried.
The day was dying, and with feeble hands
  Caressed the mountain-tops; the vales between
Darkened; the river in the meadowlands
  Sheathed itself as a sword, and was not seen.
The silence of the place was like a sleep,
  So full of rest it seemed; each passing tread
Was a reverberation from the deep
  Recesses of the ages that are dead.
For, more than thirteen centuries ago,
  Benedict fleeing from the gates of Rome,
A youth disgusted with its vice and woe,
  Sought in these mountain solitudes a home.
He founded here his Convent and his Rule
  Of prayer and work, and counted work as prayer;
The pen became a clarion, and his school
  Flamed like a beacon in the midnight air.
What though Boccaccio, in his reckless way,
  Mocking the lazy brotherhood, deplores
The illuminated manuscripts, that lay
  Torn and neglected on the dusty floors?
Boccaccio was a novelist, a child
  Of fancy and of fiction at the best!
This the urbane librarian said, and smiled
  Incredulous, as at some idle jest.
Upon such themes as these, with one young friar
  I sat conversing late into the night,
Till in its cavernous chimney the woodfire

Had burnt its heart out like an anchorite.
And then translated, in my convent cell,
  Myself yet not myself, in dreams I lay,
And, as a monk who hears the matin bell,
  Started from sleep; already it was day.
From the high window I beheld the scene
  On which Saint Benedict so oft had gazed,—
The mountains and the valley in the sheen
  Of the bright sun,—and stood as one amazed.
Gray mists were rolling, rising, vanishing;
  The woodlands glistened with their jewelled crowns;
Far off the mellow bells began to ring
  For matins in the half-awakened towns.
The conflict of the Present and the Past,
  The ideal and the actual in our life,
As on a field of battle held me fast,
  Where this world and the next world were at strife.
For, as the valley from its sleep awoke,
  I saw the iron horses of the steam
Toss to the morning air their plumes of smoke,
  And woke, as one awaketh from a dream.

AMALFI

Sweet the memory is to me Of a land beyond the sea, Where the waves and
    mountains meet, Where, amid her mulberry-trees Sits Amalfi in the heat,
    Bathing ever her white feet In the tideless summer seas.
In the middle of the town, From its fountains in the hills, Tumbling through
    the narrow gorge, The Canneto rushes down, Turns the great wheels of the
    mills, Lifts the hammers of the forge.
'T is a stairway, not a street, That ascends the deep ravine, Where the torrent
    leaps between Rocky walls that almost meet. Toiling up from stair to stair
    Peasant girls their burdens bear; Sunburnt daughters of the soil, Stately
    figures tall and straight, What inexorable fate Dooms them to this life of
    toil?
Lord of vineyards and of lands, Far above the convent stands. On its terraced
    walk aloof Leans a monk with folded hands, Placid, satisfied, serene,
    Looking down upon the scene Over wall and red-tiled roof; Wondering
    unto what good end All this toil and traffic tend, And why all men cannot
    be Free from care and free from pain, And the sordid love of gain, And as
    indolent as he.
Where are now the freighted barks From the marts of east and west? Where
    the knights in iron sarks Journeying to the Holy Land, Glove of steel upon

the hand, Cross of crimson on the breast? Where the pomp of camp and court? Where the pilgrims with their prayers? Where the merchants with their wares, And their gallant brigantines Sailing safely into port Chased by corsair Algerines?

Vanished like a fleet of cloud, Like a passing trumpet-blast, Are those splendors of the past, And the commerce and the crowd! Fathoms deep beneath the seas Lie the ancient wharves and quays, Swallowed by the engulfing waves; Silent streets and vacant halls, Ruined roofs and towers and walls; Hidden from all mortal eyes Deep the sunken city lies: Even cities have their graves!

This is an enchanted land! Round the headlands far away Sweeps the blue Salernian bay With its sickle of white sand: Further still and furthermost On the dim discovered coast Paestum with its ruins lies, And its roses all in bloom Seem to tinge the fatal skies Of that lonely land of doom.

On his terrace, high in air, Nothing doth the good monk care For such worldly themes as these, From the garden just below Little puffs of perfume blow, And a sound is in his ears Of the murmur of the bees In the shining chestnut-trees; Nothing else he heeds or hears. All the landscape seems to swoon In the happy afternoon; Slowly o'er his senses creep The encroaching waves of sleep, And he sinks as sank the town, Unresisting, fathoms down, Into caverns cool and deep!

Walled about with drifts of snow, Hearing the fierce north-wind blow, Seeing all the landscape white, And the river cased in ice, Comes this memory of delight, Comes this vision unto me Of a long-lost Paradise In the land beyond the sea.

THE SERMON OF ST. FRANCIS

Up soared the lark into the air, A shaft of song, a winged prayer, As if a soul, released from pain, Were flying back to heaven again.

St. Francis heard; it was to him An emblem of the Seraphim; The upward motion of the fire, The light, the heat, the heart's desire.

Around Assisi's convent gate The birds, God's poor who cannot wait, From moor and mere and darksome wood Came flocking for their dole of food.

"O brother birds," St. Francis said, "Ye come to me and ask for bread, But not with bread alone to-day Shall ye be fed and sent away.

"Ye shall be fed, ye happy birds, With manna of celestial words; Not mine, though mine they seem to be, Not mine, though they be spoken through me.

"O, doubly are ye bound to praise The great Creator in your lays; He giveth you your plumes of down, Your crimson hoods, your cloaks of brown.

"He giveth you your wings to fly And breathe a purer air on high, And careth for you everywhere, Who for yourselves so little care!"

With flutter of swift wings and songs Together rose the feathered throngs, And
    singing scattered far apart; Deep peace was in St. Francis' heart.
He knew not if the brotherhood His homily had understood; He only knew
    that to one ear The meaning of his words was clear.

BELISARIUS

I am poor and old and blind;
The sun burns me, and the wind
   Blows through the city gate
And covers me with dust
From the wheels of the august
   Justinian the Great.
It was for him I chased
The Persians o'er wild and waste,
   As General of the East;
Night after night I lay
In their camps of yesterday;
   Their forage was my feast.
For him, with sails of red,
And torches at mast-head,
   Piloting the great fleet,
I swept the Afric coasts
And scattered the Vandal hosts,
   Like dust in a windy street.
For him I won again
The Ausonian realm and reign,
   Rome and Parthenope;
And all the land was mine
From the summits of Apennine
   To the shores of either sea.
For him, in my feeble age,
I dared the battle's rage,
   To save Byzantium's state,
When the tents of Zabergan,
Like snow-drifts overran
   The road to the Golden Gate.
And for this, for this, behold!
Infirm and blind and old,
   With gray, uncovered head,
Beneath the very arch
Of my triumphal march,
   I stand and beg my bread!

Methinks I still can hear,
Sounding distinct and near,
  The Vandal monarch's cry,
As, captive and disgraced,
With majestic step he paced,—
  "All, all is Vanity!"
Ah! vainest of all things
Is the gratitude of kings;
  The plaudits of the crowd
Are but the clatter of feet
At midnight in the street,
  Hollow and restless and loud.
But the bitterest disgrace
Is to see forever the face
  Of the Monk of Ephesus!
The unconquerable will
This, too, can bear;—I still
  Am Belisarius!

SONGO RIVER

Nowhere such a devious stream, Save in fancy or in dream, Winding slow
  through bush and brake Links together lake and lake.

Walled with woods or sandy shelf, Ever doubling on itself Flows the stream,
  so still and slow That it hardly seems to flow.

Never errant knight of old, Lost in woodland or on wold, Such a winding path
  pursued Through the sylvan solitude.

Never school-boy in his quest After hazel-nut or nest, Through the forest in
  and out Wandered loitering thus about.

In the mirror of its tide Tangled thickets on each side Hang inverted, and
  between Floating cloud or sky serene.

Swift or swallow on the wing Seems the only living thing, Or the loon, that
  laughs and flies Down to those reflected skies.

Silent stream! thy Indian name Unfamiliar is to fame; For thou hidest here
  alone, Well content to be unknown.

But thy tranquil waters teach Wisdom deep as human speech, Moving without
  haste or noise In unbroken equipoise.

Though thou turnest no busy mill, And art ever calm and still, Even thy
  silence seems to say To the traveller on his way:—

"Traveller, hurrying from the heat Of the city, stay thy feet! Rest awhile, nor
  longer waste Life with inconsiderate haste!

"Be not like a stream that brawls Loud with shallow waterfalls, But in quiet
  self-control Link together soul and soul"

FLIGHT THE FIFTH

THE HERONS OF ELMWOOD

Warm and still is the summer night,
  As here by the river's brink I wander;
White overhead are the stars, and white
  The glimmering lamps on the hillside yonder.
Silent are all the sounds of day;
  Nothing I hear but the chirp of crickets,
And the cry of the herons winging their way
  O'er the poet's house in the Elmwood thickets.
Call to him, herons, as slowly you pass
  To your roosts in the haunts of the exiled thrushes,
Sing him the song of the green morass;
  And the tides that water the reeds and rushes.
Sing him the mystical Song of the Hern,
  And the secret that baffles our utmost seeking;
For only a sound of lament we discern,
  And cannot interpret the words you are speaking.
Sing of the air, and the wild delight
  Of wings that uplift and winds that uphold you,
The joy of freedom, the rapture of flight
  Through the drift of the floating mists that infold you.
Of the landscape lying so far below,
  With its towns and rivers and desert places;
And the splendor of light above, and the glow

Of the limitless, blue, ethereal spaces.
Ask him if songs of the Troubadours,
  Or of Minnesingers in old black-letter,
Sound in his ears more sweet than yours,
  And if yours are not sweeter and wilder and better.
Sing to him, say to him, here at his gate,
  Where the boughs of the stately elms are meeting,
Some one hath lingered to meditate,
  And send him unseen this friendly greeting;
That many another hath done the same,
  Though not by a sound was the silence broken;
The surest pledge of a deathless name
  Is the silent homage of thoughts unspoken.

A DUTCH PICTURE

Simon Danz has come home again,
  From cruising about with his buccaneers;
He has singed the beard of the King of Spain,
And carried away the Dean of Jaen
  And sold him in Algiers.
In his house by the Maese, with its roof of tiles,
  And weathercocks flying aloft in air,
There are silver tankards of antique styles,
Plunder of convent and castle, and piles
  Of carpets rich and rare.
In his tulip-garden there by the town,
  Overlooking the sluggish stream,
With his Moorish cap and dressing-gown,
The old sea-captain, hale and brown,
  Walks in a waking dream.
A smile in his gray mustachio lurks
Whenever he thinks of the King of Spain,
And the listed tulips look like Turks,
And the silent gardener as he works
  Is changed to the Dean of Jaen.
The windmills on the outermost
  Verge of the landscape in the haze,
To him are towers on the Spanish coast,
With whiskered sentinels at their post,
  Though this is the river Maese.
But when the winter rains begin,
  He sits and smokes by the blazing brands,

And old seafaring men come in,
Goat-bearded, gray, and with double chin,
  And rings upon their hands.
They sit there in the shadow and shine
  Of the flickering fire of the winter night;
Figures in color and design
Like those by Rembrandt of the Rhine,
  Half darkness and half light.
And they talk of ventures lost or won,
  And their talk is ever and ever the same,
While they drink the red wine of Tarragon,
From the cellars of some Spanish Don,
  Or convent set on flame.
Restless at times with heavy strides
  He paces his parlor to and fro;
He is like a ship that at anchor rides,
And swings with the rising and falling tides,
  And tugs at her anchor-tow.
Voices mysterious far and near,
  Sound of the wind and sound of the sea,
Are calling and whispering in his ear,
"Simon Danz! Why stayest thou here?
  Come forth and follow me!"
So he thinks he shall take to the sea again
  For one more cruise with his buccaneers,
To singe the beard of the King of Spain,
And capture another Dean of Jaen
  And sell him in Algiers.

CASTLES IN SPAIN

How much of my young heart, O Spain,
  Went out to thee in days of yore!
What dreams romantic filled my brain,
And summoned back to life again
The Paladins of Charlemagne
The Cid Campeador!
And shapes more shadowy than these,
  In the dim twilight half revealed;
Phoenician galleys on the seas,
The Roman camps like hives of bees,
The Goth uplifting from his knees
  Pelayo on his shield.

It was these memories perchance,
  From annals of remotest eld,
That lent the colors of romance
To every trivial circumstance,
And changed the form and countenance
  Of all that I beheld.
Old towns, whose history lies hid
  In monkish chronicle or rhyme,
Burgos, the birthplace of the Cid,
Zamora and Valladolid,
Toledo, built and walled amid
  The wars of Wamba's time;
The long, straight line of the high-way,
  The distant town that seems so near,
The peasants in the fields, that stay
Their toil to cross themselves and pray,
When from the belfry at midday
  The Angelus they hear;
White crosses in the mountain pass,
  Mules gay with tassels, the loud din
Of muleteers, the tethered ass
That crops the dusty wayside grass,
And cavaliers with spurs of brass
  Alighting at the inn;
White hamlets hidden in fields of wheat,
  White cities slumbering by the sea,
White sunshine flooding square and street,
Dark mountain-ranges, at whose feet
The river-beds are dry with heat,—
  All was a dream to me.
Yet something sombre and severe
  O'er the enchanted landscape reigned;
A terror in the atmosphere
As if King Philip listened near,
Or Torquemada, the austere,
  His ghostly sway maintained.
The softer Andalusian skies
  Dispelled the sadness and the gloom;
There Cadiz by the seaside lies,
And Seville's orange-orchards rise,
Making the land a paradise
  Of beauty and of bloom.
There Cordova is hidden among
  The palm, the olive, and the vine;

Gem of the South, by poets sung,
And in whose Mosque Ahmanzor hung
As lamps the bells that once had rung
  At Compostella's shrine.
But over all the rest supreme,
  The star of stars, the cynosure,
The artist's and the poet's theme,
The young man's vision, the old man's dream,—
Granada by its winding stream,
  The city of the Moor!
And there the Alhambra still recalls
  Aladdin's palace of delight;
Allah il Allah! through its halls
Whispers the fountain as it falls,
The Darro darts beneath its walls,
  The hills with snow are white.
Ah yes, the hills are white with snow,
  And cold with blasts that bite and freeze;
But in the happy vale below
The orange and pomegranate grow,
And wafts of air toss to and fro
  The blossoming almond-trees.
The Vega cleft by the Xenil,
  The fascination and allure
Of the sweet landscape chains the will;
The traveller lingers on the hill,
His parted lips are breathing still
  The last sigh of the Moor.
How like a ruin overgrown
  With flower's that hide the rents of time,
Stands now the Past that I have known,
Castles in Spain, not built of stone
But of white summer clouds, and blown
  Into this little mist of rhyme!

VITTORIA COLONNA

VITTORIA COLONNA, on the death of her husband, the Marchese di Pescara, retired to her castle at Ischia (Inarime), and there wrote the Ode upon his death, which gained her the title of Divine.

Once more, once more, Inarime,
  I see thy purple hills!—once more
I hear the billows of the bay

Wash the white pebbles on thy shore.
High o'er the sea-surge and the sands,
  Like a great galleon wrecked and cast
Ashore by storms, thy castle stands,
  A mouldering landmark of the Past.
Upon its terrace-walk I see
  A phantom gliding to and fro;
It is Colonna,—it is she
  Who lived and loved so long ago.
Pescara's beautiful young wife,
  The type of perfect womanhood,
Whose life was love, the life of life,
  That time and change and death withstood.
For death, that breaks the marriage band
  In others, only closer pressed
The wedding-ring upon her hand
  And closer locked and barred her breast.
She knew the life-long martyrdom,
  The weariness, the endless pain
Of waiting for some one to come
  Who nevermore would come again.
The shadows of the chestnut-trees,
  The odor of the orange blooms,
The song of birds, and, more than these,
  The silence of deserted rooms;
The respiration of the sea,
  The soft caresses of the air,
All things in nature seemed to be
  But ministers of her despair;
Till the o'erburdened heart, so long
  Imprisoned in itself, found vent
And voice in one impassioned song
  Of inconsolable lament.
Then as the sun, though hidden from sight,
  Transmutes to gold the leaden mist,
Her life was interfused with light,
  From realms that, though unseen, exist,
Inarime! Inarime!
  Thy castle on the crags above
In dust shall crumble and decay,
  But not the memory of her love.

THE REVENGE OF RAIN-IN-THE-FACE

In that desolate land and lone,
Where the Big Horn and Yellowstone
  Roar down their mountain path,
By their fires the Sioux Chiefs
Muttered their woes and griefs
  And the menace of their wrath.
"Revenge!" cried Rain-in-the-Face,
"Revenue upon all the race
  Of the White Chief with yellow hair!"
And the mountains dark and high
From their crags re-echoed the cry
  Of his anger and despair.
In the meadow, spreading wide
By woodland and riverside
  The Indian village stood;
All was silent as a dream,
Save the rushing a of the stream
  And the blue-jay in the wood.
In his war paint and his beads,
Like a bison among the reeds,
  In ambush the Sitting Bull
Lay with three thousand braves
Crouched in the clefts and caves,
Savage, unmerciful!
Into the fatal snare
The White Chief with yellow hair
  And his three hundred men
Dashed headlong, sword in hand;
But of that gallant band
  Not one returned again.
The sudden darkness of death
Overwhelmed them like the breath
  And smoke of a furnace fire:
By the river's bank, and between
The rocks of the ravine,
  They lay in their bloody attire.
But the foemen fled in the night,
And Rain-in-the-Face, in his flight
  Uplifted high in air
As a ghastly trophy, bore
The brave heart, that beat no more,

Of the White Chief with yellow hair.
Whose was the right and the wrong?
Sing it, O funeral song,
  With a voice that is full of tears,
And say that our broken faith
Wrought all this ruin and scathe,
  In the Year of a Hundred Years.

TO THE RIVER YVETTE

O lovely river of Yvette!
  O darling river! like a bride,
Some dimpled, bashful, fair Lisette,
  Thou goest to wed the Orge's tide.
Maincourt, and lordly Dampierre,
  See and salute thee on thy way,
And, with a blessing and a prayer,
  Ring the sweet bells of St. Forget.
The valley of Chevreuse in vain
  Would hold thee in its fond embrace;
Thou glidest from its arms again
  And hurriest on with swifter pace.
Thou wilt not stay; with restless feet
  Pursuing still thine onward flight,
Thou goest as one in haste to meet
  Her sole desire, her head's delight.
O lovely river of Yvette!
  O darling stream! on balanced wings
The wood-birds sang the chansonnette
  That here a wandering poet sings.

THE EMPEROR'S GLOVE

"Combien faudrait-il de peaux d'Espagne pour faire un gant de cette grandeur?" A
play upon the words gant, a glove, and Gand, the French for Ghent.

On St. Baron's tower, commanding
  Half of Flanders, his domain,
Charles the Emperor once was standing,
While beneath him on the landing
  Stood Duke Alva and his train.
Like a print in books of fables,
  Or a model made for show,

With its pointed roofs and gables,
Dormer windows, scrolls and labels,
  Lay the city far below.
Through its squares and streets and alleys
  Poured the populace of Ghent;
As a routed army rallies,
Or as rivers run through valleys,
  Hurrying to their homes they went
"Nest of Lutheran misbelievers!"
  Cried Duke Alva as he gazed;
"Haunt of traitors and deceivers,
Stronghold of insurgent weavers,
  Let it to the ground be razed!"
On the Emperor's cap the feather
  Nods, as laughing he replies:
"How many skins of Spanish leather,
Think you, would, if stitched together
  Make a glove of such a size?"

A BALLAD OF THE FRENCH FLEET: OCTOBER, 1746

MR. THOMAS PRINCE loquitur.

A fleet with flags arrayed
  Sailed from the port of Brest,
And the Admiral's ship displayed
  The signal: "Steer southwest."
For this Admiral D'Anville
  Had sworn by cross and crown
To ravage with fire and steel
  Our helpless Boston Town.
There were rumors in the street,
  In the houses there was fear
Of the coming of the fleet,
  And the danger hovering near.
And while from mouth to mouth
  Spread the tidings of dismay,
I stood in the Old South,
  Saying humbly: "Let us pray!
"O Lord! we would not advise;
  But if in thy Providence
A tempest should arise
  To drive the French fleet hence,
And scatter it far and wide,

Or sink it in the sea,
We should be satisfied,
  And thine the glory be."
This was the prayer I made,
  For my soul was all on flame,
And even as I prayed
  The answering tempest came;
It came with a mighty power,
  Shaking the windows and walls,
And tolling the bell in the tower,
  As it tolls at funerals.
The lightning suddenly
  Unsheathed its flaming sword,
And I cried: "Stand still, and see
  The salvation of the Lord!"
The heavens were black with cloud,
  The sea was white with hail,
And ever more fierce and loud
  Blew the October gale.
The fleet it overtook,
  And the broad sails in the van
Like the tents of Cushan shook,
  Or the curtains of Midian.
Down on the reeling decks
  Crashed the o'erwhelming seas;
Ah, never were there wrecks
  So pitiful as these!
Like a potter's vessel broke
  The great ships of the line;
They were carried away as a smoke,
  Or sank like lead in the brine.
O Lord! before thy path
  They vanished and ceased to be,
When thou didst walk in wrath
  With thine horses through the sea!

THE LEAP OF ROUSHAN BEG

Mounted on Kyrat strong and fleet,
His chestnut steed with four white feet,
  Roushan Beg, called Kurroglou,
Son of the road and bandit chief,
Seeking refuge and relief,

Up the mountain pathway flew.
Such was Kyrat's wondrous speed,
Never yet could any steed
  Reach the dust-cloud in his course.
More than maiden, more than wife,
More than gold and next to life
  Roushan the Robber loved his horse.
In the land that lies beyond
Erzeroum and Trebizond,
  Garden-girt his fortress stood;
Plundered khan, or caravan
Journeying north from Koordistan,
  Gave him wealth and wine and food.
Seven hundred and fourscore
Men at arms his livery wore,
  Did his bidding night and day.
Now, through regions all unknown,
He was wandering, lost, alone,
  Seeking without guide his way.
Suddenly the pathway ends,
Sheer the precipice descends,
  Loud the torrent roars unseen;
Thirty feet from side to side
Yawns the chasm; on air must ride
  He who crosses this ravine.
Following close in his pursuit,
At the precipice's foot,
  Reyhan the Arab of Orfah
Halted with his hundred men,
Shouting upward from the glen,
  "La Illah illa Allah!"
Gently Roushan Beg caressed
Kyrat's forehead, neck, and breast;
  Kissed him upon both his eyes;
Sang to him in his wild way,
As upon the topmost spray
  Sings a bird before it flies.
"O my Kyrat, O my steed,
Round and slender as a reed,
  Carry me this peril through!
Satin housings shall be thine,
Shoes of gold, O Kyrat mine,
  O thou soul of Kurroglou!
"Soft thy skin as silken skein,

Soft as woman's hair thy mane,
  Tender are thine eyes and true;
All thy hoofs like ivory shine,
Polished bright; O, life of mine,
  Leap, and rescue Kurroglou!"
Kyrat, then, the strong and fleet,
Drew together his four white feet,
  Paused a moment on the verge,
Measured with his eye the space,
And into the air's embrace
  Leaped as leaps the ocean surge.
As the ocean surge o'er sand
Bears a swimmer safe to land,
  Kyrat safe his rider bore;
Rattling down the deep abyss
Fragments of the precipice
  Rolled like pebbles on a shore.
Roushan's tasselled cap of red
Trembled not upon his head,
  Careless sat he and upright;
Neither hand nor bridle shook,
Nor his head he turned to look,
  As he galloped out of sight.
Flash of harness in the air,
Seen a moment like the glare
  Of a sword drawn from its sheath;
Thus the phantom horseman passed,
And the shadow that he cast
  Leaped the cataract underneath.
Reyhan the Arab held his breath
While this vision of life and death
  Passed above him. "Allahu!"
Cried he. "In all Koordistan
Lives there not so brave a man
  As this Robber Kurroglou!"

HAROUN AL RASCHID

One day, Haroun Al Raschid read A book wherein the poet said:—
"Where are the kings, and where the rest Of those who once the world
    possessed?
"They're gone with all their pomp and show, They're gone the way that thou
    shalt go.

"O thou who choosest for thy share The world, and what the world calls fair,
"Take all that it can give or lend, But know that death is at the end!"
Haroun Al Raschid bowed his head: Tears fell upon the page he read.

KING TRISANKU

Viswamitra the Magician,
  By his spells and incantations,
Up to Indra's realms elysian
  Raised Trisanku, king of nations.
Indra and the gods offended
  Hurled him downward, and descending
In the air he hung suspended,
  With these equal powers contending.
Thus by aspirations lifted,
  By misgivings downward driven,
Human hearts are tossed and drifted
  Midway between earth and heaven.

A WRAITH IN THE MIST

"Sir, I should build me a fortification, if I
came to live here." —BOSWELL'S Johnson.
On the green little isle of Inchkenneth,
  Who is it that walks by the shore,
So gay with his Highland blue bonnet,
  So brave with his targe and claymore?
His form is the form of a giant,
  But his face wears an aspect of pain;
Can this be the Laird of Inchkenneth?
  Can this be Sir Allan McLean?
Ah, no! It is only the Rambler,
  The Idler, who lives in Bolt Court,
And who says, were he Laird of Inchkenneth,
  He would wall himself round with a fort.

THE THREE KINGS

Three Kings came riding from far away,
  Melchior and Gaspar and Baltasar;
Three Wise Men out of the East were they,
And they travelled by night and they slept by day,

For their guide was a beautiful, wonderful star.
The star was so beautiful, large, and clear,
  That all the other stars of the sky
Became a white mist in the atmosphere,
And by this they knew that the coming was near
  Of the Prince foretold in the prophecy.
Three caskets they bore on their saddle-bows,
  Three caskets of gold with golden keys;
Their robes were of crimson silk with rows
Of bells and pomegranates and furbelows,
  Their turbans like blossoming almond-trees.
And so the Three Kings rode into the West,
  Through the dusk of night, over hill and dell,
And sometimes they nodded with beard on breast
And sometimes talked, as they paused to rest,
  With the people they met at some wayside well.
"Of the child that is born," said Baltasar,
  "Good people, I pray you, tell us the news;
For we in the East have seen his star,
And have ridden fast, and have ridden far,
  To find and worship the King of the Jews."
And the people answered, "You ask in vain;
  We know of no king but Herod the Great!"
They thought the Wise Men were men insane,
As they spurred their horses across the plain,
  Like riders in haste, and who cannot wait.
And when they came to Jerusalem,
  Herod the Great, who had heard this thing,
Sent for the Wise Men and questioned them;
And said, "Go down unto Bethlehem,
  And bring me tidings of this new king."
So they rode away; and the star stood still,
  The only one in the gray of morn
Yes, it stopped, it stood still of its own free will,
Right over Bethlehem on the hill,
  The city of David where Christ was born.
And the Three Kings rode through the gate and the guard,
  Through the silent street, till their horses turned
And neighed as they entered the great inn-yard;
But the windows were closed, and the doors were barred,
  And only a light in the stable burned.
And cradled there in the scented hay,
  In the air made sweet by the breath of kine,
The little child in the manger lay,

The child, that would be king one day
  Of a kingdom not human but divine.
His mother Mary of Nazareth
  Sat watching beside his place of rest,
Watching the even flow of his breath,
For the joy of life and the terror of death
  Were mingled together in her breast.
They laid their offerings at his feet:
  The gold was their tribute to a King,
The frankincense, with its odor sweet,
Was for the Priest, the Paraclete,
  The myrrh for the body's burying.
And the mother wondered and bowed her head,
  And sat as still as a statue of stone;
Her heart was troubled yet comforted,
Remembering what the Angel had said
  Of an endless reign and of David's throne.
Then the Kings rode out of the city gate,
  With a clatter of hoofs in proud array;
But they went not back to Herod the Great,
For they knew his malice and feared his hate,
  And returned to their homes by another way.

SONG

  Stay, stay at home, my heart, and rest;
  Home-keeping hearts are happiest,
  For those that wander they know not where
  Are full of trouble and full of care;
    To stay at home is best.
  Weary and homesick and distressed,
  They wander east, they wander west,
  And are baffled and beaten and blown about
  By the winds of the wilderness of doubt;
    To stay at home is best.
  Then stay at home, my heart, and rest;
  The bird is safest in its nest;
  O'er all that flutter their wings and fly
  A hawk is hovering in the sky;
    To stay at home is best.

THE WHITE CZAR

The White Czar is Peter the Great. Batyushka, Father dear, and Gosudar, Sovereign, are titles the Russian people are fond of giving to the Czar in their popular songs.

Dost thou see on the rampart's height
That wreath of mist, in the light
Of the midnight moon? O, hist!
It is not a wreath of mist;
It is the Czar, the White Czar,
   Batyushka! Gosudar!
He has heard, among the dead,
The artillery roll o'erhead;
The drums and the tramp of feet
Of his soldiery in the street;
He is awake! the White Czar,
   Batyushka! Gosudar!
He has heard in the grave the cries
Of his people: "Awake! arise!"
He has rent the gold brocade
Whereof his shroud was made;
He is risen! the White Czar,
   Batyushka! Gosudar!
From the Volga and the Don
He has led his armies on,
Over river and morass,
Over desert and mountain pass;
The Czar, the Orthodox Czar,
   Batyushka! Gosudar!
He looks from the mountain-chain
Toward the seas, that cleave in twain
The continents; his hand
Points southward o'er the land
Of Roumili! O Czar,
   Batyushka! Gosudar!
And the words break from his lips:
"I am the builder of ships,
And my ships shall sail these seas
To the Pillars of Hercules!
I say it; the White Czar,
   Batyushka! Gosudar!
"The Bosphorus shall be free;
It shall make room for me;
And the gates of its water-streets

Be unbarred before my fleets.
I say it; the White Czar,
   Batyushka! Gosudar!
"And the Christian shall no more
Be crushed, as heretofore,
Beneath thine iron rule,
O Sultan of Istamboul!
I swear it; I the Czar,
   Batyushka! Gosudar!"

DELIA

Sweet as the tender fragrance that survives,
When martyred flowers breathe out their little lives,
Sweet as a song that once consoled our pain,
But never will be sung to us again,
Is thy remembrance. Now the hour of rest
Hath come to thee. Sleep, darling; it is best.

TALES OF A WAYSIDE INN

PAUL REVERE'S RIDE, THE SAGA OF KING OLAF &
OTHER POEMS

PART FIRST

PRELUDE: THE WAYSIDE INN

One Autumn night, in Sudbury town,
Across the meadows bare and brown,
The windows of the wayside inn
Gleamed red with fire-light through the leaves
Of woodbine, hanging from the eaves
Their crimson curtains rent and thin.

As ancient is this hostelry
As any in the land may be,
Built in the old Colonial day,
When men lived in a grander way,
With ampler hospitality;
A kind of old Hobgoblin Hall,
Now somewhat fallen to decay,
With weather-stains upon the wall,
And stairways worn, and crazy doors,
And creaking and uneven floors,
And chimneys huge, and tiled and tall.

A region of repose it seems,
A place of slumber and of dreams,
Remote among the wooded hills!
For there no noisy railway speeds,

Its torch-race scattering smoke and gleeds;
But noon and night, the panting teams
Stop under the great oaks, that throw
Tangles of light and shade below,
On roofs and doors and window-sills.
Across the road the barns display
Their lines of stalls, their mows of hay,
Through the wide doors the breezes blow,
The wattled cocks strut to and fro,
And, half effaced by rain and shine,
The Red Horse prances on the sign.
Round this old-fashioned, quaint abode
Deep silence reigned, save when a gust
Went rushing down the county road,
And skeletons of leaves, and dust,
A moment quickened by its breath,
Shuddered and danced their dance of death,
And through the ancient oaks o'erhead
Mysterious voices moaned and fled.

But from the parlor of the inn
A pleasant murmur smote the ear,
Like water rushing through a weir:
Oft interrupted by the din
Of laughter and of loud applause,
And, in each intervening pause,
The music of a violin.
The fire-light, shedding over all
The splendor of its ruddy glow,
Filled the whole parlor large and low;
It gleamed on wainscot and on wall,
It touched with more than wonted grace
Fair Princess Mary's pictured face;
It bronzed the rafters overhead,
On the old spinet's ivory keys
It played inaudible melodies,
It crowned the sombre clock with flame,
The hands, the hours, the maker's name,
And painted with a livelier red
The Landlord's coat-of-arms again;
And, flashing on the window-pane,
Emblazoned with its light and shade
The jovial rhymes, that still remain,
Writ near a century ago,

By the great Major Molineaux,
Whom Hawthorne has immortal made.

Before the blazing fire of wood
Erect the rapt musician stood;
And ever and anon he bent
His head upon his instrument,
And seemed to listen, till he caught
Confessions of its secret thought,—
The joy, the triumph, the lament,
The exultation and the pain;
Then, by the magic of his art,
He soothed the throbbings of its heart,
And lulled it into peace again.

Around the fireside at their ease
There sat a group of friends, entranced
With the delicious melodies
Who from the far-off noisy town
Had to the wayside inn come down,
To rest beneath its old oak-trees.
The fire-light on their faces glanced,
Their shadows on the wainscot danced,
And, though of different lands and speech,
Each had his tale to tell, and each
Was anxious to be pleased and please.
And while the sweet musician plays,
Let me in outline sketch them all,
Perchance uncouthly as the blaze
With its uncertain touch portrays
Their shadowy semblance on the wall.

But first the Landlord will I trace;
Grave in his aspect and attire;
A man of ancient pedigree,
A Justice of the Peace was he,
Known in all Sudbury as "The Squire."
Proud was he of his name and race,
Of old Sir William and Sir Hugh,
And in the parlor, full in view,
His coat-of-arms, well framed and glazed,
Upon the wall in colors blazed;
He beareth gules upon his shield,
A chevron argent in the field,

With three wolf's heads, and for the crest
A Wyvern part-per-pale addressed
Upon a helmet barred; below
The scroll reads, "By the name of Howe."
And over this, no longer bright,
Though glimmering with a latent light,
Was hung the sword his grandsire bore
In the rebellious days of yore,
Down there at Concord in the fight.

A youth was there, of quiet ways,
A Student of old books and days,
To whom all tongues and lands were known
And yet a lover of his own;
With many a social virtue graced,
And yet a friend of solitude;
A man of such a genial mood
The heart of all things he embraced,
And yet of such fastidious taste,
He never found the best too good.
Books were his passion and delight,
And in his upper room at home
Stood many a rare and sumptuous tome,
In vellum bound, with gold bedight,
Great volumes garmented in white,
Recalling Florence, Pisa, Rome.
He loved the twilight that surrounds
The border-land of old romance;
Where glitter hauberk, helm, and lance,
And banner waves, and trumpet sounds,
And ladies ride with hawk on wrist,
And mighty warriors sweep along,
Magnified by the purple mist,
The dusk of centuries and of song.
The chronicles of Charlemagne,
Of Merlin and the Mort d'Arthure,
Mingled together in his brain
With tales of Flores and Blanchefleur,
Sir Ferumbras, Sir Eglamour,
Sir Launcelot, Sir Morgadour,
Sir Guy, Sir Bevis, Sir Gawain.

A young Sicilian, too, was there;
In sight of Etna born and bred,

Some breath of its volcanic air
Was glowing in his heart and brain,
And, being rebellious to his liege,
After Palermo's fatal siege,
Across the western seas he fled,
In good King Bomba's happy reign.
His face was like a summer night,
All flooded with a dusky light;
His hands were small; his teeth shone white
As sea-shells, when he smiled or spoke;
His sinews supple and strong as oak;
Clean shaven was he as a priest,
Who at the mass on Sunday sings,
Save that upon his upper lip
His beard, a good palm's length least,
Level and pointed at the tip,
Shot sideways, like a swallow's wings.
The poets read he o'er and o'er,
And most of all the Immortal Four
Of Italy; and next to those,
The story-telling bard of prose,
Who wrote the joyous Tuscan tales
Of the Decameron, that make
Fiesole's green hills and vales
Remembered for Boccaccio's sake.
Much too of music was his thought;
The melodies and measures fraught
With sunshine and the open air,
Of vineyards and the singing sea
Of his beloved Sicily;
And much it pleased him to peruse
The songs of the Sicilian muse,
Bucolic songs by Meli sung
In the familiar peasant tongue,
That made men say, "Behold! once more
The pitying gods to earth restore
Theocritus of Syracuse!"

A Spanish Jew from Alicant
With aspect grand and grave was there;
Vender of silks and fabrics rare,
And attar of rose from the Levant.
Like an old Patriarch he appeared,
Abraham or Isaac, or at least

Some later Prophet or High-Priest;
With lustrous eyes, and olive skin,
And, wildly tossed from cheeks and chin,
The tumbling cataract of his beard.
His garments breathed a spicy scent
Of cinnamon and sandal blent,
Like the soft aromatic gales
That meet the mariner, who sails
Through the Moluccas, and the seas
That wash the shores of Celebes.
All stories that recorded are
By Pierre Alphonse he knew by heart,
And it was rumored he could say
The Parables of Sandabar,
And all the Fables of Pilpay,
Or if not all, the greater part!
Well versed was he in Hebrew books,
Talmud and Targum, and the lore
Of Kabala; and evermore
There was a mystery in his looks;
His eyes seemed gazing far away,
As if in vision or in trance
He heard the solemn sackbut play,
And saw the Jewish maidens dance.

A Theologian, from the school
Of Cambridge on the Charles, was there;
Skilful alike with tongue and pen,
He preached to all men everywhere
The Gospel of the Golden Rule,
The New Commandment given to men,
Thinking the deed, and not the creed,
Would help us in our utmost need.
With reverent feet the earth he trod,
Nor banished nature from his plan,
But studied still with deep research
To build the Universal Church,
Lofty as in the love of God,
And ample as the wants of man.

A Poet, too, was there, whose verse
Was tender, musical, and terse;
The inspiration, the delight,
The gleam, the glory, the swift flight,

Of thoughts so sudden, that they seem
The revelations of a dream,
All these were his; but with them came
No envy of another's fame;
He did not find his sleep less sweet
For music in some neighboring street,
Nor rustling hear in every breeze
The laurels of Miltiades.
Honor and blessings on his head
While living, good report when dead,
Who, not too eager for renown,
Accepts, but does not clutch, the crown!

Last the Musician, as he stood
Illumined by that fire of wood;
Fair-haired, blue-eyed, his aspect blithe.
His figure tall and straight and lithe,
And every feature of his face
Revealing his Norwegian race;
A radiance, streaming from within,
Around his eyes and forehead beamed,
The Angel with the violin,
Painted by Raphael, he seemed.
He lived in that ideal world
Whose language is not speech, but song;
Around him evermore the throng
Of elves and sprites their dances whirled;
The Stromkarl sang, the cataract hurled
Its headlong waters from the height;
And mingled in the wild delight
The scream of sea-birds in their flight,
The rumor of the forest trees,
The plunge of the implacable seas,
The tumult of the wind at night,
Voices of eld, like trumpets blowing,
Old ballads, and wild melodies
Through mist and darkness pouring forth,
Like Elivagar's river flowing
Out of the glaciers of the North.

The instrument on which he played
Was in Cremona's workshops made,
By a great master of the past,
Ere yet was lost the art divine;

Fashioned of maple and of pine,
That in Tyrolian forests vast
Had rocked and wrestled with the blast;
Exquisite was it in design,
Perfect in each minutest part.
A marvel of the lutist's art;
And in its hollow chamber, thus,
The maker from whose hands it came
Had written his unrivalled name,—
"Antonius Stradivarius."

And when he played, the atmosphere
Was filled with magic, and the ear
Caught echoes of that Harp of Gold,
Whose music had so weird a sound,
The hunted stag forgot to bound,
The leaping rivulet backward rolled,
The birds came down from bush and tree,
The dead came from beneath the sea,
The maiden to the harper's knee!

The music ceased; the applause was loud,
The pleased musician smiled and bowed;
The wood-fire clapped its hands of flame,
The shadows on the wainscot stirred,
And from the harpsichord there came
A ghostly murmur of acclaim,
A sound like that sent down at night
By birds of passage in their flight,
From the remotest distance heard.

Then silence followed; then began
A clamor for the Landlord's tale,—
The story promised them of old,
They said, but always left untold;
And he, although a bashful man,
And all his courage seemed to fail,
Finding excuse of no avail,
Yielded; and thus the story ran.

THE LANDLORD'S TALE: PAUL REVERE'S RIDE

Listen, my children, and you shall hear

Of the midnight ride of Paul Revere,
On the eighteenth of April, in Seventy-five;
Hardly a man is now alive
Who remembers that famous day and year.

He said to his friend, "If the British march
By land or sea from the town to-night,
Hang a lantern aloft in the belfry arch
Of the North Church tower as a signal light,—
One, if by land, and two, if by sea;
And I on the opposite shore will be,
Ready to ride and spread the alarm
Through every Middlesex village and farm
For the country folk to be up and to arm,"

Then he said, "Good night!" and with muffled oar
Silently rowed to the Charlestown shore,
Just as the moon rose over the bay,
Where swinging wide at her moorings lay
The Somerset, British man-of-war;
A phantom ship, with each mast and spar
Across the moon like a prison bar,
And a huge black hulk, that was magnified
By its own reflection in the tide.

Meanwhile, his friend, through alley and street,
Wanders and watches with eager ears,
Till in the silence around him he hears
The muster of men at the barrack door,
The sound of arms, and the tramp of feet,
And the measured tread of the grenadiers,
Marching down to their boats on the shore.

Then he climbed the tower of the Old North Church,
By the wooden stairs, with stealthy tread,
To the belfry-chamber overhead,
And startled the pigeons from their perch
On the sombre rafters, that round him made
Masses and moving shapes of shade,—
By the trembling ladder, steep and tall
To the highest window in the wall,
Where he paused to listen and look down
A moment on the roofs of the town,
And the moonlight flowing over all.

Beneath, in the churchyard, lay the dead,
In their night-encampment on the hill,
Wrapped in silence so deep and still
That he could hear, like a sentinel's tread,
The watchful night-wind, as it went
Creeping along from tent to tent
And seeming to whisper, "All is well!"
A moment only he feels the spell
Of the place and the hour, and the secret dread
Of the lonely belfry and the dead;
For suddenly all his thoughts are bent
On a shadowy something far away,
Where the river widens to meet the bay,—
A line of black that bends and floats
On the rising tide, like a bridge of boats.

Meanwhile, impatient to mount and ride,
Booted and spurred, with a heavy stride
On the opposite shore walked Paul Revere.
Now he patted his horse's side,
Now gazed at the landscape far and near,
Then, impetuous, stamped the earth,
And turned and tightened his saddle-girth;
But mostly he watched with eager search
The belfry-tower of the Old North Church,
As it rose above the graves on the hill,
Lonely and spectral and sombre and still.
And lo! as he looks, on the belfry's height
A glimmer, and then a gleam of light!
He springs to the saddle, the bridle he turns,
But lingers and gazes, till full on his sight
A second lamp in the belfry burns!

A hurry of hoofs in a village street,
A shape in the moonlight, a bulk in the dark,
And beneath, from the pebbles, in passing, a spark
Struck out by a steed flying fearless and fleet:
That was all! And yet, through the gloom and the light,
The fate of a nation was riding that night;
And the spark struck out by that steed, in his flight,
Kindled the land into flame with its heat.
He has left the village and mounted the steep,
And beneath him, tranquil and broad and deep,
Is the Mystic, meeting the ocean tides;

And under the alders, that skirt its edge,
Now soft on the sand, now loud on the ledge,
Is heard the tramp of his steed as he rides.

It was twelve by the village clock
When he crossed the bridge into Medford town.
He heard the crowing of the cock,
And the barking of the farmer's dog,
And felt the damp of the river fog,
That rises after the sun goes down.

It was one by the village clock,
When he galloped into Lexington.
He saw the gilded weathercock
Swim in the moonlight as he passed,
And the meeting-house windows, blank and bare,
Gaze at him with a spectral glare,
As if they already stood aghast
At the bloody work they would look upon.

It was two by the village clock,
When he came to the bridge in Concord town.
He heard the bleating of the flock,
And the twitter of birds among the trees,
And felt the breath of the morning breeze
Blowing over the meadows brown.
And one was safe and asleep in his bed
Who at the bridge would be first to fall,
Who that day would be lying dead,
Pierced by a British musket-ball.

You know the rest. In the books you have read,
How the British Regulars fired and fled,—
How the farmers gave them ball for ball,
From behind each fence and farm-yard wall,
Chasing the red-coats down the lane,
Then crossing the fields to emerge again
Under the trees at the turn of the road,
And only pausing to fire and load.

So through the night rode Paul Revere;
And so through the night went his cry of alarm
To every Middlesex village and farm,—
A cry of defiance and not of fear,

A voice in the darkness, a knock at the door,
And a word that shall echo forevermore!
For, borne on the night-wind of the Past,
Through all our history, to the last,
In the hour of darkness and peril and need,
The people will waken and listen to hear
The hurrying hoof-beats of that steed,
And the midnight message of Paul Revere.

INTERLUDE

The Landlord ended thus his tale,
Then rising took down from its nail
The sword that hung there, dim with dust
And cleaving to its sheath with rust,
And said, "This sword was in the fight."
The Poet seized it, and exclaimed,
"It is the sword of a good knight,
Though homespun was his coat-of-mail;
What matter if it be not named
Joyeuse, Colada, Durindale,
Excalibar, or Aroundight,
Or other name the books record?
Your ancestor, who bore this sword
As Colonel of the Volunteers,
Mounted upon his old gray mare,
Seen here and there and everywhere,
To me a grander shape appears
Than old Sir William, or what not,
Clinking about in foreign lands
With iron gauntlets on his hands,
And on his head an iron pot!"

All laughed; the Landlord's face grew red
As his escutcheon on the wall;
He could not comprehend at all
The drift of what the Poet said;
For those who had been longest dead
Were always greatest in his eyes;
And he was speechless with surprise
To see Sir William's plumed head
Brought to a level with the rest,
And made the subject of a jest.

And this perceiving, to appease
The Landlord's wrath, the others' fears,
The Student said, with careless ease,
"The ladies and the cavaliers,
The arms, the loves, the courtesies,
The deeds of high emprise, I sing!
Thus Ariosto says, in words
That have the stately stride and ring
Of armed knights and clashing swords.
Now listen to the tale I bring
Listen! though not to me belong
The flowing draperies of his song,
The words that rouse, the voice that charms.
The Landlord's tale was one of arms,
Only a tale of love is mine,
Blending the human and divine,
A tale of the Decameron, told
In Palmieri's garden old,
By Fiametta, laurel-crowned,
While her companions lay around,
And heard the intermingled sound
Of airs that on their errands sped,
And wild birds gossiping overhead,
And lisp of leaves, and fountain's fall,
And her own voice more sweet than all,
Telling the tale, which, wanting these,
Perchance may lose its power to please."

THE STUDENT'S TALE: THE FALCON OF SER FEDERIGO

One summer morning, when the sun was hot,
Weary with labor in his garden-plot,
On a rude bench beneath his cottage eaves,
Ser Federigo sat among the leaves
Of a huge vine, that, with its arms outspread,
Hung its delicious clusters overhead.
Below him, through the lovely valley flowed
The river Arno, like a winding road,
And from its banks were lifted high in air
The spires and roofs of Florence called the Fair;
To him a marble tomb, that rose above
His wasted fortunes and his buried love.
For there, in banquet and in tournament,

His wealth had lavished been, his substance spent,
To woo and lose, since ill his wooing sped,
Monna Giovanna, who his rival wed,
Yet ever in his fancy reigned supreme,
The ideal woman of a young man's dream.

Then he withdrew, in poverty and pain,
To this small farm, the last of his domain,
His only comfort and his only care
To prune his vines, and plant the fig and pear;
His only forester and only guest
His falcon, faithful to him, when the rest,
Whose willing hands had found so light of yore
The brazen knocker of his palace door,
Had now no strength to lift the wooden latch,
That entrance gave beneath a roof of thatch.
Companion of his solitary ways,
Purveyor of his feasts on holidays,
On him this melancholy man bestowed
The love with which his nature overflowed.

And so the empty-handed years went round,
Vacant, though voiceful with prophetic sound,
And so, that summer morn, he sat and mused
With folded, patient hands, as he was used,
And dreamily before his half-closed sight
Floated the vision of his lost delight.
Beside him, motionless, the drowsy bird
Dreamed of the chase, and in his slumber heard
The sudden, scythe-like sweep of wings, that dare
The headlong plunge thro' eddying gulfs of air,
Then, starting broad awake upon his perch,
Tinkled his bells, like mass-bells in a church,
And, looking at his master, seemed to say,
"Ser Federigo, shall we hunt to-day?"

Ser Federigo thought not of the chase;
The tender vision of her lovely face,
I will not say he seems to see, he sees
In the leaf-shadows of the trellises,
Herself, yet not herself; a lovely child
With flowing tresses, and eyes wide and wild,
Coming undaunted up the garden walk,
And looking not at him, but at the hawk.

"Beautiful falcon!" said he, "would that I
Might hold thee on my wrist, or see thee fly!"
The voice was hers, and made strange echoes start
Through all the haunted chambers of his heart,
As an æolian harp through gusty doors
Of some old ruin its wild music pours.

"Who is thy mother, my fair boy?" he said,
His hand laid softly on that shining head.
"Monna Giovanna. Will you let me stay
A little while, and with your falcon play?
We live there, just beyond your garden wall,
In the great house behind the poplars tall."

So he spake on; and Federigo heard
As from afar each softly uttered word,
And drifted onward through the golden gleams
And shadows of the misty sea of dreams,
As mariners becalmed through vapors drift,
And feel the sea beneath them sink and lift,
And hear far off the mournful breakers roar,
And voices calling faintly from the shore!
Then, waking from his pleasant reveries
He took the little boy upon his knees,
And told him stories of his gallant bird,
Till in their friendship he became a third.

Monna Giovanna, widowed in her prime,
Had come with friends to pass the summer time
In her grand villa, half-way up the hill,
O'erlooking Florence, but retired and still;
With iron gates, that opened through long lines
Of sacred ilex and centennial pines,
And terraced gardens, and broad steps of stone,
And sylvan deities, with moss o'ergrown,
And fountains palpitating in the heat,
And all Val d'Arno stretched beneath its feet.
Here in seclusion, as a widow may,
The lovely lady whiled the hours away,
Pacing in sable robes the statued hall,
Herself the stateliest statue among all,
And seeing more and more, with secret joy,
Her husband risen and living in her boy,
Till the lost sense of life returned again,

Not as delight, but as relief from pain.
Meanwhile the boy, rejoicing in his strength,
Stormed down the terraces from length to length;
The screaming peacock chased in hot pursuit,
And climbed the garden trellises for fruit.
But his chief pastime was to watch the flight
Of a gerfalcon, soaring into sight,
Beyond the trees that fringed the garden wall,
Then downward stooping at some distant call;
And as he gazed full often wondered he
Who might the master of the falcon be,
Until that happy morning, when he found
Master and falcon in the cottage ground.

And now a shadow and a terror fell
On the great house, as if a passing-bell
Tolled from the tower, and filled each spacious room
With secret awe, and preternatural gloom;
The petted boy grew ill, and day by day
Pined with mysterious malady away.
The mother's heart would not be comforted;
Her darling seemed to her already dead,
And often, sitting by the sufferer's side,
"What can I do to comfort thee?" she cried.
At first the silent lips made no reply,
But moved at length by her importunate cry,
"Give me," he answered, with imploring tone,
"Ser Federigo's falcon for my own!"
No answer could the astonished mother make;
How could she ask, e'en for her darling's sake,
Such favor at a luckless lover's hand,
Well knowing that to ask was to command?
Well knowing, what all falconers confessed,
In all the land that falcon was the best,
The master's pride and passion and delight,
And the sole pursuivant of this poor knight.
But yet, for her child's sake, she could no less
Than give assent to soothe his restlessness,
So promised, and then promising to keep
Her promise sacred, saw him fall asleep.

The morrow was a bright September morn;
The earth was beautiful as if new-born;
There was that nameless splendor everywhere,

That wild exhilaration in the air,
Which makes the passers in the city street
Congratulate each other as they meet.
Two lovely ladies, clothed in cloak and hood,
Passed through the garden gate into the wood,
Under the lustrous leaves, and through the sheen
Of dewy sunshine showering down between.

The one, close-hooded, had the attractive grace
Which sorrow sometimes lends a woman's face;
Her dark eyes moistened with the mists that roll
From the gulf-stream of passion in the soul;
The other with her hood thrown back, her hair
Making a golden glory in the air,
Her cheeks suffused with an auroral blush,
Her young heart singing louder than the thrush.
So walked, that morn, through mingled light and shade,
Each by the other's presence lovelier made,
Monna Giovanna and her bosom friend,
Intent upon their errand and its end.

They found Ser Federigo at his toil,
Like banished Adam, delving in the soil;
And when he looked and these fair women spied,
The garden suddenly was glorified;
His long-lost Eden was restored again,
And the strange river winding through the plain
No longer was the Arno to his eyes,
But the Euphrates watering Paradise!

Monna Giovanna raised her stately head,
And with fair words of salutation said:
"Ser Federigo, we come here as friends,
Hoping in this to make some poor amends
For past unkindness. I who ne'er before
Would even cross the threshold of your door,
I who in happier days such pride maintained,
Refused your banquets, and your gifts disdained,
This morning come, a self-invited guest,
To put your generous nature to the test,
And breakfast with you under your own vine."
To which he answered: "Poor desert of mine,
Not your unkindness call it, for if aught
Is good in me of feeling or of thought,

From you it comes, and this last grace outweighs
All sorrows, all regrets of other days."

And after further compliment and talk,
Among the asters in the garden walk
He left his guests; and to his cottage turned,
And as he entered for a moment yearned
For the lost splendors of the days of old,
The ruby glass, the silver and the gold,
And felt how piercing is the sting of pride,
By want embittered and intensified.
He looked about him for some means or way
To keep this unexpected holiday;
Searched every cupboard, and then searched again,
Summoned the maid, who came, but came in vain;
"The Signor did not hunt to-day," she said,
"There's nothing in the house but wine and bread."

Then suddenly the drowsy falcon shook
His little bells, with that sagacious look,
Which said, as plain as language to the ear,
"If anything is wanting, I am here!"
Yes, everything is wanting, gallant bird!
The master seized thee without further word.
Like thine own lure, he whirled thee round; ah me!
The pomp and flutter of brave falconry,
The bells, the jesses, the bright scarlet hood,
The flight and the pursuit o'er field and wood,
All these forevermore are ended now;
No longer victor, but the victim thou!

Then on the board a snow-white cloth he spread,
Laid on its wooden dish the loaf of bread,
Brought purple grapes with autumn sunshine hot,
The fragrant peach, the juicy bergamot;
Then in the midst a flask of wine he placed,
And with autumnal flowers the banquet graced.
Ser Federigo, would not these suffice
Without thy falcon stuffed with cloves and spice?

When all was ready, and the courtly dame
With her companion to the cottage came,
Upon Ser Federigo's brain there fell
The wild enchantment of a magic spell!

The room they entered, mean and low and small,
Was changed into a sumptuous banquet-hall,
With fanfares by aerial trumpets blown;
The rustic chair she sat on was a throne;
He ate celestial food, and a divine
Flavor was given to his country wine,
And the poor falcon, fragrant with his spice,
A peacock was, or bird of paradise!

When the repast was ended, they arose
And passed again into the garden-close.
Then said the lady, "Far too well I know
Remembering still the days of long ago,
Though you betray it not with what surprise
You see me here in this familiar wise.
You have no children, and you cannot guess
What anguish, what unspeakable distress
A mother feels, whose child is lying ill,
Nor how her heart anticipates his will.
And yet for this, you see me lay aside
All womanly reserve and check of pride,
And ask the thing most precious in your sight,
Your falcon, your sole comfort and delight,
Which if you find it in your heart to give,
My poor, unhappy boy perchance may live."

Ser Federigo listens, and replies,
With tears of love and pity in his eyes:
"Alas, dear lady! there can be no task
So sweet to me, as giving when you ask.
One little hour ago, if I had known
This wish of yours, it would have been my own.
But thinking in what manner I could best
Do honor to the presence of my guest,
I deemed that nothing worthier could be
Than what most dear and precious was to me,
And so my gallant falcon breathed his last
To furnish forth this morning our repast."

In mute contrition, mingled with dismay,
The gentle lady tuned her eyes away,
Grieving that he such sacrifice should make,
And kill his falcon for a woman's sake,
Yet feeling in her heart a woman's pride,

That nothing she could ask for was denied;
Then took her leave, and passed out at the gate
With footstep slow and soul disconsolate.

Three days went by, and lo! a passing-bell
Tolled from the little chapel in the dell;
Ten strokes Ser Federigo heard, and said,
Breathing a prayer, "Alas! her child is dead!"
Three months went by; and lo! a merrier chime
Rang from the chapel bells at Christmas time;
The cottage was deserted, and no more
Ser Federigo sat beside its door,
But now, with servitors to do his will,
In the grand villa, half-way up the hill,
Sat at the Christmas feast, and at his side
Monna Giovanna, his beloved bride,
Never so beautiful, so kind, so fair,
Enthroned once more in the old rustic chair,
High-perched upon the back of which there stood
The image of a falcon carved in wood,
And underneath the inscription, with date,
"All things come round to him who will but wait."

INTERLUDE

Soon as the story reached its end,
One, over eager to commend,
Crowned it with injudicious praise;
And then the voice of blame found vent,
And fanned the embers of dissent
Into a somewhat lively blaze.

The Theologian shook his head;
"These old Italian tales," he said,
"From the much-praised Decameron down
Through all the rabble of the rest,
Are either trifling, dull, or lewd;
The gossip of a neighborhood
In some remote provincial town,
A scandalous chronicle at best!
They seem to me a stagnant fen,
Grown rank with rushes and with reeds,
Where a white lily, now and then,

Blooms in the midst of noxious weeds
And deadly nightshade on its banks."

To this the Student straight replied,
"For the white lily, many thanks!
One should not say, with too much pride,
Fountain, I will not drink of thee!
Nor were it grateful to forget,
That from these reservoirs and tanks
Even imperial Shakespeare drew
His Moor of Venice, and the Jew,
And Romeo and Juliet,
And many a famous comedy."

Then a long pause; till some one said,
"An Angel is flying overhead!"
At these words spake the Spanish Jew,
And murmured with an inward breath:
"God grant, if what you say be true,
It may not be the Angel of Death!"
And then another pause; and then,
Stroking his beard, he said again:
"This brings back to my memory
A story in the Talmud told,
That book of gems, that book of gold,
Of wonders many and manifold,
A tale that often comes to me,
And fills my heart, and haunts my brain,
And never wearies nor grows old."

THE SPANISH JEW'S TALE: THE LEGEND OF RABBI BEN LEVI

Rabbi Ben Levi, on the Sabbath, read
A volume of the Law, in which it said,
"No man shall look upon my face and live."
And as he read, he prayed that God would give
His faithful servant grace with mortal eye
To look upon His face and yet not die.

Then fell a sudden shadow on the page,
And, lifting up his eyes, grown dim with age
He saw the Angel of Death before him stand,
Holding a naked sword in his right hand.

Rabbi Ben Levi was a righteous man,
Yet through his veins a chill of terror ran.
With trembling voice he said, "What wilt thou here?"
The angel answered, "Lo! the time draws near
When thou must die; yet first, by God's decree,
Whate'er thou askest shall be granted thee."
Replied the Rabbi, "Let these living eyes
First look upon my place in Paradise."

Then said the Angel, "Come with me and look."
Rabbi Ben Levi closed the sacred book,
And rising, and uplifting his gray head,
"Give me thy sword," he to the Angel said,
"Lest thou shouldst fall upon me by the way."
The angel smiled and hastened to obey,
Then led him forth to the Celestial Town,
And set him on the wall, whence, gazing down,
Rabbi Ben Levi, with his living eyes,
Might look upon his place in Paradise.

Then straight into the city of the Lord
The Rabbi leaped with the Death-Angel's sword,
And through the streets there swept a sudden breath
Of something there unknown, which men call death.
Meanwhile the Angel stayed without and cried,
"Come back!" To which the Rabbi's voice replied,
"No! in the name of God, whom I adore,
I swear that hence I will depart no more!"

Then all the Angels cried, "O Holy One,
See what the son of Levi here hath done!
The kingdom of Heaven he takes by violence,
And in Thy name refuses to go hence!"
The Lord replied, "My Angels, be not wroth;
Did e'er the son of Levi break his oath?
Let him remain; for he with mortal eye
Shall look upon my face and yet not die."

Beyond the outer wall the Angel of Death
Heard the great voice, and said, with panting breath,
"Give back the sword, and let me go my way."
Whereat the Rabbi paused, and answered, "Nay!
Anguish enough already hath it caused
Among the sons of men." And while he paused

He heard the awful mandate of the Lord
Resounding through the air, "Give back the sword!"

The Rabbi bowed his head in silent prayer;
Then said he to the dreadful Angel, "Swear,
No human eye shall look on it again;
But when thou takest away the souls of men,
Thyself unseen, and with an unseen sword,
Thou wilt perform the bidding of the Lord."
The Angel took the sword again, and swore,
And walks on earth unseen forevermore.

INTERLUDE

He ended: and a kind of spell
Upon the silent listeners fell.
His solemn manner and his words
Had touched the deep, mysterious chords,
That vibrate in each human breast
Alike, but not alike confessed.
The spiritual world seemed near;
And close above them, full of fear,
Its awful adumbration passed,
A luminous shadow, vague and vast.
They almost feared to look, lest there,
Embodied from the impalpable air,
They might behold the Angel stand,
Holding the sword in his right hand.

At last, but in a voice subdued,
Not to disturb their dreamy mood,
Said the Sicilian: "While you spoke,
Telling your legend marvellous,
Suddenly in my memory woke
The thought of one, now gone from us,—
An old Abate, meek and mild,
My friend and teacher, when a child,
Who sometimes in those days of old
The legend of an Angel told,
Which ran, as I remember, thus."

THE SICILIAN'S TALE: KING ROBERT OF SICILY

Robert of Sicily, brother of Pope Urbane
And Valmond, Emperor of Allemaine,
Apparelled in magnificent attire,
With retinue of many a knight and squire,
On St. John's eve, at vespers, proudly sat
And heard the priests chant the Magnificat,
And as he listened, o'er and o'er again
Repeated, like a burden or refrain,
He caught the words, "*Deposuit potentes*
De sede, et exaltavit humiles;"
And slowly lifting up his kingly head
He to a learned clerk beside him said,
"What mean these words?" The clerk made answer meet,
"He has put down the mighty from their seat,
And has exalted them of low degree."
Thereat King Robert muttered scornfully,
"'T is well that such seditious words are sung
Only by priests and in the Latin tongue;
For unto priests and people be it known,
There is no power can push me from my throne!"
And leaning back, he yawned and fell asleep,
Lulled by the chant monotonous and deep.

When he awoke, it was already night;
The church was empty, and there was no light,
Save where the lamps, that glimmered few and faint,
Lighted a little space before some saint.
He started from his seat and gazed around,
But saw no living thing and heard no sound.
He groped towards the door, but it was locked;
He cried aloud, and listened, and then knocked,
And uttered awful threatenings and complaints,
And imprecations upon men and saints.
The sounds re-echoed from the roof and walls
As if dead priests were laughing in their stalls.

At length the sexton, hearing from without
The tumult of the knocking and the shout,
And thinking thieves were in the house of prayer,
Came with his lantern, asking, "Who is there?"
Half choked with rage, King Robert fiercely said,

"Open: 'tis I, the King! Art thou afraid?"
The frightened sexton, muttering, with a curse,
"This is some drunken vagabond, or worse!"
Turned the great key and flung the portal wide;
A man rushed by him at a single stride,
Haggard, half naked, without hat or cloak,
Who neither turned, nor looked at him, nor spoke,
But leaped into the blackness of the night,
And vanished like a spectre from his sight.

Robert of Sicily, brother of Pope Urbane
And Valmond, Emperor of Allemaine,
Despoiled of his magnificent attire,
Bareheaded, breathless, and besprent with mire,
With sense of wrong and outrage desperate,
Strode on and thundered at the palace gate;
Rushed through the courtyard, thrusting in his rage
To right and left each seneschal and page,
And hurried up the broad and sounding stair,
His white face ghastly in the torches' glare.
From hall to hall he passed with breathless speed;
Voices and cries he heard, but did not heed,
Until at last he reached the banquet-room,
Blazing with light and breathing with perfume.

There on the dais sat another king,
Wearing his robes, his crown, his signet-ring,
King Robert's self in features, form, and height,
But all transfigured with angelic light!
It was an Angel; and his presence there
With a divine effulgence filled the air,
An exaltation, piercing the disguise,
Though none the hidden Angel recognize.

A moment speechless, motionless, amazed,
The throneless monarch on the Angel gazed,
Who met his look of anger and surprise
With the divine compassion of his eyes;
Then said, "Who art thou? and why com'st thou here?"
To which King Robert answered, with a sneer,
"I am the King, and come to claim my own
From an impostor, who usurps my throne!"
And suddenly, at these audacious words,
Up sprang the angry guests, and drew their swords;

The Angel answered, with unruffled brow,
"Nay, not the King, but the King's Jester, thou
Henceforth shall wear the bells and scalloped cape,
And for thy counsellor shalt lead an ape;
Thou shalt obey my servants when they call,
And wait upon my henchmen in the hall!"

Deaf to King Robert's threats and cries and prayers,
They thrust him from the hall and down the stairs;
A group of tittering pages ran before,
And as they opened wide the folding door,
His heart failed, for he heard, with strange alarms,
The boisterous laughter of the men-at-arms,
And all the vaulted chamber roar and ring
With the mock plaudits of "Long live the King!"

Next morning, waking with the day's first beam,
He said within himself, "It was a dream!"
But the straw rustled as he turned his head,
There were the cap and bells beside his bed,
Around him rose the bare, discolored walls,
Close by, the steeds were champing in their stalls,
And in the corner, a revolting shape,
Shivering and chattering sat the wretched ape.
It was no dream; the world he loved so much
Had turned to dust and ashes at his touch!

Days came and went; and now returned again
To Sicily the old Saturnian reign;
Under the Angel's governance benign
The happy island danced with corn and wine,
And deep within the mountain's burning breast
Enceladus, the giant, was at rest.

Meanwhile King Robert yielded to his fate,
Sullen and silent and disconsolate.
Dressed in the motley garb that Jesters wear,
With look bewildered and a vacant stare,
Close shaven above the ears, as monks are shorn,
By courtiers mocked, by pages laughed to scorn,
His only friend the ape, his only food
What others left,—he still was unsubdued.
And when the Angel met him on his way,
And half in earnest, half in jest, would say

Sternly, though tenderly, that he might feel
The velvet scabbard held a sword of steel,
"Art thou the King?" the passion of his woe
Burst from him in resistless overflow,
And, lifting high his forehead, he would fling
The haughty answer back, "I am, I am the King!"

Almost three years were ended; when there came
Ambassadors of great repute and name
From Valmond, Emperor of Allemaine,
Unto King Robert, saying that Pope Urbane
By letter summoned them forthwith to come
On Holy Thursday to his city of Rome.
The Angel with great joy received his guests,
And gave them presents of embroidered vests,
And velvet mantles with rich ermine lined,
And rings and jewels of the rarest kind.
Then he departed with them o'er the sea
Into the lovely land of Italy,
Whose loveliness was more resplendent made
By the mere passing of that cavalcade,
With plumes, and cloaks, and housings, and the stir
Of jewelled bridle and of golden spur.
And lo! among the menials, in mock state,
Upon a piebald steed, with shambling gait,
His cloak of fox-tails flapping in the wind,
The solemn ape demurely perched behind,
King Robert rode, making huge merriment
In all the country towns through which they went.

The Pope received them with great pomp and blare
Of bannered trumpets, on Saint Peter's square,
Giving his benediction and embrace,
Fervent, and full of apostolic grace.
While with congratulations and with prayers
He entertained the Angel unawares,
Robert, the Jester, bursting through the crowd,
Into their presence rushed, and cried aloud,
"I am the King! Look, and behold in me
Robert, your brother, King of Sicily!
This man, who wears my semblance to your eyes,
Is an impostor in a king's disguise.
Do you not know me? does no voice within
Answer my cry, and say we are akin?"

The Pope in silence, but with troubled mien,
Gazed at the Angel's countenance serene;
The Emperor, laughing, said, "It is strange sport
To keep a mad man for thy Fool at court!"
And the poor, baffled Jester in disgrace
Was hustled back among the populace.

In solemn state the Holy Week went by,
And Easter Sunday gleamed upon the sky;
The presence of the Angel, with its light,
Before the sun rose, made the city bright,
And with new fervor filled the hearts of men,
Who felt that Christ indeed had risen again.
Even the Jester, on his bed of straw,
With haggard eyes the unwonted splendor saw,
He felt within a power unfelt before,
And, kneeling humbly on his chamber floor,
He heard the rushing garments of the Lord
Sweep through the silent air, ascending heavenward.

And now the visit ending, and once more
Valmond returning to the Danube's shore,
Homeward the Angel journeyed, and again
The land was made resplendent with his train,
Flashing along the towns of Italy
Unto Salerno, and from thence by sea.
And when once more within Palermo's wall,
And, seated on the throne in his great hall,
He heard the Angelus from convent towers,
As if the better world conversed with ours,
He beckoned to King Robert to draw nigher,
And with a gesture bade the rest retire;
And when they were alone, the Angel said,
"Art thou the King?" Then, bowing down his head,
King Robert crossed both hands upon his breast,
And meekly answered him: "Thou knowest best!
My sins as scarlet are; let me go hence,
And in some cloister's school of penitence,
Across those stones, that pave the way to heaven,
Walk barefoot, till my guilty soul be shriven!"

The Angel smiled, and from his radiant face
A holy light illumined all the place,
And through the open window, loud and clear,

They heard the monks chant in the chapel near,
Above the stir and tumult of the street:
"He has put down the mighty from their seat,
And has exalted them of low degree!"
And through the chant a second melody
Rose like the throbbing of a single string:
"I am an Angel, and thou art the King!"

King Robert, who was standing near the throne,
Lifted his eyes, and lo! he was alone!
But all apparelled as in days of old,
With ermined mantle and with cloth of gold;
And when his courtiers came, they found him there
Kneeling upon the floor, absorbed in, silent prayer.

INTERLUDE

And then the blue-eyed Norseman told
A Saga of the days of old.
"There is," said he, "a wondrous book
Of Legends in the old Norse tongue,
Of the dead kings of Norroway,—
Legends that once were told or sung
In many a smoky fireside nook
Of Iceland, in the ancient day,
By wandering Saga-man or Scald;
Heimskringla is the volume called;
And he who looks may find therein
The story that I now begin."

And in each pause the story made
Upon his violin he played,
As an appropriate interlude,
Fragments of old Norwegian tunes
That bound in one the separate runes,
And held the mind in perfect mood,
Entwining and encircling all
The strange and antiquated rhymes
with melodies of olden times;
As over some half-ruined wall,
Disjointed and about to fall,
Fresh woodbines climb and interlace,
And keep the loosened stones in place.

THE MUSICIAN'S TALE: THE SAGA OF KING OLAF

I. THE CHALLENGE OF THOR

I am the God Thor,
I am the War God,
I am the Thunderer!
Here in my Northland,
My fastness and fortress,
Reign I forever!

Here amid icebergs
Rule I the nations;
This is my hammer,
Miölner the mighty;
Giants and sorcerers
Cannot withstand it!

These are the gauntlets
Wherewith I wield it,
And hurl it afar off;
This is my girdle;
Whenever I brace it,
Strength is redoubled!

The light thou beholdest
Stream through the heavens,
In flashes of crimson,
Is but my red beard
Blown by the night-wind,
Affrighting the nations!

Jove is my brother;
Mine eyes are the lightning;
The wheels of my chariot
Roll in the thunder,
The blows of my hammer
Ring in the earthquake!

Force rules the world still,
Has ruled it, shall rule it;
Meekness is weakness,
Strength is triumphant,

Over the whole earth
Still is it Thor's-Day!

Thou art a God too,
O Galilean!
And thus single-handed
Unto the combat,
Gauntlet or Gospel,
Here I defy thee!

II. KING OLAF'S RETURN

And King Olaf heard the cry,
Saw the red light in the sky,
  Laid his hand upon his sword,
As he leaned upon the railing,
And his ships went sailing, sailing
  Northward into Drontheim fiord.

There he stood as one who dreamed;
And the red light glanced and gleamed
  On the armor that he wore;
And he shouted, as the rifled
Streamers o'er him shook and shifted,
  "I accept thy challenge, Thor!"

To avenge his father slain,
And reconquer realm and reign,
  Came the youthful Olaf home,
Through the midnight sailing, sailing,
Listening to the wild wind's wailing,
  And the dashing of the foam.

To his thoughts the sacred name
Of his mother Astrid came,
  And the tale she oft had told
Of her flight by secret passes
Through the mountains and morasses,
  To the home of Hakon old.

Then strange memories crowded back
Of Queen Gunhild's wrath and wrack,
  And a hurried flight by sea;
Of grim Vikings, and the rapture

Of the sea-fight, and the capture,
   And the life of slavery.

How a stranger watched his face
In the Esthonian market-place,
   Scanned his features one by one,
Saying, "We should know each other;
I am Sigurd, Astrid's brother,
   Thou art Olaf, Astrid's son!"

Then as Queen Allogia's page,
Old in honors, young in age,
   Chief of all her men-at-arms;
Till vague whispers, and mysterious,
Reached King Valdemar, the imperious,
   Filling him with strange alarms.

Then his cruisings o'er the seas,
Westward to the Hebrides,
   And to Scilly's rocky shore;
And the hermit's cavern dismal,
Christ's great name and rites baptismal
   in the ocean's rush and roar.

All these thoughts of love and strife
Glimmered through his lurid life,
   As the stars' intenser light
Through the red flames o'er him trailing,
As his ships went sailing, sailing,
   Northward in the summer night.

Trained for either camp or court,
Skilful in each manly sport,
   Young and beautiful and tall;
Art of warfare, craft of chases,
Swimming, skating, snow-shoe races
   Excellent alike in all.

When at sea, with all his rowers,
He along the bending oars
   Outside of his ship could run.
He the Smalsor Horn ascended,
And his shining shield suspended,
On its summit, like a sun.

On the ship-rails he could stand,
Wield his sword with either hand,
     And at once two javelins throw;
At all feasts where ale was strongest
Sat the merry monarch longest,
     First to come and last to go.

Norway never yet had seen
One so beautiful of mien,
     One so royal in attire,
When in arms completely furnished,
Harness gold-inlaid and burnished,
     Mantle like a flame of fire.

Thus came Olaf to his own,
When upon the night-wind blown
     Passed that cry along the shore;
And he answered, while the rifted
Streamers o'er him shook and shifted,
     "I accept thy challenge, Thor!"

III. THORA OF RIMOL

"Thora of Rimol! hide me! hide me!
Danger and shame and death betide me!
For Olaf the King is hunting me down
Through field and forest, through thorp and town!"
     Thus cried Jarl Hakon
     To Thora, the fairest of women.

Hakon Jarl! for the love I bear thee
Neither shall shame nor death come near thee!
But the hiding-place wherein thou must lie
Is the cave underneath the swine in the sty."
     Thus to Jarl Hakon
     Said Thora, the fairest of women.

So Hakon Jarl and his base thrall Karker
Crouched in the cave, than a dungeon darker,
As Olaf came riding, with men in mail,
Through the forest roads into Orkadale,
     Demanding Jarl Hakon
     Of Thora, the fairest of women.

"Rich and honored shall be whoever
The head of Hakon Jarl shall dissever!"
Hakon heard him, and Karker the slave,
Through the breathing-holes of the darksome cave.
    Alone in her chamber
    Wept Thora, the fairest of women.

Said Karker, the crafty, "I will not slay thee!
For all the king's gold I will never betray thee!"
"Then why dost thou turn so pale, O churl,
And then again black as the earth?" said the Earl.
    More pale and more faithful
    Was Thora, the fairest of women.

From a dream in the night the thrall started, saying,
"Round my neck a gold ring King Olaf was laying!"
And Hakon answered, "Beware of the king!
He will lay round thy neck a blood-red ring."
    At the ring on her finger
    Gazed Thora, the fairest of women.

At daybreak slept Hakon, with sorrows encumbered,
But screamed and drew up his feet as he slumbered;
The thrall in the darkness plunged with his knife,
And the Earl awakened no more in this life.
    But wakeful and weeping
    Sat Thora, the fairest of women.

At Nidarholm the priests are all singing,
Two ghastly heads on the gibbet are swinging;
One is Jarl Hakon's and one is his thrall's,
And the people are shouting from windows and walls;
    While alone in her chamber
    Swoons Thora, the fairest of women.

IV. QUEEN SIGRID THE HAUGHTY

Queen Sigrid the Haughty sat proud and aloft
In her chamber, that looked over meadow and croft.
   Heart's dearest,
   Why dost thou sorrow so?

The floor with tassels of fir was besprent,
Filling the room with their fragrant scent.

She heard the birds sing, she saw the sun shine,
The air of summer was sweeter than wine.

Like a sword without scabbard the bright river lay
Between her own kingdom and Norroway.

But Olaf the King had sued for her hand,
The sword would be sheathed, the river be spanned.

Her maidens were seated around her knee,
Working bright figures in tapestry.

And one was singing the ancient rune
Of Brynhilda's love and the wrath of Gudrun.

And through it, and round it, and over it all
Sounded incessant the waterfall.

The Queen in her hand held a ring of gold,
From the door of Lade's Temple old.

King Olaf had sent her this wedding gift,
But her thoughts as arrows were keen and swift.

She had given the ring to her goldsmiths twain,
Who smiled, as they handed it back again.

And Sigrid the Queen, in her haughty way,
Said, "Why do you smile, my goldsmiths, say?"

And they answered: "O Queen! if the truth must be told,
The ring is of copper, and not of gold!"

The lightning flashed o'er her forehead and cheek,

She only murmured, she did not speak:

"If in his gifts he can faithless be,
There will be no gold in his love to me."

A footstep was heard on the outer stair,
And in strode King Olaf with royal air.

He kissed the Queen's hand, and he whispered of love,
And swore to be true as the stars are above.

But she smiled with contempt as she answered: "O King,
Will you swear it, as Odin once swore, on the ring?"

And the King: "O speak not of Odin to me,
The wife of King Olaf a Christian must be."

Looking straight at the King, with her level brows,
She said, "I keep true to my faith and my vows."

Then the face of King Olaf was darkened with gloom,
He rose in his anger and strode through the room.

"Why, then, should I care to have thee?" he said,—
"A faded old woman, a heathenish jade!"

His zeal was stronger than fear or love,
And he struck the Queen in the face with his glove.

Then forth from the chamber in anger he fled,
And the wooden stairway shook with his tread.

Queen Sigrid the Haughty said under her breath,
"This insult, King Olaf, shall be thy death!"
    Heart's dearest,
    Why dost thou sorrow so?

V. THE SKERRY OF SHRIEKS

Now from all King Olaf's farms
    His men-at-arms
Gathered on the Eve of Easter;
To his house at Angvalds-ness
    Fast they press,

Drinking with the royal feaster.

Loudly through the wide-flung door
    Came the roar
Of the sea upon the Skerry;
And its thunder loud and near
    Reached the ear,
Mingling with their voices merry.

"Hark!" said Olaf to his Scald,
    Halfred the Bald,
"Listen to that song, and learn it!
Half my kingdom would I give,
    As I live,
If by such songs you would earn it!
"For of all the runes and rhymes
    Of all times,
Best I like the ocean's dirges,
When the old harper heaves and rocks,
    His hoary locks
Flowing and flashing in the surges!"

Halfred answered: "I am called
    The Unappalled!
Nothing hinders me or daunts me.
Hearken to me, then, O King,
    While I sing
The great Ocean Song that haunts me."

"I will hear your song sublime
    Some other time,"
Says the drowsy monarch, yawning,
And retires; each laughing guest
    Applauds the jest;
Then they sleep till day is dawning.

Pacing up and down the yard,
    King Olaf's guard
Saw the sea-mist slowly creeping
O'er the sands, and up the hill,
    Gathering still
Round the house where they were sleeping.

It was not the fog he saw,

Nor misty flaw,
That above the landscape brooded;
It was Eyvind Kallda's crew
    Of warlocks blue
With their caps of darkness hooded!

Round and round the house they go,
    Weaving slow
Magic circles to encumber
And imprison in their ring
    Olaf the King,
As he helpless lies in slumber.

Then athwart the vapors dun
    The Easter sun
Streamed with one broad track of splendor!
in their real forms appeared
    The warlocks weird,
Awful as the Witch of Endor.

Blinded by the light that glared,
    They groped and stared
Round about with steps unsteady;
From his window Olaf gazed,
    And, amazed,
"Who are these strange people?" said he.
"Eyvind Kallda and his men!"
    Answered then
From the yard a sturdy farmer;
While the men-at-arms apace
    Filled the place,
Busily buckling on their armor.

From the gates they sallied forth,
    South and north,
Scoured the island coast around them,
Seizing all the warlock band,
    Foot and hand
On the Skerry's rocks they bound them.

And at eve the king again
    Called his train,
And, with all the candles burning,
Silent sat and heard once more

The sullen roar
Of the ocean tides returning.

Shrieks and cries of wild despair
    Filled the air,
Growing fainter as they listened;
Then the bursting surge alone
    Sounded on;—
Thus the sorcerers were christened!

"Sing, O Scald, your song sublime,
    Your ocean-rhyme,"
Cried King Olaf: "it will cheer me!"
Said the Scald, with pallid cheeks,
    "The Skerry of Shrieks
Sings too loud for you to hear me!"

VI. THE WRAITH OF ODIN

The guests were loud, the ale was strong,
King Olaf feasted late and long;
The hoary Scalds together sang;
O'erhead the smoky rafters rang.
    Dead rides Sir Morten of Fogelsang.

The door swung wide, with creak and din;
A blast of cold night-air came in,
And on the threshold shivering stood
A one-eyed guest, with cloak and hood.
    Dead rides Sir Morten of Fogelsang.

The King exclaimed, "O graybeard pale!
Come warm thee with this cup of ale."
The foaming draught the old man quaffed,
The noisy guests looked on and laughed.
    Dead rides Sir Morten of Fogelsang.

Then spake the King: "Be not afraid;
Sit here by me." The guest obeyed,
And, seated at the table, told
Tales of the sea, and Sagas old.
    Dead rides Sir Morten of Fogelsang.

And ever, when the tale was o'er,

The King demanded yet one more;
Till Sigurd the Bishop smiling said,
"'T is late, O King, and time for bed."
    Dead rides Sir Morten of Fogelsang.

The King retired; the stranger guest
Followed and entered with the rest;
The lights were out, the pages gone,
But still the garrulous guest spake on.
    Dead rides Sir Morten of Fogelsang.

As one who from a volume reads,
He spake of heroes and their deeds,
Of lands and cities he had seen,
And stormy gulfs that tossed between.
    Dead rides Sir Morten of Fogelsang.

Then from his lips in music rolled
The Havamal of Odin old,
With sounds mysterious as the roar
Of billows on a distant shore.
    Dead rides Sir Morten of Fogelsang.

"Do we not learn from runes and rhymes
Made by the gods in elder times,
And do not still the great Scalds teach
That silence better is than speech?"
    Dead rides Sir Morten of Fogelsang.

Smiling at this, the King replied,
"Thy lore is by thy tongue belied;
For never was I so enthralled
Either by Saga-man or Scald,"
    Dead rides Sir Morten of Fogelsang.

The Bishop said, "Late hours we keep!
Night wanes, O King! 't is time for sleep!"
Then slept the King, and when he woke
The guest was gone, the morning broke.
    Dead rides Sir Morten of Fogelsang.

They found the doors securely barred,
They found the watch-dog in the yard,
There was no footprint in the grass,

And none had seen the stranger pass.
    Dead rides Sir Morten of Fogelsang.

King Olaf crossed himself and said:
"I know that Odin the Great is dead;
Sure is the triumph of our Faith,
The one-eyed stranger was his wraith."
    Dead rides Sir Morten of Fogelsang.

VII. IRON-BEARD

    Olaf the King, one summer morn,
    Blew a blast on his bugle-horn,
Sending his signal through the land of Drontheim.

    And to the Hus-Ting held at Mere
    Gathered the farmers far and near,
With their war weapons ready to confront him.

    Ploughing under the morning star,
    Old Iron-Beard in Yriar
Heard the summons, chuckling with a low laugh.

    He wiped the sweat-drops from his brow,
    Unharnessed his horses from the plough,
And clattering came on horseback to King Olaf.

    He was the churliest of the churls;
    Little he cared for king or earls;
Bitter as home-brewed ale were his foaming passions.

    Hodden-gray was the garb he wore,
    And by the Hammer of Thor he swore;
He hated the narrow town, and all its fashions.

    But he loved the freedom of his farm,
    His ale at night, by the fireside warm,
Gudrun his daughter, with her flaxen tresses.

    He loved his horses and his herds,
    The smell of the earth, and the song of birds,
His well-filled barns, his brook with its water-cresses.

    Huge and cumbersome was his frame;

His beard, from which he took his name,
Frosty and fierce, like that of Hymer the Giant.

So at the Hus-Ting he appeared,
    The farmer of Yriar, Iron-Beard,
On horseback, in an attitude defiant.

And to King Olaf he cried aloud,
    Out of the middle of the crowd,
That tossed about him like a stormy ocean:

"Such sacrifices shalt thou bring;
    To Odin and to Thor, O King,
As other kings have done in their devotion!"

King Olaf answered: "I command
    This land to be a Christian land;
Here is my Bishop who the folk baptizes!

"But if you ask me to restore
    Your sacrifices, stained with gore,
Then will I offer human sacrifices!

"Not slaves and peasants shall they be,
    But men of note and high degree,
Such men as Orm of Lyra and Kar of Gryting!"

Then to their Temple strode he in,
    And loud behind him heard the din
Of his men-at-arms and the peasants fiercely fighting.

There in the Temple, carved in wood,
    The image of great Odin stood,
And other gods, with Thor supreme among them.

King Olaf smote them with the blade
    Of his huge war-axe, gold inlaid,
And downward shattered to the pavement flung them.

At the same moment rose without,
    From the contending crowd, a shout,
A mingled sound of triumph and of wailing.

And there upon the trampled plain

The farmer iron-Beard lay slain,
Midway between the assailed and the assailing.

King Olaf from the doorway spoke.
"Choose ye between two things, my folk,
To be baptized or given up to slaughter!"

And seeing their leader stark and dead,
The people with a murmur said,
"O King, baptize us with thy holy water";

So all the Drontheim land became
A Christian land in name and fame,
In the old gods no more believing and trusting.

And as a blood-atonement, soon
King Olaf wed the fair Gudrun;
And thus in peace ended the Drontheim Hus-Ting!

VIII. GUDRUN

On King Olaf's bridal night
Shines the moon with tender light,
And across the chamber streams
    Its tide of dreams.

At the fatal midnight hour,
When all evil things have power,
In the glimmer of the moon
    Stands Gudrun.

Close against her heaving breast
Something in her hand is pressed
Like an icicle, its sheen
    Is cold and keen.

On the cairn are fixed her eyes
Where her murdered father lies,
And a voice remote and drear
    She seems to hear.

What a bridal night is this!
Cold will be the dagger's kiss;
Laden with the chill of death

Is its breath.

Like the drifting snow she sweeps
To the couch where Olaf sleeps;
Suddenly he wakes and stirs,
   His eyes meet hers.

"What is that," King Olaf said,
"Gleams so bright above thy head?
Wherefore standest thou so white
   In pale moonlight?"

"'T is the bodkin that I wear
When at night I bind my hair;
It woke me falling on the floor;
   'T is nothing more."

"Forests have ears, and fields have eyes;
Often treachery lurking lies
Underneath the fairest hair!
   Gudrun beware!"

Ere the earliest peep of morn
Blew King Olaf's bugle-horn;
And forever sundered ride
   Bridegroom and bride!

IX. THANGBRAND THE PRIEST

Short of stature, large of limb,
  Burly face and russet beard,
All the women stared at him,
  When in Iceland he appeared.
    "Look!" they said,
    With nodding head,
"There goes Thangbrand, Olaf's Priest."

All the prayers he knew by rote,
  He could preach like Chrysostome,
From the Fathers he could quote,
  He had even been at Rome,
    A learned clerk,
    A man of mark,
Was this Thangbrand, Olaf's Priest.

He was quarrelsome and loud,
  And impatient of control,
Boisterous in the market crowd,
  Boisterous at the wassail-bowl,
    Everywhere
    Would drink and swear,
Swaggering Thangbrand, Olaf's Priest.

In his house this malcontent
  Could the King no longer bear,
So to Iceland he was sent
  To convert the heathen there,
    And away
    One summer day
Sailed this Thangbrand, Olaf's Priest.

There in Iceland, o'er their books
  Pored the people day and night,
But he did not like their looks,
  Nor the songs they used to write.
    "All this rhyme
    Is waste of time!"
Grumbled Thangbrand, Olaf's Priest.

To the alehouse, where he sat
  Came the Scalds and Saga-men;
Is it to be wondered at,
  That they quarrelled now and then,
    When o'er his beer
    Began to leer
Drunken Thangbrand, Olaf's Priest?

All the folk in Altafiord
  Boasted of their island grand;
Saying in a single word,
  "Iceland is the finest land
    That the sun
    Doth shine upon!"
Loud laughed Thangbrand, Olaf's Priest.

And he answered: "What's the use
  Of this bragging up and down,
When three women and one goose
  Make a market in your town!"

Every Scald
Satires scrawled
On poor Thangbrand, Olaf's Priest.

Something worse they did than that;
  And what vexed him most of all
Was a figure in shovel hat,
  Drawn in charcoal on the wall;
    With words that go
    Sprawling below,
"This is Thangbrand, Olaf's Priest."

Hardly knowing what he did,
  Then he smote them might and main,
Thorvald Veile and Veterlid
  Lay there in the alehouse slain.
    "To-day we are gold,
    To-morrow mould!"
Muttered Thangbrand, Olaf's Priest.

Much in fear of axe and rope,
  Back to Norway sailed he then.
"O, King Olaf! little hope
  Is there of these Iceland men!"
    Meekly said,
    With bending head,
Pious Thangbrand, Olaf's Priest.

X. RAUD THE STRONG

"All the old gods are dead,
All the wild warlocks fled;
But the White Christ lives and reigns,
And throughout my wide domains
His Gospel shall be spread!"
  On the Evangelists
  Thus swore King Olaf.

But still in dreams of the night
Beheld he the crimson light,
And heard the voice that defied
Him who was crucified,
And challenged him to the fight.
  To Sigurd the Bishop

King Olaf confessed it.

And Sigurd the Bishop said,
"The old gods are not dead,
For the great Thor still reigns,
And among the Jarls and Thanes
The old witchcraft still is spread."
 Thus to King Olaf
 Said Sigurd the Bishop.

"Far north in the Salten Fiord,
By rapine, fire, and sword,
Lives the Viking, Raud the Strong;
All the Godoe Isles belong
To him and his heathen horde."
 Thus went on speaking
 Sigurd the Bishop.

"A warlock, a wizard is he,
And lord of the wind and the sea;
And whichever way he sails,
He has ever favoring gales,
By his craft in sorcery."
 Here the sign of the cross
 Made devoutly King Olaf.

"With rites that we both abhor,
He worships Odin and Thor;
So it cannot yet be said,
That all the old gods are dead,
And the warlocks are no more,"
 Flushing with anger
 Said Sigurd the Bishop.

Then King Olaf cried aloud:
"I will talk with this mighty Raud,
And along the Salten Fiord
Preach the Gospel with my sword,
Or be brought back in my shroud!"
 So northward from Drontheim
 Sailed King Olaf!

XI. BISHOP SIGURD AT SALTEN FIORD

Loud the angry wind was wailing
As King Olaf's ships came sailing
Northward out of Drontheim haven
  To the mouth of Salten Fiord.

Though the flying sea-spray drenches
Fore and aft the rowers' benches,
Not a single heart is craven
  Of the champions there on board.

All without the Fiord was quiet
But within it storm and riot,
Such as on his Viking cruises
  Raud the Strong was wont to ride.

And the sea through all its tide-ways
Swept the reeling vessels sideways,
As the leaves are swept through sluices,
  When the flood-gates open wide.

"'T is the warlock! 't is the demon
Raud!" cried Sigurd to the seamen;
"But the Lord is not affrighted
  By the witchcraft of his foes."

To the ship's bow he ascended,
By his choristers attended,
Round him were the tapers lighted,
  And the sacred incense rose.

On the bow stood Bishop Sigurd,
In his robes, as one transfigured,
And the Crucifix he planted
  High amid the rain and mist.

Then with holy water sprinkled
All the ship; the mass-bells tinkled;
Loud the monks around him chanted,
  Loud he read the Evangelist.

As into the Fiord they darted,
On each side the water parted;
Down a path like silver molten
  Steadily rowed King Olaf's ships;

Steadily burned all night the tapers,
And the White Christ through the vapors
Gleamed across the Fiord of Salten,
  As through John's Apocalypse,—

Till at last they reached Raud's dwelling
On the little isle of Gelling;
Not a guard was at the doorway,
  Not a glimmer of light was seen.

But at anchor, carved and gilded,
Lay the dragon-ship he builded;
'T was the grandest ship in Norway,
  With its crest and scales of green.

Up the stairway, softly creeping,
To the loft where Raud was sleeping,
With their fists they burst asunder
  Bolt and bar that held the door.

Drunken with sleep and ale they found him,
Dragged him from his bed and bound him,
While he stared with stupid wonder,
  At the look and garb they wore.

Then King Olaf said: "O Sea-King!
Little time have we for speaking,
Choose between the good and evil;
  Be baptized, or thou shalt die!

But in scorn the heathen scoffer
Answered: "I disdain thine offer;
Neither fear I God nor Devil;
  Thee and thy Gospel I defy!"

Then between his jaws distended,
When his frantic struggles ended,
Through King Olaf's horn an adder,
  Touched by fire, they forced to glide.

Sharp his tooth was as an arrow,
As he gnawed through bone and marrow;
But without a groan or shudder,
  Raud the Strong blaspheming died.

Then baptized they all that region,
Swarthy Lap and fair Norwegian,
Far as swims the salmon, leaping,
   Up the streams of Salten Fiord.

In their temples Thor and Odin
Lay in dust and ashes trodden,
As King Olaf, onward sweeping,
   Preached the Gospel with his sword.

Then he took the carved and gilded
Dragon-ship that Raud had builded,
And the tiller single-handed,
   Grasping, steered into the main.

Southward sailed the sea-gulls o'er him,
Southward sailed the ship that bore him,
Till at Drontheim haven landed
   Olaf and his crew again.

XII. KING OLAF'S CHRISTMAS

At Drontheim, Olaf the King
Heard the bells of Yule-tide ring,
   As he sat in his banquet-hall,
Drinking the nut-brown ale,
With his bearded Berserks hale
   And tall.

Three days his Yule-tide feasts
He held with Bishops and Priests,
   And his horn filled up to the brim;
But the ale was never too strong,
Nor the Saga-man's tale too long,
   For him.

O'er his drinking-horn, the sign
He made of the cross divine,
As he drank, and muttered his prayers;
But the Berserks evermore
Made the sign of the Hammer of Thor
   Over theirs.

The gleams of the fire-light dance

Upon helmet and hauberk and lance,
   And laugh in the eyes of the King;
And he cries to Halfred the Scald,
Gray-bearded, wrinkled, and bald,
   "Sing!"

"Sing me a song divine,
With a sword in every line,
   And this shall be thy reward."
And he loosened the belt at his waist,
And in front of the singer placed
   His sword.

"Quern-biter of Hakon the Good,
Wherewith at a stroke he hewed
   The millstone through and through,
And Foot-breadth of Thoralf the Strong,
Were neither so broad nor so long,
   Nor so true."

Then the Scald took his harp and sang,
And loud though the music rang
   The sound of that shining word;
And the harp-strings a clangor made,
As if they were struck with the blade
   Of a sword.

And the Berserks round about
Broke forth into a shout
   That made the rafters ring:
They smote with their fists on the board,
And shouted, "Long live the Sword,
   And the King!"

But the King said, "O my son,
I miss the bright word in one
   Of thy measures and thy rhymes."
And Halfred the Scald replied,
"In another 't was multiplied
   Three times."

Then King Olaf raised the hilt
Of iron, cross-shaped and gilt,
   And said, "Do not refuse;

Count well the gain and the loss,
Thor's hammer or Christ's cross:
    Choose!"

And Halfred the Scald said, "This
In the name of the Lord I kiss,
    Who on it was crucified!"
And a shout went round the board,
"In the name of Christ the Lord,
    Who died!"

Then over the waste of snows
The noonday sun uprose,
    Through the driving mists revealed,
Like the lifting of the Host,
By incense-clouds almost
    Concealed.

On the shining wall a vast
And shadowy cross was cast
    From the hilt of the lifted sword,
And in foaming cups of ale
The Berserks drank "Was-hael!
    To the Lord!"

XIII. THE BUILDING OF THE LONG SERPENT

Thorberg Skafting, master-builder,
    In his ship-yard by the sea,
Whistling, said, "It would bewilder
Any man but Thorberg Skafting,
    Any man but me!"

Near him lay the Dragon stranded,
    Built of old by Raud the Strong,
And King Olaf had commanded
He should build another Dragon,
    Twice as large and long.

Therefore whistled Thorberg Skafting,
    As he sat with half-closed eyes,
And his head turned sideways, drafting
That new vessel for King Olaf
    Twice the Dragon's size.

Round him busily hewed and hammered
   Mallet huge and heavy axe;
Workmen laughed and sang and clamored;
Whirred the wheels, that into rigging
   Spun the shining flax!

All this tumult heard the master,—
   It was music to his ear;
Fancy whispered all the faster,
"Men shall hear of Thorberg Skafting
   For a hundred year!"

Workmen sweating at the forges
   Fashioned iron bolt and bar,
Like a warlock's midnight orgies
Smoked and bubbled the black caldron
   With the boiling tar.

Did the warlocks mingle in it,
   Thorberg Skafting, any curse?
Could you not be gone a minute
But some mischief must be doing,
   Turning bad to worse?

'T was an ill wind that came wafting,
   From his homestead words of woe
To his farm went Thorberg Skafting,
Oft repeating to his workmen,
   Build ye thus and so.

After long delays returning
   Came the master back by night
To his ship-yard longing, yearning,
Hurried he, and did not leave it
   Till the morning's light.

"Come and see my ship, my darling"
   On the morrow said the King;
"Finished now from keel to carling;
Never yet was seen in Norway
   Such a wondrous thing!"

In the ship-yard, idly talking,
   At the ship the workmen stared:

Some one, all their labor balking,
Down her sides had cut deep gashes,
    Not a plank was spared!

"Death be to the evil-doer!"
    With an oath King Olaf spoke;
"But rewards to his pursuer
And with wrath his face grew redder
    Than his scarlet cloak.

Straight the master-builder, smiling,
    Answered thus the angry King:
"Cease blaspheming and reviling,
Olaf, it was Thorberg Skafting
    Who has done this thing!"

Then he chipped and smoothed the planking,
    Till the King, delighted, swore,
With much lauding and much thanking,
"Handsomer is now my Dragon
    Than she was before!"

Seventy ells and four extended
    On the grass the vessel's keel;
High above it, gilt and splendid,
Rose the figure-head ferocious
    With its crest of steel.

Then they launched her from the tressels,
    In the ship-yard by the sea;
She was the grandest of all vessels,
Never ship was built in Norway
    Half so fine as she!

The Long Serpent was she christened,
    'Mid the roar of cheer on cheer!
They who to the Saga listened
Heard the name of Thorberg Skafting
    For a hundred year!

XIV. THE CREW OF THE LONG SERPENT

Safe at anchor in Drontheim bay
King Olaf's fleet assembled lay,

And, striped with white and blue,
Downward fluttered sail and banner,
As alights the screaming lanner;
Lustily cheered, in their wild manner,
  The Long Serpent's crew.

Her forecastle man was Ulf the Red,
Like a wolf's was his shaggy head,
  His teeth as large and white;
His beard, of gray and russet blended,
Round as a swallow's nest descended;
As standard-bearer he defended
  Olaf's flag in the fight.

Near him Kolbiorn had his place,
Like the King in garb and face,
  So gallant and so hale;
Every cabin-boy and varlet
Wondered at his cloak of scarlet;
Like a river, frozen and star-lit,
  Gleamed his coat of mail.

By the bulkhead, tall and dark,
Stood Thrand Rame of Thelemark,
  A figure gaunt and grand;
On his hairy arm imprinted
Was an anchor, azure-tinted;
Like Thor's hammer, huge and dinted
  Was his brawny hand.

Einar Tamberskelver, bare
To the winds his golden hair,
  By the mainmast stood;
Graceful was his form, and slender,
And his eyes were deep and tender
As a woman's, in the splendor
  Of her maidenhood.

In the fore-hold Biorn and Bork
Watched the sailors at their work:
  Heavens! how they swore!
Thirty men they each commanded,
Iron-sinewed, horny-handed,
Shoulders broad, and chests expanded.

Tugging at the oar.

These, and many more like these,
With King Olaf sailed the seas,
  Till the waters vast
Filled them with a vague devotion,
With the freedom and the motion,
With the roll and roar of ocean
  And the sounding blast.

When they landed from the fleet,
How they roared through Drontheim's street,
  Boisterous as the gale!
How they laughed and stamped and pounded,
Till the tavern roof resounded,
And the host looked on astounded
  As they drank the ale!

Never saw the wild North Sea
Such a gallant company
  Sail its billows blue!
Never, while they cruised and quarrelled,
Old King Gorm, or Blue-Tooth Harald,
Owned a ship so well apparelled,
  Boasted such a crew!

XV. A LITTLE BIRD IN THE AIR

A little bird in the air
Is singing of Thyri the fair,
  The sister of Svend the Dane;
And the song of the garrulous bird
In the streets of the town is heard,
  And repeated again and again.
    Hoist up your sails of silk,
    And flee away from each other.

To King Burislaf, it is said,
Was the beautiful Thyri wed,
  And a sorrowful bride went she;
And after a week and a day,
She has fled away and away,
  From his town by the stormy sea.
    Hoist up your sails of silk,

And flee away from each other.

They say, that through heat and through cold,
Through weald, they say, and through wold,
  By day and by night, they say,
She has fled; and the gossips report
She has come to King Olaf's court,
  And the town is all in dismay.
    Hoist up your sails of silk,
    And flee away from each other.

It is whispered King Olaf has seen,
  Has talked with the beautiful Queen;
  And they wonder how it will end;
For surely, if here she remain,
It is war with King Svend the Dane,
  And King Burislaf the Vend!
    Hoist up your sails of silk,
    And flee away from each other.

O, greatest wonder of all!
It is published in hamlet and hall,
  It roars like a flame that is fanned!
The King—yes, Olaf the King—
Has wedded her with his ring,
  And Thyri is Queen in the land!
    Hoist up your sails of silk,
    And flee away from each other.

XVI. QUEEN THYRI AND THE ANGELICA STALKS

Northward over Drontheim,
Flew the clamorous sea-gulls,
Sang the lark and linnet
  From the meadows green;

Weeping in her chamber,
Lonely and unhappy,
Sat the Drottning Thyri,
  Sat King Olaf's Queen.

In at all the windows
Streamed the pleasant sunshine,
On the roof above her

Softly cooed the dove;

But the sound she heard not,
Nor the sunshine heeded,
For the thoughts of Thyri
  Were not thoughts of love.

Then King Olaf entered,
Beautiful as morning,
Like the sun at Easter
  Shone his happy face;

In his hand he carried
Angelicas uprooted,
With delicious fragrance
  Filling all the place.

Like a rainy midnight
Sat the Drottning Thyri,
Even the smile of Olaf
  Could not cheer her gloom;

Nor the stalks he gave her
With a gracious gesture,
And with words as pleasant
  As their own perfume.

In her hands he placed them,
And her jewelled fingers
Through the green leaves glistened
  Like the dews of morn;

But she cast them from her,
Haughty and indignant,
On the floor she threw them
  With a look of scorn.

"Richer presents," said she,
"Gave King Harald Gormson
To the Queen, my mother,
  Than such worthless weeds;

"When he ravaged Norway,
Laying waste the kingdom,

Seizing scatt and treasure
  For her royal needs.

"But thou darest not venture
Through the Sound to Vendland,
My domains to rescue
  From King Burislaf;

"Lest King Svend of Denmark,
Forked Beard, my brother,
Scatter all thy vessels
  As the wind the chaff."

Then up sprang King Olaf,
Like a reindeer bounding,
With an oath he answered
  Thus the luckless Queen:

"Never yet did Olaf
Fear King Svend of Denmark;
This right hand shall hale him
  By his forked chin!"

Then he left the chamber,
Thundering through the doorway,
Loud his steps resounded
  Down the outer stair.

Smarting with the insult,
Through the streets of Drontheim
Strode he red and wrathful,
  With his stately air.

All his ships he gathered,
Summoned all his forces,
Making his war levy
  In the region round;

Down the coast of Norway,
Like a flock of sea-gulls,
Sailed the fleet of Olaf
  Through the Danish Sound.

With his own hand fearless,

Steered he the Long Serpent,
Strained the creaking cordage,
  Bent each boom and gaff;

Till in Venland landing,
The domains of Thyri
He redeemed and rescued
  From King Burislaf.

Then said Olaf, laughing,
"Not ten yoke of oxen
Have the power to draw us
  Like a woman's hair!

"Now will I confess it,
Better things are jewels
Than angelica stalks are
  For a Queen to wear."

XVII. KING SVEND OF THE FORKED BEAR

Loudly the sailors cheered
Svend of the Forked Beard,
As with his fleet he steered
  Southward to Vendland;
Where with their courses hauled
All were together called,
Under the Isle of Svald
  Near to the mainland.

After Queen Gunhild's death,
So the old Saga saith,
Plighted King Svend his faith
  To Sigrid the Haughty;
And to avenge his bride,
Soothing her wounded pride,
Over the waters wide
  King Olaf sought he.

Still on her scornful face,
Blushing with deep disgrace,
Bore she the crimson trace
  Of Olaf's gauntlet;
Like a malignant star,

Blazing in heaven afar,
Red shone the angry scar
  Under her frontlet.

Oft to King Svend she spake,
"For thine own honor's sake
Shalt thou swift vengeance take
  On the vile coward!"
Until the King at last,
Gusty and overcast,
Like a tempestuous blast
  Threatened and lowered.

Soon as the Spring appeared,
Svend of the Forked Beard
High his red standard reared,
  Eager for battle;
While every warlike Dane,
Seizing his arms again,
Left all unsown the grain,
  Unhoused the cattle.

Likewise the Swedish King
Summoned in haste a Thing,
Weapons and men to bring
  In aid of Denmark;
Erie the Norseman, too,
As the war-tidings flew,
Sailed with a chosen crew
  From Lapland and Finmark.

So upon Easter day
Sailed the three kings away,
Out of the sheltered bay,
  In the bright season;
With them Earl Sigvald came,
Eager for spoil and fame;
Pity that such a name
  Stooped to such treason!

Safe under Svald at last,
Now were their anchors cast,
Safe from the sea and blast,
  Plotted the three kings;

While, with a base intent,
Southward Earl Sigvald went,
On a foul errand bent,
  Unto the Sea-kings.

Thence to hold on his course,
Unto King Olaf's force,
Lying within the hoarse
  Mouths of Stet-haven;
Him to ensnare and bring,
Unto the Danish king,
Who his dead corse would fling
  Forth to the raven!

XVIII. KING OLAF AND EARL SIGVALD

On the gray sea-sands
King Olaf stands,
Northward and seaward
He points with his hands.

With eddy and whirl
The sea-tides curl,
Washing the sandals
Of Sigvald the Earl.

The mariners shout,
The ships swing about,
The yards are all hoisted,
The sails flutter out.

The war-horns are played,
The anchors are weighed,
Like moths in the distance
The sails flit and fade.

The sea is like lead
The harbor lies dead,
As a corse on the sea-shore,
Whose spirit has fled!

On that fatal day,
The histories say,
Seventy vessels

Sailed out of the bay.

But soon scattered wide
O'er the billows they ride,
While Sigvald and Olaf
Sail side by side.

Cried the Earl: "Follow me!
I your pilot will be,
For I know all the channels
Where flows the deep sea!"

So into the strait
Where his foes lie in wait,
Gallant King Olaf
Sails to his fate!

Then the sea-fog veils
The ships and their sails;
Queen Sigrid the Haughty,
Thy vengeance prevails!

XIX. KING OLAF'S WAR-HORNS

"Strike the sails!" King Olaf said;
"Never shall men of mine take flight;
Never away from battle I fled,
Never away from my foes!
    Let God dispose
Of my life in the fight!"

"Sound the horns!" said Olaf the King;
And suddenly through the drifting brume
The blare of the horns began to ring,
Like the terrible trumpet shock
    Of Regnarock,
On the Day of Doom!

Louder and louder the war-horns sang
Over the level floor of the flood;
All the sails came down with a clang,
And there in the mist overhead
    The sun hung red
As a drop of blood.

Drifting down on the Danish fleet
Three together the ships were lashed,
So that neither should turn and retreat;
In the midst, but in front of the rest
   The burnished crest
Of the Serpent flashed.

King Olaf stood on the quarter-deck,
With bow of ash and arrows of oak,
His gilded shield was without a fleck,
His helmet inlaid with gold,
   And in many a fold
Hung his crimson cloak.

On the forecastle Ulf the Red
Watched the lashing of the ships;
"If the Serpent lie so far ahead,
We shall have hard work of it here,
   Said he with a sneer
On his bearded lips.

King Olaf laid an arrow on string,
"Have I a coward on board?" said he.
"Shoot it another way, O King!"
Sullenly answered Ulf,
   The old sea-wolf;
"You have need of me!"

In front came Svend, the King of the Danes,
Sweeping down with his fifty rowers;
To the right, the Swedish king with his thanes;
And on board of the Iron Beard
   Earl Eric steered
To the left with his oars.

"These soft Danes and Swedes," said the King,
"At home with their wives had better stay,
Than come within reach of my Serpent's sting:
But where Eric the Norseman leads
   Heroic deeds
Will be done to-day!"

Then as together the vessels crashed,
Eric severed the cables of hide,

With which King Olaf's ships were lashed,
And left them to drive and drift
    With the currents swift
Of the outward tide.

Louder the war-horns growl and snarl,
Sharper the dragons bite and sting!
Eric the son of Hakon Jarl
A death-drink salt as the sea
    Pledges to thee,
Olaf the King!

XX. EINAR TAMBERSKELVER

It was Einar Tamberskelver
    Stood beside the mast;
From his yew-bow, tipped with silver,
    Flew the arrows fast;

Aimed at Eric unavailing,
    As he sat concealed,
Half behind the quarter-railing,
    Half behind his shield.

First an arrow struck the tiller,
    Just above his head;
"Sing, O Eyvind Skaldaspiller,"
    Then Earl Eric said.

"Sing the song of Hakon dying,
    Sing his funeral wail!"
And another arrow flying
    Grazed his coat of mail.

Turning to a Lapland yeoman,
    As the arrow passed,
Said Earl Eric, "Shoot that bowman
    Standing by the mast."

Sooner than the word was spoken
    Flew the yeoman's shaft;
Einar's bow in twain was broken,
    Einar only laughed.

"What was that?" said Olaf, standing
  On the quarter-deck.
"Something heard I like the stranding
  Of a shattered wreck."

Einar then, the arrow taking
  From the loosened string,
Answered, "That was Norway breaking
  From thy hand, O King!"

"Thou art but a poor diviner,"
  Straightway Olaf said;
"Take my bow, and swifter, Einar,
  Let thy shafts be sped."

Of his bows the fairest choosing,
  Reached he from above;
Einar saw the blood-drops oozing
  Through his iron glove.

But the bow was thin and narrow;
  At the first assay,
O'er its head he drew the arrow,
  Flung the bow away;

Said, with hot and angry temper
  Flushing in his cheek,
"Olaf! for so great a Kamper
  Are thy bows too weak!"

Then, with smile of joy defiant
  On his beardless lip,
Scaled he, light and self-reliant,
  Eric's dragon-ship.

Loose his golden locks were flowing,
  Bright his armor gleamed;
Like Saint Michael overthrowing
  Lucifer he seemed.

XXI. KING OLAF'S DEATH-DRINK

All day has the battle raged,
All day have the ships engaged,

But not yet is assuaged
  The vengeance of Eric the Earl.

The decks with blood are red,
The arrows of death are sped,
The ships are filled with the dead,
  And the spears the champions hurl.

They drift as wrecks on the tide,
The grappling-irons are plied,
The boarders climb up the side,
  The shouts are feeble and few.

Ah! never shall Norway again
See her sailors come back o'er the main;
They all lie wounded or slain,
  Or asleep in the billows blue!

On the deck stands Olaf the King,
Around him whistle and sing
The spears that the foemen fling,
  And the stones they hurl with their hands.

In the midst of the stones and the spears,
Kolbiorn, the marshal, appears,
His shield in the air he uprears,
  By the side of King Olaf he stands.

Over the slippery wreck
Of the Long Serpent's deck
Sweeps Eric with hardly a check,
  His lips with anger are pale;

He hews with his axe at the mast,
Till it falls, with the sails overcast,
Like a snow-covered pine in the vast
  Dim forests of Orkadale.

Seeking King Olaf then,
He rushes aft with his men,
As a hunter into the den
  Of the bear, when he stands at bay.

"Remember Jarl Hakon!" he cries;

When lo! on his wondering eyes,
Two kingly figures arise,
  Two Olaf's in warlike array!

Then Kolbiorn speaks in the ear
Of King Olaf a word of cheer,
In a whisper that none may hear,
  With a smile on his tremulous lip;

Two shields raised high in the air,
Two flashes of golden hair,
Two scarlet meteors' glare,
  And both have leaped from the ship.

Earl Eric's men in the boats
Seize Kolbiorn's shield as it floats,
And cry, from their hairy throats,
  "See! it is Olaf the King!"

While far on the opposite side
Floats another shield on the tide,
Like a jewel set in the wide
  Sea-current's eddying ring.

There is told a wonderful tale,
How the King stripped off his mail,
Like leaves of the brown sea-kale,
  As he swam beneath the main;

But the young grew old and gray,
And never, by night or by day,
In his kingdom of Norroway
  Was King Olaf seen again!

XXII. THE NUN OF NIDAROS

In the convent of Drontheim,
Alone in her chamber
Knelt Astrid the Abbess,
At midnight, adoring,
Beseeching, entreating
The Virgin and Mother.

She heard in the silence

The voice of one speaking,
Without in the darkness,
In gusts of the night-wind
Now louder, now nearer,
Now lost in the distance.

The voice of a stranger
It seemed as she listened,
Of some one who answered,
Beseeching, imploring,
A cry from afar off
She could not distinguish.

The voice of Saint John,
The beloved disciple,
Who wandered and waited
The Master's appearance.
Alone in the darkness,
Unsheltered and friendless.

"It is accepted
The angry defiance
The challenge of battle!
It is accepted,
But not with the weapons
Of war that thou wieldest!

"Cross against corselet,
Love against hatred,
Peace-cry for war-cry!
Patience is powerful;
He that o'ercometh
Hath power o'er the nations!

"As torrents in summer,
Half dried in their channels,
Suddenly rise, though the
Sky is still cloudless,
For rain has been falling
Far off at their fountains;

So hearts that are fainting
Grow full to o'erflowing,
And they that behold it

Marvel, and know not
That God at their fountains
Far off has been raining!

"Stronger than steel
Is the sword of the Spirit;
Swifter than arrows
The light of the truth is,
Greater than anger
Is love, and subdueth!

"Thou art a phantom,
A shape of the sea-mist,
A shape of the brumal
Rain, and the darkness
Fearful and formless;
Day dawns and thou art not!

"The dawn is not distant,
Nor is the night starless;
Love is eternal!
God is still God, and
His faith shall not fail us
Christ is eternal!"

INTERLUDE

A strain of music closed the tale,
A low, monotonous, funeral wail,
That with its cadence, wild and sweet,
Made the long Saga more complete.

"Thank God," the Theologian said,
"The reign of violence is dead,
Or dying surely from the world;
While Love triumphant reigns instead,
And in a brighter sky o'erhead
His blessed banners are unfurled.
And most of all thank God for this:
The war and waste of clashing creeds
Now end in words, and not in deeds,
And no one suffers loss, or bleeds,
For thoughts that men call heresies.

"I stand without here in the porch,
I hear the bell's melodious din,
I hear the organ peal within,
I hear the prayer, with words that scorch
Like sparks from an inverted torch,
I hear the sermon upon sin,
With threatenings of the last account.
And all, translated in the air,
Reach me but as our dear Lord's Prayer,
And as the Sermon on the Mount.

"Must it be Calvin, and not Christ?
Must it be Athanasian creeds,
Or holy water, books, and beads?
Must struggling souls remain content
With councils and decrees of Trent?
And can it be enough for these
The Christian Church the year embalms
With evergreens and boughs of palms,
And fills the air with litanies?

"I know that yonder Pharisee
Thanks God that he is not like me;
In my humiliation dressed,
I only stand and beat my breast,
And pray for human charity.

"Not to one church alone, but seven,
The voice prophetic spake from heaven;
And unto each the promise came,
Diversified, but still the same;
For him that overcometh are
The new name written on the stone,
The raiment white, the crown, the throne,
And I will give him the Morning Star!

"Ah! to how many Faith has been
No evidence of things unseen,
But a dim shadow, that recasts
The creed of the Phantasiasts,
For whom no Man of Sorrows died,
For whom the Tragedy Divine
Was but a symbol and a sign,
And Christ a phantom crucified!

"For others a diviner creed
Is living in the life they lead.
The passing of their beautiful feet
Blesses the pavement of the street
And all their looks and words repeat
Old Fuller's saying, wise and sweet,
Not as a vulture, but a dove,
The Holy Ghost came from above.

"And this brings back to me a tale
So sad the hearer well may quail,
And question if such things can be;
Yet in the chronicles of Spain
Down the dark pages runs this stain,
And naught can wash them white again,
So fearful is the tragedy."

THE THEOLOGIAN'S TALE: TORQUEMADA

In the heroic days when Ferdinand
And Isabella ruled the Spanish land,
And Torquemada, with his subtle brain,
Ruled them, as Grand Inquisitor of Spain,
In a great castle near Valladolid,
Moated and high and by fair woodlands hid,
There dwelt as from the chronicles we learn,
An old Hidalgo proud and taciturn,
Whose name has perished, with his towers of stone,
And all his actions save this one alone;
This one, so terrible, perhaps 't were best
If it, too, were forgotten with the rest;
Unless, perchance, our eyes can see therein
The martyrdom triumphant o'er the sin;
A double picture, with its gloom and glow,
The splendor overhead, the death below.

This sombre man counted each day as lost
On which his feet no sacred threshold crossed;
And when he chanced the passing Host to meet,
He knelt and prayed devoutly in the street;
Oft he confessed; and with each mutinous thought,
As with wild beasts at Ephesus, he fought.
In deep contrition scourged himself in Lent,

Walked in processions, with his head down bent,
At plays of Corpus Christi oft was seen,
And on Palm Sunday bore his bough of green.
His sole diversion was to hunt the boar
Through tangled thickets of the forest hoar,
Or with his jingling mules to hurry down
To some grand bull-fight in the neighboring town,
Or in the crowd with lighted taper stand,
When Jews were burned, or banished from the land.
Then stirred within him a tumultuous joy;
The demon whose delight is to destroy
Shook him, and shouted with a trumpet tone,
Kill! kill! and let the Lord find out his own!"

And now, in that old castle in the wood,
His daughters, in the dawn of womanhood,
Returning from their convent school, had made
Resplendent with their bloom the forest shade,
Reminding him of their dead mother's face,
When first she came into that gloomy place,—
A memory in his heart as dim and sweet
As moonlight in a solitary street,
Where the same rays, that lift the sea, are thrown
Lovely but powerless upon walls of stone.
These two fair daughters of a mother dead
Were all the dream had left him as it fled.
A joy at first, and then a growing care,
As if a voice within him cried, "Beware
A vague presentiment of impending doom,
Like ghostly footsteps in a vacant room,
Haunted him day and night; a formless fear
That death to some one of his house was near,
With dark surmises of a hidden crime,
Made life itself a death before its time.
Jealous, suspicious, with no sense of shame,
A spy upon his daughters he became;
With velvet slippers, noiseless on the floors,
He glided softly through half-open doors;
Now in the room, and now upon the stair,
He stood beside them ere they were aware;
He listened in the passage when they talked,
He watched them from the casement when they walked,
He saw the gypsy haunt the river's side,
He saw the monk among the cork-trees glide;

And, tortured by the mystery and the doubt
Of some dark secret, past his finding out,
Baffled he paused; then reassured again
Pursued the flying phantom of his brain.
He watched them even when they knelt in church;
And then, descending lower in his search,
Questioned the servants, and with eager eyes
Listened incredulous to their replies;
The gypsy? none had seen her in the wood!
The monk? a mendicant in search of food!

At length the awful revelation came,
Crushing at once his pride of birth and name;
The hopes his yearning bosom forward cast,
And the ancestral glories of the vast,
All fell together, crumbling in disgrace,
A turret rent from battlement to base.
His daughters talking in the dead of night
In their own chamber, and without a light,
Listening, as he was wont, he overheard,
And learned the dreadful secret, word by word;
And hurrying from his castle, with a cry
He raised his hands to the unpitying sky,
Repeating one dread word, till bush and tree
Caught it, and shuddering answered, "Heresy!"

Wrapped in his cloak, his hat drawn o'er his face,
Now hurrying forward, now with lingering pace,
He walked all night the alleys of his park,
With one unseen companion in the dark,
The Demon who within him lay in wait,
And by his presence turned his love to hate,
Forever muttering in an undertone,
"Kill! kill! and let the Lord find out his own!"

Upon the morrow, after early Mass,
While yet the dew was glistening on the grass,
And all the woods were musical with birds,
The old Hidalgo, uttering fearful words,
Walked homeward with the Priest, and in his room
Summoned his trembling daughters to their doom.
When questioned, with brief answers they replied,
Nor when accused evaded or denied;
Expostulations, passionate appeals,

All that the human heart most fears or feels,
In vain the Priest with earnest voice essayed;
In vain the father threatened, wept, and prayed;
Until at last he said, with haughty mien,
"The Holy Office, then, must intervene!"

And now the Grand Inquisitor of Spain,
With all the fifty horsemen of his train,
His awful name resounding, like the blast
Of funeral trumpets, as he onward passed,
Came to Valladolid, and there began
To harry the rich Jews with fire and ban.
To him the Hidalgo went, and at the gate
Demanded audience on affairs of state,
And in a secret chamber stood before
A venerable graybeard of fourscore,
Dressed in the hood and habit of a friar;
Out of his eyes flashed a consuming fire,
And in his hand the mystic horn he held,
Which poison and all noxious charms dispelled.
He heard in silence the Hidalgo's tale,
Then answered in a voice that made him quail:
"Son of the Church! when Abraham of old
To sacrifice his only son was told,
He did not pause to parley nor protest
But hastened to obey the Lord's behest.
In him it was accounted righteousness;
The Holy Church expects of thee no less!"

A sacred frenzy seized the father's brain,
And Mercy from that hour implored in vain.
Ah! who will e'er believe the words I say?
His daughters he accused, and the same day
They both were cast into the dungeon's gloom,
That dismal antechamber of the tomb,
Arraigned, condemned, and sentenced to the flame,
The secret torture and the public shame.

Then to the Grand Inquisitor once more
The Hidalgo went, more eager than before,
And said: "When Abraham offered up his son,
He clave the wood wherewith it might be done.
By his example taught, let me too bring
Wood from the forest for my offering!"

And the deep voice, without a pause, replied:
"Son of the Church! by faith now justified,
Complete thy sacrifice, even as thou wilt;
The Church absolves thy conscience from all guilt!"

Then this most wretched father went his way
Into the woods, that round his castle lay,
Where once his daughters in their childhood played
With their young mother in the sun and shade.
Now all the leaves had fallen; the branches bare
Made a perpetual moaning in the air,
And screaming from their eyries overhead
The ravens sailed athwart the sky of lead.
With his own hands he lopped the boughs and bound
Fagots, that crackled with foreboding sound,
And on his mules, caparisoned and gay
With bells and tassels, sent them on their way.

Then with his mind on one dark purpose bent,
Again to the Inquisitor he went, And said:
"Behold, the fagots I have brought,
And now, lest my atonement be as naught,
Grant me one more request, one last desire,—
With my own hand to light the funeral fire!"
And Torquemada answered from his seat,
"Son of the Church! Thine offering is complete;
Her servants through all ages shall not cease
To magnify thy deed. Depart in peace!"

Upon the market-place, builded of stone
The scaffold rose, whereon Death claimed his own.
At the four corners, in stern attitude,
Four statues of the Hebrew Prophets stood,
Gazing with calm indifference in their eyes
Upon this place of human sacrifice,
Round which was gathering fast the eager crowd,
With clamor of voices dissonant and loud,
And every roof and window was alive
With restless gazers, swarming like a hive.

The church-bells tolled, the chant of monks drew near,
Loud trumpets stammered forth their notes of fear,
A line of torches smoked along the street,
There was a stir, a rush, a tramp of feet,

And, with its banners floating in the air,
Slowly the long procession crossed the square,
And, to the statues of the Prophets bound,
The victims stood, with fagots piled around.
Then all the air a blast of trumpets shook,
And louder sang the monks with bell and book,
And the Hidalgo, lofty, stern, and proud,
Lifted his torch, and, bursting through the crowd,
Lighted in haste the fagots, and then fled,
Lest those imploring eyes should strike him dead!

O pitiless skies! why did your clouds retain
For peasants' fields their floods of hoarded rain?
O pitiless earth! why open no abyss
To bury in its chasm a crime like this?

That night a mingled column of fire and smoke
Prom the dark thickets of the forest broke,
And, glaring o'er the landscape leagues away,
Made all the fields and hamlets bright as day.
Wrapped in a sheet of flame the castle blazed,
And as the villagers in terror gazed,
They saw the figure of that cruel knight
Lean from a window in the turret's height,
His ghastly face illumined with the glare,
His hands upraised above his head in prayer,
Till the floor sank beneath him, and he fell
Down the black hollow of that burning well.

Three centuries and more above his bones
Have piled the oblivious years like funeral stones;
His name has perished with him, and no trace
Remains on earth of his afflicted race;
But Torquemada's name, with clouds o'ercast,
Looms in the distant landscape of the Past,
Like a burnt tower upon a blackened heath,
Lit by the fires of burning woods beneath!

INTERLUDE

Thus closed the tale of guilt and gloom,
That cast upon each listener's face
Its shadow, and for some brief space

Unbroken silence filled the room.
The Jew was thoughtful and distressed;
Upon his memory thronged and pressed
The persecution of his race,
Their wrongs and sufferings and disgrace;
His head was sunk upon his breast,
And from his eyes alternate came
Flashes of wrath and tears of shame.

The student first the silence broke,
As one who long has lain in wait
With purpose to retaliate,
And thus he dealt the avenging stroke.
"In such a company as this,
A tale so tragic seems amiss,
That by its terrible control
O'ermasters and drags down the soul
Into a fathomless abyss.
The Italian Tales that you disdain,
Some merry Night of Straparole,
Or Machiavelli's Belphagor,
Would cheer us and delight us more,
Give greater pleasure and less pain
Than your grim tragedies of Spain!"

And here the Poet raised his hand,
With such entreaty and command,
It stopped discussion at its birth,
And said: "The story I shall tell
Has meaning in it, if not mirth;
Listen, and hear what once befell
The merry birds of Killingworth!"

THE POET'S TALE: THE BIRDS OF KILLINGWORTH

It was the season, when through all the land
  The merle and mavis build, and building sing
Those lovely lyrics, written by His hand,
  Whom Saxon Caedmon calls the Blitheheart King;
When on the boughs the purple buds expand,
  The banners of the vanguard of the Spring,
And rivulets, rejoicing, rush and leap,
And wave their fluttering signals from the steep.

The robin and the bluebird, piping loud,
  Filled all the blossoming orchards with their glee;
The sparrows chirped as if they still were proud
  Their race in Holy Writ should mentioned be;
And hungry crows assembled in a crowd,
  Clamored their piteous prayer incessantly,
Knowing who hears the ravens cry, and said:
"Give us, O Lord, this day our daily bread!"

Across the Sound the birds of passage sailed,
  Speaking some unknown language strange and sweet
Of tropic isle remote, and passing hailed
  The village with the cheers of all their fleet;
Or quarrelling together, laughed and railed
  Like foreign sailors, landed in the street
Of seaport town, and with outlandish noise
Of oaths and gibberish frightening girls and boys.

Thus came the jocund Spring in Killingworth,
  In fabulous day; some hundred years ago;
And thrifty farmers, as they tilled the earth,
  Heard with alarm the cawing of the crow,
That mingled with the universal mirth,
  Cassandra-like, prognosticating woe;
They shook their heads, and doomed with dreadful words
To swift destruction the whole race of birds.

And a town-meeting was convened straightway
  To set a price upon the guilty heads
Of these marauders, who, in lieu of pay,
  Levied black-mail upon the garden beds
And cornfields, and beheld without dismay
  The awful scarecrow, with his fluttering shreds;
The skeleton that waited at their feast,
Whereby their sinful pleasure was increased.

Then from his house, a temple painted white,
  With fluted columns, and a roof of red,
The Squire came forth, august and splendid sight!
  Slowly descending, with majestic tread,
Three flights of steps, nor looking left nor right,
  Down the long street he walked, as one who said,
"A town that boasts inhabitants like me
Can have no lack of good society!"

The Parson, too, appeared, a man austere,
  The instinct of whose nature was to kill;
The wrath of God he preached from year to year,
  And read, with fervor, Edwards on the Will;
His favorite pastime was to slay the deer
  In Summer on some Adirondac hill;
E'en now, while walking down the rural lane,
He lopped the wayside lilies with his cane.

From the Academy, whose belfry crowned
  The hill of Science with its vane of brass,
Came the Preceptor, gazing idly round,
  Now at the clouds, and now at the green grass,
And all absorbed in reveries profound
  Of fair Almira in the upper class,
Who was, as in a sonnet he had said,
As pure as water, and as good as bread.

And next the Deacon issued from his door,
  In his voluminous neck-cloth, white as snow;
A suit of sable bombazine he wore;
  His form was ponderous, and his step was slow;
There never was so wise a man before;
  He seemed the incarnate "Well, I told you so!"
And to perpetuate his great renown
There was a street named after him in town.

These came together in the new town-hall,
  With sundry farmers from the region round.
The Squirt presided, dignified and tall,
  His air impressive and his reasoning sound;
Ill fared it with the birds, both great and small;
  Hardly a friend in all that crowd they found,
But enemies enough, who every one
Charged them with all the crimes beneath the sun.

When they had ended, from his place apart,
  Rose the Preceptor, to redress the wrong,
And, trembling like a steed before the start,
  Looked round bewildered on the expectant throng;
Then thought of fair Almira, and took heart
  To speak out what was in him, clear and strong,
Alike regardless of their smile or frown,
And quite determined not to be laughed down.

"Plato, anticipating the Reviewers,
　From his Republic banished without pity
The Poets; in this little town of yours,
　You put to death, by means of a Committee,
The ballad-singers and the Troubadours,
　The street-musicians of the heavenly city,
The birds, who make sweet music for us all
In our dark hours, as David did for Saul.

"The thrush that carols at the dawn of day
　From the green steeples of the piny wood;
The oriole in the elm; the noisy jay,
　Jargoning like a foreigner at his food;
The bluebird balanced on some topmost spray,
　Flooding with melody the neighborhood;
Linnet and meadow-lark, and all the throng
That dwell in nests, and have the gift of song.

"You slay them all! and wherefore! for the gain
　Of a scant handful more or less of wheat,
Or rye, or barley, or some other grain,
　Scratched up at random by industrious feet,
Searching for worm or weevil after rain!
　Or a few cherries, that are not so sweet
As are the songs these uninvited guests,
Sing at their feast with comfortable breasts.

"Do you ne'er think what wondrous beings these?
　Do you ne'er think who made them and who taught
The dialect they speak, where melodies
　Alone are the interpreters of thought?
Whose household words are songs in many keys,
　Sweeter than instrument of man e'er caught!
Whose habitations in the tree-tops even
Are half-way houses on the road to heaven!

"Think, every morning when the sun peeps through
　The dim, leaf-latticed windows of the grove,
How jubilant the happy birds renew
　Their old, melodious madrigals of love!
And when you think of this, remember too
　'T is always morning somewhere, and above
The awakening continent; from shore to shore,
Somewhere the birds are singing evermore.

"Think of your woods and orchards without birds!
  Of empty nests that cling to boughs and beams
As in an idiot's brain remembered words
  Hang empty 'mid the cobwebs of his dreams!
Will bleat of flocks or bellowing of herds
  Make up for the lost music, when your teams
Drag home the stingy harvest, and no more
The feathered gleaners follow to your door?

"What! would you rather see the incessant stir
  Of insects in the windrows of the hay,
And hear the locust and the grasshopper
  Their melancholy hurdy-gurdies play?
Is this more pleasant to you than the whir
  Of meadow-lark, and her sweet roundelay,
Or twitter of little field-fares, as you take
Your nooning in the shade of bush and brake?

"You call them thieves and pillagers; but know,
  They are the winged wardens of your farms,
Who from the cornfields drive the insidious foe,
  And from your harvests keep a hundred harms;
Even the blackest of them all, the crow,
  Renders good service as your man-at-arms,
Crushing the beetle in his coat of mail,
And crying havoc on the slug and snail.

"How can I teach your children gentleness,
  And mercy to the weak, and reverence
For Life, which, in its weakness or excess,
  Is still a gleam of God's omnipotence,
Or Death, which, seeming darkness, is no less
  The selfsame light, although averted hence,
When by your laws, your actions, and your speech,
You contradict the very things I teach?"

With this he closed; and through the audience went
  A murmur, like the rustle of dead leaves;
The farmers laughed and nodded, and some bent
  Their yellow heads together like their sheaves;
Men have no faith in fine-spun sentiment
  Who put their trust in bullocks and in beeves.
The birds were doomed; and, as the record shows,
A bounty offered for the heads of crows.

There was another audience out of reach,
  Who had no voice nor vote in making laws,
But in the papers read his little speech,
  And crowned his modest temples with applause;
They made him conscious, each one more than each,
  He still was victor, vanquished in their cause.
Sweetest of all the applause he won from thee,
O fair Almira at the Academy!

And so the dreadful massacre began;
  O'er fields and orchards, and o'er woodland crests,
The ceaseless fusillade of terror ran.
  Dead fell the birds, with blood-stains on their breasts,
Or wounded crept away from sight of man,
  While the young died of famine in their nests;
A slaughter to be told in groans, not words,
The very St. Bartholomew of Birds!

The Summer came, and all the birds were dead;
  The days were like hot coals; the very ground
Was burned to ashes; in the orchards fed
  Myriads of caterpillars, and around
The cultivated fields and garden beds
  Hosts of devouring insects crawled, and found
No foe to check their march, till they had made
The land a desert without leaf or shade.

Devoured by worms, like Herod, was the town,
  Because, like Herod, it had ruthlessly
Slaughtered the Innocents. From the trees spun down
  The canker-worms upon the passers-by,
Upon each woman's bonnet, shawl, and gown,
  Who shook them off with just a little cry
They were the terror of each favorite walk,
The endless theme of all the village talk.

The farmers grew impatient but a few
  Confessed their error, and would not complain,
For after all, the best thing one can do
  When it is raining, is to let it rain.
Then they repealed the law, although they knew
  It would not call the dead to life again;
As school-boys, finding their mistake too late,
Draw a wet sponge across the accusing slate.

That year in Killingworth the Autumn came
  Without the light of his majestic look,
The wonder of the falling tongues of flame,
  The illumined pages of his Doom's-Day book.
A few lost leaves blushed crimson with their shame,
  And drowned themselves despairing in the brook,
While the wild wind went moaning everywhere,
Lamenting the dead children of the air!

But the next Spring a stranger sight was seen,
  A sight that never yet by bard was sung,
As great a wonder as it would have been
  If some dumb animal had found a tongue!
A wagon, overarched with evergreen,
  Upon whose boughs were wicker cages hung,
All full of singing birds, came down the street,
Filling the air with music wild and sweet.

From all the country round these birds were brought,
  By order of the town, with anxious quest,
And, loosened from their wicker prisons, sought
  In woods and fields the places they loved best,
Singing loud canticles, which many thought
  Were satires to the authorities addressed,
While others, listening in green lanes, averred
Such lovely music never had been heard!

But blither still and louder carolled they
  Upon the morrow, for they seemed to know
It was the fair Almira's wedding-day,
  And everywhere, around, above, below,
When the Preceptor bore his bride away,
  Their songs burst forth in joyous overflow,
And a new heaven bent over a new earth
Amid the sunny farms of Killingworth.

FINALE

The hour was late; the fire burned low,
The Landlord's eyes were closed in sleep,
And near the story's end a deep
Sonorous sound at times was heard,
As when the distant bagpipes blow.

At this all laughed; the Landlord stirred,
As one awaking from a swound,
And, gazing anxiously around,
Protested that he had not slept,
But only shut his eyes, and kept
His ears attentive to each word.

Then all arose, and said "Good Night."
Alone remained the drowsy Squire
To rake the embers of the fire,
And quench the waning parlor light.
While from the windows, here and there,
The scattered lamps a moment gleamed,
And the illumined hostel seemed
The constellation of the Bear,
Downward, athwart the misty air,
Sinking and setting toward the sun,
Far off the village clock struck one.

PART SECOND

A cold, uninterrupted rain,
That washed each southern window-pane,
And made a river of the road;
A sea of mist that overflowed
The house, the barns, the gilded vane,
And drowned the upland and the plain,
Through which the oak-trees, broad and high,
Like phantom ships went drifting by;
And, hidden behind a watery screen,
The sun unseen, or only seen
As a faint pallor in the sky;—
Thus cold and colorless and gray,
The morn of that autumnal day,
As if reluctant to begin,
Dawned on the silent Sudbury Inn,
And all the guests that in it lay.

Full late they slept. They did not hear
The challenge of Sir Chanticleer,
Who on the empty threshing-floor,
Disdainful of the rain outside,
Was strutting with a martial stride,
As if upon his thigh he wore

The famous broadsword of the Squire,
And said, "Behold me, and admire!"

Only the Poet seemed to hear,
In drowse or dream, more near and near
Across the border-land of sleep
The blowing of a blithesome horn,
That laughed the dismal day to scorn;
A splash of hoofs and rush of wheels
Through sand and mire like stranding keels,
As from the road with sudden sweep
The Mail drove up the little steep,
And stopped beside the tavern door;
A moment stopped, and then again
With crack of whip and bark of dog
Plunged forward through the sea of fog,
And all was silent as before,—
All silent save the dripping rain.

Then one by one the guests came down,
And greeted with a smile the Squire,
Who sat before the parlor fire,
Reading the paper fresh from town.
First the Sicilian, like a bird,
Before his form appeared, was heard
Whistling and singing down the stair;
Then came the Student, with a look
As placid as a meadow-brook;
The Theologian, still perplexed
With thoughts of this world and the next;
The Poet then, as one who seems
Walking in visions and in dreams;
Then the Musician, like a fair
Hyperion from whose golden hair
The radiance of the morning streams;
And last the aromatic Jew
Of Alicant, who, as he threw
The door wide open, on the air
Breathed round about him a perfume
Of damask roses in full bloom,
Making a garden of the room.

The breakfast ended, each pursued
The promptings of his various mood;

Beside the fire in silence smoked
The taciturn, impassive Jew,
Lost in a pleasant revery;
While, by his gravity provoked,
His portrait the Sicilian drew,
And wrote beneath it "Edrehi,
At the Red Horse in Sudbury."

By far the busiest of them all,
The Theologian in the hall
Was feeding robins in a cage,—
Two corpulent and lazy birds,
Vagrants and pilferers at best,
If one might trust the hostler's words,
Chief instrument of their arrest;
Two poets of the Golden Age,
Heirs of a boundless heritage
Of fields and orchards, east and west,
And sunshine of long summer days,
Though outlawed now and dispossessed!—
Such was the Theologian's phrase.

Meanwhile the Student held discourse
With the Musician, on the source
Of all the legendary lore
Among the nations, scattered wide
Like silt and seaweed by the force
And fluctuation of the tide;
The tale repeated o'er and o'er,
With change of place and change of name,
Disguised, transformed, and yet the same
We've heard a hundred times before.

The Poet at the window mused,
And saw, as in a dream confused,
The countenance of the Sun, discrowned,
And haggard with a pale despair,
And saw the cloud-rack trail and drift
Before it, and the trees uplift
Their leafless branches, and the air
Filled with the arrows of the rain,
And heard amid the mist below,
Like voices of distress and pain,
That haunt the thoughts of men insane,

The fateful cawings of the crow.

Then down the road, with mud besprent,
And drenched with rain from head to hoof,
The rain-drops dripping from his mane
And tail as from a pent-house roof,
A jaded horse, his head down bent,
Passed slowly, limping as he went.

The young Sicilian—who had grown
Impatient longer to abide
A prisoner, greatly mortified
To see completely overthrown
His plans for angling in the brook,
And, leaning o'er the bridge of stone,
To watch the speckled trout glide by,
And float through the inverted sky,
Still round and round the baited hook—
Now paced the room with rapid stride,
And, pausing at the Poet's side,
Looked forth, and saw the wretched steed,
And said: "Alas for human greed,
That with cold hand and stony eye
Thus turns an old friend out to die,
Or beg his food from gate to gate!
This brings a tale into my mind,
Which, if you are not disinclined
To listen, I will now relate."

All gave assent; all wished to hear,
Not without many a jest and jeer,
The story of a spavined steed;
And even the Student with the rest
Put in his pleasant little jest
Out of Malherbe, that Pegasus
Is but a horse that with all speed
Bears poets to the hospital;
While the Sicilian, self-possessed,
After a moment's interval
Began his simple story thus.

THE SICILIAN'S TALE: THE BELL OF ATRI

At Atri in Abruzzo, a small town
Of ancient Roman date, but scant renown,
One of those little places that have run
Half up the hill, beneath a blazing sun,
And then sat down to rest, as if to say,
"I climb no farther upward, come what may,"—
The Re Giovanni, now unknown to fame,
So many monarchs since have borne the name,
Had a great bell hung in the market-place
Beneath a roof, projecting some small space,
By way of shelter from the sun and rain.
Then rode he through the streets with all his train,
And, with the blast of trumpets loud and long,
Made proclamation, that whenever wrong
Was done to any man, he should but ring
The great bell in the square, and he, the King,
Would cause the Syndic to decide thereon.
Such was the proclamation of King John.

How swift the happy days in Atri sped,
What wrongs were righted, need not here be said.
Suffice it that, as all things must decay,
The hempen rope at length was worn away,
Unravelled at the end, and, strand by strand,
Loosened and wasted in the ringer's hand,
Till one, who noted this in passing by,
Mended the rope with braids of briony,
So that the leaves and tendrils of the vine
Hung like a votive garland at a shrine.

By chance it happened that in Atri dwelt
A knight, with spur on heel and sword in belt,
Who loved to hunt the wild-boar in the woods,
Who loved his falcons with their crimson hoods,
Who loved his hounds and horses, and all sports
And prodigalities of camps and courts;—
Loved, or had loved them; for at last, grown old,
His only passion was the love of gold.

He sold his horses, sold his hawks and hounds,
Rented his vineyards and his garden-grounds,

Kept but one steed, his favorite steed of all,
To starve and shiver in a naked stall,
And day by day sat brooding in his chair,
Devising plans how best to hoard and spare.

At length he said: "What is the use or need
To keep at my own cost this lazy steed,
Eating his head off in my stables here,
When rents are low and provender is dear?
Let him go feed upon the public ways;
I want him only for the holidays."
So the old steed was turned into the heat
Of the long, lonely, silent, shadeless street;
And wandered in suburban lanes forlorn,
Barked at by dogs, and torn by brier and thorn.

One afternoon, as in that sultry clime
It is the custom in the summer time,
With bolted doors and window-shutters closed,
The inhabitants of Atri slept or dozed;
When suddenly upon their senses fell
The loud alarum of the accusing bell!
The Syndic started from his deep repose,
Turned on his couch, and listened, and then rose
And donned his robes, and with reluctant pace
Went panting forth into the market-place,
Where the great bell upon its cross-beam swung
Reiterating with persistent tongue,
In half-articulate jargon, the old song:
"Some one hath done a wrong, hath done a wrong!"

But ere he reached the belfry's light arcade
He saw, or thought he saw, beneath its shade,
No shape of human form of woman born,
But a poor steed dejected and forlorn,
Who with uplifted head and eager eye
Was tugging at the vines of briony.
"Domeneddio!" cried the Syndie straight,
"This is the Knight of Atri's steed of state!
He calls for justice, being sore distressed,
And pleads his cause as loudly as the best."

Meanwhile from street and lane a noisy crowd
Had rolled together like a summer cloud,

And told the story of the wretched beast
In five-and-twenty different ways at least,
With much gesticulation and appeal
To heathen gods, in their excessive zeal.
The Knight was called and questioned; in reply
Did not confess the fact, did not deny;
Treated the matter as a pleasant jest,
And set at naught the Syndic and the rest,
Maintaining, in an angry undertone,
That he should do what pleased him with his own.

And thereupon the Syndic gravely read
The proclamation of the King; then said:
"Pride goeth forth on horseback grand and gay,
But cometh back on foot, and begs its way;
Fame is the fragrance of heroic deeds,
Of flowers of chivalry and not of weeds!
These are familiar proverbs; but I fear
They never yet have reached your knightly ear.
What fair renown, what honor, what repute
Can come to you from starving this poor brute?
He who serves well and speaks not, merits more
Than they who clamor loudest at the door.
Therefore the law decrees that as this steed
Served you in youth, henceforth you shall take heed
To comfort his old age, and to provide
Shelter in stall an food and field beside."

The Knight withdrew abashed; the people all
Led home the steed in triumph to his stall.
The King heard and approved, and laughed in glee
And cried aloud: "Right well it pleaseth me!
Church-bells at best but ring us to the door;
But go not in to mass; my bell doth more:
It cometh into court and pleads the cause
Of creatures dumb and unknown to the laws;
And this shall make, in every Christian clime,
The Bell of Atri famous for all time."

INTERLUDE

"Yes, well your story pleads the cause
Of those dumb mouths that have no speech,

Only a cry from each to each
In its own kind, with its own laws;
Something that is beyond the reach
Of human power to learn or teach,—
An inarticulate moan of pain,
Like the immeasurable main
Breaking upon an unknown beach."

Thus spake the Poet with a sigh;
Then added, with impassioned cry,
As one who feels the words he speaks,
The color flushing in his cheeks,
The fervor burning in his eye:
"Among the noblest in the land,
Though he may count himself the least,
That man I honor and revere
Who without favor, without fear,
In the great city dares to stand
The friend of every friendless beast,
And tames with his unflinching hand
The brutes that wear our form and face,
The were-wolves of the human race!"
Then paused, and waited with a frown,
Like some old champion of romance,
Who, having thrown his gauntlet down,
Expectant leans upon his lance;
But neither Knight nor Squire is found
To raise the gauntlet from the ground,
And try with him the battle's chance.

"Wake from your dreams, O Edrehi!
Or dreaming speak to us, and make
A feint of being half awake,
And tell us what your dreams may be.
Out of the hazy atmosphere
Of cloud-land deign to reappear
Among us in this Wayside Inn;
Tell us what visions and what scenes
Illuminate the dark ravines
In which you grope your way. Begin!"

Thus the Sicilian spake. The Jew
Made no reply, but only smiled,
As men unto a wayward child,

Not knowing what to answer, do.
As from a cavern's mouth, o'ergrown
With moss and intertangled vines,
A streamlet leaps into the light
And murmurs over root and stone
In a melodious undertone;
Or as amid the noonday night
Of sombre and wind-haunted pines,
There runs a sound as of the sea;
So from his bearded lips there came
A melody without a name,
A song, a tale, a history,
Or whatsoever it may be,
Writ and recorded in these lines.

THE SPANISH JEW'S TALE: KAMBALU

Into the city of Kambalu,
By the road that leadeth to Ispahan,
At the head of his dusty caravan,
Laden with treasure from realms afar,
Baldacca and Kelat and Kandahar,
Rode the great captain Alau.

The Khan from his palace-window gazed,
And saw in the thronging street beneath,
In the light of the setting sun, that blazed
Through the clouds of dust by the caravan raised,
The flash of harness and jewelled sheath,
And the shining scymitars of the guard,
And the weary camels that bared their teeth,
As they passed and passed through the gates unbarred
Into the shade of the palace-yard.

Thus into the city of Kambalu
Rode the great captain Alau;
And he stood before the Khan, and said:
"The enemies of my lord are dead;
All the Kalifs of all the West
Bow and obey thy least behest;
The plains are dark with the mulberry-trees,
The weavers are busy in Samarcand,
The miners are sifting the golden sand,

The divers plunging for pearls in the seas,
And peace and plenty are in the land.

"Baldacca's Kalif, and he alone,
Rose in revolt against thy throne:
His treasures are at thy palace-door,
With the swords and the shawls and the jewels he wore;
His body is dust o'er the desert blown.

"A mile outside of Baldacca's gate
I left my forces to lie in wait,
Concealed by forests and hillocks of sand,
And forward dashed with a handful of men,
To lure the old tiger from his den
Into the ambush I had planned.
Ere we reached the town the alarm was spread,
For we heard the sound of gongs from within;
And with clash of cymbals and warlike din
The gates swung wide; and we turned and fled;
And the garrison sallied forth and pursued,
With the gray old Kalif at their head,
And above them the banner of Mohammed:
So we snared them all, and the town was subdued.

"As in at the gate we rode, behold,
A tower that is called the Tower of Gold!
For there the Kalif had hidden his wealth,
Heaped and hoarded and piled on high,
Like sacks of wheat in a granary;
And thither the miser crept by stealth
To feel of the gold that gave him health,
And to gaze and gloat with his hungry eye
On jewels that gleamed like a glow-worm's spark,
Or the eyes of a panther in the dark.

"I said to the Kalif: 'Thou art old,
Thou hast no need of so much gold.
Thou shouldst not have heaped and hidden it here,
Till the breath of battle was hot and near,
But have sown through the land these useless hoards
To spring into shining blades of swords,
And keep thine honor sweet and clear.
These grains of gold are not grains of wheat;
These bars of silver thou canst not eat;

These jewels and pearls and precious stones
Cannot cure the aches in thy bones,
Nor keep the feet of Death one hour
From climbing the stairways of thy tower!'

"Then into his dungeon I locked the drone,
And left him to feed there all alone
In the honey-cells of his golden hive:
Never a prayer, nor a cry, nor a groan
Was heard from those massive walls of stone,
Nor again was the Kalif seen alive!

"When at last we unlocked the door,
We found him dead upon the floor;
The rings had dropped from his withered hands,
His teeth were like bones in the desert sands:
Still clutching his treasure he had died;
And as he lay there, he appeared
A statue of gold with a silver beard,
His arms outstretched as if crucified."

This is the story, strange and true,
That the great captain Alau
Told to his brother the Tartar Khan,
When he rode that day into Kambalu
By the road that leadeth to Ispahan.

INTERLUDE

"I thought before your tale began,"
The Student murmured, "we should have
Some legend written by Judah Rav
In his Gemara of Babylon;
Or something from the Gulistan,—
The tale of the Cazy of Hamadan,
Or of that King of Khorasan
Who saw in dreams the eyes of one
That had a hundred years been dead
Still moving restless in his head,
Undimmed, and gleaming with the lust
Of power, though all the rest was dust.

"But lo! your glittering caravan

On the road that leadeth to Ispahan
Hath led us farther to the East
Into the regions of Cathay.
Spite of your Kalif and his gold,
Pleasant has been the tale you told,
And full of color; that at least
No one will question or gainsay.
And yet on such a dismal day
We need a merrier tale to clear
The dark and heavy atmosphere.
So listen, Lordlings, while I tell,
Without a preface, what befell
A simple cobbler, in the year —
No matter; it was long ago;
And that is all we need to know."

THE STUDENT'S TALE: THE COBBLER OF HAGENAU

I trust that somewhere and somehow
You all have heard of Hagenau,
A quiet, quaint, and ancient town
Among the green Alsatian hills,
A place of valleys, streams, and mills,
Where Barbarossa's castle, brown
With rust of centuries, still looks down
On the broad, drowsy land below,—
On shadowy forests filled with game,
And the blue river winding slow
Through meadows, where the hedges grow
That give this little town its name.

It happened in the good old times,
While yet the Master-singers filled
The noisy workshop and the guild
With various melodies and rhymes,
That here in Hagenau there dwelt
A cobbler,—one who loved debate,
And, arguing from a postulate,
Would say what others only felt;
A man of forecast and of thrift,
And of a shrewd and careful mind
In this world's business, but inclined
Somewhat to let the next world drift.

Hans Sachs with vast delight he read,
And Regenbogen's rhymes of love,
For their poetic fame had spread
Even to the town of Hagenau;
And some Quick Melody of the
Plough, Or Double Harmony of the Dove,
Was always running in his head.
He kept, moreover, at his side,
Among his leathers and his tools,
Reynard the Fox, the Ship of Fools,
Or Eulenspiegel, open wide;
With these he was much edified:
He thought them wiser than the Schools.

His good wife, full of godly fear,
Liked not these worldly themes to hear;
The Psalter was her book of songs;
The only music to her ear
Was that which to the Church belongs,
When the loud choir on Sunday chanted,
And the two angels carved in wood,
That by the windy organ stood,
Blew on their trumpets loud and clear,
And all the echoes, far and near,
Gibbered as if the church were haunted.
Outside his door, one afternoon,
This humble votary of the muse
Sat in the narrow strip of shade
By a projecting cornice made,
Mending the Burgomaster's shoes,
And singing a familiar tune:—

"Our ingress into the world
    Was naked and bare;
Our progress through the world
    Is trouble and care;
Our egress from the world
    Will be nobody knows where;
But if we do well here
    We shall do well there;
And I could tell you no more,
    Should I preach a whole year!"

Thus sang the cobbler at his work;

And with his gestures marked the time
Closing together with a jerk
Of his waxed thread the stitch and rhyme.
Meanwhile his quiet little dame
Was leaning o'er the window-sill,
Eager, excited, but mouse-still,
Gazing impatiently to see
What the great throng of folk might be
That onward in procession came,
Along the unfrequented street,
With horns that blew, and drums that beat,
And banners flying, and the flame
Of tapers, and, at times, the sweet
Voices of nuns; and as they sang
Suddenly all the church-bells rang.

In a gay coach, above the crowd,
There sat a monk in ample hood,
Who with his right hand held aloft
A red and ponderous cross of wood,
To which at times he meekly bowed.
In front three horsemen rode, and oft,
With voice and air importunate,
A boisterous herald cried aloud:
"The grace of God is at your gate!"
So onward to the church they passed.

The cobbler slowly tuned his last,
And, wagging his sagacious head,
Unto his kneeling housewife said:
"'Tis the monk Tetzel. I have heard
The cawings of that reverend bird.
Don't let him cheat you of your gold;
Indulgence is not bought and sold."

The church of Hagenau, that night,
Was full of people, full of light;
An odor of incense filled the air,
The priest intoned, the organ groaned
Its inarticulate despair;
The candles on the altar blazed,
And full in front of it upraised
The red cross stood against the glare.
Below, upon the altar-rail

Indulgences were set to sale,
Like ballads at a country fair.
A heavy strong-box, iron-bound
And carved with many a quaint device,
Received, with a melodious sound,
The coin that purchased Paradise.

Then from the pulpit overhead,
Tetzel the monk, with fiery glow,
Thundered upon the crowd below.
"Good people all, draw near!" he said;
"Purchase these letters, signed and sealed,
By which all sins, though unrevealed
And unrepented, are forgiven!
Count but the gain, count not the loss
Your gold and silver are but dross,
And yet they pave the way to heaven.
I hear your mothers and your sires
Cry from their purgatorial fires,
And will ye not their ransom pay?
O senseless people! when the gate
Of heaven is open, will ye wait?
Will ye not enter in to-day?
To-morrow it will be too late;
I shall be gone upon my way.
Make haste! bring money while ye may!'

The women shuddered, and turned pale;
Allured by hope or driven by fear,
With many a sob and many a tear,
All crowded to the altar-rail.
Pieces of silver and of gold
Into the tinkling strong-box fell
Like pebbles dropped into a well;
And soon the ballads were all sold.
The cobbler's wife among the rest
Slipped into the capacious chest
A golden florin; then withdrew,
Hiding the paper in her breast;
And homeward through the darkness went
Comforted, quieted, content;
She did not walk, she rather flew,
A dove that settles to her nest,
When some appalling bird of prey

That scared her has been driven away.

The days went by, the monk was gone,
The summer passed, the winter came;
Though seasons changed, yet still the same
The daily round of life went on;
The daily round of household care,
The narrow life of toil and prayer.
But in her heart the cobbler's dame
Had now a treasure beyond price,
A secret joy without a name,
The certainty of Paradise. Alas, alas!
Dust unto dust! Before the winter wore away,
Her body in the churchyard lay,
Her patient soul was with the Just!
After her death, among the things
That even the poor preserve with care,—
Some little trinkets and cheap rings,
A locket with her mother's hair,
Her wedding gown, the faded flowers
She wore upon her wedding day,—
Among these memories of past hours,
That so much of the heart reveal,
Carefully kept and put away,
The Letter of Indulgence lay
Folded, with signature and seal.

Meanwhile the Priest, aggrieved and pained,
Waited and wondered that no word
Of mass or requiem he heard,
As by the Holy Church ordained;
Then to the Magistrate complained,
That as this woman had been dead
A week or more, and no mass said,
It was rank heresy, or at least
Contempt of Church; thus said the Priest;
And straight the cobbler was arraigned.

He came, confiding in his cause,
But rather doubtful of the laws.
The Justice from his elbow-chair
Gave him a look that seemed to say:
"Thou standest before a Magistrate,
Therefore do not prevaricate!"

Then asked him in a business way,
Kindly but cold: "Is thy wife dead?"
The cobbler meekly bowed his head;
"She is," came struggling from his throat
Scarce audibly. The Justice wrote
The words down in a book, and then
Continued, as he raised his pen:
"She is; and hath a mass been said
For the salvation of her soul?
Come, speak the truth! confess the whole!"
The cobbler without pause replied:
"Of mass or prayer there was no need;
For at the moment when she died
Her soul was with the glorified!"
And from his pocket with all speed
He drew the priestly title-deed,
And prayed the Justice he would read.

The Justice read, amused, amazed;
And as he read his mirth increased;
At times his shaggy brows he raised,
Now wondering at the cobbler gazed,
Now archly at the angry Priest.
"From all excesses, sins, and crimes
Thou hast committed in past times
Thee I absolve! And furthermore,
Purified from all earthly taints,
To the communion of the Saints
And to the sacraments restore!
All stains of weakness, and all trace
Of shame and censure I efface;
Remit the pains thou shouldst endure,
And make thee innocent and pure,
So that in dying, unto thee
The gates of heaven shall open be!
Though long thou livest, yet this grace
Until the moment of thy death
Unchangeable continueth!"

Then said he to the Priest: "I find
This document is duly signed
Brother John Tetzel, his own hand.
At all tribunals in the land
In evidence it may be used;

Therefore acquitted is the accused."
Then to the cobbler turned: "My friend,
Pray tell me, didst thou ever read
Reynard the Fox?"—"O yes, indeed!"—
"I thought so. Don't forget the end."

INTERLUDE

"What was the end? I am ashamed
Not to remember Reynard's fate;
I have not read the book of late;
Was he not hanged?" the Poet said.
The Student gravely shook his head,
And answered: "You exaggerate.
There was a tournament proclaimed,
And Reynard fought with Isegrim
The Wolf, and having vanquished him,
Rose to high honor in the State,
And Keeper of the Seals was named!"
At this the gay Sicilian laughed:
"Fight fire with fire, and craft with craft;
Successful cunning seems to be
The moral of your tale," said he.
"Mine had a better, and the Jew's
Had none at all, that I could see;
His aim was only to amuse."

Meanwhile from out its ebon case
His violin the Minstrel drew,
And having tuned its strings anew,
Now held it close in his embrace,
And poising in his outstretched hand
The bow, like a magician's wand,
He paused, and said, with beaming face:
"Last night my story was too long;
To-day I give you but a song,
An old tradition of the North;
But first, to put you in the mood,
I will a little while prelude,
And from this instrument draw forth
Something by way of overture."

He played; at first the tones were pure

And tender as a summer night,
The full moon climbing to her height,
The sob and ripple of the seas,
The flapping of an idle sail;
And then by sudden and sharp degrees
The multiplied, wild harmonies
Freshened and burst into a gale;
A tempest howling through the dark,
A crash as of some shipwrecked bark.
A loud and melancholy wail.

Such was the prelude to the tale
Told by the Minstrel; and at times
He paused amid its varying rhymes,
And at each pause again broke in
The music of his violin,
With tones of sweetness or of fear,
Movements of trouble or of calm,
Creating their own atmosphere;
As sitting in a church we hear
Between the verses of the psalm
The organ playing soft and clear,
Or thundering on the startled ear.

THE MUSICIAN'S TALE: THE BALLAD OF CARMILHAN

I.

At Stralsund, by the Baltic Sea,
  Within the sandy bar,
At sunset of a summer's day,
Ready for sea, at anchor lay
  The good ship Valdemar.
The sunbeams danced upon the waves,
  And played along her side;
And through the cabin windows streamed
In ripples of golden light, that seemed
  The ripple of the tide.

There sat the captain with his friends,
  Old skippers brown and hale,
Who smoked and grumbled o'er their grog,
And talked of iceberg and of fog,

Of calm and storm and gale.

And one was spinning a sailor's yarn
  About Klaboterman,
The Kobold of the sea; a spright
Invisible to mortal sight,
  Who o'er the rigging ran.

Sometimes he hammered in the hold,
  Sometimes upon the mast,
Sometimes abeam, sometimes abaft,
Or at the bows he sang and laughed,
  And made all tight and fast.

He helped the sailors at their work,
  And toiled with jovial din;
He helped them hoist and reef the sails,
He helped them stow the casks and bales,
  And heave the anchor in.

But woe unto the lazy louts,
  The idlers of the crew;
Them to torment was his delight,
And worry them by day and night,
  And pinch them black and blue.

And woe to him whose mortal eyes
  Klaboterman behold.
It is a certain sign of death!—
The cabin-boy here held his breath,
  He felt his blood run cold.

II.

The jolly skipper paused awhile,
  And then again began;
"There is a Spectre Ship," quoth he,
"A ship of the Dead that sails the sea,
  And is called the Carmilhan.

"A ghostly ship, with a ghostly crew,
  In tempests she appears;
And before the gale, or against the gale,
She sails without a rag of sail,

Without a helmsman steers.

"She haunts the Atlantic north and south,
  But mostly the mid-sea,
Where three great rocks rise bleak and bare
Like furnace-chimneys in the air,
  And are called the Chimneys Three.

"And ill betide the luckless ship
  That meets the Carmilhan;
Over her decks the seas will leap,
She must go down into the deep,
  And perish mouse and man."

The captain of the Valdemar
  Laughed loud with merry heart.
"I should like to see this ship," said he;
"I should like to find these Chimneys Three,
  That are marked down in the chart.

"I have sailed right over the spot," he said
  "With a good stiff breeze behind,
When the sea was blue, and the sky was clear,—
You can follow my course by these pinholes here,—
  And never a rock could find."

And then he swore a dreadful oath,
  He swore by the Kingdoms Three,
That, should he meet the Carmilhan,
He would run her down, although he ran
  Right into Eternity!

All this, while passing to and fro,
  The cabin-boy had heard;
He lingered at the door to hear,
And drank in all with greedy ear,
  And pondered every word.

He was a simple country lad,
  But of a roving mind.
"O, it must be like heaven," thought he,
"Those far-off foreign lands to see,
  And fortune seek and find!"

But in the fo'castle, when he heard
  The mariners blaspheme,
He thought of home, he thought of God,
And his mother under the churchyard sod,
  And wished it were a dream.

One friend on board that ship had he;
  'T was the Klaboterman,
Who saw the Bible in his chest,
And made a sign upon his breast,
  All evil things to ban.

III.

The cabin windows have grown blank
  As eyeballs of the dead;
No more the glancing sunbeams burn
On the gilt letters of the stern,
  But on the figure-head;

On Valdemar Victorious,
  Who looketh with disdain
To see his image in the tide
Dismembered float from side to side,
  And reunite again.

"It is the wind," those skippers said,
  "That swings the vessel so;
It is the wind; it freshens fast,
'T is time to say farewell at last
  'T is time for us to go."

They shook the captain by the hand,
  "Goodluck! goodluck!" they cried;
Each face was like the setting sun,
As, broad and red, they one by one
  Went o'er the vessel's side.

The sun went down, the full moon rose,
  Serene o'er field and flood;
And all the winding creeks and bays
And broad sea-meadows seemed ablaze,
  The sky was red as blood.

The southwest wind blew fresh and fair,
  As fair as wind could be;
Bound for Odessa, o'er the bar,
With all sail set, the Valdemar
  Went proudly out to sea.

The lovely moon climbs up the sky
  As one who walks in dreams;
A tower of marble in her light,
A wall of black, a wall of white,
  The stately vessel seems.

Low down upon the sandy coast
  The lights begin to burn;
And now, uplifted high in air,
They kindle with a fiercer glare,
  And now drop far astern.

The dawn appears, the land is gone,
  The sea is all around;
Then on each hand low hills of sand
Emerge and form another land;
  She steereth through the Sound.

Through Kattegat and Skager-rack
  She flitteth like a ghost;
By day and night, by night and day,
She bounds, she flies upon her way
  Along the English coast.

Cape Finisterre is drawing near,
  Cape Finisterre is past;
Into the open ocean stream
She floats, the vision of a dream
  Too beautiful to last.

Suns rise and set, and rise, and yet
  There is no land in sight;
The liquid planets overhead
Burn brighter now the moon is dead,
  And longer stays the night.

IV.

And now along the horizon's edge
  Mountains of cloud uprose,
Black as with forests underneath,
Above their sharp and jagged teeth
  Were white as drifted snows.

Unseen behind them sank the sun,
  But flushed each snowy peak
A little while with rosy light
That faded slowly from the sight
  As blushes from the cheek.

Black grew the sky,—all black, all black;
  The clouds were everywhere;
There was a feeling of suspense
In nature, a mysterious sense
  Of terror in the air.

And all on board the Valdemar
  Was still as still could be;
Save when the dismal ship-bell tolled,
As ever and anon she rolled,
  And lurched into the sea.

The captain up and down the deck
  Went striding to and fro;
Now watched the compass at the wheel,
Now lifted up his hand to feel
  Which way the wind might blow.

And now he looked up at the sails,
  And now upon the deep;
In every fibre of his frame
He felt the storm before it came,
  He had no thought of sleep.

Eight bells! and suddenly abaft,
  With a great rush of rain,
Making the ocean white with spume,
In darkness like the day of doom,
  On came the hurricane.

The lightning flashed from cloud to cloud,
  And rent the sky in two;

A jagged flame, a single jet
Of white fire, like a bayonet
    That pierced the eyeballs through.

Then all around was dark again,
    And blacker than before;
But in that single flash of light
He had beheld a fearful sight,
    And thought of the oath he swore.

For right ahead lay the Ship of the Dead,
    The ghostly Carmilhan!
Her masts were stripped, her yards were bare,
And on her bowsprit, poised in air,
    Sat the Klaboterman.

Her crew of ghosts was all on deck
    Or clambering up the shrouds;
The boatswain's whistle, the captain's hail,
Were like the piping of the gale,
    And thunder in the clouds.

And close behind the Carmilhan
    There rose up from the sea,
As from a foundered ship of stone,
Three bare and splintered masts alone:
    They were the Chimneys Three.

And onward dashed the Valdemar
    And leaped into the dark;
A denser mist, a colder blast,
A little shudder, and she had passed
    Right through the Phantom Bark.

She cleft in twain the shadowy hulk,
    But cleft it unaware;
As when, careering to her nest,
The sea-gull severs with her breast
    The unresisting air.

Again the lightning flashed; again
    They saw the Carmilhan,
Whole as before in hull and spar;
But now on board of the Valdemar

Stood the Klaboterman.

And they all knew their doom was sealed;
  They knew that death was near;
Some prayed who never prayed before,
And some they wept, and some they swore,
  And some were mute with fear.

Then suddenly there came a shock,
  And louder than wind or sea
A cry burst from the crew on deck,
As she dashed and crashed, a hopeless wreck,
  Upon the Chimneys Three.

The storm and night were passed, the light
  To streak the east began;
The cabin-boy, picked up at sea,
Survived the wreck, and only he,
  To tell of the Carmilhan.

INTERLUDE

When the long murmur of applause
That greeted the Musician's lay
Had slowly buzzed itself away,
And the long talk of Spectre Ships
That followed died upon their lips
And came unto a natural pause,
"These tales you tell are one and all
Of the Old World," the Poet said,
"Flowers gathered from a crumbling wall,
Dead leaves that rustle as they fall;
Let me present you in their stead
Something of our New England earth,
A tale which, though of no great worth,
Has still this merit, that it yields
A certain freshness of the fields,
A sweetness as of home-made bread."

The Student answered: "Be discreet;
For if the flour be fresh and sound,
And if the bread be light and sweet,
Who careth in what mill 't was ground,

Or of what oven felt the heat,
Unless, as old Cervantes said,
You are looking after better bread
Than any that is made of wheat?
You know that people nowadays
To what is old give little praise;
All must be new in prose and verse:
They want hot bread, or something worse,
Fresh every morning, and half baked;
The wholesome bread of yesterday,
Too stale for them, is thrown away,
Nor is their thirst with water slaked.

As oft we see the sky in May
Threaten to rain, and yet not rain,
The Poet's face, before so gay,
Was clouded with a look of pain,
But suddenly brightened up again;
And without further let or stay
He told his tale of yesterday.

THE POET'S TALE: LADY WENTWORTH

One hundred years ago, and something more,
In Queen Street, Portsmouth, at her tavern door,
Neat as a pin, and blooming as a rose,
Stood Mistress Stavers in her furbelows,
Just as her cuckoo-clock was striking nine.
Above her head, resplendent on the sign,
The portrait of the Earl of Halifax,
In scarlet coat and periwig of flax,
Surveyed at leisure all her varied charms,
Her cap, her bodice, her white folded arms,
And half resolved, though he was past his prime,
And rather damaged by the lapse of time,
To fall down at her feet and to declare
The passion that had driven him to despair.
For from his lofty station he had seen
Stavers, her husband, dressed in bottle-green,
Drive his new Flying Stage-coach, four in hand,
Down the long lane, and out into the land,
And knew that he was far upon the way
To Ipswich and to Boston on the Bay!

Just then the meditations of the Earl
Were interrupted by a little girl,
Barefooted, ragged, with neglected hair,
Eyes full of laughter, neck and shoulders bare,
A thin slip of a girl, like a new moon,
Sure to be rounded into beauty soon,
A creature men would worship and adore,
Though now in mean habiliments she bore
A pail of water, dripping, through the street
And bathing, as she went her naked feet.

It was a pretty picture, full of grace,—
The slender form, the delicate, thin face;
The swaying motion, as she hurried by;
The shining feet, the laughter in her eye,
That o'er her face in ripples gleamed and glanced,
As in her pail the shifting sunbeam danced:
And with uncommon feelings of delight
The Earl of Halifax beheld the sight.
Not so Dame Stavers, for he heard her say
These words, or thought he did, as plain as day:
"O Martha Hilton! Fie! how dare you go
About the town half dressed, and looking so!"
At which the gypsy laughed, and straight replied:
"No matter how I look; I yet shall ride
In my own chariot, ma'am." And on the child
The Earl of Halifax benignly smiled,
As with her heavy burden she passed on,
Looked back, then turned the corner, and was gone.

What next, upon that memorable day,
Arrested his attention was a gay
And brilliant equipage, that flashed and spun,
The silver harness glittering in the sun,
Outriders with red jackets, lithe and lank,
Pounding the saddles as they rose and sank,
While all alone within the chariot sat
A portly person with three-cornered hat,
A crimson velvet coat, head high in air,
Gold-headed cane, and nicely powdered hair,
And diamond buckles sparkling at his knees,
Dignified, stately, florid, much at ease.
Onward the pageant swept, and as it passed,
Fair Mistress Stavers courtesied low and fast;

For this was Governor Wentworth, driving down
To Little Harbor, just beyond the town,
Where his Great House stood looking out to sea,
A goodly place, where it was good to be.

It was a pleasant mansion, an abode
Near and yet hidden from the great high-road,
Sequestered among trees, a noble pile,
Baronial and colonial in its style;
Gables and dormer-windows everywhere,
And stacks of chimneys rising high in air,—
Pandaean pipes, on which all winds that blew
Made mournful music the whole winter through.
Within, unwonted splendors met the eye,
Panels, and floors of oak, and tapestry;
Carved chimney-pieces, where on brazen dogs
Revelled and roared the Christmas fires of logs;
Doors opening into darkness unawares,
Mysterious passages, and flights of stairs;
And on the walls, in heavy gilded frames,
The ancestral Wentworths with Old-Scripture names.

Such was the mansion where the great man dwelt.
A widower and childless; and he felt
The loneliness, the uncongenial gloom,
That like a presence haunted ever room;
For though not given to weakness, he could feel
The pain of wounds, that ache because they heal.

The years came and the years went,—seven in all,
And passed in cloud and sunshine o'er the Hall;
The dawns their splendor through its chambers shed,
The sunsets flushed its western windows red;
The snow was on its roofs, the wind, the rain;
Its woodlands were in leaf and bare again;
Moons waxed and waned, the lilacs bloomed and died,
In the broad river ebbed and flowed the tide,
Ships went to sea, and ships came home from sea,
And the slow years sailed by and ceased to be.

And all these years had Martha Hilton served
In the Great House, not wholly unobserved:
By day, by night, the silver crescent grew,
Though hidden by clouds, her light still shining through;

A maid of all work, whether coarse or fine,
A servant who made service seem divine!
Through her each room was fair to look upon;
The mirrors glistened, and the brasses shone,
The very knocker on the outer door,
If she but passed, was brighter than before.

And now the ceaseless turning of the mill
Of Time, that never for an hour stands still,
Ground out the Governor's sixtieth birthday,
And powdered his brown hair with silver-gray.
The robin, the forerunner of the spring,
The bluebird with his jocund carolling,
The restless swallows building in the eaves,
The golden buttercups, the grass, the leaves,
The lilacs tossing in the winds of May,
All welcomed this majestic holiday!
He gave a splendid banquet served on plate,
Such as became the Governor of the State,
Who represented England and the King,
And was magnificent in everything.
He had invited all his friends and peers,—
The Pepperels, the Langdons, and the Lears,
The Sparhawks, the Penhallows, and the rest;
For why repeat the name of every guest?
But I must mention one, in bands and gown,
The rector there, the Reverend Arthur Brown
Of the Established Church; with smiling face
He sat beside the Governor and said grace;
And then the feast went on, as others do,
But ended as none other I e'er knew.

When they had drunk the King, with many a cheer,
The Governor whispered in a servant's ear,
Who disappeared and presently there stood
Within the room, in perfect womanhood,
A maiden, modest and yet self-possessed,
Youthful and beautiful, and simply dressed.
Can this be Martha Hilton? It must be!
Yes, Martha Hilton, and no other she!
Dowered with the beauty of her twenty years,
How ladylike, how queenlike she appears;
The pale, thin crescent of the days gone by
Is Dian now in all her majesty!

Yet scarce a guest perceived that she was there,
Until the Governor, rising from his chair,
Played slightly with his ruffles, then looked down,
And said unto the Reverend Arthur Brown:
"This is my birthday: it shall likewise be
My wedding-day; and you shall marry me!"

The listening guests were greatly mystified,
None more so than the rector, who replied:
"Marry you? Yes, that were a pleasant task,
Your Excellency; but to whom? I ask."
The Governor answered: "To this lady here"
And beckoned Martha Hilton to draw near.
She came and stood, all blushes, at his side.
The rector paused. The impatient Governor cried:
"This is the lady; do you hesitate?
Then I command you as Chief Magistrate."
The rector read the service loud and clear:
"Dearly beloved, we are gathered here,"
And so on to the end. At his command
On the fourth finger of her fair left hand
The Governor placed the ring; and that was all:
Martha was Lady Wentworth of the Hall!

INTERLUDE

Well pleased the audience heard the tale.
The Theologian said: "Indeed,
To praise you there is little need;
One almost hears the farmers flail
Thresh out your wheat, nor does there fail
A certain freshness, as you said,
And sweetness as of home-made bread.
But not less sweet and not less fresh
Are many legends that I know,
Writ by the monks of long-ago,
Who loved to mortify the flesh,
So that the soul might purer grow,
And rise to a diviner state;
And one of these—perhaps of all
Most beautiful—I now recall,
And with permission will narrate;
Hoping thereby to make amends

For that grim tragedy of mine,
As strong and black as Spanish wine,
I told last night, and wish almost
It had remained untold, my friends;
For Torquemada's awful ghost
Came to me in the dreams I dreamed,
And in the darkness glared and gleamed
Like a great lighthouse on the coast."

The Student laughing said: "Far more
Like to some dismal fire of bale
Flaring portentous on a hill;
Or torches lighted on a shore
By wreckers in a midnight gale.
No matter; be it as you will,
Only go forward with your tale."

THE THEOLOGIAN'S TALE: THE LEGEND BEAUTIFUL

"Hads't thou stayed, I must have fled!"
That is what the Vision said.

In his chamber all alone,
Kneeling on the floor of stone,
Prayed the Monk in deep contrition
For his sins of indecision,
Prayed for greater self-denial
In temptation and in trial;
It was noonday by the dial,
And the Monk was all alone.

Suddenly, as if it lightened,
An unwonted splendor brightened
All within him and without him
In that narrow cell of stone;
And he saw the Blessed Vision
Of our Lord, with light Elysian
Like a vesture wrapped about him,
Like a garment round him thrown.

Not as crucified and slain,
Not in agonies of pain,
Not with bleeding hands and feet,

Did the Monk his Master see;
But as in the village street,
In the house or harvest-field,
Halt and lame and blind he healed,
When he walked in Galilee.

In an attitude imploring,
Hands upon his bosom crossed,
Wondering, worshipping, adoring,
Knelt the Monk in rapture lost.
Lord, he thought, in heaven that reignest,
Who am I, that thus thou deignest
To reveal thyself to me?
Who am I, that from the centre
Of thy glory thou shouldst enter
This poor cell, my guest to be?

Then amid his exaltation,
Loud the convent bell appalling,
From its belfry calling, calling,
Rang through court and corridor
With persistent iteration
He had never heard before.
It was now the appointed hour
When alike in shine or shower,
Winter's cold or summer's heat,
To the convent portals came
All the blind and halt and lame,
All the beggars of the street,
For their daily dole of food
Dealt them by the brotherhood;
And their almoner was he
Who upon his bended knee,
Rapt in silent ecstasy
Of divinest self-surrender,
Saw the Vision and the Splendor.

Deep distress and hesitation
Mingled with his adoration;
Should he go, or should he stay?
Should he leave the poor to wait
Hungry at the convent gate,
Till the Vision passed away?
Should he slight his radiant guest,

Slight this visitant celestial,
For a crowd of ragged, bestial
Beggars at the convent gate?
Would the Vision there remain?
Would the Vision come again?
Then a voice within his breast
Whispered, audible and clear
As if to the outward ear:
"Do thy duty; that is best;
Leave unto thy Lord the rest!"

Straightway to his feet he started,
And with longing look intent
On the Blessed Vision bent,
Slowly from his cell departed,
Slowly on his errand went.

At the gate the poor were waiting,
Looking through the iron grating,
With that terror in the eye
That is only seen in those
Who amid their wants and woes
Hear the sound of doors that close,
And of feet that pass them by;
Grown familiar with disfavor,
Grown familiar with the savor
Of the bread by which men die!
But to-day, they knew not why,
Like the gate of Paradise
Seemed the convent sate to rise,
Like a sacrament divine
Seemed to them the bread and wine.
In his heart the Monk was praying,
Thinking of the homeless poor,
What they suffer and endure;
What we see not, what we see;
And the inward voice was saying:
"Whatsoever thing thou doest
To the least of mine and lowest,
That thou doest unto me!"

Unto me! but had the Vision
Come to him in beggar's clothing,
Come a mendicant imploring,

Would he then have knelt adoring,
Or have listened with derision,
And have turned away with loathing.

Thus his conscience put the question,
Full of troublesome suggestion,
As at length, with hurried pace,
Towards his cell he turned his face,
And beheld the convent bright
With a supernatural light,
Like a luminous cloud expanding
Over floor and wall and ceiling.

But he paused with awe-struck feeling
At the threshold of his door,
For the Vision still was standing
As he left it there before,
When the convent bell appalling,
From its belfry calling, calling,
Summoned him to feed the poor.
Through the long hour intervening
It had waited his return,
And he felt his bosom burn,
Comprehending all the meaning,
When the Blessed Vision said,
"Hadst thou stayed, I must have fled!"

INTERLUDE

All praised the Legend more or less;
Some liked the moral, some the verse;
Some thought it better, and some worse
Than other legends of the past;
Until, with ill-concealed distress
At all their cavilling, at last
The Theologian gravely said:
"The Spanish proverb, then, is right;
Consult your friends on what you do,
And one will say that it is white,
And others say that it is red."
And "Amen!" quoth the Spanish Jew.

"Six stories told! We must have seven,

A cluster like the Pleiades,
And lo! it happens, as with these,
That one is missing from our heaven.
Where is the Landlord? Bring him here;
Let the Lost Pleiad reappear."

Thus the Sicilian cried, and went
Forthwith to seek his missing star,
But did not find him in the bar,
A place that landlords most frequent,
Nor yet beside the kitchen fire,
Nor up the stairs, nor in the hall;
It was in vain to ask or call,
There were no tidings of the Squire.

So he came back with downcast head,
Exclaiming: "Well, our bashful host
Hath surely given up the ghost.
Another proverb says the dead
Can tell no tales; and that is true.
It follows, then, that one of you
Must tell a story in his stead.
You must," he to the Student said,
"Who know so many of the best,
And tell them better than the rest."
Straight by these flattering words beguiled,
The Student, happy as a child
When he is called a little man,
Assumed the double task imposed,
And without more ado unclosed
His smiling lips, and thus began.

THE STUDENT'S SECOND TALE: THE BARON OF ST. CASTINE

Baron Castine of St. Castine
Has left his chateau in the Pyrenees,
And sailed across the western seas.
When he went away from his fair demesne
The birds were building, the woods were green;
And now the winds of winter blow
Round the turrets of the old chateau,
The birds are silent and unseen,
The leaves lie dead in the ravine,

And the Pyrenees are white with snow.

His father, lonely, old, and gray,
Sits by the fireside day by day,
Thinking ever one thought of care;
Through the southern windows, narrow and tall,
The sun shines into the ancient hall,
And makes a glory round his hair.
The house-dog, stretched beneath his chair,
Groans in his sleep as if in pain
Then wakes, and yawns, and sleeps again,
So silent is it everywhere,—
So silent you can hear the mouse
Run and rummage along the beams
Behind the wainscot of the wall;
And the old man rouses from his dreams,
And wanders restless through the house,
As if he heard strange voices call.

His footsteps echo along the floor
Of a distant passage, and pause awhile;
He is standing by an open door
Looking long, with a sad, sweet smile,
Into the room of his absent son.
There is the bed on which he lay,
There are the pictures bright and gay,
Horses and hounds and sun-lit seas;
There are his powder-flask and gun,
And his hunting-knives in shape of a fan;
The chair by the window where he sat,
With the clouded tiger-skin for a mat,
Looking out on the Pyrenees,
Looking out on Mount Marbore
And the Seven Valleys of Lavedan.
Ah me! he turns away and sighs;
There is a mist before his eyes.

At night whatever the weather be,
Wind or rain or starry heaven,
Just as the clock is striking seven,
Those who look from the windows see
The village Curate, with lantern and maid,
Come through the gateway from the park
And cross the courtyard damp and dark,—

A ring of light in a ring of shade.

And now at the old man's side he stands,
His voice is cheery, his heart expands,
He gossips pleasantly, by the blaze
Of the fire of fagots, about old days,
And Cardinal Mazarin and the Fronde,
And the Cardinal's nieces fair and fond,
And what they did, and what they said,
When they heard his Eminence was dead.

And after a pause the old man says,
His mind still coming back again
To the one sad thought that haunts his brain,
"Are there any tidings from over sea?
Ah, why has that wild boy gone from me?"
And the Curate answers, looking down,
Harmless and docile as a lamb,
"Young blood! young blood! It must so be!"
And draws from the pocket of his gown
A handkerchief like an oriflamb,
And wipes his spectacles, and they play
Their little game of lansquenet
In silence for an hour or so,
Till the clock at nine strikes loud and clear
From the village lying asleep below,
And across the courtyard, into the dark
Of the winding pathway in the park,
Curate and lantern disappear,
And darkness reigns in the old chateau.

The ship has come back from over sea,
She has been signalled from below,
And into the harbor of Bordeaux
She sails with her gallant company.
But among them is nowhere seen
The brave young Baron of St. Castine;
He hath tarried behind, I ween,
In the beautiful land of Acadie!

And the father paces to and fro
Through the chambers of the old chateau,
Waiting, waiting to hear the hum
Of wheels on the road that runs below,

Of servants hurrying here and there,
The voice in the courtyard, the step on the stair,
Waiting for some one who doth not come!
But letters there are, which the old man reads
To the Curate, when he comes at night
Word by word, as an acolyte
Repeats his prayers and tells his beads;
Letters full of the rolling sea,
Full of a young man's joy to be
Abroad in the world, alone and free;
Full of adventures and wonderful scenes
Of hunting the deer through forests vast
In the royal grant of Pierre du Gast;
Of nights in the tents of the Tarratines;
Of Madocawando the Indian chief,
And his daughters, glorious as queens,
And beautiful beyond belief;
And so soft the tones of their native tongue,
The words are not spoken, they are sung!

And the Curate listens, and smiling says:
"Ah yes, dear friend! in our young days
We should have liked to hunt the deer
All day amid those forest scenes,
And to sleep in the tents of the Tarratines;
But now it is better sitting here
Within four walls, and without the fear
Of losing our hearts to Indian queens;
For man is fire and woman is tow,
And the Somebody comes and begins to blow."
Then a gleam of distrust and vague surmise
Shines in the father's gentle eyes,
As fire-light on a window-pane
Glimmers and vanishes again;
But naught he answers; he only sighs,
And for a moment bows his head;
Then, as their custom is, they play
Their little gain of lansquenet,
And another day is with the dead.

Another day, and many a day
And many a week and month depart,
When a fatal letter wings its way
Across the sea, like a bird of prey,

422 | HENRY WADSWORTH LONGFELLOW

And strikes and tears the old man's heart.
Lo! the young Baron of St. Castine,
Swift as the wind is, and as wild,
Has married a dusky Tarratine,
Has married Madocawando's child!

The letter drops from the father's hand;
Though the sinews of his heart are wrung,
He utters no cry, he breathes no prayer,
No malediction falls from his tongue;
But his stately figure, erect and grand,
Bends and sinks like a column of sand
In the whirlwind of his great despair.
Dying, yes, dying! His latest breath
Of parley at the door of death
Is a blessing on his wayward son.
Lower and lower on his breast
Sinks his gray head; he is at rest;
No longer he waits for any one;

For many a year the old chateau
Lies tenantless and desolate;
Rank grasses in the courtyard grow,
About its gables caws the crow;
Only the porter at the gate
Is left to guard it, and to wait
The coming of the rightful heir;
No other life or sound is there;
No more the Curate comes at night,
No more is seen the unsteady light,
Threading the alleys of the park;
The windows of the hall are dark,
The chambers dreary, cold, and bare!

At length, at last, when the winter is past,
And birds are building, and woods are green,
With flying skirts is the Curate seen
Speeding along the woodland way,
Humming gayly, "No day is so long
But it comes at last to vesper-song."
He stops at the porter's lodge to say
That at last the Baron of St. Castine
Is coming home with his Indian queen,
Is coming without a week's delay;

And all the house must be swept and clean,
And all things set in good array!
And the solemn porter shakes his head;
And the answer he makes is: "Lackaday!
We will see, as the blind man said!"

Alert since first the day began,
The cock upon the village church
Looks northward from his airy perch,
As if beyond the ken of man
To see the ships come sailing on,
And pass the isle of Oleron,
And pass the Tower of Cordouan.

In the church below is cold in clay
The heart that would have leaped for joy—
O tender heart of truth and trust!—
To see the coming of that day;
In the church below the lips are dust;
Dust are the hands, and dust the feet,
That would have been so swift to meet
The coming of that wayward boy.

At night the front of the old chateau
Is a blaze of light above and below;
There's a sound of wheels and hoofs in the street,
A cracking of whips, and scamper of feet,
Bells are ringing, and horns are blown,
And the Baron hath come again to his own.
The Curate is waiting in the hall,
Most eager and alive of all
To welcome the Baron and Baroness;
But his mind is full of vague distress,
For he hath read in Jesuit books
Of those children of the wilderness,
And now, good, simple man! he looks
To see a painted savage stride
Into the room, with shoulders bare,
And eagle feathers in her hair,
And around her a robe of panther's hide.

Instead, he beholds with secret shame
A form of beauty undefined,
A loveliness with out a name,

Not of degree, but more of kind;
Nor bold nor shy, nor short nor tall,
But a new mingling of them all.
Yes, beautiful beyond belief,
Transfigured and transfused, he sees
The lady of the Pyrenees,
The daughter of the Indian chief.

Beneath the shadow of her hair
The gold-bronze color of the skin
Seems lighted by a fire within,
As when a burst of sunlight shines
Beneath a sombre grove of pines,—
A dusky splendor in the air.
The two small hands, that now are pressed
In his, seem made to be caressed,
They lie so warm and soft and still,
Like birds half hidden in a nest,
Trustful, and innocent of ill.
And ah! he cannot believe his ears
When her melodious voice he hears
Speaking his native Gascon tongue;
The words she utters seem to be
Part of some poem of Goudouli,
They are not spoken, they are sung!
And the Baron smiles, and says,
"You see, I told you but the simple truth;
Ah, you may trust the eyes of youth!"

Down in the village day by day
The people gossip in their way,
And stare to see the Baroness pass
On Sunday morning to early Mass;
And when she kneeleth down to pray,
They wonder, and whisper together, and say,
"Surely this is no heathen lass!"
And in course of time they learn to bless
The Baron and the Baroness.

And in course of time the Curate learns
A secret so dreadful, that by turns
He is ice and fire, he freezes and burns.
The Baron at confession hath said,
That though this woman be his wife,

He bath wed her as the Indians wed,
He hath bought her for a gun and a knife!
And the Curate replies: "O profligate,
O Prodigal Son! return once more
To the open arms and the open door
Of the Church, or ever it be too late.
Thank God, thy father did not live
To see what he could not forgive;
On thee, so reckless and perverse,
He left his blessing, not his curse.
But the nearer the dawn the darker the night,
And by going wrong all things come right;
Things have been mended that were worse,
And the worse, the nearer they are to mend.
For the sake of the living and the dead,
Thou shalt be wed as Christians wed,
And all things come to a happy end."

O sun, that followest the night,
In yon blue sky, serene and pure,
And pourest thine impartial light
Alike on mountain and on moor,
Pause for a moment in thy course,
And bless the bridegroom and the bride!
O Gave, that from thy hidden source
In you mysterious mountain-side
Pursuest thy wandering way alone,
And leaping down its steps of stone,
Along the meadow-lands demure
Stealest away to the Adour,
Pause for a moment in thy course
To bless the bridegroom and the bride!

The choir is singing the matin song,
The doors of the church are opened wide,
The people crowd, and press, and throng
To see the bridegroom and the bride.
They enter and pass along the nave;
They stand upon the father's grave;
The bells are ringing soft and slow;
The living above and the dead below
Give their blessing on one and twain;
The warm wind blows from the hills of Spain,
The birds are building, the leaves are green,

And Baron Castine of St. Castine
Hath come at last to his own again.

FINALE

"Nunc plaudite!" the Student cried,
When he had finished; "now applaud,
As Roman actors used to say
At the conclusion of a play";
And rose, and spread his hands abroad,
And smiling bowed from side to side,
As one who bears the palm away.
And generous was the applause and loud,
But less for him than for the sun,
That even as the tale was done
Burst from its canopy of cloud,
And lit the landscape with the blaze
Of afternoon on autumn days,
And filled the room with light, and made
The fire of logs a painted shade.

A sudden wind from out the west
Blew all its trumpets loud and shrill;
The windows rattled with the blast,
The oak-trees shouted as it passed,
And straight, as if by fear possessed,
The cloud encampment on the hill
Broke up, and fluttering flag and tent
Vanished into the firmament,
And down the valley fled amain
The rear of the retreating rain.

Only far up in the blue sky
A mass of clouds, like drifted snow
Suffused with a faint Alpine glow,
Was heaped together, vast and high,
On which a shattered rainbow hung,
Not rising like the ruined arch
Of some aerial aqueduct,
But like a roseate garland plucked
From an Olympian god, and flung
Aside in his triumphal march.

Like prisoners from their dungeon gloom,
Like birds escaping from a snare,
Like school-boys at the hour of play,
All left at once the pent-up room,
And rushed into the open air;
And no more tales were told that day.

PART THIRD

The evening came; the golden vane
A moment in the sunset glanced,
Then darkened, and then gleamed again,
As from the east the moon advanced
And touched it with a softer light;
While underneath, with flowing mane,
Upon the sign the Red Horse pranced,
And galloped forth into the night.

But brighter than the afternoon
That followed the dark day of rain,
And brighter than the golden vane
That glistened in the rising moon,
Within the ruddy fire-light gleamed;
And every separate window-pane,
Backed by the outer darkness, showed
A mirror, where the flamelets gleamed
And flickered to and fro, and seemed
A bonfire lighted in the road.

Amid the hospitable glow,
Like an old actor on the stage,
With the uncertain voice of age,

The singing chimney chanted low
The homely songs of long ago.

The voice that Ossian heard of yore,
When midnight winds were in his hall;
A ghostly and appealing call,
A sound of days that are no more!
And dark as Ossian sat the Jew,
And listened to the sound, and knew
The passing of the airy hosts,
The gray and misty cloud of ghosts
In their interminable flight;
And listening muttered in his beard,
With accent indistinct and weird,
"Who are ye, children of the Night?"

Beholding his mysterious face,
"Tell me," the gay Sicilian said,
"Why was it that in breaking bread
At supper, you bent down your head
And, musing, paused a little space,
As one who says a silent grace?"

The Jew replied, with solemn air,
"I said the Manichaean's prayer.
It was his faith,—perhaps is mine,—
That life in all its forms is one,
And that its secret conduits run
Unseen, but in unbroken line,
From the great fountain-head divine
Through man and beast, through grain and grass.
Howe'er we struggle, strive, and cry,
From death there can be no escape,
And no escape from life, alas
Because we cannot die, but pass
From one into another shape:
It is but into life we die.

"Therefore the Manichaean said
This simple prayer on breaking bread,
Lest he with hasty hand or knife
Might wound the incarcerated life,
The soul in things that we call dead:
'I did not reap thee, did not bind thee,

I did not thrash thee, did not grind thee,
Nor did I in the oven bake thee!
It was not I, it was another
Did these things unto thee, O brother;
I only have thee, hold thee, break thee!'"

"That birds have souls I can concede,"
The poet cried, with glowing cheeks;
"The flocks that from their beds of reed
Uprising north or southward fly,
And flying write upon the sky
The biforked letter of the Greeks,
As hath been said by Rucellai;
All birds that sing or chirp or cry,
Even those migratory bands,
The minor poets of the air,
The plover, peep, and sanderling,
That hardly can be said to sing,
But pipe along the barren sands,—
All these have souls akin to ours;
So hath the lovely race of flowers:
Thus much I grant, but nothing more.
The rusty hinges of a door
Are not alive because they creak;
This chimney, with its dreary roar,
These rattling windows, do not speak!"
"To me they speak," the Jew replied;
"And in the sounds that sink and soar,
I hear the voices of a tide
That breaks upon an unknown shore!"

Here the Sicilian interfered:
"That was your dream, then, as you dozed
A moment since, with eyes half-closed,
And murmured something in your beard."
The Hebrew smiled, and answered, "Nay;
Not that, but something very near;
Like, and yet not the same, may seem
The vision of my waking dream;
Before it wholly dies away,
Listen to me, and you shall hear."

THE SPANISH JEW'S TALE: AZRAEL

King Solomon, before his palace gate
At evening, on the pavement tessellate
Was walking with a stranger from the East,
Arrayed in rich attire as for a feast,
The mighty Runjeet-Sing, a learned man,
And Rajah of the realms of Hindostan.
And as they walked the guest became aware
Of a white figure in the twilight air,
Gazing intent, as one who with surprise
His form and features seemed to recognize;
And in a whisper to the king he said:
"What is yon shape, that, pallid as the dead,
Is watching me, as if he sought to trace
In the dim light the features of my face?"

The king looked, and replied: "I know him well;
It is the Angel men call Azrael,
'T is the Death Angel; what hast thou to fear?"
And the guest answered: "Lest he should come near,
And speak to me, and take away my breath!
Save me from Azrael, save me from death!
O king, that hast dominion o'er the wind,
Bid it arise and bear me hence to Ind."

The king gazed upward at the cloudless sky,
Whispered a word, and raised his hand on high,
And lo! the signet-ring of chrysoprase
On his uplifted finger seemed to blaze
With hidden fire, and rushing from the west
There came a mighty wind, and seized the guest
And lifted him from earth, and on they passed,
His shining garments streaming in the blast,
A silken banner o'er the walls upreared,
A purple cloud, that gleamed and disappeared.
Then said the Angel, smiling: "If this man
Be Rajah Runjeet-Sing of Hindostan,
Thou hast done well in listening to his prayer;
I was upon my way to seek him there."

INTERLUDE

"O Edrehi, forbear to-night
Your ghostly legends of affright,
And let the Talmud rest in peace;
Spare us your dismal tales of death
That almost take away one's breath;
So doing, may your tribe increase."

Thus the Sicilian said; then went
And on the spinet's rattling keys
Played Marianina, like a breeze
From Naples and the Southern seas,
That brings us the delicious scent
Of citron and of orange trees,
And memories of soft days of ease
At Capri and Amalfi spent.

"Not so," the eager Poet said;
"At least, not so before I tell
The story of my Azrael,
An angel mortal as ourselves,
Which in an ancient tome I found
Upon a convent's dusty shelves,
Chained with an iron chain, and bound
In parchment, and with clasps of brass,
Lest from its prison, some dark day,
It might be stolen or steal away,
While the good friars were singing mass.

"It is a tale of Charlemagne,
When like a thunder-cloud, that lowers
And sweeps from mountain-crest to coast,
With lightning flaming through its showers,
He swept across the Lombard plain,
Beleaguering with his warlike train
Pavia, the country's pride and boast,
The City of the Hundred Towers."
Thus heralded the tale began,
And thus in sober measure ran.

THE POET'S TALE: CHARLEMAGNE

Olger the Dane and Desiderio,
King of the Lombards, on a lofty tower
Stood gazing northward o'er the rolling plains,
League after league of harvests, to the foot
Of the snow-crested Alps, and saw approach
A mighty army, thronging all the roads
That led into the city. And the King
Said unto Olger, who had passed his youth
As hostage at the court of France, and knew
The Emperor's form and face "Is Charlemagne
Among that host?" And Olger answered: "No."

And still the innumerable multitude
Flowed onward and increased, until the King
Cried in amazement: "Surely Charlemagne
Is coming in the midst of all these knights!"
And Olger answered slowly: "No; not yet;
He will not come so soon." Then much disturbed
King Desiderio asked: "What shall we do,
If he approach with a still greater army!"
And Olger answered: "When he shall appear,
You will behold what manner of man he is;
But what will then befall us I know not."

Then came the guard that never knew repose,
The Paladins of France; and at the sight
The Lombard King o'ercome with terror cried:
"This must be Charlemagne!" and as before
Did Olger answer: "No; not yet, not yet."

And then appeared in panoply complete
The Bishops and the Abbots and the Priests
Of the imperial chapel, and the Counts
And Desiderio could no more endure
The light of day, nor yet encounter death,
But sobbed aloud and said: "Let us go down
And hide us in the bosom of the earth,
Far from the sight and anger of a foe
So terrible as this!" And Olger said:
"When you behold the harvests in the fields
Shaking with fear, the Po and the Ticino

Lashing the city walls with iron waves,
Then may you know that Charlemagne is come.
And even as he spake, in the northwest,
Lo! there uprose a black and threatening cloud,
Out of whose bosom flashed the light of arms
Upon the people pent up in the city;
A light more terrible than any darkness;
And Charlemagne appeared;—a Man of Iron!

His helmet was of iron, and his gloves
Of iron, and his breastplate and his greaves
And tassets were of iron, and his shield.
In his left hand he held an iron spear,
In his right hand his sword invincible.
The horse he rode on had the strength of iron,
And color of iron. All who went before him
Beside him and behind him, his whole host,
Were armed with iron, and their hearts within them
Were stronger than the armor that they wore.
The fields and all the roads were filled with iron,
And points of iron glistened in the sun
And shed a terror through the city streets.

This at a single glance Olger the Dane
Saw from the tower, and turning to the King
Exclaimed in haste: "Behold! this is the man
You looked for with such eagerness!" and then
Fell as one dead at Desiderio's feet.

INTERLUDE

Well pleased all listened to the tale,
That drew, the Student said, its pith
And marrow from the ancient myth
Of some one with an iron flail;
Or that portentous Man of Brass
Hephæstus made in days of yore,
Who stalked about the Cretan shore,
And saw the ships appear and pass,
And threw stones at the Argonauts,
Being filled with indiscriminate ire
That tangled and perplexed his thoughts;
But, like a hospitable host,

When strangers landed on the coast,
Heated himself red-hot with fire,
And hugged them in his arms, and pressed
Their bodies to his burning breast.

The Poet answered: "No, not thus
The legend rose; it sprang at first
Out of the hunger and the thirst
In all men for the marvellous.
And thus it filled and satisfied
The imagination of mankind,
And this ideal to the mind
Was truer than historic fact.
Fancy enlarged and multiplied
The tenors of the awful name
Of Charlemagne, till he became
Armipotent in every act,
And, clothed in mystery, appeared
Not what men saw, but what they feared.
Besides, unless my memory fail,
Your some one with an iron flail
Is not an ancient myth at all,
But comes much later on the scene
As Talus in the Faerie Queene,
The iron groom of Artegall,
Who threshed out falsehood and deceit,
And truth upheld, and righted wrong,
As was, as is the swallow, fleet,
And as the lion is, was strong."

The Theologian said: "Perchance
Your chronicler in writing this
Had in his mind the Anabasis,
Where Xenophon describes the advance
Of Artaxerxes to the fight;
At first the low gray cloud of dust,
And then a blackness o'er the fields
As of a passing thunder-gust,
Then flash of brazen armor bright,
And ranks of men, and spears up-thrust,
Bowmen and troops with wicker shields,
And cavalry equipped in white,
And chariots ranged in front of these
With scythes upon their axle-trees."

To this the Student answered: "Well,
I also have a tale to tell
Of Charlemagne; a tale that throws
A softer light, more tinged with rose,
Than your grim apparition cast
Upon the darkness of the past.
Listen, and hear in English rhyme
What the good Monk of Lauresheim
Gives as the gossip of his time,
In mediaeval Latin prose."

THE STUDENT'S TALE: EMMA AND EGINHARD

When Alcuin taught the sons of Charlemagne,
In the free schools of Aix, how kings should reign,
And with them taught the children of the poor
How subjects should be patient and endure,
He touched the lips of some, as best befit,
With honey from the hives of Holy Writ;
Others intoxicated with the wine
Of ancient history, sweet but less divine;
Some with the wholesome fruits of grammar fed;
Others with mysteries of the stars o'er-head,
That hang suspended in the vaulted sky
Like lamps in some fair palace vast and high.

In sooth, it was a pleasant sight to see
That Saxon monk, with hood and rosary,
With inkhorn at his belt, and pen and book,
And mingled lore and reverence in his look,
Or hear the cloister and the court repeat
The measured footfalls of his sandaled feet,
Or watch him with the pupils of his school,
Gentle of speech, but absolute of rule.

Among them, always earliest in his place.
Was Eginhard, a youth of Frankish race,
Whose face was bright with flashes that forerun
The splendors of a yet unrisen sun.
To him all things were possible, and seemed
Not what he had accomplished, but had dreamed,
And what were tasks to others were his play,
The pastime of an idle holiday.

Smaragdo, Abbot of St. Michael's, said,
With many a shrug and shaking of the head,
Surely some demon must possess the lad,
Who showed more wit than ever schoolboy had,
And learned his Trivium thus without the rod;
But Alcuin said it was the grace of God.

Thus he grew up, in Logic point-device,
Perfect in Grammar, and in Rhetoric nice;
Science of Numbers, Geometric art,
And lore of Stars, and Music knew by heart;
A Minnesinger, long before the times
Of those who sang their love in Suabian rhymes.

The Emperor, when he heard this good report
Of Eginhard much buzzed about the court,
Said to himself, "This stripling seems to be
Purposely sent into the world for me;
He shall become my scribe, and shall be schooled
In all the arts whereby the world is ruled."
Thus did the gentle Eginhard attain
To honor in the court of Charlemagne;
Became the sovereign's favorite, his right hand,
So that his fame was great in all the land,
And all men loved him for his modest grace
And comeliness of figure and of face.
An inmate of the palace, yet recluse,
A man of books, yet sacred from abuse
Among the armed knights with spur on heel,
The tramp of horses and the clang of steel;
And as the Emperor promised he was schooled
In all the arts by which the world is ruled.
But the one art supreme, whose law is fate,
The Emperor never dreamed of till too late.

Home from her convent to the palace came
The lovely Princess Emma, whose sweet name,
Whispered by seneschal or sung by bard,
Had often touched the soul of Eginhard.
He saw her from his window, as in state
She came, by knights attended through the gate;
He saw her at the banquet of that day,
Fresh as the morn, and beautiful as May;
He saw her in the garden, as she strayed

Among the flowers of summer with her maid,
And said to him, "O Eginhard, disclose
The meaning and the mystery of the rose";
And trembling he made answer: "In good sooth,
Its mystery is love, its meaning youth!"

How can I tell the signals and the signs
By which one heart another heart divines?
How can I tell the many thousand ways
By which it keeps the secret it betrays?

O mystery of love! O strange romance!
Among the Peers and Paladins of France,
Shining in steel, and prancing on gay steeds,
Noble by birth, yet nobler by great deeds,
The Princess Emma had no words nor looks
But for this clerk, this man of thought and books.

The summer passed, the autumn came; the stalks
Of lilies blackened in the garden walks;
The leaves fell, russet-golden and blood-red,
Love-letters thought the poet fancy-led,
Or Jove descending in a shower of gold
Into the lap of Danae of old;
For poets cherish many a strange conceit,
And love transmutes all nature by its heat.

No more the garden lessons, nor the dark
And hurried meetings in the twilight park;
But now the studious lamp, and the delights
Of firesides in the silent winter nights,
And watching from his window hour by hour
The light that burned in Princess Emma's tower.

At length one night, while musing by the fire,
O'ercome at last by his insane desire,—
For what will reckless love not do and dare?—
He crossed the court, and climbed the winding stair,
With some feigned message in the Emperor's name;
But when he to the lady's presence came
He knelt down at her feet, until she laid
Her hand upon him, like a naked blade,
And whispered in his ear: "Arise, Sir Knight,
To my heart's level, O my heart's delight."

And there he lingered till the crowing cock,
The Alectryon of the farmyard and the flock,
Sang his aubade with lusty voice and clear,
To tell the sleeping world that dawn was near.
And then they parted; but at parting, lo!
They saw the palace courtyard white with snow,
And, placid as a nun, the moon on high
Gazing from cloudy cloisters of the sky.
"Alas!" he said, "how hide the fatal line
Of footprints leading from thy door to mine,
And none returning!" Ah, he little knew
What woman's wit, when put to proof, can do!

That night the Emperor, sleepless with the cares
And troubles that attend on state affairs,
Had risen before the dawn, and musing gazed
Into the silent night, as one amazed
To see the calm that reigned o'er all supreme,
When his own reign was but a troubled dream.
The moon lit up the gables capped with snow,
And the white roofs, and half the court below,
And he beheld a form, that seemed to cower
Beneath a burden, come from Emma's tower,—
A woman, who upon her shoulders bore
Clerk Eginhard to his own private door,
And then returned in haste, but still essayed
To tread the footprints she herself had made;
And as she passed across the lighted space,
The Emperor saw his daughter Emma's face!

He started not; he did not speak or moan,
But seemed as one who hath been turned to stone;
And stood there like a statue, nor awoke
Out of his trance of pain, till morning broke,
Till the stars faded, and the moon went down,
And o'er the towers and steeples of the town
Came the gray daylight; then the sun, who took
The empire of the world with sovereign look,
Suffusing with a soft and golden glow
All the dead landscape in its shroud of snow,
Touching with flame the tapering chapel spires,
Windows and roofs, and smoke of household fires,
And kindling park and palace as he came;
The stork's nest on the chimney seemed in flame.

And thus he stood till Eginhard appeared,
Demure and modest with his comely beard
And flowing flaxen tresses, come to ask,
As was his wont, the day's appointed task.

The Emperor looked upon him with a smile,
And gently said: "My son, wait yet awhile;
This hour my council meets upon some great
And very urgent business of the state.
Come back within the hour. On thy return
The work appointed for thee shalt thou learn.

Having dismissed this gallant Troubadour,
He summoned straight his council, and secure
And steadfast in his purpose, from the throne
All the adventure of the night made known;
Then asked for sentence; and with eager breath
Some answered banishment, and others death.

Then spake the king: "Your sentence is not mine;
Life is the gift of God, and is divine;
Nor from these palace walls shall one depart
Who carries such a secret in his heart;
My better judgment points another way.
Good Alcuin, I remember how one day
When my Pepino asked you, 'What are men?'
You wrote upon his tablets with your pen,
'Guests of the grave and travellers that pass!'
This being true of all men, we, alas!
Being all fashioned of the selfsame dust,
Let us be merciful as well as just;
This passing traveller, who hath stolen away
The brightest jewel of my crown to-day,
Shall of himself the precious gem restore;
By giving it, I make it mine once more.
Over those fatal footprints I will throw
My ermine mantle like another snow."

Then Eginhard was summoned to the hall,
And entered, and in presence of them all,
The Emperor said: "My son, for thou to me
Hast been a son, and evermore shalt be,
Long hast thou served thy sovereign, and thy zeal
Pleads to me with importunate appeal,

While I have been forgetful to requite
Thy service and affection as was right.
But now the hour is come, when I, thy Lord,
Will crown thy love with such supreme reward,
A gift so precious kings have striven in vain
To win it from the hands of Charlemagne."

Then sprang the portals of the chamber wide,
And Princess Emma entered, in the pride
Of birth and beauty, that in part o'er-came
The conscious terror and the blush of shame.
And the good Emperor rose up from his throne,
And taking her white hand within his own
Placed it in Eginhard's, and said: "My son
This is the gift thy constant zeal hath won;
Thus I repay the royal debt I owe,
And cover up the footprints in the snow."

INTERLUDE

Thus ran the Student's pleasant rhyme
Of Eginhard and love and youth;
Some doubted its historic truth,
But while they doubted, ne'ertheless
Saw in it gleams of truthfulness,
And thanked the Monk of Lauresheim.

This they discussed in various mood;
Then in the silence that ensued
Was heard a sharp and sudden sound
As of a bowstring snapped in air;
And the Musician with a bound
Sprang up in terror from his chair,
And for a moment listening stood,
Then strode across the room, and found
His dear, his darling violin
Still lying safe asleep within
Its little cradle, like a child
That gives a sudden cry of pain,
And wakes to fall asleep again;
And as he looked at it and smiled,
By the uncertain light beguiled,
Despair! two strings were broken in twain.

While all lamented and made moan,
With many a sympathetic word
As if the loss had been their own,
Deeming the tones they might have heard
Sweeter than they had heard before,
They saw the Landlord at the door,
The missing man, the portly Squire!
He had not entered, but he stood
With both arms full of seasoned wood,
To feed the much-devouring fire,
That like a lion in a cage
Lashed its long tail and roared with rage.

The missing man! Ah, yes, they said,
Missing, but whither had he fled?
Where had he hidden himself away?
No farther than the barn or shed;
He had not hidden himself, nor fled;
How should he pass the rainy day
But in his barn with hens and hay,
Or mending harness, cart, or sled?
Now, having come, he needs must stay
And tell his tale as well as they.

The Landlord answered only: "These
Are logs from the dead apple-trees
Of the old orchard planted here
By the first Howe of Sudbury.
Nor oak nor maple has so clear
A flame, or burns so quietly,
Or leaves an ash so clean and white";
Thinking by this to put aside
The impending tale that terrified;
When suddenly, to his delight,
The Theologian interposed,
Saying that when the door was closed,
And they had stopped that draft of cold,
Unpleasant night air, he proposed
To tell a tale world-wide apart
From that the Student had just told;
World-wide apart, and yet akin,
As showing that the human heart
Beats on forever as of old,
As well beneath the snow-white fold

Of Quaker kerchief, as within
Sendal or silk or cloth of gold,
And without preface would begin.

And then the clamorous clock struck eight,
Deliberate, with sonorous chime
Slow measuring out the march of time,
Like some grave Consul of old Rome
In Jupiter's temple driving home
The nails that marked the year and date.
Thus interrupted in his rhyme,
The Theologian needs must wait;
But quoted Horace, where he sings
The dire Necessity of things,
That drives into the roofs sublime
Of new-built houses of the great
The adamantine nails of Fate.

When ceased the little carillon
To herald from its wooden tower
The important transit of the hour,
The Theologian hastened on,
Content to be all owed at last
To sing his Idyl of the Past.

THE THEOLOGIAN'S TALE: ELIZABETH

I.

"Ah, how short are the days! How soon the night overtakes us!
In the old country the twilight is longer; but here in the forest
Suddenly comes the dark, with hardly a pause in its coming,
Hardly a moment between the two lights, the day and the lamplight;
Yet how grand is the winter! How spotless the snow is, and perfect!"

  Thus spake Elizabeth Haddon at nightfall to Hannah the housemaid,
As in the farm-house kitchen, that served for kitchen and parlor,
By the window she sat with her work, and looked on a landscape
White as the great white sheet that Peter saw in his vision,
By the four corners let down and descending out of the heavens.
Covered with snow were the forests of pine, and the fields and the meadows.
Nothing was dark but the sky, and the distant Delaware flowing
Down from its native hills, a peaceful and bountiful river.

   Then with a smile on her lips made answer Hannah the housemaid:
"Beautiful winter! yea, the winter is beautiful, surely,
If one could only walk like a fly with one's feet on the ceiling.
But the great Delaware River is not like the Thames, as we saw it
Out of our upper windows in Rotherhithe Street in the Borough,
Crowded with masts and sails of vessels coming and going;
Here there is nothing but pines, with patches of snow on their branches.
There is snow in the air, and see! it is falling already;
All the roads will be blocked, and I pity Joseph to-morrow,
Breaking his way through the drifts, with his sled and oxen; and then, too,
How in all the world shall we get to Meeting on First-Day?"

   But Elizabeth checked her, and answered, mildly reproving:
"Surely the Lord will provide; for unto the snow he sayeth,
Be thou on the earth, the good Lord sayeth; he is it
Giveth snow like wool, like ashes scatters the hoar-frost."
So she folded her work and laid it away in her basket.

   Meanwhile Hannah the housemaid had closed and fastened the shutters,
Spread the cloth, and lighted the lamp on the table, and placed there
Plates and cups from the dresser, the brown rye loaf, and the butter
Fresh from the dairy, and then, protecting her hand with a holder,
Took from the crane in the chimney the steaming and simmering kettle,
Poised it aloft in the air, and filled up the earthen teapot,
Made in Delft, and adorned with quaint and wonderful figures.

   Then Elizabeth said, "Lo! Joseph is long on his errand.
I have sent him away with a hamper of food and of clothing
For the poor in the village. A good lad and cheerful is Joseph;
In the right place is his heart, and his hand is ready and willing."

   Thus in praise of her servant she spake, and Hannah the housemaid
Laughed with her eyes, as she listened, but governed her tongue, and was
      silent,
While her mistress went on: "The house is far from the village;
We should be lonely here, were it not for Friends that in passing
Sometimes tarry o'ernight, and make us glad by their coming."

   Thereupon answered Hannah the housemaid, the thrifty, the frugal:
"Yea, they come and they tarry, as if thy house were a tavern;
Open to all are its doors, and they come and go like the pigeons
In and out of the holes of the pigeon-house over the hayloft,
Cooing and smoothing their feathers and basking themselves in the sunshine."

But in meekness of spirit, and calmly, Elizabeth answered:
"All I have is the Lord's, not mine to give or withhold it;
I but distribute his gifts to the poor, and to those of his people
Who in journeyings often surrender their lives to his service.
His, not mine, are the gifts, and only so far can I make them
Mine, as in giving I add my heart to whatever is given.
Therefore my excellent father first built this house in the clearing;
Though he came not himself, I came; for the Lord was my guidance,
Leading me here for this service. We must not grudge, then, to others
Ever the cup of cold water, or crumbs that fall from our table."

   Thus rebuked, for a season was silent the penitent housemaid;
And Elizabeth said in tones even sweeter and softer:
"Dost thou remember, Hannah, the great May-Meeting in London,
When I was still a child, how we sat in the silent assembly,
Waiting upon the Lord in patient and passive submission?
No one spake, till at length a young man, a stranger, John Estaugh,
Moved by the Spirit, rose, as if he were John the Apostle,
Speaking such words of power that they bowed our hearts, as a strong wind
Bends the grass of the fields, or grain that is ripe for the sickle.
Thoughts of him to-day have been oft borne inward upon me,
Wherefore I do not know; but strong is the feeling within me
That once more I shall see a face I have never forgotten."

II.

E'en as she spake they heard the musical jangle of sleigh-bells,
First far off, with a dreamy sound and faint in the distance,
Then growing nearer and louder, and turning into the farmyard,
Till it stopped at the door, with sudden creaking of runners.
Then there were voices heard as of two men talking together,
And to herself, as she listened, upbraiding said Hannah the housemaid,
"It is Joseph come back, and I wonder what stranger is with him?"

   Down from its nail she took and lighted the great tin lantern
Pierced with holes, and round, and roofed like the top of a lighthouse,
And went forth to receive the coming guest at the doorway,
Casting into the dark a network of glimmer and shadow
Over the falling snow, the yellow sleigh, and the horses,
And the forms of men, snow-covered, looming gigantic.
Then giving Joseph the lantern, she entered the house with the stranger.
Youthful he was and tall, and his cheeks aglow with the night air;
And as he entered, Elizabeth rose, and, going to meet him,
As if an unseen power had announced and preceded his presence,

And he had come as one whose coming had long been expected,
Quietly gave him her hand, and said, "Thou art welcome, John Estaugh."
And the stranger replied, with staid and quiet behavior,
"Dost thou remember me still, Elizabeth? After so many
Years have passed, it seemeth a wonderful thing that I find thee.
Surely the hand of the Lord conducted me here to thy threshold.
For as I journeyed along, and pondered alone and in silence
On his ways, that are past finding out, I saw in the snow-mist,
Seemingly weary with travel, a wayfarer, who by the wayside
Paused and waited. Forthwith I remembered Queen Candace's eunuch,
How on the way that goes down from Jerusalem unto Gaza,
Reading Esaias the Prophet, he journeyed, and spake unto Philip,
Praying him to come up and sit in his chariot with him.
So I greeted the man, and he mounted the sledge beside me,
And as we talked on the way he told me of thee and thy homestead,
How, being led by the light of the Spirit, that never deceiveth,
Full of zeal for the work of the Lord, thou hadst come to this country.
And I remembered thy name, and thy father and mother in England,
And on my journey have stopped to see thee, Elizabeth Haddon.
Wishing to strengthen thy hand in the labors of love thou art doing."

   And Elizabeth answered with confident voice, and serenely
Looking into his face with her innocent eyes as she answered,
"Surely the hand of the Lord is in it; his Spirit hath led thee
Out of the darkness and storm to the light and peace of my fireside."

   Then, with stamping of feet, the door was opened, and Joseph
Entered, bearing the lantern, and, carefully blowing the light out,
Rung it up on its nail, and all sat down to their supper;
For underneath that roof was no distinction of persons,
But one family only, one heart, one hearth and one household.

   When the supper was ended they drew their chairs to the fireplace,
Spacious, open-hearted, profuse of flame and of firewood,
Lord of forests unfelled, and not a gleaner of fagots,
Spreading its arms to embrace with inexhaustible bounty
All who fled from the cold, exultant, laughing at winter!
Only Hannah the housemaid was busy in clearing the table,
Coming and going, and hustling about in closet and chamber.

   Then Elizabeth told her story again to John Estaugh,
Going far back to the past, to the early days of her childhood;
How she had waited and watched, in all her doubts and besetments
Comforted with the extendings and holy, sweet inflowings

Of the spirit of love, till the voice imperative sounded,
And she obeyed the voice, and cast in her lot with her people
Here in the desert land, and God would provide for the issue.

　Meanwhile Joseph sat with folded hands, and demurely
Listened, or seemed to listen, and in the silence that followed
Nothing was heard for a while but the step of Hannah the housemaid
Walking the floor overhead, and setting the chambers in order.
And Elizabeth said, with a smile of compassion, "The maiden
Hath a light heart in her breast, but her feet are heavy and awkward."
Inwardly Joseph laughed, but governed his tongue, and was silent.

　Then came the hour of sleep, death's counterfeit, nightly rehearsal
Of the great Silent Assembly, the Meeting of shadows, where no man
Speaketh, but all are still, and the peace and rest are unbroken!
Silently over that house the blessing of slumber descended.
But when the morning dawned, and the sun uprose in his splendor,
Breaking his way through clouds that encumbered his path in the heavens,
Joseph was seen with his sled and oxen breaking a pathway
Through the drifts of snow; the horses already were harnessed,
And John Estaugh was standing and taking leave at the threshold,
Saying that he should return at the Meeting in May; while above them
Hannah the housemaid, the homely, was looking out of the attic,
Laughing aloud at Joseph, then suddenly closing the casement,
As the bird in a cuckoo-clock peeps out of its window,
Then disappears again, and closes the shutter behind it.

III.

Now was the winter gone, and the snow; and Robin the Redbreast,
Boasted on bush and tree it was he, it was he and no other
That had covered with leaves the Babes in the Wood, and blithely
All the birds sang with him, and little cared for his boasting,
Or for his Babes in the Wood, or the Cruel Uncle, and only
Sang for the mates they had chosen, and cared for the nests they were
　　building.
With them, but more sedately and meekly, Elizabeth Haddon
Sang in her inmost heart, but her lips were silent and songless.
Thus came the lovely spring with a rush of blossoms and music,
Flooding the earth with flowers, and the air with melodies vernal.

　Then it came to pass, one pleasant morning, that slowly
Up the road there came a cavalcade, as of pilgrims
Men and women, wending their way to the Quarterly Meeting

In the neighboring town; and with them came riding John Estaugh.
At Elizabeth's door they stopped to rest, and alighting
Tasted the currant wine, and the bread of rye, and the honey
Brought from the hives, that stood by the sunny wall of the garden;
Then remounted their horses, refreshed, and continued their journey,
And Elizabeth with them, and Joseph, and Hannah the housemaid.
But, as they started, Elizabeth lingered a little, and leaning
Over her horse's neck, in a whisper said to John Estaugh
"Tarry awhile behind, for I have something to tell thee,
Not to be spoken lightly, nor in the presence of others;
Them it concerneth not, only thee and me it concerneth."
And they rode slowly along through the woods, conversing together.
It was a pleasure to breathe the fragrant air of the forest;
It was a pleasure to live on that bright and happy May morning!

    Then Elizabeth said, though still with a certain reluctance,
As if impelled to reveal a secret she fain would have guarded:
"I will no longer conceal what is laid upon me to tell thee;
I have received from the Lord a charge to love thee, John Estaugh."

    And John Estaugh made answer, surprised by the words she had spoken,
"Pleasant to me are thy converse, thy ways, thy meekness of spirit;
Pleasant thy frankness of speech, and thy soul's immaculate whiteness,
Love without dissimulation, a holy and inward adorning.
But I have yet no light to lead me, no voice to direct me.
When the Lord's work is done, and the toil and the labor completed
He hath appointed to me, I will gather into the stillness
Of my own heart awhile, and listen and wait for his guidance."

    Then Elizabeth said, not troubled nor wounded in spirit,
"So is it best, John Estaugh. We will not speak of it further.
It hath been laid upon me to tell thee this, for to-morrow
Thou art going away, across the sea, and I know not
When I shall see thee more; but if the Lord hath decreed it,
Thou wilt return again to seek me here and to find me."
And they rode onward in silence, and entered the town with the others.

IV.

Ships that pass in the night, and speak each other in passing,
Only a signal shown and a distant voice in the darkness;
So on the ocean of life we pass and speak one another,
Only a look and a voice, then darkness again and a silence.

Now went on as of old the quiet life of the homestead.
Patient and unrepining Elizabeth labored, in all things
Mindful not of herself, but bearing the burdens of others,
Always thoughtful and kind and untroubled; and Hannah the housemaid
Diligent early and late, and rosy with washing and scouring,
Still as of old disparaged the eminent merits of Joseph,
And was at times reproved for her light and frothy behavior,
For her shy looks, and her careless words, and her evil surmisings,
Being pressed down somewhat like a cart with sheaves overladen,
As she would sometimes say to Joseph, quoting the Scriptures.

Meanwhile John Estaugh departed across the sea, and departing
Carried hid in his heart a secret sacred and precious,
Filling its chambers with fragrance, and seeming to him in its sweetness
Mary's ointment of spikenard, that filled all the house with its odor.
O lost days of delight, that are wasted in doubting and waiting!
O lost hours and days in which we might have been happy!
But the light shone at last, and guided his wavering footsteps,
And at last came the voice, imperative, questionless, certain.

Then John Estaugh came back o'er the sea for the gift that was offered,
Better than houses and lands, the gift of a woman's affection.
And on the First-Day that followed, he rose in the Silent Assembly,
Holding in his strong hand a hand that trembled a little,
Promising to be kind and true and faithful in all things.
Such were the marriage-rites of John and Elizabeth Estaugh.

And not otherwise Joseph, the honest, the diligent servant,
Sped in his bashful wooing with homely Hannah the housemaid;
For when he asked her the question, she answered, "Nay"; and then added
"But thee may make believe, and see what will come of it, Joseph."

INTERLUDE

"A pleasant and a winsome tale,"
The Student said, "though somewhat pale
And quiet in its coloring,
As if it caught its tone and air
From the gray suits that Quakers wear;
Yet worthy of some German bard,
Hebel, or Voss, or Eberhard,
Who love of humble themes to sing,
In humble verse; but no more true

Than was the tale I told to you."

The Theologian made reply,
And with some warmth, "That I deny;
'T is no invention of my own,
But something well and widely known
To readers of a riper age,
Writ by the skilful hand that wrote
The Indian tale of Hobomok,
And Philothea's classic page.
I found it like a waif afloat
Or dulse uprooted from its rock,
On the swift tides that ebb and flow
In daily papers, and at flood
Bear freighted vessels to and fro,
But later, when the ebb is low, Leave a long waste of sand and mud."

"It matters little," quoth the Jew;
"The cloak of truth is lined with lies,
Sayeth some proverb old and wise;
And Love is master of all arts,
And puts it into human hearts
The strangest things to say and do."

And here the controversy closed
Abruptly, ere 't was well begun;
For the Sicilian interposed
With, "Lordlings, listen, every one
That listen may, unto a tale
That's merrier than the nightingale;
A tale that cannot boast, forsooth,
A single rag or shred of truth;
That does not leave the mind in doubt
As to the with it or without;
A naked falsehood and absurd
As mortal ever told or heard.
Therefore I tell it; or, maybe,
Simply because it pleases me."

THE SICILIAN'S TALE: THE MONK OF CASAL-MAGGIORE

Once on a time, some centuries ago,
  In the hot sunshine two Franciscan friars

Wended their weary way with footsteps slow
  Back to their convent, whose white walls and spires
Gleamed on the hillside like a patch of snow;
  Covered with dust they were, and torn by briers,
And bore like sumpter-mules upon their backs
The badge of poverty, their beggar's sacks.

The first was Brother Anthony, a spare
  And silent man, with pallid cheeks and thin,
Much given to vigils, penance, fasting, prayer,
  Solemn and gray, and worn with discipline,
As if his body but white ashes were,
  Heaped on the living coals that glowed within;
A simple monk, like many of his day,
Whose instinct was to listen and obey.

A different man was Brother Timothy,
  Of larger mould and of a coarser paste;
A rubicund and stalwart monk was he,
  Broad in the shoulders, broader in the waist,
Who often filled the dull refectory
  With noise by which the convent was disgraced,
But to the mass-book gave but little heed,
By reason he had never learned to read.

Now, as they passed the outskirts of a wood,
  They saw, with mingled pleasure and surprise,
Fast tethered to a tree an ass, that stood
  Lazily winking his large, limpid eyes.
The farmer Gilbert of that neighborhood
  His owner was, who, looking for supplies
Of fagots, deeper in the wood had strayed,
Leaving his beast to ponder in the shade.

As soon as Brother Timothy espied
  The patient animal, he said: "Good-lack!
Thus for our needs doth Providence provide;
  We'll lay our wallets on the creature's back."
This being done, he leisurely untied
  From head and neck the halter of the jack,
And put it round his own, and to the tree
Stood tethered fast as if the ass were he.

And, bursting forth into a merry laugh,

He cried to Brother Anthony: "Away!
And drive the ass before you with your staff;
  And when you reach the convent you may say
You left me at a farm, half tired and half
  Ill with a fever, for a night and day,
And that the farmer lent this ass to bear
Our wallets, that are heavy with good fare."

Now Brother Anthony, who knew the pranks
  Of Brother Timothy, would not persuade
Or reason with him on his quirks and cranks,
  But, being obedient, silently obeyed;
And, smiting with his staff the ass's flanks,
  Drove him before him over hill and glade,
Safe with his provend to the convent gate,
Leaving poor Brother Timothy to his fate.

Then Gilbert, laden with fagots for his fire,
  Forth issued from the wood, and stood aghast
To see the ponderous body of the friar
  Standing where he had left his donkey last.
Trembling he stood, and dared not venture nigher,
  But stared, and gaped, and crossed himself full fast;
For, being credulous and of little wit,
He thought it was some demon from the pit.

While speechless and bewildered thus he gazed,
  And dropped his load of fagots on the ground,
Quoth Brother Timothy: "Be not amazed
  That where you left a donkey should be found
A poor Franciscan friar, half-starved and crazed,
  Standing demure and with a halter bound;
But set me free, and hear the piteous story
Of Brother Timothy of Casal-Maggiore.

"I am a sinful man, although you see
  I wear the consecrated cowl and cape;
You never owned an ass, but you owned me,
  Changed and transformed from my own natural shape
All for the deadly sin of gluttony,
  From which I could not otherwise escape,
Than by this penance, dieting on grass,
And being worked and beaten as an ass.

"Think of the ignominy I endured;
  Think of the miserable life I led,
The toil and blows to which I was inured,
  My wretched lodging in a windy shed,
My scanty fare so grudgingly procured,
  The damp and musty straw that formed my bed!
But, having done this penance for my sins,
My life as man and monk again begins."

The simple Gilbert, hearing words like these,
  Was conscience-stricken, and fell down apace
Before the friar upon his bended knees,
  And with a suppliant voice implored his grace;
And the good monk, now very much at ease,
  Granted him pardon with a smiling face,
Nor could refuse to be that night his guest,
It being late, and he in need of rest.

Upon a hillside, where the olive thrives,
  With figures painted on its white-washed walls,
The cottage stood; and near the humming hives
  Made murmurs as of far-off waterfalls;
A place where those who love secluded lives
  Might live content, and, free from noise and brawls,
Like Claudian's Old Man of Verona here
Measure by fruits the slow-revolving year.

And, coming to this cottage of content
  They found his children, and the buxom wench
His wife, Dame Cicely, and his father, bent
  With years and labor, seated on a bench,
Repeating over some obscure event
  In the old wars of Milanese and French;
All welcomed the Franciscan, with a sense
Of sacred awe and humble reverence.

When Gilbert told them what had come to pass,
  How beyond question, cavil, or surmise,
Good Brother Timothy had been their ass,
  You should have seen the wonder in their eyes;
You should have heard them cry, "Alas! alas!
  Have heard their lamentations and their sighs!
For all believed the story, and began
To see a saint in this afflicted man.

Forthwith there was prepared a grand repast,
  To satisfy the craving of the friar
After so rigid and prolonged a fast;
  The bustling housewife stirred the kitchen fire;
Then her two barnyard fowls, her best and last,
  Were put to death, at her express desire,
And served up with a salad in a bowl,
And flasks of country wine to crown the whole.

It would not be believed should I repeat
  How hungry Brother Timothy appeared;
It was a pleasure but to see him eat,
  His white teeth flashing through his russet beard,
His face aglow and flushed with wine and meat,
  His roguish eyes that rolled and laughed and leered!
Lord! how he drank the blood-red country wine
As if the village vintage were divine!

And all the while he talked without surcease,
  And told his merry tales with jovial glee
That never flagged, but rather did increase,
  And laughed aloud as if insane were he,
And wagged his red beard, matted like a fleece,
  And cast such glances at Dame Cicely
That Gilbert now grew angry with his guest,
And thus in words his rising wrath expressed.

"Good father," said he, "easily we see
  How needful in some persons, and how right,
Mortification of the flesh may be.
  The indulgence you have given it to-night,
After long penance, clearly proves to me
  Your strength against temptation is but slight,
And shows the dreadful peril you are in
Of a relapse into your deadly sin.

"To-morrow morning, with the rising sun,
  Go back unto your convent, nor refrain
From fasting and from scourging, for you run
  Great danger to become an ass again,
Since monkish flesh and asinine are one;
  Therefore be wise, nor longer here remain,
Unless you wish the scourge should be applied
By other hands, that will not spare your hide."

When this the monk had heard, his color fled
  And then returned, like lightning in the air,
Till he was all one blush from foot to head,
  And even the bald spot in his russet hair
Turned from its usual pallor to bright red!
  The old man was asleep upon his chair.
Then all retired, and sank into the deep
And helpless imbecility of sleep.

They slept until the dawn of day drew near,
  Till the cock should have crowed, but did not crow,
For they had slain the shining chanticleer
  And eaten him for supper, as you know.
The monk was up betimes and of good cheer,
  And, having breakfasted, made haste to go,
As if he heard the distant matin bell,
And had but little time to say farewell.

Fresh was the morning as the breath of kine;
  Odors of herbs commingled with the sweet
Balsamic exhalations of the pine;
  A haze was in the air presaging heat;
Uprose the sun above the Apennine,
  And all the misty valleys at its feet
Were full of the delirious song of birds,
Voices of men, and bells, and low of herds.

All this to Brother Timothy was naught;
  He did not care for scenery, nor here
His busy fancy found the thing it sought;
  But when he saw the convent walls appear,
And smoke from kitchen chimneys upward caught
  And whirled aloft into the atmosphere,
He quickened his slow footsteps, like a beast
That scents the stable a league off at least.

And as he entered though the convent gate
  He saw there in the court the ass, who stood
Twirling his ears about, and seemed to wait,
  Just as he found him waiting in the wood;
And told the Prior that, to alleviate
  The daily labors of the brotherhood,
The owner, being a man of means and thrift,
Bestowed him on the convent as a gift.

And thereupon the Prior for many days
  Revolved this serious matter in his mind,
And turned it over many different ways,
  Hoping that some safe issue he might find;
But stood in fear of what the world would say,
  If he accepted presents of this kind,
Employing beasts of burden for the packs,
That lazy monks should carry on their backs.

Then, to avoid all scandal of the sort,
  And stop the mouth of cavil, he decreed
That he would cut the tedious matter short,
  And sell the ass with all convenient speed,
Thus saving the expense of his support,
  And hoarding something for a time of need.
So he despatched him to the neighboring Fair,
And freed himself from cumber and from care.

It happened now by chance, as some might say,
  Others perhaps would call it destiny,
Gilbert was at the Fair; and heard a bray,
  And nearer came, and saw that it was he,
And whispered in his ear, "Ah, lackaday!
  Good father, the rebellious flesh, I see,
Has changed you back into an ass again,
And all my admonitions were in vain."

The ass, who felt this breathing in his ear,
  Did not turn round to look, but shook his head,
As if he were not pleased these words to hear,
  And contradicted all that had been said.
And this made Gilbert cry in voice more clear,
  "I know you well; your hair is russet-red;
Do not deny it; for you are the same
Franciscan friar, and Timothy by name."

The ass, though now the secret had come out,
  Was obstinate, and shook his head again;
Until a crowd was gathered round about
  To hear this dialogue between the twain;
And raised their voices in a noisy shout
  When Gilbert tried to make the matter plain,
And flouted him and mocked him all day long
With laughter and with jibes and scraps of song.

"If this be Brother Timothy," they cried,
  "Buy him, and feed him on the tenderest grass;
Thou canst not do too much for one so tried
  As to be twice transformed into an ass."
So simple Gilbert bought him, and untied
  His halter, and o'er mountain and morass
He led him homeward, talking as he went
Of good behavior and a mind content.

The children saw them coming, and advanced,
  Shouting with joy, and hung about his neck,—
Not Gilbert's, but the ass's,—round him danced,
  And wove green garlands where-withal to deck
His sacred person; for again it chanced
  Their childish feelings, without rein or check,
Could not discriminate in any way
A donkey from a friar of Orders Gray.

"O Brother Timothy," the children said,
  "You have come back to us just as before;
We were afraid, and thought that you were dead,
  And we should never see you any more."
And then they kissed the white star on his head,
  That like a birth-mark or a badge he wore,
And patted him upon the neck and face,
And said a thousand things with childish grace.

Thenceforward and forever he was known
  As Brother Timothy, and led alway
A life of luxury, till he had grown
  Ungrateful being stuffed with corn and hay,
And very vicious. Then in angry tone,
  Rousing himself, poor Gilbert said one day
"When simple kindness is misunderstood
A little flagellation may do good."

His many vices need not here be told;
  Among them was a habit that he had
Of flinging up his heels at young and old,
  Breaking his halter, running off like mad
O'er pasture-lands and meadow, wood and wold,
  And other misdemeanors quite as bad;
But worst of all was breaking from his shed
At night, and ravaging the cabbage-bed.

So Brother Timothy went back once more
　To his old life of labor and distress;
Was beaten worse than he had been before.
　And now, instead of comfort and caress,
Came labors manifold and trials sore;
　And as his toils increased his food grew less,
Until at last the great consoler, Death,
Ended his many sufferings with his breath.

Great was the lamentation when he died;
　And mainly that he died impenitent;
Dame Cicely bewailed, the children cried,
　The old man still remembered the event
In the French war, and Gilbert magnified
　His many virtues, as he came and went,
And said: "Heaven pardon Brother Timothy,
And keep us from the sin of gluttony."

INTERLUDE

"Signor Luigi," said the Jew,
When the Sicilian's tale was told,
"The were-wolf is a legend old,
But the were-ass is something new,
And yet for one I think it true.
The days of wonder have not ceased
If there are beasts in forms of men,
As sure it happens now and then,
Why may not man become a beast,
In way of punishment at least?

"But this I will not now discuss,
I leave the theme, that we may thus
Remain within the realm of song.
The story that I told before,
Though not acceptable to all,
At least you did not find too long.
I beg you, let me try again,
With something in a different vein,
Before you bid the curtain fall.
Meanwhile keep watch upon the door,
Nor let the Landlord leave his chair,
Lest he should vanish into air,

And thus elude our search once more."

Thus saying, from his lips he blew
A little cloud of perfumed breath,
And then, as if it were a clew
To lead his footsteps safely through,
Began his tale as followeth.

THE SPANISH JEW'S SECOND TALE: SCANDERBEG

The battle is fought and won
By King Ladislaus the Hun,
In fire of hell and death's frost,
On the day of Pentecost.
And in rout before his path
From the field of battle red
Flee all that are not dead
Of the army of Amurath.

In the darkness of the night
Iskander, the pride and boast
Of that mighty Othman host,
With his routed Turks, takes flight
From the battle fought and lost
On the day of Pentecost;
Leaving behind him dead
The army of Amurath,
The vanguard as it led,
The rearguard as it fled,
Mown down in the bloody swath
Of the battle's aftermath.

But he cared not for Hospodars,
Nor for Baron or Voivode,
As on through the night he rode
And gazed at the fateful stars,
That were shining overhead
But smote his steed with his staff,
And smiled to himself, and said;
"This is the time to laugh."

In the middle of the night,
In a halt of the hurrying flight,

There came a Scribe of the King
Wearing his signet ring,
And said in a voice severe:
"This is the first dark blot
On thy name, George Castriot!
Alas why art thou here,
And the army of Amurath slain,
And left on the battle plain?"

And Iskander answered and said:
"They lie on the bloody sod
By the hoofs of horses trod;
But this was the decree
Of the watchers overhead;
For the war belongeth to God,
And in battle who are we,
Who are we, that shall withstand
The wind of his lifted hand?"

Then he bade them bind with chains
This man of books and brains;
And the Scribe said: "What misdeed
Have I done, that, without need,
Thou doest to me this thing?"
And Iskander answering
Said unto him: "Not one
Misdeed to me hast thou done;
But for fear that thou shouldst run
And hide thyself from me,
Have I done this unto thee.

"Now write me a writing, O Scribe,
And a blessing be on thy tribe!
A writing sealed with thy ring,
To King Amurath's Pasha
In the city of Croia,
The city moated and walled,
That he surrender the same
In the name of my master, the King;
For what is writ in his name
Can never be recalled."

And the Scribe bowed low in dread,
And unto Iskander said:

"Allah is great and just,
But we are as ashes and dust;
How shall I do this thing,
When I know that my guilty head
Will be forfeit to the King?"

Then swift as a shooting star
The curved and shining blade
Of Iskander's scimetar
From its sheath, with jewels bright,
Shot, as he thundered: "Write!"
And the trembling Scribe obeyed,
And wrote in the fitful glare
Of the bivouac fire apart,
With the chill of the midnight air
On his forehead white and bare,
And the chill of death in his heart.

Then again Iskander cried:
"Now follow whither I ride,
For here thou must not stay.
Thou shalt be as my dearest friend,
And honors without end
Shall surround thee on every side,
And attend thee night and day."
But the sullen Scribe replied
"Our pathways here divide;
Mine leadeth not thy way."

And even as he spoke
Fell a sudden scimetar-stroke,
When no one else was near;
And the Scribe sank to the ground,
As a stone, pushed from the brink
Of a black pool, might sink
With a sob and disappear;
And no one saw the deed;
And in the stillness around
No sound was heard but the sound
Of the hoofs of Iskander's steed,
As forward he sprang with a bound.

Then onward he rode and afar,
With scarce three hundred men,

Through river and forest and fen,
O'er the mountains of Argentar;
And his heart was merry within,
When he crossed the river Drin,
And saw in the gleam of the morn
The White Castle Ak-Hissar,
The city Croia called,
The city moated and walled,
The city where he was born,—
And above it the morning star.

Then his trumpeters in the van
On their silver bugles blew,
And in crowds about him ran
Albanian and Turkoman,
That the sound together drew.
And he feasted with his friends,
And when they were warm with wine,
He said: "O friends of mine,
Behold what fortune sends,
And what the fates design!
King Amurath commands
That my father's wide domain,
This city and all its lands,
Shall be given to me again."

Then to the Castle White
He rode in regal state,
And entered in at the gate
In all his arms bedight,
And gave to the Pasha
Who ruled in Croia
The writing of the King,
Sealed with his signet ring.
And the Pasha bowed his head,
And after a silence said:
"Allah is just and great!
I yield to the will divine,
The city and lands are thine;
Who shall contend with fate?"

Anon from the castle walls
The crescent banner falls,
And the crowd beholds instead,

Like a portent in the sky,
Iskander's banner fly,
The Black Eagle with double head;
And a shout ascends on high,
For men's souls are tired of the Turks,
And their wicked ways and works,
That have made of Ak-Hissar
A city of the plague;
And the loud, exultant cry
That echoes wide and far
Is: "Long live Scanderbeg!"

It was thus Iskander came
Once more unto his own;
And the tidings, like the flame
Of a conflagration blown
By the winds of summer, ran,
Till the land was in a blaze,
And the cities far and near,
Sayeth Ben Joshua Ben Meir,
In his Book of the Words of the Days,
"Were taken as a man
Would take the tip of his ear."

INTERLUDE

"Now that is after my own heart,"
The Poet cried; "one understands
Your swarthy hero Scanderbeg,
Gauntlet on hand and boot on leg,
And skilled in every warlike art,
Riding through his Albanian lands,
And following the auspicious star
That shone for him o'er Ak-Hissar."

The Theologian added here
His word of praise not less sincere,
Although he ended with a jibe;
"The hero of romance and song
Was born," he said, "to right the wrong;
And I approve; but all the same
That bit of treason with the Scribe
Adds nothing to your hero's fame."

The Student praised the good old times
And liked the canter of the rhymes,
That had a hoofbeat in their sound;
But longed some further word to hear
Of the old chronicler Ben Meir,
And where his volume might he found.

The tall Musician walked the room
With folded arms and gleaming eyes,
As if he saw the Vikings rise,
Gigantic shadows in the gloom;
And much he talked of their emprise,
And meteors seen in Northern skies,
And Heimdal's horn, and day of doom
But the Sicilian laughed again;
"This is the time to laugh," he said,
For the whole story he well knew
Was an invention of the Jew,
Spun from the cobwebs in his brain,
And of the same bright scarlet thread
As was the Tale of Kambalu.

Only the Landlord spake no word;
'T was doubtful whether he had heard
The tale at all, so full of care
Was he of his impending fate,
That, like the sword of Damocles,
Above his head hung blank and bare,
Suspended by a single hair,
So that he could not sit at ease,
But sighed and looked disconsolate,
And shifted restless in his chair,
Revolving how he might evade
The blow of the descending blade.

The Student came to his relief
By saying in his easy way
To the Musician: "Calm your grief,
My fair Apollo of the North,
Balder the Beautiful and so forth;
Although your magic lyre or lute
With broken strings is lying mute,
Still you can tell some doleful tale
Of shipwreck in a midnight gale,

Or something of the kind to suit
The mood that we are in to-night
For what is marvellous and strange;
So give your nimble fancy range,
And we will follow in its flight."

But the Musician shook his head;
"No tale I tell to-night," he said,
"While my poor instrument lies there,
Even as a child with vacant stare
Lies in its little coffin dead."

Yet, being urged, he said at last:
"There comes to me out of the Past
A voice, whose tones are sweet and wild,
Singing a song almost divine,
And with a tear in every line;
An ancient ballad, that my nurse
Sang to me when I was a child,
In accents tender as the verse;
And sometimes wept, and sometimes smiled
While singing it, to see arise
The look of wonder in my eyes,
And feel my heart with tenor beat.
This simple ballad I retain
Clearly imprinted on my brain,
And as a tale will now repeat"

THE MUSICIAN'S TALE: THE MOTHER'S GHOST

Svend Dyring he rideth adown the glade;
   I myself was young!
There he hath wooed him so winsome a maid;
   Fair words gladden so many a heart.

Together were they for seven years,
And together children six were theirs.

Then came Death abroad through the land,
And blighted the beautiful lily-wand.

Svend Dyring he rideth adown the glade,
And again hath he wooed him another maid,

He hath wooed him a maid and brought home a bride,
But she was bitter and full of pride.

When she came driving into the yard,
There stood the six children weeping so hard.

There stood the small children with sorrowful heart;
From before her feet she thrust them apart.

She gave to them neither ale nor bread;
"Ye shall suffer hunger and hate," she said.

She took from them their quilts of blue,
And said: "Ye shall lie on the straw we strew."

She took from them the great waxlight;
"Now ye shall lie in the dark at night."

In the evening late they cried with cold;
The mother heard it under the mould.

The woman heard it the earth below:
"To my little children I must go."

She standeth before the Lord of all:
"And may I go to my children small?"

She prayed him so long, and would not cease,
Until he bade her depart in peace.

"At cock-crow thou shalt return again;
Longer thou shalt not there remain!"

She girded up her sorrowful bones,
And rifted the walls and the marble stones.

As through the village she flitted by,
The watch-dogs howled aloud to the sky.

When she came to the castle gate,
There stood her eldest daughter in wait.

"Why standest thou here, dear daughter mine?
How fares it with brothers and sisters thine?"

"Never art thou mother of mine,
For my mother was both fair and fine.

"My mother was white, with cheeks of red,
But thou art pale, and like to the dead."

"How should I be fair and fine?
I have been dead; pale cheeks are mine.

"How should I be white and red,
So long, so long have I been dead?"

When she came in at the chamber door,
There stood the small children weeping sore.

One she braided, another she brushed,
The third she lifted, the fourth she hushed.

The fifth she took on her lap and pressed,
As if she would suckle it at her breast.

Then to her eldest daughter said she,
"Do thou bid Svend Dyring come hither to me."

Into the chamber when he came
She spake to him in anger and shame.

"I left behind me both ale and bread;
My children hunger and are not fed.

"I left behind me quilts of blue;
My children lie on the straw ye strew.

"I left behind me the great waxlight;
My children lie in the dark at night.

"If I come again unto your hall, A
s cruel a fate shall you befall!

"Now crows the cock with feathers red;
Back to the earth must all the dead.

"Now crows the cock with feathers swart;
The gates of heaven fly wide apart.

"Now crows the cock with feathers white;
I can abide no longer to-night."

Whenever they heard the watch-dogs wail,
They gave the children bread and ale.

Whenever they heard the watch-dogs bay,
They feared lest the dead were on their way.

Whenever they heard the watch-dogs bark;
　I myself was young!
They feared the dead out there in the dark.
　Fair words gladden so many a heart.

INTERLUDE

Touched by the pathos of these rhymes,
The Theologian said: "All praise
Be to the ballads of old times
And to the bards of simple ways,
Who walked with Nature hand in hand,
Whose country was their Holy Land,
Whose singing robes were homespun brown
From looms of their own native town,
Which they were not ashamed to wear,
And not of silk or sendal gay,
Nor decked with fanciful array
Of cockle-shells from Outre-Mer."

To whom the Student answered:
"Yes; All praise and honor! I confess
That bread and ale, home-baked, home-brewed,
Are wholesome and nutritious food,
But not enough for all our needs;
Poets—the best of them—are birds
Of passage; where their instinct leads
They range abroad for thoughts and words,
And from all climes bring home the seeds
That germinate in flowers or weeds.
They are not fowls in barnyards born
To cackle o'er a grain of corn;
And, if you shut the horizon down
To the small limits of their town,

What do you but degrade your bard
Till he at last becomes as one
Who thinks the all-encircling sun
Rises and sets in his back yard?"

The Theologian said again:
"It may be so; yet I maintain
That what is native still is best,
And little care I for the rest.
'T is a long story; time would fail
To tell it, and the hour is late;
We will not waste it in debate,
But listen to our Landlord's tale."

And thus the sword of Damocles
Descending not by slow degrees,
But suddenly, on the Landlord fell,
Who blushing, and with much demur
And many vain apologies,
Plucking up heart, began to tell
The Rhyme of one Sir Christopher.

THE LANDLORD'S TALE: THE RHYME OF SIR CHRISTOPHER

It was Sir Christopher Gardiner,
Knight of the Holy Sepulchre,
From Merry England over the sea,
Who stepped upon this continent
As if his august presence lent
A glory to the colony.

You should have seen him in the street
Of the little Boston of Winthrop's time,
His rapier dangling at his feet
Doublet and hose and boots complete,
Prince Rupert hat with ostrich plume,
Gloves that exhaled a faint perfume,
Luxuriant curls and air sublime,
And superior manners now obsolete!

He had a way of saying things
That made one think of courts and kings,
And lords and ladies of high degree;

So that not having been at court
Seemed something very little short
Of treason or lese-majesty,
Such an accomplished knight was he.

His dwelling was just beyond the town,
At what he called his country-seat;
For, careless of Fortune's smile or frown,
And weary grown of the world and its ways,
He wished to pass the rest of his days
In a private life and a calm retreat.

But a double life was the life he led,
And, while professing to be in search
Of a godly course, and willing, he said,
Nay, anxious to join the Puritan church,
He made of all this but small account,
And passed his idle hours instead
With roystering Morton of Merry Mount,
That pettifogger from Furnival's Inn,
Lord of misrule and riot and sin,
Who looked on the wine when it was red.

This country-seat was little more
Than a cabin of log's; but in front of the door
A modest flower-bed thickly sown
With sweet alyssum and columbine
Made those who saw it at once divine
The touch of some other hand than his own.
And first it was whispered, and then it was known,
That he in secret was harboring there
A little lady with golden hair,
Whom he called his cousin, but whom he had wed
In the Italian manner, as men said,
And great was the scandal everywhere.

But worse than this was the vague surmise,
Though none could vouch for it or aver,
That the Knight of the Holy Sepulchre
Was only a Papist in disguise;
And the more to imbitter their bitter lives,
And the more to trouble the public mind,
Came letters from England, from two other wives,
Whom he had carelessly left behind;

Both of them letters of such a kind
As made the governor hold his breath;
The one imploring him straight to send
The husband home, that he might amend;
The other asking his instant death,
As the only way to make an end.

The wary governor deemed it right,
When all this wickedness was revealed,
To send his warrant signed and sealed,
And take the body of the knight.
Armed with this mighty instrument,
The marshal, mounting his gallant steed,
Rode forth from town at the top of his speed,
And followed by all his bailiffs bold,
As if on high achievement bent,
To storm some castle or stronghold,
Challenge the warders on the wall,
And seize in his ancestral hall
A robber-baron grim and old.

But when though all the dust and heat
He came to Sir Christopher's country-seat,
No knight he found, nor warder there,
But the little lady with golden hair,
Who was gathering in the bright sunshine
The sweet alyssum and columbine;
While gallant Sir Christopher, all so gay,
Being forewarned, through the postern gate
Of his castle wall had tripped away,
And was keeping a little holiday
In the forests, that bounded his estate.

Then as a trusty squire and true
The marshal searched the castle through,
Not crediting what the lady said;
Searched from cellar to garret in vain,
And, finding no knight, came out again
And arrested the golden damsel instead,
And bore her in triumph into the town,
While from her eyes the tears rolled down
On the sweet alyssum and columbine,
That she held in her fingers white and fine.

The governor's heart was moved to see
So fair a creature caught within
The snares of Satan and of sin,
And he read her a little homily
On the folly and wickedness of the lives
Of women, half cousins and half wives;
But, seeing that naught his words availed,
He sent her away in a ship that sailed
For Merry England over the sea,
To the other two wives in the old countree,
To search her further, since he had failed
To come at the heart of the mystery.

Meanwhile Sir Christopher wandered away
Through pathless woods for a month and a day,
Shooting pigeons, and sleeping at night
With the noble savage, who took delight
In his feathered hat and his velvet vest,
His gun and his rapier and the rest.
But as soon as the noble savage heard
That a bounty was offered for this gay bird,
He wanted to slay him out of hand,
And bring in his beautiful scalp for a show,
Like the glossy head of a kite or crow,
Until he was made to understand
They wanted the bird alive, not dead;
Then he followed him whithersoever he fled,
Through forest and field, and hunted him down,
And brought him prisoner into the town.

Alas! it was a rueful sight,
To see this melancholy knight
In such a dismal and hapless case;
His hat deformed by stain and dent,
His plumage broken, his doublet rent,
His beard and flowing locks forlorn,
Matted, dishevelled, and unshorn,
His boots with dust and mire besprent;
But dignified in his disgrace,
And wearing an unblushing face.
And thus before the magistrate
He stood to hear the doom of fate.
In vain he strove with wonted ease
To modify and extenuate

His evil deeds in church and state,
For gone was now his power to please;
And his pompous words had no more weight
Than feathers flying in the breeze.

With suavity equal to his own
The governor lent a patient ear
To the speech evasive and highflown,
In which he endeavored to make clear
That colonial laws were too severe
When applied to a gallant cavalier,
A gentleman born, and so well known,
And accustomed to move in a higher sphere.

All this the Puritan governor heard,
And deigned in answer never a word;
But in summary manner shipped away,
In a vessel that sailed from Salem bay,
This splendid and famous cavalier,
With his Rupert hat and his popery,
To Merry England over the sea,
As being unmeet to inhabit here.

Thus endeth the Rhyme of Sir Christopher,
Knight of the Holy Sepulchre,
The first who furnished this barren land
With apples of Sodom and ropes of sand.

FINALE

These are the tales those merry guests
Told to each other, well or ill;
Like summer birds that lift their crests
Above the borders of their nests
And twitter, and again are still.

These are the tales, or new or old,
In idle moments idly told;
Flowers of the field with petals thin,
Lilies that neither toil nor spin,
And tufts of wayside weeds and gorse
Hung in the parlor of the inn
Beneath the sign of the Red Horse.

And still, reluctant to retire,
The friends sat talking by the fire
And watched the smouldering embers burn
To ashes, and flash up again
Into a momentary glow,
Lingering like them when forced to go,
And going when they would remain;
For on the morrow they must turn
Their faces homeward, and the pain
Of parting touched with its unrest
A tender nerve in every breast.

But sleep at last the victory won;
They must be stirring with the sun,
And drowsily good night they said,
And went still gossiping to bed,
And left the parlor wrapped in gloom.
The only live thing in the room
Was the old clock, that in its pace
Kept time with the revolving spheres
And constellations in their flight,
And struck with its uplifted mace
The dark, unconscious hours of night,
To senseless and unlistening ears.

Uprose the sun; and every guest,
Uprisen, was soon equipped and dressed
For journeying home and city-ward;
The old stage-coach was at the door,
With horses harnessed, long before
The sunshine reached the withered sward
Beneath the oaks, whose branches hoar
Murmured: "Farewell forevermore."

"Farewell!" the portly Landlord cried;
"Farewell!" the parting guests replied,
But little thought that nevermore
Their feet would pass that threshold o'er;
That nevermore together there
Would they assemble, free from care,
To hear the oaks' mysterious roar,
And breathe the wholesome country air.

Where are they now? What lands and skies

Paint pictures in their friendly eyes?
What hope deludes, what promise cheers,
What pleasant voices fill their ears?
Two are beyond the salt sea waves,
And three already in their graves.
Perchance the living still may look
Into the pages of this book,
And see the days of long ago
Floating and fleeting to and fro,
As in the well-remembered brook
They saw the inverted landscape gleam,
And their own faces like a dream
Look up upon them from below.

Made in United States
North Haven, CT
29 July 2023

39697501R00289